From Salvation
to Spirituality

JAPANESE SOCIETY SERIES

General Editor: Yoshio Sugimoto

From Salvation to Spirituality

Popular Religious Movements in Modern Japan

Susumu Shimazono

Trans Pacific Press

Melbourne

This English edition first published in 2004 by
Trans Pacific Press, PO Box 120, Rosanna, Melbourne, Victoria 3084, Australia
Telephone: +61 3 9459 3021 Fax: +61 3 9457 5923
Email: info@transpacificpress.com
Web: http://www.transpacificpress.com

Copyright © Trans Pacific Press 2004

Designed and set by digital environs Melbourne. enquiries@digitalenvirons.com

Printed by BPA Digital, Burwood, Victoria, Australia

Distributors

Australia
Bushbooks
PO Box 1958, Gosford, NSW 2250
Telephone: (02) 4323-3274
Fax: (02) 4323-3223
Email: bushbook@ozemail.com.au

USA and Canada
International Specialized Book
Services (ISBS)
920 NE 58th Avenue, Suite 300
Portland, Oregon 97213-3786
USA
Telephone: (800) 944-6190
Fax: (503) 280-8832
Email: orders@isbs.com
Web: http://www.isbs.com

UK and Europe
Asian Studies Book Services
Franseweg 55B, 3921 DE Elst, Utrecht, The
Netherlands
Telephone: +31 318 470 030
Fax: +31 318 470 073
Email: info@asianstudiesbooks.com
Web: http://www.asianstudiesbooks.com

Japan
Kyoto University Press
Kyodai Kaikan
15-9 Yoshida Kawara-cho
Sakyo-ku, Kyoto 606-8305
Telephone: (075) 761-6182
Fax: (075) 761-6190
Email: sales@kyoto-up.gr.jp
Web: http://www.kyoto-up.gr.jp

Japan, Asia and the Pacific
Kinokuniya Company Ltd.
Head office:
38-1 Sakuragaoka 5-chome, Setagaya-ku,
Tokyo 156-8691, Japan
Phone: +81 (0)3 3439 0161
Fax: +81 (0)3 3439 0839
Email: bkimp@kinokuniya.co.jp
Web: www.kinokuniya.co.jp
Asia-Pacific office:
Kinokuniya Book Stores of Singapore Pte., Ltd.
391B Orchard Road #13-06/07/08
Ngee Ann City Tower B
Singapore 238874
Tel: +65 6276 5558
Fax: +65 6276 5570
Email: SSO@kinokuniya.co.jp

ISBN   1–8768–4312–8 (Hardback)
ISBN   1–8768–4313–6 (Paperback)

National Library of Australia Cataloging in Publication Data

Shimazono Susumu, 1948–.
    From salvation to spirituality : popular religious
    movements in modern Japan.

    Bibliography.
    Includes index.
    ISBN 1 876843 12 8.
    ISBN 1 876843 13 6 (pbk.).

    1. Sects - Japan. 2. Japan - Religion. 3. Japan -
    Religion - Social aspects. I. Title. (Series : Japanese
    society series).

299.56

Contents

Tables

Figures

Acknowledgements

The papers compiled in this book were selected from papers first written between the late 1970s and 2003 in Japanese or in English. Many of those written in Japanese were translated into English and published in various journals and books. The following is a list of the English version of the papers published.

Introduction
'New Religions and Christianity,' in Mark Mullins ed., *Handbook of Christianity in Japan (Handbook of Oriental Studies, vol. Ten)*, Leiden: Brill, 2003, pp.277–294.

Part I Japan's New Religions in the Broader Scheme

Chapter 1 New Religions and the Sociology of Religion in Japan
'Asian Religions and Sociology: The Case of New Religion Studies in Japan,' in Liliane Voye and Jack Billiet, eds., *Sociology and Religions: An Ambiguous Relationship*, Louven University Press, 1999, pp.183–93

Chapter 2 Religious Influences on Japan's Modernization
'Religious Influence on Japan's Modernization,' *Japanese Journal of Religious Studies*, vol.8, Nos. 3–4, September–December 1981, pp.207–223

Chapter 3 On Contemporary Salvation Religion
'On Contemporary Salvation Religion,' *Tenri Journal of Religion*, No.25, March 1997, pp.41–57

Part II Popular Buddhist Movements and Nationalism

Chapter 4 Crisis of Authority and the Lotus Sutra-Based New Religions
(unpublished)

Chapter 5 Popularism Derived from the Lotus Sutra Tradition
'The Popularism of New Religions Derived from the Lotus Sutra: The Early Reiyukai's Philosophy of Independence and Self-Help and Its

View of History,' *Acta Asiatica: Bulletin of the Institute of Eastern Culture*, No.75, 1998, pp.110–28

Ch.6 Soka Gakkai and the Modern Reformation of Buddhism
'Soka Gakkai and the Modern Reformation of Buddhism', in Takeuchi Yoshinori, ed., *Buddhist Spirituality: Later China, Korea, Japan and the Modern World*, The Crossroad Publishing Company, 1999, pp.435–454

Part III Perspectives on Religious and Spiritual Movements

Ch.7 Millennialism
'The Development of Millennialistic Thought in Japan's New Religions; From Tenrikyo to Honmichi,' in James A. Beckford, ed., *New Religious Movements and Rapid Social Change*, Sage, 1986, pp. 55–86

Ch.8 Spirit Belief
'Spirit-Belief in New Religious Movements and Popular Culture: The Case of Japan's New Religions,' *The Journal of Oriental Studies*, vol.26. no.1, 1987, pp. 90–100

Ch.9 Conversion Stories
'Conversion Stories and their Popularization in Japan's New Religions,' *Japanese Journal of Religious Studies*, vol.13, nos. 2–3, June–September 1986, pp. 157–175

Ch.10 Alternative Knowledge
'Alternative Knowledge Movements as Religion: An Alternative Farming Movement in Japan,' *Social Compass*, vol.43, no.1, 1996, pp.47–63

Ch.11 From Religion to Psychotherapy
'From Religion to Psychotherapy: Yoshimoto Ishin's *Naikan* or "Method of Inner Observation,"' in Eileen Barker et al. eds., *Secularization, Rationalism and Sectarianism*, Clarendon Press, 1993, pp. 223–239

Part IV Religious and Spiritual Movements after 1970s

Ch.12 The Post-1970 Situation
'Introduction to Part 4: New Religious Movements,' in Mark Mullins

et al., eds., *Religion and Society in Modern Japan*, Asian Humanities Press, 1993, pp221–230

Ch.13 The Expansion of New Religions Overseas
'The Expansion of Japan's New Religions into Foreign Cultures,' *Japanese Journal of Religious Studies*, vol.18, nos. 2–3, June–September 1991, pp.105–132

Ch.14 New New Religions and This World
'New New Religions and This World: Religious Movements in Japan after the 1970s and their Beliefs about Salvation,' *Social Compass*, vol.42, no.2, 1995, pp.193–05

Ch.15 New Spirituality Movements and the Spiritual Intellectuals
'New Age and New Spiritual Movements: The Role of Spiritual Intellectuals,'*SYZYGY: Journal of Alternative Religion and Culture*, vol.2, no.12, Winter/Spring 1993, pp.9–22

Ch.16 'New Age Movements' or 'New Spirituality Movements and Culture'
'"New Age Movement" or "New Spiritual Movements and Culture"?' *Social Compass*, vol.46, no.2, 1999, pp.121–3

Many of the chapters have also been published as chapters in three of my books in Japanese:
- *Gendai kyūsai shūkyō ron* (On Contemporary Salvation Religion), Tokyo: Seikyūsha, 1992 – Chapters 2, 3, 4, and 13.
- *Seishin sekai no yukue* (Whither the Spiritual World?), Tokyo: Tōkyōdō Shuppan, 1996 – Chapters 10 and 15.
- *Posutomodan no shinshūkyō* (New Religions in the Postmodern Era), Tokyo: Tōkyōdō Shuppan, 2001 – Chapters 12 and 14.

Brill Publisher and Louven University Press kindly gave permission to use the text included in the Introduction and the whole text of Chapter 1. I thank Sage Publications and Oxford University Press for permitting to reprint the Chapters 7 and 11. My thanks is also due to Nanzan Insttitute for Religion and Culture and Asian Humanities Press for the permission to reprint the text of Chapter 12. Some of the chapters, including the Introduction and Chapter 12, were revised or enlarged when included in this volume.

I am indebted to so many colleagues for their advice and assistance in writing these chapters that I cannot list all the names here. I would like to express my sincere thanks to them all. The names of the translators of some of the original papers are given in the Notes.

My greatest debt is due to two people who have helped translating my papers and editing them. Ms. Hayashi Chine has long been helping me in translating my papers into English. Without her expertise I could not have produced many of my papers. Dr. Robert Kisala, who has long been working on new religions in Japan and who understands my academic interest very well, has helped not only in the translation of my texts but also revising and editing all the texts of this volume. I am indebted to Mr. Watanabe Yū for indexing this book with great care and attention to detail. Finally, without Professor Yoshio Sugimoto's proposal to publish a book in English I would not have thought of the possibility of publishing a book in this way.

Introduction: Salvation Religion, New Religions, and New Spirituality

This book is a compilation of papers presented by the author in recent years on the religions and spirituality of people in modern Japan. Religion in modern Japan is a complicated subject, requiring consideration from multiple perspectives. In this book, focus is placed on the phenomenon called 'new religions.' The intention is not simply to provide an explanation for new religions, but, rather, the author also tries to see new religions from a certain theoretical perspective in order to shed light on some characteristics of the religious history of Japan and of modern Japan. The real intention is to ask this question, 'What is a religion?', and to offer some hints for reflection on the cultural and philosophical environment in which we live. The theses proposed here have been motivated by a quest for the state of mind of modern people in a post-new religion era.

The author offers 'salvation' as the key concept for this quest. Following the realization that the human being lives in fear of death, disease, and other problematic situations, salvation in a religious context is defined as teaching individuals how to face these situations squarely, and to reach a higher level of life beyond these limits, or at least to try to do so. The concept of salvation is the central element of many religions. These religions encourage individuals to make a decision to lead a new life and aim for a universalistic goal, and to expand their sense of solidarity beyond the geographical, cultural, and communal frameworks of their lives. What are called 'world religions' – Buddhism, Christianity and Islam – are typical 'salvation' religions. New religions that have emerged in Japan and other places of the world can also be called salvation religions. In contemporary industrialized societies, in which wealth and power and cultural resources have come to be concentrated in cities, salvation religions have continued to play an important role. Although salvation religions have been somewhat relativized in modern society, where the social status of elites who do not have faith in salvation religions is enhanced, nevertheless the foundations of the spiritual culture in many parts of the world continue to find support in salvation religions. In Islamic societies, for example, where we see a 'return to the religion,' the power of salvation religion continues to be apparent. In contrast, the further the process of modernization progresses the more people appear to be alienated from the concept of salvation or the institution of salvation religions. Europe is a typical example of this.

What is the situation in Japan? Before the modern period, the concepts and practices of salvation religion were prevalent in the domain of popular religion, characterized by a syncretic blend of Buddhism and Shinto. In the early modern period, i.e. from the mid-16th to the mid-19th centuries, Confucianism and Shinto gained strength. Although Confucianism can be considered a religion, it is difficult to define it as a salvation religion. Salvational elements are contained in Shinto, but other aspects are given a higher priority. Some religious historians argue that Buddhism lost its influence during this period, and this process has continued and deepened with the development of modernization. However, a consideration of Japanese religious history from the viewpoint of new religions offers a different point of view. The modern period is characterized by the development of salvation religion under the guise of the new religions, and the early modern period can be seen as a preparatory phase for this later religious development. New religions in Japan are salvation religions in which ordinary people are the main players. Japan is similar to the United States in that many popular salvational religious movements have developed, leading to a competition for supremacy among these religious organizations. In the world at large, it is Islam and Christianity that have shown the most growth as salvation religions from the end of the 20th century to the beginning of the 21st century. In addition to Islam and Christianity, new religions that emerged in East Asia can also be considered, as part of this expanse in salvation religions that dates back to the middle of the 20th century. For that reason, one focus of this introduction will be a comparison of the new religions and Christianity.

The focus of interest of this book is not, however, limited to new religions as salvation religions. It further attempts to look at the 'post-new religion' religious development. As mentioned above, in some areas of the world the concept of 'salvation' is relativized, and people are alienated from salvation religions. This does not mean that they have given up on all things religious. There are not a few people who are skeptical about modern science and rationalism, and who pursue a worldview that is neither 'scientific' nor 'religious.' Such a tendency has been notable in Japan since the 1970s. The focal word in this tendency is 'spirituality' instead of 'salvation.' In the period following that of salvation religions and modern civilization, 'new spirituality' is pursued. In the final section of this book these trends in the 'post-salvation' period will be considered.

What are new religions?

When people use the term 'new religion' they generally mean a religion that came into existence in their own lifetime, or, more commonly, the term refers to a comparatively recent religion, seen from the perspective of modern times.[1] In this latter case, the problem that arises is determining how long ago a religion could have started and yet still be described as 'new.' In Europe, people are more likely to refer to religious groups that began spreading in the 1960s when they speak of new religions, whereas in the Americas, Japan, and Korea, religious groups founded anytime after the beginning of the nineteenth century are more likely to be called new religions. The latter are religious groups that have to a certain extent become independent of established religious traditions and that have developed on their own in step with the establishment of a modern nation state. In Japan this use of the term is far more common than any other. The Mormons in the United States, the Baha'i Faith in Iran, and Chondokyō in Korea are early examples of such new religions.

The earliest of the new religions in Japan was Nyoraikyō, a group that emerged in the early nineteenth century. It was followed by Kurozumikyō, Misogikyō, Tenrikyō, Konkōkyō, Honmon Butsuryūshū, and others. By the 1870s the fact that they were a force to reckon with on the religious scene was recognized, and even the central government considered it advisable to assign them some sort of institutional place in the bureaucratic scheme of things. They were followed in the first half of the twentieth century by more new religions such as Ōmotokyō, Hitonomichi Kyōdan (later renamed PL Kyōdan), and Reiyūkai. These latter had developed so quickly that in the first half of the 1930s they were a major force behind popular movements. In the second half of the 1930s most of these religious groups were subjected to strict regulation by the government and their activities were curbed, so that they could not interfere with the prosecution of the government's war objectives, but after the end of the Second World War freedom of religion was guaranteed and these groups grew more rapidly than ever before.

By the end of the 1960s Sōka Gakkai could claim more than fifteen million followers. It was joined by other religious groups that each claimed to have several million followers, although the number is highly exagerrated. During the 1960s Sōka Gakkai formed its own political party, Kōmeito; most of the other religious groups formed links with the Liberal Democratic Party, or other parties, in a bid to assure themselves of political protection. At the same time, the political parties came to look upon the religious groups as powerful backers, because of the huge numbers of votes each group was capable of directing their way.

During the 1970s, however, the impressive growth of Sōka Gakkai and other already established new religions came to a halt, and newer new religions began to emerge. In the 1980s an increasing number of these latter groups, dubbed 'new new religions,' 'cults,' and the like, became conspicuous for their friction with the wider community. Many of them proclaimed a vision of reform of the Establishment and came into conflict with the modern State. Among them was Aum Shinrikyō, which even resorted to terrorism and mass murder, with the result that new religions began to draw renewed attention – as groups that were capable of threatening the freedom of large numbers of the nation's citizenry.

It is extremely difficult to estimate the number of new religious groups or the numbers of their followers. The *Shinshūkyō Jiten* (Dictionary of New Religions) published in 1984 describes approximately two hundred of these groups in some detail, but it says the total number of such groups 'probably exceeds two or three thousand' (Matsuno 1984: i). As regards the total number of followers of such groups, I would put the number at somewhere between ten and twenty percent of the total population.

There appear to be three main religio-historical sources of the new religions: (1) the groups of folk religions that used Shinto shrines and Buddhist temples equally as centers for pilgrimage and accepted the *yamabushi, gyōja,* and other folk-belief practitioners as intermediaries, supporting people who gathered in *kō* (religious associations); we can call this source the 'syncretic cult' tradition; (2) the *kō* (religious associations) in the Nichiren tradition, in which family groups of lay followers actively participated; (3) popular movements stressing self-discipline and the cultivation of virtue, such as Sekimon Shingaku.

The majority of Japan's new religions would, when they were formed, inherit one or the other of these religious traditions coming down from early modern times, but the closer we come to the present day, the more the new religions would select bits and pieces of the religions, learning, thought, and ideology that spread through the country after the Meiji Restoration. Christianity would become one of the important modern sources for such eclectic new religions. The new religions have taken their nourishment from a truly wide variety of sources.

The special feature of the religious thought of the new religions can be summarized in the concept of 'this-worldly salvation.' Whereas the view of salvation in Buddhism, which was dominant until the appearance of the new religions, was this-world renouncing and oriented to the next world, the new religions preach that improvement of a person's immediate life in this world itself leads to ultimate happiness. They were not too interested in death or the world after death, and even when they did show interest in the world after death, they had a strong tendency to be concerned about the next world only insofar as it had an effect on happiness in this life.

Some take as their main object of devotion an Oyagami (Parent God) or 'Buddha,' but often enough the main object of devotion is also referred to as the 'Great Life of the Universe.' According to the typical teaching on the subject, all things in the universe, including human beings, have sprung from the same Great Life of the Universe, and a person can achieve union with the life force of the universe by forging harmonious relations with other people and with one's environment. The key to forging harmonious relations lies in each individual's 'heart.' Most of these new religions also share in common a teaching called *kokoro naoshi* (transformation of the heart), which holds that, by preserving a pure, unclouded heart, a heart that is rich in love and enjoys serene tranquility, one can realize a happy life in which there is an outpouring of universal life. These teachings constitute what can be called 'a vitalistic conception of salvation' (Tsushima et al. 1979). Inasmuch as vitalism finds life in all beings, it is possible to conclude that the new religions have inherited the animistic beliefs of folk religions. We can also discover in them the influences of Shinto and Neo-Confucianism, as well as the influence of 'original enlightenment' (*hongaku*) thought that was very strong within Japan's Buddhist tradition.

Most of the new religious groups hold that a person's life is naturally brought to fulfillment in the person's family, and harmony within the family is highly esteemed. Many of the groups treasure the ancestors as guardians of the family. A typical example of such groups would be those in the Reiyūkai line; they require that each family have a 'combined posthumous Buddhist name' to honor all the ancestors on both the husband's and the wife's sides of the family. Through the giving of new posthumous names to as many of the deceased family members as possible and the performance of rites for them, adherents hope that the ancestors will enter paradise and do what they can to guard both their descendants' families and their country.

We can also find in these groups a widespread nationalism, in that they believe Japan is a special country with a special mission, but the groups that revere and worship the emperor are not necessarily in the majority. Many of them do worship their founders or the founders' successors in a manner approaching that of living deities. Finding sanctity in things of this world (such as the family or a living deity) is a special characteristic of the new religions; at the same time it is also a special characteristic of Japan's folk religions, of Shinto, and of Japanese Buddhism with its heavy dependence on original enlightenment thought.

Some of the religious groups, touting *yonaoshi* (rectification of the world), look forward with great expectation to a fundamental renewal of this world's order. Tenrikyō, Maruyamakyō, Ōmotokyō, and Honmichi are examples of such groups. At one time the Buddhist-based Sōka Gakkai and Reiyūkai also were heavily colored by a strong expectation of the coming of an ideal world. Words like 'heaven on earth' were used, and some looked upon their group's holy land as a miniature replica of this heaven on earth. In Ōmotokyō and Honmichi we also find influences of the folk religion idea of 'the world of Miroku (Maitreya).'

The motivation for joining a new religion is often summarized in three words: poverty, sickness, and strife. These indicate how common it is for very concrete worries and concerns in present people's daily lives to serve as the trigger for starting religious activities. Especially frequent are cases in which someone suffering from an illness has experienced relief from it after a healing ceremony in a new religion and then goes on to become a fervent believer. The practice of healing does in fact occupy an extremely important place within the activities of new religions. The Sekai Kyūseikyō introduced a method of healing in which a protective amulet called *ohikari* (sacred light) is hung around the believer's neck and a hand is laid upon the believer to 'cleanse the spirit.' This healing technique has gained wide support and been adopted by numerous groups, including Mahikarikyō (Sekai Mahikari Bunmei Kyōdan and Sūkyō Mahikari).

Frequent family meetings conducted by small local groups is another feature of the new religions. At such meetings everyone has a chance to talk with others and learn from them in the presence of a local religious leader. Representative examples of such sessions are the *hōza* of Risshō Kōseikai and the *zadankai* of Sōka Gakkai. These can be seen as successors to the *kō* (religious associations) that once were common in folk religions, Pure Land Shin Sect, and Nichiren Sect. Up until the 1960s these small local groups made up of people with close daily contacts formed the foundation upon which the structure of many of the religious groups was built. From the 1970s, however, there has been a growing tendency for the religious group to be controlled by a centralized organization, in which all authority lies with the head of the group. More and more religious groups are being organized along the lines of business corporations. The Unification Church and Aum Shinrikyō are good examples of new religion groups that are organized this way.

The connection between new religions and Christianity

The new religions and Christianity have in common the fact that they were both guaranteed some freedom after the Meiji Restoration, gradually increasing the number of their adherents, and became influential religious forces. Another similarity is that they preach the salvation of the individual, urge the believer to undergo a trans-formation of heart, and require entry into a group of believers that revolves around a local leader. The concept of 'salvation' presupposes the idea that from the start humanity is living in the midst of an adverse situation that makes salvation necessary. Before salvation can be experienced as something real, the person has to realize that the human person's life is circumscribed by limitations that cannot easily be overcome by a person's ordinary powers. Once such a realization is gained, eyes are set on some being that transcends human powers and the person tries, with the aid of that transcendent power, to draw near to the state of supreme bliss that transcends the aforesaid limitations – in other words, tries to draw near to 'salvation.'

In pre-modern Japan Buddhism was the major salvation religion, and as such it played an important role in Japanese society. From the beginning of the Edo period, however, the Buddhist temples belonging to the principal sects came to focus their activities on the performance of funeral services, and Buddhism in Japan took on more and more the character of a religion devoted to rituals promoting the unity of the *ie* (household, family). This character grew even stronger in modern times, to the extent that Buddhism would be given the label 'funeral

Buddhism' or 'ancestor rite.' What this also meant is that its function as a religion of salvation of the individual progressively diminished. Meanwhile, in the Edo period, Confucianism and Shinto made great progress, but even though they sometimes carried out functions that had something to do with the salvation of the individual, this facet was not a significant part of their work. What did develop in the late Edo period as a powerful religious force that dealt with the salvation of the individual were folk religion groups. However, many of these groups were dealt a severe blow at the time of the Meiji Restoration by the policy of the separation of Shinto and Buddhism and similar measures.

From the Meiji Restoration on, then, conditions were spreading that would prevent the religions that had taken root before the modern period from being able fully to carry out their functions as salvation religions. Furthermore, after the Meiji Restoration autonomy and independence of the individual would be encouraged, and opportunities would increase for people to leave their traditional regional communities and lead new lives as individuals; both these factors raised people's felt need for a salvation religion that looked to the salvation of the individual. The new religions and Christianity would come to play an extremely important role in this situation, thanks to their being salvation religions that were new on the religious scene.

This situation is similar to the one in South Korea. There, too, new religions and Christianity came to enjoy tremendous development because of the fact that Confucianism and the other religions passed down from Yi Dynasty times were incapable of functioning fully in the process of modernization. But, whereas in South Korea it was Christianity that made the greater advances, in Japan it was the new religions that gained most ground. In Japan Christianity had infiltrated by way of the samurai stratum, and from then on it tended very much to win the support of people from the upper strata of Japanese society. On the other hand, in South Korea Christianity came to gain the support of the masses. In Japan the masses flocked to the new religions, and so Christianity had only limited success in getting through to them. What no doubt happened in Japan was that Buddhism and folk religions still remained powerful influences at the time modernization was beginning, and when the new religions were formed they inherited some of that energy.

When one thus compares the situation of the new religions and of Christianity in Japanese society, one sees that, though both groups were alike in being religions devoted to the salvation of the individual, at the same time they differed in several important respects. The difference in the social strata of their adherents is an important consideration. According to an analysis made by Morioka Kiyomi (1970: 193), the social strata of Christians went through three stages during the Meiji period: (1) the first converts were drawn largely from the samurai class, particularly those individuals who lost their social status as a result of the Meiji Restoration; (2) in the next phase, progressive small capitalists and wealthy farmers (1870s) turned to Christianity; and (3) from the 1880s the new middle-class intellectuals made up of people earning salaries, and their successors (high school and university graduates) were drawn to the Christian churches. In each of these three stages Christianity was accepted in the context of a foreign language and associated with cultural refinement obtained through a high level of education. Morioka draws upon the words of Honda Yōichi (1848–1912), a samurai Christian, to confirm what he says about these social-strata features:

> Even though the ordinary people in Japan are not deep thinkers and have many superstitions, they do entertain a certain amount of religiosity. For this reason [sic] Christianity is not readily accepted by them. But Japan has a social class, that of the samurai. They are self-reliant people who are comparatively culturally refined, independent of spirit, and somewhat proud. When the Meiji Restoration brought on a breakdown of the old order, they discovered that there were many problems, both to do with themselves and to do with society in general, requiring a solution. This realization made them feel there was something lacking, and this feeling was also shared among many ambitious young samurai who embraced the same feeling. They were proud, true, but they sensed an emptiness deep in their hearts. The spaces of this emptiness could be filled up by Christianity. Also, in their somewhat proud philosophy of life, they recognize a being that, simple as it may be, is to be revered; it is referred to as the Way of Heaven, the Disposition of Heaven, and so on (it is not extremely concrete, as it would be among common folk). Also, while among the great masses the only measures of human life are simply advantage and loss, this samurai class has the attitude that losing one's life for the sake of honor and uprightness is a virtue, so Christianity's teachings about the existence of God and service to others had a profound appeal. At the same time, because the samurai had the inner force to resist what was common, they managed to see creative possibilities within difficulties. Again, because they wanted to learn once more what was happening in the world, and how they could bring

their beloved country up to a par with the major powers and restore the Emperor to his rightful place, and because they believed that it was Christianity that animated Western civilization, they wasted no time in adopting it (Morioka 1970: 192–93).[2]

On the basis of his investigations, Morioka concludes that 'the social stratum that supported the Christian church in our country was not that of working farmers or craftsmen, nor even of factory laborers, but, right from its first beginnings, the intellectual stratum' (194).

The principal supporters of the new religions, in contrast, were the middle and low strata of the population. In the case of Tenrikyō, which is representative of Meiji-period new religions, there is no mistaking the fact that the poorest stratum was included among the principal targets of its propagation, as is easily seen from the fact that the founder himself, heeding the command of God ('Abandon thyself to poverty'), was drawing near to the lifestyle of the poorest stratum in society, and from her prophesying that the control of the 'high mountains' would finally end and the hopes of the 'bottoms of the valleys' would be realized. Its teachings were couched in easily understood everyday language, and they have been characterized ever since the founder's times as 'teachings in kana.'[3]

We also have a study on the characteristics of Sōka Gakkai membership in Fukuoka City around 1960 (Suzuki 1968: 25–26). It lists membership as: (a) people in their thirties and forties; (b) more women than men; (c) of low educational background; (d) of lower middle class, lower-class laborers, simple and irregular laborers; (e) urban residents; and (f) increasing suddenly since 1955. In a 1967 public opinion survey (White 1970), ordinary members of the public (= A) and Sōka Gakkai members (= B) were asked how far they had completed their education. The results (White 1970: 64) were as follows:

	(A)	(B)
Graduated from elementary school	21%	19%
Graduated from junior high school	41%	55%
Graduated from senior high school	29%	18%
Graduated from university	8%	4%

Though the findings cited above apply only to Tenrikyō and Sōka Gakkai, and the membership of some of the new religions are thought to consist of higher social strata, the overall tendency in new religions in respect to social strata is believed to approximate that of these two groups.

Another matter that is important when looking at the difference between the functions of Christianity and the new religions within Japanese society is the difference in their views of the world and in their views of salvation. In the new religions the attitude is that human beings are by nature good, and that by purifying their hearts through their own efforts they can go on to draw nearer to a happy life.

And in this world the family is linked with salvation, in that becoming happy together with the people around one is considered to be the highest goal in life. As was pointed out before, the salvation of the new religions is this-world affirming, humankind affirming. One might say it prefers to turn its eyes to the brighter, more positive things about human beings and life. Let us look at this characteristic as it shows up in Tenrikyō.

> Because Parent God wanted to see joyous life and to share this joy with someone else, he created man. For this reason, bringing this desire of Parent God to fulfillment is the meaning of human life and the ultimate goal of the human race.
>
> *No matter how long you believe,*
> *Let it always be with a heart full of joy.*
>
> A bright, cheerful heart – that is a happy heart. True happiness, and worthwhile living, are to be found in spending all one's days with a joyous heart. No matter how long the road one trods, if the heart is not cheerful, is gloomy, it is not in tune with the heart of Parent God. Living every day in joy and pleasure, safe in the protection of Parent God, is an experience that cannot be surpassed in this world. When one opens the closed windows of one's heart and receives the infinite light of Parent God upon oneself, the dark clouds of confusion disperse of themselves and one stands in a circle of bright joy. What is meant by a happy existence is a life full of pleasure (Tenri-kyō Kyōkai Honbu 1949: 92–93).

> The fact that Parent God allows us to experience so many different fates stems from the desire of Parent Heart to use them to make people change their hearts, or to cheer them up, so that they will have a happy existence. Even when Parent God allows us to experience unpleasant fates, it is not from a desire to make us suffer or cause us trouble. No matter what situation we find ourselves in, if we lean upon the Parent Heart that leads us to good and if we keep our hearts calm as we pass through the situation, everything will be restored to the original fate of a happy existence, the limitless blessings of Parent God will flow without end to the person, and his heart will become brighter and more cheerful.

A person's happiness does not lie in his surroundings; the pains and pleasures of human life are not determined by external appearances. All things depend on the way each person keeps his heart. Correcting the way one keeps one's heart and living every day in cheerful joy, that is the way of the believing heart (*ibid.*: 71–72).

In the above text the words 'correcting the way one keeps one's heart' refer to the clearing away of the blemishes of the heart that are represented by the 'eight blemishes' of 'begrudging, wanting, judging ugly, judging pretty, envying, being angry, being greedy, being proud' – in other words, they refer to cleansing of the heart. It is believed that one can head in the direction of 'a happy existence' by having one's own heart made pure through being filled with the cleansing action of God.

How does this compare with Christianity? Let us turn to one Yamamuro Gunpei (1872–1940), who devoted his whole life to bringing the Gospel to the common people and preached the teachings of Christianity in easily understood language.

In olden times a man named Shokusanjin made up his mind to stay away from all alcohol. Two days, three days passed, and already he couldn't stand it anymore, so he promptly broke his resolve. When he did so he wrote a poem on the paper door next to where he sat: 'My vow not to drink has ended up a tattered garment; come on, pour me another drink!' Now, this story of spineless failure is not a story of Shokusanjin alone; the world is full of such people...This is the way it goes with something as simple as alcohol or tobacco. When it comes to all the different kinds of sins like pride, servility, deceit, lechery, insincerity, laziness, jealousy, thievery, unkindness, impiety, and other vices, how can a person be expected to win against them on his own power?

There are those people who, in the inner rooms of their houses, do things that are unpardonable, but out where other people can see them they pretend to be oh-so-perfect – I'm talking about hypocrites. But people like this are like the whitened sepulchers that Christ spoke about; no matter how fine they are on the outside, inside they are full of rotting and dead bones. You can be sure that, in the presence of God, who sees to the very core of man's being, they are not worth a plug nickel. Then what should we do? Clumsiness in being honest is far better than skillfulness in deceit. The only way we can be saved from the likes of sin is, along with King David of ancient times, bemoaning the way

we are and, relying on God the Father in Heaven, allowing ourselves
to be saved by his power. (Yamamuro 1899 [1992]: 39–41)

Obviously, Tenrikyō is only one example of the new religions, but
still the general framework of its views of the world and of salvation
is similar to that of many of the other new religions. Within that
framework you see that a person changes into a good person in this
world by his own power, and expectations are placed on becoming
happy in this world by doing so. Sometimes the world after death is
believed to be important, but even in such cases it is not believed that
the ultimate good life will be realized in the world after death. In
contrast to this, in Christianity the human person is fundamentally
a deeply sinful being, the evil that humanity produces is something
difficult to remove, and this evil can only be overcome by the power
of God. And ultimately the only way humanity can be cleansed from
sin is in the next world, after death.

Yamamuro, who was an officer in the Salvation Army, stressed that
the believer could undergo change in this world through the process
of sanctification, a belief he inherited from the Arminian theology of
the Methodist tradition. As a person who carried out a propagation of
the Gospel that was deeply rooted in the lives of the common people,
Yamamuro was someone within Christianity who had a keen interest
in self-reformation in the present world. In spite of this, he stressed the
deep sinfulness of humanity and rarely referred to happiness in this
life. One of the reasons for this, no doubt, is the difference between
Christianity, which stresses the break between God and humanity,
and Japan's religious tradition, which accepts as perfectly natural a
continuity between the gods and the human person. Another reason
is that, in Japan, traditional Buddhism, particularly the Pure Land
sects, represents a this-world-denying doctrine, and people feel this is
something they can relate to because of their familiarity with funeral
Buddhism and traditional culture. The new religions that appeared
on the scene in modern times presented an alternative to that familiar
this-world-denying view of salvation, and they no doubt built up a
relationship with funeral Buddhism in which they each catered for
different aspects of religion.

Christianity within the new religions

The earliest of the new religions, Nyoraikyō, founded by Isson Nyorai
Kino (1756–1826), is more similar to Christianity than other new

religions, and at one time there were those who argued that Christian influences could be found in it. Ishibashi Tomonobu, a religion scholar specializing in Old Testament studies, published in 1927 an essay entitled 'A Hidden Messiah Religion in Japan,' thus bringing Nyoraikyō to the world's attention.

> Just as Jesus, conscious of himself as the Messiah, the savior of the world who would redeem it from sin, was worshipped after death as the son of God, the Christ, and overseas there arose the Christian religion (a Messiah religion) that reveres and prays to that Messiah (Christ), so too over here the woman 'Kino,' who ended her days in the world as the sin-redeeming Lord and Messiah who suffered tribulations, and who was also called Ryūzen, is now worshipped, revered, and prayed to as 'Ryūzen Nyorai,' and at the present time there is this hidden Messiah teaching being followed in our country. This is a really amazing similarity. The fact that it has, however, obviously not received any influence from the Christian religion whatsoever, that it is purely made-in-Japan, a domestic product, makes it all the more fascinating from the standpoint of comparative religion studies. (Ishibashi 1927a: 504)

If we look for a similarity on the score of 'a founder who suffered tribulations,' then other examples exist as well. Ishibashi has noted that Nyoraikyō also has creation myths, but these can be found in other groups as well. Tenrikyō and other new religions also teach about the ordeals of their founders, and they have creation myths. Still, in the case of Nyoraikyō we find other features as well – an idea of original sin and an orientation toward the world to come – that make the resemblance to Christianity striking. In this new religion that appeared on the scene slightly earlier than the other new religions, there is a this-world-denying way of thinking that is deeply colored, experts believe, by the influence of Buddhism, particularly that of the Pure Land sect. Commenting on this point, Ishibashi says:

> Mankind is evil. Right from birth, all man does is heap evil upon evil. There is not a single good person. Even the ancestors 'are unworthy to enter the Good Land [the Pure Land].' The world of man is nothing but a world of sin. 'In this Valley of Tears peace of mind and freedom from care are impossible.' There is no salvation, no hope. Wishing for salvation is useless – the more dire the situation, the more useless the wish.
>
> There are many gods in the world, but only Nyorai is incomparably high. It is Nyorai who creates the human race and the world and disposes

all things. Who is all-knowing, all-powerful to the highest degree. Whose heart is love, and who therefore undergoes all kinds of suffering for the sake of the salvation of the sinful world, sinful offspring. Who, moreover, exists in the transcendent reaches of the upper world, continuing to agonize for the sake of delivering this lower world from its sins.

It is believed that it is the foundress to whom the agonizing heart of Nyorai was revealed and who accomplished the salvation that the loving Nyorai agonized over. Accomplishing Nyorai's salvation and thus becoming the savior, revealing the Nyorai of love and thus held to be Nyorai in another form, the foundress is now revered as Ryūzen Nyorai.

Taking this Nyorai as the only support, abandoning all consideration of devices based on self-power, turning away from cleverness and resourcefulness, believing wholeheartedly in Nyorai's salvation, taking on the love of Nyorai, putting love into practice, storing up good, hoping in this way to reach in the next world the 'boundless Good Land' at the side of Nyorai, keeping Nyorai in mind at all times, being unrelenting in effort – this is what it is to be a follower of the Nyorai teaching of Ryūzen Nyorai, this is the Isson teaching that takes Isson as its founder (Ishibashi 1927b: 126).

Ishibashi came to the conclusion that there was no influence of Christianity on Nyoraikyō, but Murakami Shigeyoshi (1971b) thought there was a possibility of influence by the Kirishitan (Christians who had been forced into hiding by severe persecution in the seventeenth century) who were living in the part of Japan where Nyoraikyō originated.

The divine status of Nyorai as supreme god, creator god, and savior god is nearer to the view of the God of Christianity than to the divine status of the monotheistic Amida Buddha. Konpira, the messenger of Nyorai who visits Kino, corresponds to the concept and the role of the angel that is a feature of the monotheism of the Semite line: Judaism, Christianity, Islam, etc. The concept of sin is completely alien to the traditional view of sin and evil in Japanese society, that is, the optimistic view that sin and uncleanness are things that adhere from the outside and that sin is removed by being brushed away or washed off. Whereas Tenrikyō, which carried on from Nyoraikyō, formed the idea of 'blemish' along the lines of 'sin' and 'uncleanness,' Kino's theory of original sin is a pessimistic philosophy of redemption from sin that considers this world a place for 'Buddhist asceticism.' This view of sin and evil is closer to the idea

of Christianity than to Shinran's idea of evil human beings full of sins
and bad karma. These ideas are said to stem from the influence of the
Kirishitan upon Nyoraikyō, an influence that is amply conceivable from
a religious history standpoint (Murakami 1971b: 585–86).

Later, Kanda Hideo, a scholar who conducted the most comprehensive
research on Nyoraikyō, would conclude that a Christian influence
on Nyoraikyō is unlikely (Kanda 1990: 133–35). What had strongly
influenced Nyoraikyō had been Pure Land teachings, the Nichiren
Sect, Shugendō, Konpira belief, and so on. According to Kanda, the
more likely interpretation is that these sources provided a seedbed in
Japan's commoner society from the end of the eighteenth century to
the beginning of the nineteenth century from which sprang a salvation
religion that closely resembled Christianity.

It was after the middle of the nineteenth century that Christianity
would again reveal itself to Japanese society as a living religion instead
of a body of knowledge encased in written documents. And from this
period on, the gap between the new religions and Christianity would
proceed to widen. This can be seen from the fact that the period of
establishment and development of Christianity in Japan overlaps
the period of establishment and development of Tenrikyō, the new
religion that is typical of the early new religions with their 'joyous
life' teaching. Its foundation as a religious body firmly established
in the 1860s, Tenrikyō would be able to claim over four million
followers in 1929 (Tenrikyō Dōyusha 1929: 286). It was just at this
time, when the emphasis on sin and the idea of salvation in the next
world that were so prominent in the heyday of Nyoraikyō would be
receding into the background in the new religions, that Christianity
began propagating its teachings in Japan. It would be wrong, however,
to think that the common people in Japan turned wholeheartedly to
this-world-affirming views of salvation, because at this very same
time Pure Land Shin sect was also still going strong.

When one looks at the development of the new religions after this
time, one finds that Christianity and the new religions developed along
parallel paths. There were, however, a few times when the two paths
fused to result in a 'Christian new religion' or in a 'new-religion-like
Christianity.' Let us briefly touch, then, on the two questions of how
new religions made contact with Christianity, and how Christianity
developed into new religions.

Both Deguchi Onisaburō (1871–1948) of Ōmotokyō and Taniguchi Masaharu (1893–1985) of Seichō no Ie knew quite a lot about

Christianity. The religious world of Ōmotokyō was shaped by Deguchi Nao (1836–1918) and Onisaburō, but nothing connected with Christianity comes from the writings left by Nao, who had very little acquaintance with written culture. Wherever the contents of Christian teachings appear in Ōmotokyō materials, it is almost always in the writings of Onisaburō. One reason the latter had such a strong interest in Christianity was, as he himself said, that he wanted to explain the connection between the God of Judaism and Christianity and the god of Ōmotokyō.

We can refer to some of the modern doctrinal texts as we pick out the main lines of Onisaburō's thought. The god of Ōmotokyō is called Sushin (= Lord God). This is 'the true god that is the original source of the universe...In order for this true god to save the human race of the present times from great danger, the persons especially possessed by the god were the Foundress [i.e., Deguchi Nao] and the Holy Teacher [i.e., Deguchi Onisaburō]' (Ōmoto Honbu 1975: 46). Through these 'two great god-humans,' the two great scriptures of *Ōmoto shin'yu* and *Reikai monogatari* were revealed to the human race. When one reinterprets the sacred scriptures of the past in the light of these two works, one realizes that the former were only expressing the truth imperfectly. Still, many religions do talk about the true god; in Japan's *Kojiki* the true god is called Ame-no-minaka-nushi-no-kami, and in the Bible it is called Jehovah. Moses was correct in understanding the true god to be the only god, but his way of explaining the 'divine virtues' of this god was mistaken.

The view that Ōmotokyō and Christianity worship the same god is connected with the idea of 'thousands of religions, one root' (Tsushima 1989). 'Thousands of religions, one root' holds that all religions have the same root source; the idea is that truth is contained to a certain extent in other religions, and for that reason they have a certain value, but because they all are imperfect, they have to be united by Ōmoto. Thus it is that Christianity is seen as one of the religions that has a certain amount of significance and ought to be united into Ōmoto, and for this reason it is the object of Ōmoto interest. Indeed, Christianity would take a place alongside Buddhism as the most frequently mentioned religion in Ōmoto commentaries. The case of Ōmoto shows, one can safely say, the classical pattern of what happens when a new religion draws near to Christianity. While on the one hand Christianity is perceived as a formidable opponent attacking one's position from the outside, it is treated as something that has to be absorbed by taking in as much of its doctrinal content as possible.

Having looked at an example of a new religion making contact with Christianity, we now need to look at 'Christianity within the new religions' from the opposite direction, that of a Christian group developing into a new religion. This is closely connected with the indigenous Christian movements discussed in Mark Mullins' work *Christianity Made in Japan* (Mullins 1998). These indigenous movements are religious groups that, while possessing a Christian framework (at least in the beginning), took on other elements as well and more or less ended up being distinguished from traditional Christianity. These groups stand somewhere between Christianity and the new religions. If you imagine a coordinate axis running between the two opposite poles of Christianity and new religions in Japan, you can visualize these groups as moving away from the Christian pole and nearer to the new religion pole, the more non-Christian elements take over positions of dominance. Thus, for example, while the Nonchurch Movement, the Original Gospel, and the Okinawa Christian Gospel are close to traditional Christianity, The Way, Christ Heart Church, and the Holy Ecclesia of Jesus are nearer the new religion pole. Whether to call them new religions or not depends (among other things) on how one defines a new religion. In the case of The Way (Dōkai), even were one to adopt a very narrow definition, it would almost certainly be classed as a new religion. Most of these indigenous movements could easily be called Christian new religions.

The Christian new religions also include some that are imports. Jehovah's Witnesses, the Unification Church, and the Mormons are groups that have achieved considerable success. Their growth since 1970 has been remarkable. The Jehovah's Witnesses, for example, began preaching in Japan in 1911; in 1933 and 1939 they were subjected to official regulation and their activities suspended; after the Second World War they began missionary work again under prodding from the United States, but as of 1966 they had only 4112 followers. Their numbers increased rapidly after that, and by 1975 they numbered approximately 33,000, then 108,000 in 1986, and finally approximately 223,000 in 1999 (these figures are based on Numata 1988 and materials provided by the Watchtower Bible and Tract Society). Many of the new religions that made progress during this period are referred to as 'new new religions' (*shin shin shūkyō*). It was not until after the beginning of the 1970s that the Christianity-related new religions made rapid progress and came to hold a large share of the religious pie. To put it another way, Christianity-related new religions figure quite prominently among the new new religions, and this is one significant difference from the situation among earlier new religions.

From the end of the eighteenth century and in the early nineteenth century, before the beginning of modernization, a small new religious group called Nyoraikyō preached a this-world-denying, pessimistic view of salvation that had many features similar to Christianity. But it was followed by new religions in which a this-world-affirming, human-being-affirming view of salvation became dominant, and the distance between the new religions and Christianity widened. Sometimes a new religion drew near to Christianity and sometimes the opposite occurred, but in neither case was there sufficient impetus to fill in the divide separating both sides, and nothing much ever came of these exercises. But then the period beginning with the1970s came along, a period in which a new generation of new religions, called new new religions, would evolve, and for the first time Christian new religions would form a major influence. Imported Christian new religions like the Unification Church and Jehovah's Witnesses must be reevaluated as religious groups that have an important significance from the standpoint of the history of Christianity in Japan. This is because of the possibility that the great success enjoyed by these groups indicates that the time has arrived when the this-world-denying view of salvation preached by Christianity once more looks appealing – this time not to Japan's intellectuals, but to the ordinary common folk.

Beyond new religions and Christianity

In Japan, the concept of salvation contained in new religions came closer to that of Christianity after the 1970s. On the other hand, however, people who were discontent with the concept of 'salvation' itself, or with organized salvation religions, increased, and the trend away from salvation religions became apparent. In Western countries, about the same time increasing numbers of people became detached from Christianity and found themselves unconvinced by modern rationalism as well, and they became interested in something religious in a broad sense. The fashion of meditation and drug use that developed in the counter-culture movement of the 1960s anticipated this change. Young people in the West in those days became suspicious of Western civilization that had sought 'progress' by rational and efficient production and scientific technology that supported such production, and came to seek a new way of life. What they sought was a third way, departing both from Christianity and modern rationalism. While some people who place some expectations in a third way directed their interest to Buddhism and other Eastern religions or new religions, others are disappointed with salvation religions or organized religions in general and seek something like a post-religious worldview. In the West, this movement is usually called the 'New Age' movement.

The term 'New Age' has not taken root in Japan, and instead, the term 'Spiritual World' has come to be used widely. The 'Spiritual World' in Japan and the 'New Age' in the West are not identical phenomena. It is misleading to apply the local term 'New Age' to generalized phenomena of a different character that can be found in different regions of the world. Even in the West, some people who are part of the movement do not find it appropriate to be embraced under the term of 'New Age.' Rather than using a term specific to the thought of a certain group of people, it is better to apply a simple term to express the characteristics of the movement objectively. With this thought in mind, the author advocates the term of 'new spirituality movements/culture,' as he considers that a 'new spirituality' is the central characteristic of this movement (see Ch. 15 and 16).

What then does this 'new spirituality movement/culture' mean? Its outline is explicated in Part 4. Here, views of two sympathizers of the movement, taken from *Shūkyō Jidai* (Religious Age) (1988), a collection of interviews by Yoneyama Yoshio and others are presented.

Ms. A.K., age 22

Profile: After graduating from high school, she went to the USA to study. Upon returning to Japan, she worked as a bartender in a disco and a translator for video programs. Currently, she works as a stylist and free-lance writer for magazines.

> I began to hang out when I was in junior high school. I often had quarrels outside, and wouldn't get home until early the next morning. My parents did not scold me. But when I was a second year student in high school, I realized that I should not continue living in that way, and began reading books. The first book I read was *Vibration* by Ramakrishna. I was impressed by the phrase that says something like 'every person should accept what one is.' I felt very relaxed and relieved.
>
> I found a very good episode in this book. One day, a person asked for a ride on a cart to a town. While he was moving to the pitching and rolling of the cart, he came to feel high, and began singing. Then the carter also

joined him singing. Both forgot to go to the town and continued dancing and walking to their songs.

Don't you like that story? They are so in tune to their own feelings, wonderfully optimistic. I feel that we need to live with more optimism.

I took part in a twenty-day fasting course, and reached a calm state of mind. I experienced changes in my emotions, and I did not get angry as easily as before. While fasting, I had for a moment the feeling that I am the same as the universe. 'You see, the universe exists within a human being. A human being is a part of the universe. When you free your mind from everything, and when you act naturally, the universe within you and the external universe are united.'

For two years now I have been visiting a Kung-fu training class run by Kozo Nishino. During the class, Nishino sends *qui* (life energy) to me, and I can feel the power of the universe. After learning a correct method of breathing, I can feel oneness with the universe. I can recall that I had stronger *qui* than any one else when I was a child, and now I understand why mysterious things happened to me in my childhood.

Be it while enjoying sexual intercourse, or being high on a drug, the feeling of ecstasy is the shortest way to feel oneness with the universe. Love, or sex, might be better than drugs because they are more natural. Everyone has a chance to feel ecstasy. So I hope that all people will realize this and try to find it.

I don't like religions, because they are pushy. I don't like having someone tell me what to do. It is waste of time and energy to force yourself to do something, and go through stoic training. I can be more natural in enjoying life, and being optimistic. Being natural is the best way to live. Nobody should force someone to do something.

Mr. K.S., age 39

Profile: Since he traveled to Bali, Indonesia, for the first time five years ago, he has been visiting there twice a year on average. He quit his job with a trading firm, and left Tokyo. He now lives in Nagano prefecture growing vegetables on an organic farm. He is preparing himself to open and manage a pension for tourists.

I made frequent visits to the United States as a trading company employee. I tried various kinds of drugs. When I went to Bali for the first time, I wanted to try 'magic mushrooms.' While visiting there, I came across people who were meditating. They appeared so refreshed and calm.

I wondered why and imagined that they were doing something very comfortable. I became more interested in meditation, and my interest in drugs was turned into one in meditation.

This did not mean that my values changed. The principle in my life is that I want to do something comfortable, and that something comfortable just changed from substances to something mental.

I came to study Hinduism through books. I was attracted by the folklorist Yanagita Kunio while studying at university, and I have kept my interest in folk religions. However, whatever great amount of knowledge you accumulate through reading, your understanding about anything is much less than what you learn from experience. I realized this after I met Wayan.

Wayan is a Bali magician who can speak English. When he visited Japan, I accompanied him for two weeks. While living together with him, I was strongly inspired by his spirituality and his way of living. I attempted the meditation that he taught me, and had new experiences. I felt my finger tips get hot as if they were electrified, then fell into a swoon and felt comfortable and calm. So I meditated every night. About a week later, I had a mysterious experience, seeing in a vision the supreme deity of Bali. Weeks later, I had another experience of being filled with a sense of ecstasy. It was such a pleasant feeling, and I noticed that my body was swaying and giving voice to that feeling.

One of the reasons for my sympathy with the Hinduism of Bali is that the religion is not dichotomous, dividing things into black or white, good or bad. Just as religions in Japan developed while syncretizing various religions on the base of animism, religions in Bali are syncretic. A painting illustrates the story that Buddhism has expelled Hinduism. In the picture, a dragon (Buddhism) swallows the moon (Hinduism), but the moon is emitting shining rays in the belly of the dragon. It implies that it is worthless to stick to the 'win or lose' concept in your life. In the present religion boom in Japan, there is no tolerance between believers of different religions. Yet in Bali, people are tolerant. In Bali, I can find religious scenes that existed in earlier Japan.

The above interviews were taken during the period when new new religions, including Aum Shinrikyō, were gathering strength. Many believers of Aum Shirikyō had harbored strong interest in the new spirituality movements/culture before entering the group. It was in 1978 that a corner devoted to the 'Spiritual World' was allocated a place besides the 'religion' shelf in large bookstores. From around this year until the early 90s, the Spiritual World boom was at its peak, when many people were attracted to yoga, *qigong*, meditation, healing, psychological therapy, near-death experience, self-enlightenment seminars, mysticism, alchemy and the like.

After Aum Shinrikyō released sarin on the Tokyo subway in 1995, some religious organizations such as Life Space, which insisted that the corpse of one of its member was still alive (2000), and Pana Wave, whose members wore completely white uniforms and insisted electromagnetic waves were causing great harm and that the earth was in crisis (2003), were the object of widespread scorn. These incidents cannot be understood without knowledge of the boom of the 'Spiritual World.' Can these strange phenomena be considered as the end result of the new spirituality movements/culture that was popular at one time? Is the new spirituality movements/culture becoming more subdued? Was it only a short-lived flower that bloomed briefly at the end of the period of rapid economic growth? After the Aum-related incidents, have people's minds been cleared and have they come to find more value in rational thinking?

It would appear not. Books on the Spiritual World still occupy considerable space in bookstores even today. People's interest in the Spiritual World continues and develops further, although in somewhat different ways from before. Interest in 'healing' and 'spirituality' is seen broadly among people in developed countries. What is common in these terms is a desire to seek something different from institutionalized religions. It may happen to develop into a closed new new religion such as Aum Shinrikyō, or into a cult movement. The general tendency among participants in the new spirituality movements/culture is that they do not like institutionalized religious organizations or firmly established institutions. They rather prefer aiming for self-transformation and spiritual growth in a loose network on an individual basis. In the 21st century they are the successors of the youth culture of the 1970s, and they likewise value strongly the independent activities of individuals and avoid organizational and hierarchical orders. Many individuals reflect upon themselves in search of their self-identity, and extend their interest in domains where science or rationalism cannot intervene.

As they do not establish churches or organizations, it is difficult to identify where groups are and what kind of bonds hold the members together. However, as we can see from books and other material on these movements, as well as from conversations with members, the concept and way of living advocated by the new spirituality movements/culture deeply permeates the daily living of those who participate in these movements and culture. As such, interest in the 'Spiritual World' and 'spirituality' is a continuing phenomenon. After the 1990s, the materialistic characteristic of consumer society that extols individual freedom has weakened, giving rise to a simpler way of life in which only the basic needs of life are met.

Typical examples are grief-work transformation meetings held by the Association of People Thinking about Life and Death to nurture an attitude of facing death squarely, and self-help groups organized by people with disabilities or those suffering from various diseases. People suffering from neurosis, alcoholism, eating disorders, and discrimination gather together to seek ways to heal themselves. Through interacting with people who share the same problem and feel the same anxiety, members feel that they can rid themselves of their obsession, and that they are communicating with something greater than themselves. Prayer is a part of these activities and enlightenment a result. Without keeping this background in mind, we cannot understand the meaning behind the continuing popularity of works of art and entertainment containing spiritual themes, such movies like 'Mononoke Hime' and 'Harry Potter,' and children's stories by Kenji Miyazawa.

Both young and old, highly educated and those not so, seek to find meaning in life and reasons for living. They all need support to cope with death, the loss of loved ones, and various other kinds of suffering. The role long played by religion is now fulfilled by cultural resources and networks that have something 'religious' and 'spiritual' in their activities. Musicians, therapists, children's story writers, volunteers, people with disabilities as well as people who have lost a loved one can tell more heart-rending stories than those who belong to religious organizations. Thirty years after its appearance in the 1970s, the Spiritual World continues to spread widely in various forms into people's lives, even more persistently than before.

In many industrialized countries, including Japan, the culture in which high-ranking religious leaders and rationally thinking individuals who have studied science at higher educational institutes monopolized spiritual authority has collapsed in the final quarter of the 20th century. The new spirituality movements/culture provide us with signs that allow us to predict the characteristics of an emerging worldview, self-development activities, and a system to control one's mental and physical activities. The author himself as well as every reader of this book are interested parties in this long-term cultural transformation.

Part I:
Japan's New Religions in the Broader Scheme

1 New Religions and the Sociology of Religion in Japan

Diversity and complexity of religious culture in Japan

Asia is wide, and there is a diversity of religions and social scientific studies of religion in the various sub-regions of the continent. For the purpose of this chapter, the area under discussion is limited to Japan.[1] The relationship in Japan between religions and the sociology of religion in a broad sense will be considered, with an emphasis on the new religions. One of the reasons for this emphasis is that the study of new religions has been a major subject in the sociology of religion in Japan in the past few decades. In this section, the reason why the study of new religions has become an important subject will be explained, and the problems involved in the relationship between new religious organizations and religious researchers will then be discussed. While keeping the focus on new religions, care will be taken to give a broader view of the entire picture of the relationship between religions and the sociology of religion in its wider sense.

Japanese culture, in comparison to that of other countries in Asia, is often considered homogeneous. Indeed, it does have a more homogeneous culture and less diversity in language than China and India, whose huge expanses embrace multiple ethnic groups and religions, or the Philippines, Indonesia, and Thailand, which are smaller but equally diverse. Apart from the Okinawan population, Korean residents, and small numbers of overseas Chinese and indigenous Ainu people, there are few distinctive ethnic communities. From this fact, it might easily be inferred that Japanese religious culture is also homogeneous. In fact, it is not. Buddhism, although the strongest religious organization, is divided into multiple sects, and the differences in theory and practice among these sects are so great as to be almost inconceivable. Shinto has a weak cohesive power but its influence permeates people's daily life and customs and, at this point, it is no less influential than Buddhism. Confucianism is hardly to be found as a system of theory or practice, but Confucian thought, and the prescriptions based on Confucianism regarding the relationship with others are deeply rooted in the life of the people. Various systems of folk religious practice, such as Shamanism and mountain religions, and Western religions such as the Catholic, Protestant and Russian Orthodox churches have also had some influence. As such, the religious culture of Japan is very diverse and complex.

What caused this diverse and complex religious structure of Japan to become even more so was the emergence of new religions, which achieved remarkable growth from the 19th century through the 20th century. The 'new religions' in Japan are defined as the great number of religious groups that developed beginning with the transition from the early modern period to the modern period, or from the first half of the 19th century. The number of these groups in the 19th century was several dozens at most. But the number increased gradually from the 1920s and remarkably after 1945 when freedom of belief was guaranteed in the post-war Constitution. Sōka Gakkai, the largest new religious organization, claimed to have 7.5 million households among its followers in the 1970s. Although this figure is somewhat exaggerated, it is estimated that between three and four million people, or about three percent of the population, are conscientious followers of Sōka Gakkai. The total number of new religious organizations is unknown. The *New Religion Encyclopedia* (Inoue et al., eds. 1990) contains data on more than 300 organizations. I estimate the total body of followers of new religions to be between ten and twenty percent of the population. Public surveys show that about twenty-five percent of respondents answer 'yes' to the question of whether they believe in a specific religion. Therefore, according to my estimate, roughly half of the Japanese who have definite religious beliefs can be regarded as followers of the new religions.

New religions have developed based on the traditions of long-established religions – such as Buddhism, Shinto, Confucianism, Christianity or folk religions – into which new ideas and practical methodology were incorporated. For example, Western science, psychology, nationalism and utopian idealism, ideas that became influential in modern times, have been introduced, and new communication media and organizational or management theories have been adopted. There are also imported new religions that have been successfully transplanted in Japan such as the Jehovah's Witnesses, Mormons, Unification Church, Rajneesh Movement, Scientology and so on. New religions do not receive high respect from the public equal to that accorded to established religious organizations that have centuries-old traditions. While regarded as culturally deviant from the intellectual mainstream, these new religions have been supported mainly by relatively lower middle-class people, but also by other strata of society. In postwar Japan, they have certainly come to occupy an important place in the religious life of the people (Inoue 1992).

An important component of the modernization process of a country is the popularization or democratization of culture. In Japan, the popularization or democratization of religious organizations is seen in the evolution of new religions (Shimazono 1992a). In the United States, popular participation in Christian churches was encouraged on the basis of the diversity of the religious communities that came along with immigrants from Europe, which in turn promoted the birth of new sects and new religious organizations. Likewise in Japan, new religions have added to the diversity and complexity of traditional religious culture. Although they are similar in that they are religious organizations with popular participation, they have amplified the diverse and complex culture further in other aspects such as doctrines and practices. As a result, the structure of religious culture has today become increasingly complex.

Sociology of religion and the importance of folk religions and new religions in Japan

From around 1910 modern research on religions based on fieldwork was started in Japan. The range covered by the sociology of religion may be defined in many ways, and the wide variety of subjects and styles of study may be included. Research based on fieldwork constitutes an important method whereby a researcher seeks contact with people in those strata of society where people's views and practices are not sufficiently expressed in written texts, in order to comprehend their meaning and explicate their cultural background. Researchers of Japanese religions using a fieldwork-based approach are represented by Yanagita Kunio (1875–1962), Orikuchi Shinobu (1886–1953) and other folklorists. Their research on folk religions was successful as an approach to the religious culture of Japan, and exercised great influence on later social-scientific studies of religion. In later years, exchanges between folklorists, on the one hand, and sociologists, religious studies scholars, and cultural anthropologists, on the other, became frequent, so that social-scientific studies of religion now transcend the narrow boundary of the study of Japanese culture. Before the sociology of religion developed as a rigorous discipline, the study of folk religions in Japan had already yielded rich results. On the basis of these results, religious studies and cultural anthropology were intertwined, widening the direction of the development of sociology of religion.[2]

Religious studies in a narrow sense began to appear from around 1930 focusing on the structure of religious organizations, the quantitative measurement of concepts and the behavior of people, or a Weberian search into the relation between modernization and religion. Many excellent achievements were obtained in the following few decades, and these are often used as reference points today. Among them, Naito Kanji noticed that in the Ohmi district east of Kyoto, which produced many successful merchants, there was strong influence from the Jōdo Shin Sect of Buddhism, and explained how the doctrine of the sect was related to the virtues demanded of merchants, such as hard work and thrift (Naito 1941). Morioka Kiyomi illustrated that the organizational structure of the Jōdo Shin Sect took the form of a federation of households, and attempted to prove that the organizational character of this religious body was based on the principles of the organizational structure of Japanese society as a whole (Morioka 1962). Suzuki Hiroshi conducted research tracing the way in which the largest new religion, Sōka Gakkai, had been propagated in Fukuoka prefecture in northern Kyushu, and sought to demonstrate that this religion was a movement coinciding with the needs of lower-class people in large cities (Suzuki 1963–1964). These studies are a few examples that, using orthodox Western sociological concepts and methodologies, greatly contributed to the progress of sociological studies of religion in Japan.

The impact of Western sociology of religion became more apparent in the 1970s. Secularization theory, modernization theory, sects and new religions, and statistical analyses of various religious practices were studied, while the achievements of the sociology of religion in Europe and North America were also absorbed. The impact was most noticeable in the studies of religions that had well-established organizations or doctrines and ritual systems. In spite of the strong influence of Western sociology of religion, however, folk religion studies undertaken by native folklore scholars since the 1910s, as well as the influence of research by religious studies scholars and cultural anthropologists, have continued in importance. For example, ancestor worship, shamanism and belief in spirit possession are prominent in the religious tradition of Japan. If a name were to be given to a system of concepts and practices that embraces these elements as one category, it might be folk religion, popular religion or new religion. In Europe and North America, sociological studies of these types of religious phenomena have been made by cultural anthropologists or social anthropologists, rather than by sociologists. In Japan, these phenomena have been addressed in folklore studies, cultural anthropology, and religious studies.

From the 1910s to around 1930, folklorists such as Yanagita Kunio and Nakayama Tarō laid the foundation for studies on shamanism and spirit possession beliefs(Yanagita 1913–1914, Nakayama 1930). Their achievements were developed further by the religious scholar, Hori Ichirō, the folklorist, Sakurai Tokutarō, and the cultural anthropologist, Sasaki Kokan, in the 1960s and later (Hori 1971, Sakurai 1974 and 1977, Sasaki 1980). Among studies by scholars from Europe and America, Carmen Blacker's work is important (Blacker 1975). Her work was based on an approach from the viewpoint of folklore or anthropology of religion rather than from that of sociology of religion in its narrow sense. In taking up the study of shamanism and spirit possession beliefs today, new religions cannot be excluded. Those who study new religions have an interest in shamanism and beliefs regarding spirit possession, and one of the 'must read' books for them is *Ecstatic Religion* by the British anthropologist, I. M. Lewis (1971). Studies of folk religion and new religions are more prominent in the social-scientific study of religion in Japan. Those engaged in these studies belong under the umbrella of the social science disciplines, that is, to sociology, and even more to cultural anthropology, folklore, and religious studies. In the latter disciplines, the cultural aspects of phenomena are emphasized more than the sociological. In other words, an understanding of the meaning of a phenomenon is valued in these studies. Such understanding can be obtained through interpreting written texts as well as by communicating with the persons concerned. Methodologically, understanding, interpretation and dialogues through participatory observation, interview and text decipherment are emphasized. Instead of objectifying the persons to be studied as a quantitatively measurable entity, the researcher is urged to interact with the object of study and to regard those studied as dialogue partners. These researchers have a strong inclination toward interpretive study.

The position of new religions in culture and the development of studies on new religions

New religions in Europe and North America tend to indicate religious groups that uphold philosophies and practices clearly different from the mainstream religious tradition of each country or from the major religious traditions of the world. It would be misleading if new religions in Japan were perceived in the same way. Rather, new religions in Japan are much closer to the mainstream religious traditions of the population (Shimazono 1992a; Mullins et al. 1993). New religions are to some extent related to the traditions of Buddhism, Shinto and folk religions in Japan, and above all they are most closely associated with folk religion. If a female shaman attracts many followers, for example, this phenomenon is seen initially as part of existing folk religion. But as this group of followers comes to have regular, frequent meetings, as the founder's words are compiled in printed materials, as group behavior is codified, and as responsibilities are divided among followers in an organized manner, then, such a group approaches the category of new religion.

For this reason, new religions are often considered as groups that have close associations with the predominant character of Japanese religious culture, and many of the phenomena associated with them are not seen as deviating very much from the mainstream religious tradition of Japan. Just as storefront churches are a common phenomenon with deep associations with the mainstream American Protestant tradition, so new religions in Japan are seen as common phenomena of the Japanese religious scene, even though they have some extreme elements in the way they think and act. Hence, new religions attract the interest of researchers of the history and character of Japanese culture, just as Japanese folklorists sought to explicate the religious consciousness of the Japanese common people through studying festivals, rituals and oral tradition.

Although they have not deviated so radically from the mainstream religions, new religions have a strong sense of mission and pride in themselves. They also approach the public positively in order to increase their membership, and while doing so they are often involved in serious conflicts with the wider society. Since the beginning of the 19th century, when new religions began to be founded, fierce conflicts have been recurrent between emerging religious organizations, intent on expanding their membership, and the government, police, media, and existing religious organizations concerned about their expansion. There is, for example, the case of Ōmotokyō, which was suppressed by the government twice, in 1921 and 1935, or the cases of Renmonkyō and Jiu, which were attacked by the media and investigated by the police in the 1890s and 1940s respectively. The two latter have both almost ceased to exist. In turn, there are people who feel that they have been the victims of new religions and their beliefs. At times, new religions are seen as deviant from generally accepted values and mores.

Sociological research on new religions has been conducted in the environment described above. Some new religions, such as Tenrikyō, Konkōkyō and Sōka Gakkai, have universities or research institutes within their organizations in which follower-researchers conduct more or less scientific studies of religion in general or of their own religion in particular. However, on the whole, there is little active research within the new religions. There are only a few researchers who themselves are members of a new religion and who belong to a university or a research institute specializing in the study of new religions. In comparison with the number of amount of research published by researchers with backgrounds in Buddhism, Shinto, and Christianity who have studied their own religion, the output of researchers affiliated with new religions is very limited. It is generally the case that journalists or other writers who describe a specific new religion in some detail do so with the intention of either supporting or criticizing it. Researchers belonging to universities and other authorized institutes often take up the subject from a social-scientific point of view, after the public's evaluation on the new religion is already formed.

Research on new religions increased rapidly since the 1950s, and it developed around opposing views of the new religions. Positive views include the opinion that they offer a critique of existing discriminatory and oppressive social structures and seek to realize a freer and more equal society, or that they attempt to revitalize, in modern society, important aspects of the Japanese religious tradition. Negative views on new religions maintain that they encourage the irrational cultural aspects of the pre-modern period that need to be relinquished in the modern world; that they turn people's eyes away from the real causes of social problems; or that they are dangerous groups attempting to propagate exclusively self-righteous, or even totalitarian concepts and systems. Some researchers adopt a position that includes both of these views, but others put stronger emphasis on either one or the other. Representative works that emphasize the former view are Kano Masanao's *The Sense of Order during the Formation Period of Capitalism* (1969) and Yasumaru Yoshio's *Deguchi Nao* (1977); those which emphasize the negative view are Saki Akio's *Newly Risen Religions* (1960) and Murakami Shigeyoshi's *Sōka Gakkai: Kōmei Party* (1967). Yasumaru's *Japan's Modernization and Popular Thought* and Murakami's *A Study of the History of Modern*

Popular Religions (1958, 1963) are more complex and include both viewpoints.

Since the latter half of the 1970s, there has been an increase in research activity on new religions, and during this time what has been stressed is the need to take a neutral stance on value judgments. This occurred because many researchers from sociology and cultural anthropology place a strong emphasis on neutrality. The most influential researcher to promote this was Morioka Kiyomi, who insisted on neutrality in value judgment and who practiced a research method that stressed the accumulation of objective evidence. Representative of his work is *The Developmental Processes of A New Religious Movement* (1989). Another example of this tendency was the work of a group of researchers born in the 1940s, including the present author, who jointly compiled *A Handbook for Survey and Research on New Religions* (Inoue et al. 1981), and *New Religion Encyclopedia* (Inoue et al. 1990). These researchers regarded it as important to acquire a deeper understanding of the facts concerning new religions before making hasty value judgments, and expended much energy in accumulating data and information through field research and gathering other research materials. They were, indeed, influenced by a positivistic sociological method.

On the other hand, there were researchers critical of positivism who were conscious of the need to understand the world of meaning of others and the need to examine problems arising from that world (Shūkyō Shakaigaku Kenkyūkai 1992). They were affected by the tradition of folk religious studies and earlier studies of new religions that had accorded high value to understanding the meaning system of those studied, and used interactive approaches to the people being studied. However, when researchers of new religions were about to begin a consideration of methodological approaches in the latter half of the 1980s, conflicts between new religious organizations and the public grew increasingly serious, and researchers became involved in these conflicts.

The intensification of conflicts surrounding new religions and the involvement of researchers

Up to the present, not a few new religious organizations have caused serious troubles for non-members. In the past, however, when new religious groups were exposed to strong public criticism, they tended to mitigate their aggressive attitudes and attempted to compromise with the general public. Before 1945, religious organizations that were regarded as dangerous elements in society were often kept under governmental control. Since then, with 'freedom of belief' guaranteed by the Constitution, it is understood that all religious bodies would be treated equally, and that control by the government would be limited to financial scandals or other such cases. Religious organizations acquired the ability to counterattack media assaults by legal procedures and by using media strategies. Thus, the situation changed, and the conflict with society was prolonged while new religious groups reacted to the criticism and assaults from the public with resistance and repeated counterattacks.

Long-term serious conflicts between new religions and the public began first in the 1960s with Sōka Gakkai, and then with the Unification Church. They grew increasingly serious from the 1970s to the 1980s, and finally became an outstanding social phenomenon toward the end of the 1980s.[3] Some major incidents in this process were as follows: Prior to the publication of *Criticizing Sōka Gakkai* by Fujiwara Kotatsu (Nisshin Hodo Shuppanbu, 1969), Sōka Gakkai put strong pressure on the publishing house and the author to halt publication of the book, invoking severe public criticism of its actions (Murakami 1979). During the same period, the Unification Church induced young members to live together in a commune, completely severing contact with their families and with the wider society for long periods of time. As a result, they came to be involved in heated conflict with parents and those who eventually left the group (Waga 1978). Since the Unification Church was strongly anti-communist, it attracted conservative politicians and scholars to its side, thus causing a greater confrontation with reformist parties. This may have been a factor that prevented the depth of the conflict from being revealed at the time.

In the 1980s, the Unification Church followers induced people to make large donations through deceptive sales of merchandise called *reikan shōhō* (sales based on extra-sensory perception) and were severely criticized for this practice (Naruse 1989, Yamaguchi 1993). *Reikan shōhō* is a method of selling that puts strong psychological pressure on ordinary people to buy, at extraordinarily high prices, seals, ceramic pots, and so on, said to possess some spiritual power. After a while, many of those who had bought these items brought law suits for alleged fraudulent fund-raising activities. In 1989, when the Cold War was ending, an incident concerning the match-making and subsequent marriage of well-known TV performers in a group-wedding ceremony held by the organization, as well as a further incident concerning a famous TV performer who left the organization as the result of persistent persuasion by her relatives, gave further impetus to the already strong criticism of the Unification Church. In 1991, another new religion, Kōfuku no Kagaku (Institute for Research inHuman Happiness, IRH) launched a major protest against a publishing company that had printed in its magazine articles critical of its founder. A large number of protest messages were sent by fax to the company. Following this protest, public criticism against this organization increased (Shimada 1992). Furthermore, public criticism of World Mate, Hō no Hana Sanpōgyō, and other new religious groups continued because of their coercive efforts to induce the donation of large amounts of money.

By far the greatest conflicts between the public and a religious organization were those caused by Aum Shinrikyō (Egawa 1991, Shimazono 1992a and 1995a, Reader 1996). Since around 1989, Aum Shinrikyō had been criticized for forcing followers to make huge financial contributions, and to adopt a hermit-like lifestyle after breaking away from their families. In response to public criticism, the founder and leaders tried to counterattack, and secretly murdered the family of a lawyer who had been working for those opposed to Aum's activities. Although the public suspected they had been involved in the murders, they continued to deny it. In February 1990, the founder and other leaders of the group stood as candidates for the House of Councilors and staged showy election campaigns. But, contrary to the founder's personal expectations, they suffered a crushing defeat. From that time, they became an increasingly closed community, and began building ashrams at various locations in the country for the followers to live a hermetic life. Local people began protesting against the building of Aum's facilities in their neighborhoods and conflicts increased (Kumamoto Nichinichi Shinbun 1992). While they became more isolated from the public, they made full use of the media in an attempt to gain public support by having the leaders appear in a positive light on TV programs, or arranging interviews between the founder and scholars or writers that were printed in popular magazines. In 1994, intending to kill the judges dealing with a lawsuit against Aum, they released sarin gas in Matsumoto city and killed seven people. They then began to insist that they themselves were victims of poisonous gas attacks, thereby arousing public suspicion that they were responsible for releasing the gas. Families of followers who had been forcibly taken to ashrams took legal steps against Aum Shinrikyō, causing the police to take decisive action. Conscious of an impending disaster in such an unfavorable climate, the group reacted. On 20 March 1995, they released sarin gas in the Tokyo subway, killing eleven people and injuring thousands more.

In the course of these conflicts between Aum Shinrikyō and the public, the media occasionally asked sociologists of religion for information about this organization, for comment on the lawsuits, or for explanations regarding the actions of the organization. Many scholars and writers were critical of the organization, while others attempted to keep a distance from both sides involved in the conflicts. There were, however, also scholars and writers who were influenced by the organization, or who expressed some apprehension about potential religious oppression. Professor Shimada Hiromi of Japan Women's University, a researcher who had been active in the field of sociology of religion, supported Aum Shinrikyō (Shimada 1992 and 1997). After the sarin incident, Shimada was severely criticized by the public and as a result resigned as professor in the autumn of 1995. The scope of Aum Shinrikyō-related incidents and Shimada's resignation posed serious questions regarding the social responsibility of religious scholars and sociologists of religion who have extensive knowledge concerning religious groups.

Responsibilities of sociologists of religion concerning religious groups

The relationship between the Japanese public and religious or-ganizations, especially new religious organizations, underwent a major change from the 1980s to 1995. Since the 1950s, when the system guaranteeing the freedom of belief was stabilized, there were always conditions that could stimulate conflict between religious groups and the public. When criticized by the public, religious organizations would compromise and make certain concessions. While aware that they might at any time be criticized again, they maintained a relatively stable existence based on the judgment that they were, to a certain extent, accepted by the public. Since the 1980s, however, sharp confrontations between religious organizations and major critical groups became common, and lawsuits were filed one after another. As a result of Aum's crimes, we even saw the forced intervention by the government in the affairs of a religious organization. Now many people make the claim that they have been the victim of the harmful practices of religious organizations. As seen most clearly in the case of Aum Shinrikyō, obvious evidence of damage is revealed to the public.

Sociologists of religion cannot help but become conscious that their research and the publication of their results is being conducted in environment of conflict. Sociologists of religion are now being urged to reconsider the methods of their research in this era of new religious conflicts (Fujiwara 1995). There have been two major streams in sociology of religion in Japan. One stream is based on the tradition of positivistic sociology emphasizing neutrality in value judgment. The other one is based on the methodological consideration of recent social science emphasizing the understanding of meaning and a dialogical approach based on the tradition of approaching the study of religious culture through religious studies, folklore and cultural anthropology. Researchers belonging to both streams should find something new to learn from the current state of religious conflict.

Researchers in the former group who claim to be positivists presenting only neutral, objective facts are now challenged to consider whether that method of research remains feasible. In order to do research on a religious organization, you must collect information. And for this, you need to develop relationships with those who have an interest in the organization. The quality and quantity of the information will vary depending on those with whom you come into contact. Inevitably, your own subjective nature and the nature of your relationship with the informants will be reflected in your research. There is a necessary limit, even if you attempt to obtain fair and objective information. Publishing the result of your research may affect people with an interest in the religious organization to some degree. When a religious organization is a party to a suit filed by a former believer, for example, an academic report by a religious sociologist may be used to favor either one or the other of the parties. Sociologists of religion cannot pretend to take a purely objective stance. Rather, they need to be well aware of their own standpoint when establish contacts with informers and when they select what information to use for their research. It may be appropriate to express what value-premises underlie their research. The value-neutrality that Max Weber referred to needs to be reevaluated.

Researchers of the latter group who place emphasis on under-standing meaning and dialogue with the persons studied may claim that they are aware of the fact that subjective elements are included in the information they gather and that the interaction between them and those studied may be reflected in their research results. They need to examine, however, to what degree they are conscious of all the interests involved in their understanding of meaning and dialogue. It is important for them to know that they may not have full insight into the area that they are researching. Researchers can never hear the voices of all the people concerned. Indeed, they cannot always be attentive even to the major interests of important persons of the target group. Ideally, dialogue should be held with as many people as possible, but there is always a limit. Sociologists of religion should be fully conscious of this fact, and should be open-minded in listening to the views of others.

However, a consciousness of such limits does not mean that researchers should drop their interest in religious organizations. Certainly, one of the functions of scholars is to offer more objective perceptions and information regarding the targets of their research. Therefore, they should keep a certain distance from the object of their research, and present objective and proven information. However, they are able to make certain value judgments based on academic knowledge, something other people do not have the tools to do. When disclosure of a value judgment is required, sociologists of religion should be willing, especially in a situation of conflict, to present clearly the reasons for their judgment.

Researchers must be aware of the bias of their own viewpoints and conscious of the limitations of their awareness. Even so, when necessary they must be willing to present clear value judgments to the public. By doing so, sociologists of religion interested in religious organizations will be fulfilling the social responsibility that goes along with their social status. Sociologists of religion still have much to learn from the incidents involving Aum Shinrikyō.

2 Religious Influences on Japan's Modernization

Modernization and religion

The Weberian view and popular thought

Max Weber's *The Protestant Ethic and the Spirit of Capitalism* remains an important starting point in considerations of the relationship between religion and modernization in any society. This is primarily because of the following two points that he makes: first, in the background of Western modernization, especially in capitalistic industrialization, there rushes a torrid current of popular ethical reform that supported that modernization; and second, this popular ethical reform movement is linked to Western religious tradition and to the modernistic reform movements within that tradition, and was given direction by both.

In other words, Weber's essay is an attempt to interpret the Western 'human fundamentals of modernization' (Otsuka 1948) from the background of religious history, and we cannot ignore its perspectives even when we are studying the modernization of non-Western societies.

When one attempts to apply the ideas in Weber's essay to non-Western geographical areas, however, several problems arise, and we can easily see that it is necessary to make several adjustments to Weber's theoretical framework. In this sense Japan should prove a particularly interesting case in point. Weber thought that the 'human fundamentals of modernization' developed only with the concurrent evolution of Western religion, and he attempted to explain this evolution in terms of the peculiarities of the history of Western spiritual development. He believed that other geographical areas did not experience similar evolutions in religious tradition.

There is certainly no room to doubt that we will find no evolution of broad religious traditions similar to ascetic Protestantism in the Japanese modernization process. At the same time, however, it is clear that Japanese society did somehow manage to modernize and that in the background of this process we can find religious concepts exerting influence. This means, in my view, that we cannot content ourselves with calling Japan's modernization 'distorted,' but we must also point to the problems in the theoretical framework of Weber's essay.

For example, Weber gives particular weight to ascetic Protestantism, especially the Calvinistic dogma, as having exemplary significance. This is because he thought of Calvinism as being the most appropriate religious thought for bringing forth the 'human fundamentals of modernization.' At the core of Calvinism is the idea that salvation depends not so much on a person's inner qualities as it does on the will of a basically unfathomable God, and Weber explicates the significance of this predestination theory from the perspective of cultural history:

> That great historic process in the development of religions, the *elimination of magic from the world* which had begun with the old Hebrew prophets and, in conjunction with Hellenistic scientific thought, had repudiated all magical means to salvation as superstition and sin, came here to its logical conclusion. The genuine Puritan even rejected all signs of religious ceremony at the grave and buried his nearest and dearest without song or ritual in order that no superstition, no trust in the effects of magical and sacramental forces on salvation, should creep in.
>
> There was not only no magical means of attaining the grace of God for those to whom God had decided to deny it, but no means whatever. Combined with the harsh doctrines of the absolute transcendentality of God and the corruption of everything pertaining to the flesh, this inner isolation of the individual contains, on the one hand, the reason for the entirely negative attitude of Puritanism to all the sensuous and emotional elements in culture and religion...Thus it provides a basis for a fundamental antagonism to sensuous culture of all kinds. On the other hand, it forms one of the roots of that disillusioned and pessimistically inclined individualism which can even today be identified in the national characters and institutions of the peoples with a Puritan past...(Weber 1958: 105, emphasis added).

I would like to point out that with these words Weber shows he thought 'elimination of magic' and 'inner isolation' were at the base of the modern popular ethical reformation movement.

I believe that even though the relationship between religion and ethics noted here might represent one pattern of a reform movement in popular ethics that has been given motivation by religion during the modernization process, it is not the only gauge for judging the position of other examples. One must, insofar as one is looking at the Japanese modernization process, recognize that there are other patterns of relationships between religion and ethics, and religion and modernization, than those Weber noted.

Most of the scholars who have attempted to analyze Japan's modernization from a Weberian perspective have failed to think in these terms. The main reason for this is that they have clung to a view that emphasizes the pre-modern and unprogressive nature of Japanese society and have advocated a modernism bent on conquering this through use of the Western model. They have failed to appreciate the fact that there was a current of popular ethical reform in Japan and that this played an important role in the formation of the ethics of modern Japanese because they believe that most of the Japanese people were wandering lost in an 'enchanted garden.'

Yasumaru's contributions

Some significant changes in this way of thinking have come about since the appearance of the work of R. Bellah (1957) and Yasumaru Yoshio (1974). Yasumaru in particular has made it clear through ample documentation that the Japanese modernization process was in fact supported by a powerful movement of popular ethical reform, and he has done much to rectify the errors in the 'modernist' position.

According to Yasumaru, the Japanese people refined themselves ethically through the implementation of 'popular morality,' exemplified by virtues such as diligence, thrift, humility and filial piety. These virtues themselves he holds to be traditional, but says that in the crises of daily life, which accompanied social differentiations that came to be established among the merchant and independent farmer classes, their actual practice was pushed to the limits, and this resulted in the formation of an ethical self that worked to destroy traditional attitudes. This trend to build up a self based on 'popular morality' began in the seventeenth century in the major urban areas of Japan. By the nineteenth century it had spread throughout the country, and by the end of that century had taken root at the very depths of popular culture. Yasumaru says its contents can be seen in the 'popular thought' growing out of such phenomena as the *Sekkimon Shingaku*, *Hōtoku* and late Edo National Learning (*kokugaku*) movements; Ōhara Yūgaku; popular religions; the *myōkōnin*; the moralistic old farmers (*rōnō*); the leaders of the farmers' uprisings in the nineteenth century, and the like.

Yasumaru searches for the core of such popular thought in what he terms 'the philosophy of the heart' (*kokoro no tetsugaku*). This 'philosophy of the heart' is a spiritualistic worldview, holding that the human heart has unlimited potentiality: 'All things spring from the heart' (Ishida Baigan), 'Life and death, wealth and poverty, everything/ all comes from the use of the heart' (Kurozumi Munetada). This is something born from the realization of the power of one's own spirit and comes as the result of wholehearted practice of the 'popular morality.' In addition to reflecting the powerful self-affirmation of the populace it has contributed to the formation of the ethical self because it is a wholly coherent worldview. Yasumaru says that when viewed as social thought this idea on the one hand underscores the abstract equality of all humans, for all possess a 'heart;' on the other hand, however, it has the tendency to become a philosophy of resignation and forbearance, laying misfortune on the 'heart.'

I think that Yasumaru's research contains a corrective of the Weberian view of the nature of the popular ethical reform that supported modernization. Perhaps because he considered the ethical reform of the emerging bourgeoisie as typical, Weber treated the ethical reforms of the working classes as one part of this, but Yasumaru's research gives us another model, that of the populace (in which workers form an important element). When we attempt to understand the relationships between modernization and religion in these terms we need a different theoretical framework than that provided by Weber. Yasumaru himself, however, does not, in his writings, pay a great amount of attention to this point.

Yasumaru's views of religion

Yasumaru does not see religion in Japan – which lacks a transcendental deity in its religious traditions – as playing a very positive role in popular ethical reform. Indeed, the popular ethical reform brought about by the 'philosophy of the heart' is regaraded to be closer to atheism, and he says there is denial of magic due precisely to the tendency of the ideas to be human-centered. For example, he says the true significance in the ideas of the reformer of the Mt. Fuji cult, Jikigyō Miroku (1671–1733), lies in the fact that he reformed the existing Fuji cult 'from something ascetical and magical...to something that put the affirmation of popular morality at its center' (Yasumaru 1974: 100), and that this was an attempt to supplant the authority of magic with the authority of the 'heart.' The authority of magic was an 'unexplicable, all-powerful strength, existing apart from humans, which controls humans' (Yasumaru 1974: 32), and Yasumaru sees the central figure of worship of the Fuji cult, the Great Bodhisattva Sengen, as having been such a figure. Thus liberation from magic is tantamount to liberation from the worship of Shinto and Buddhist deities.

If we take such a viewpoint, how should we consider the new religions (popular religions), which worship deities who exist on a plane higher than that of humans and in which magical elements play such a crucial role? It can be said that all of the new religions contain elements such as magic and spells, charms, sacred rice and sacred water for the purpose of healing illness, although sometimes they are given new non-magical interpretations. In spite of this, it is true – as Yasumaru himself stresses – that these new religions contributed to the popular ethical reform movement. How, then, should we interpret the coexistence in the new religions of the promotion of an ethical self and of magic?

All the answers Yasumaru has given to these questions are fragmentary. He has said, for example, 'Magic has played an important role in the cases of the various popular religions, sometimes even becoming a determining stage in their propagation. Even so, there are also cases such as that of Konkōkyō, which, in the process of strengthening their characters as monotheistic religions, rejected magic' (1974: 32). Here he suggests that magical elements were 'a stage in propagation' having no connection with the original doctrine, and that there were new religions that clearly rejected magic. The place held by magical elements is, however, rather too large for it to be called a mere stage, and furthermore, even in the case of Konkōkyō (especially in that aspect of it that has generated so many new converts), elements such as belief in sacred rice and the worship of the head of the church clearly reveal a magical character.

Additionally, when discussing new religions such as Maruyamakyō or Ōmotokyō, which have a strong tendency toward social reform, Yasumaru has said that magico-religious elements such as spirit possession or violent ecstasy are necessary in order that the 'popular morality' might extend itself to social criticism. These elements enabled such religions to identify themselves with an absolute authority and hence to deny the established secular authority, and thus provided them with a magico-religious foundation on which to base their social criticism. Here Yasumaru recognizes, however negatively, a meaning in the magical elements, but he limits it to the element of social criticism. A separate explanation is necessary for those magical elements that fall outside the realm of social criticism.

I believe it is necessary to reexamine the whole question of whether the denial of magic is indeed one of the most important trends in popular thought based on 'popular morality.' In that he sees popular ethical reform and magical elements at opposite ends of the spectrum, Yasumaru has taken a position similar to that of Weber. For this reason he has, I believe, overlooked the question of how his suggestive new views concerning the content of popular ethical reform have been brought to bear on the problem of the relationship between modernization and religion. In what follows I will deal positively with the meaning of magical elements in religion and explore how they are connected to popular ethical reform; this is basically an attempt to add the views of a specialist in religion to the picture of popular thought painted by Yasumaru.

Popular ethical reform and magico-religious elements in new religions

Akazawa Bunji and Konkōkyō

Weber and Yasumaru do not precisely fail to define magic as 'an attempt, for whatever purpose, to utilize the assistance of a supernatural entity (deities, spirits and the like) or magical power in order to cause various phenomena, or the belief systems associated with such acts' (Yoshida 1973), but in their cases it is necessary to take 'associated beliefs' in a rather broad sense. As expressed by the term 'enchanted garden,' this does not differ significantly from animism or primal belief in their widest senses, and contains such elements as taboos, fortune telling and shamanism. I will refer to this as the 'magico-religious factor.' In this section I would like to deal with the power of this magico-religious factor to bring about popular ethical reform through the use of two or three examples.

Let us look first at Akazawa Bunji (1814–1883), the founder of Konkōkyō, a new religion that Yasumaru uses as an example of the tendency of the new religions to reject magic (see Konkōkyō Honbu Kyōchō 1953 and Shimazono 1980). When Bunji deepened his respect for the deities and grew resolute in his efforts to lead a life consistent with his beliefs the most important factor in this process was none other than the magico-religious one. From about the time he turned forty Bunji strengthened his ties with popular religion and it was through the divine words of a *sendatsu* (leader) of the mountain cult Ishizuchikō and those of a practitioner who worshiped the popular deity Konjin that he came to discover the religious reply to his several years of pain and doubt. During these years of religious questioning he had been sustained by a belief in the benevolence (*okage*) of the deities. He first received this deep belief in the benevolence of the deities when he was confined to bed with an illness and heard the promise of succor from a possessed *sendatsu* of the Ishizuchikō. One of the things that impressed Bunji at that time was when the *sendatsu*, acting for the deity, attached rice and beans to a sacred wand (*gohei*), then ordered Bunji to make them into a gruel and eat it. This act was at the same time a miracle that demonstrated the power of the deity, and also contained a magical significance concerning the living of a robust life. Later Bunji was to encourage the establishment of a personal belief among the populace with words such as *'Ikigami* (living god) Konkō Daijin [the founding deity] and Tenchi Kane no Kami [the parent deity]: In single-heartedness offer your prayers to them. God's benevolence dwells in your heart; pray this very day' (*Tenchi kakitsuki*). Standing behind such a statement is, of course, a strong belief in the magical/religious nature of the deity's benevolence.

That the establishment of such a personal belief stood in intimate connection with ethical reform we can tell from the example of Saitō Jūemon (1823–1859), one of the early converts to the religion, who entered after his wife had been saved from postnatal hemorrhage (see Aoki 1955). One of the things that lodged in Jūemon's heart after he first visited the house of the founder were Bunji's words, 'Belief, in all events, is a matter of having a pure heart – be filial to your parents, respectful and honest to people, treat your family business as important, and do not treat the deities poorly. Even if it should be an unimportant deity, remember that calamities come from below and that one should never treat any deity poorly' (Aoki 1955: 43). Hearing these words Jūemon looked back on his own life: 'Well then, well, what manner of a shallow human being I was! I was one who could not hear properly what people were saying to me, one who was, until today, causing all my own problems' (Aoki 1955: 43). His meeting with Bunji and his coming to know the power of the deities was tantamount to an ethical awakening for Jūemon.

The magico-religious factor in Tenrikyō

The magico-religious factor in Tenrikyō is even more obvious. Tenrikyō believers deepen their faith in their deity through *tsutome* (service) and *sazuke* (divine granting), times of magical-emotional exchange with the deity. *Tsutome* is a ritual performed daily, and also monthly, for the 'harmony between the deity and the people' (*shinjin waraku*), in which the 'sacred songs' (*mikagura uta*) are combined with 'hand dancing' (*te odori*) and sacred dancing (*kagura*); *sazuke*, which is performed for those suffering from illness, is a magical ceremony:

> First we clap the hands twice and call the deity down to us, then we report the name, age, sex and illness of the patient to the deity and pray for the success of the ritual, then, while reciting three times, 'expel the evil, please help us, oh Lord of Tenri,' and at the end of the third waving of the hands, we hold our palms as though we have received something from above, and are transferring it to the afflicted area of the patient. Then, while chanting three times, 'Assist us, we pray, oh Lord of Tenri,' we stroke the patient from top to bottom and at the third repetition we wave our hands and stroke. Then we (again) stroke the patient three times, then the arms three times, and repeat this all three times, bringing the ritual to an end. We once again pray for the success of the ritual, and clap the hands twice in order to send the deity back to above. Finally (or before this) we face the patient and explicate the doctrine, explaining the illness by using the doctrine, and encourage the practice of the doctrine (Ushio 1934: 99–100).

The function of the deity who gives birth to, protects and loves human beings is brought to life through such magical rituals, and the ritual elicits the deep respect of the people.

Of course faith is also supported by doctrine, a more prosaic, less emotionally intense form, and for that very reason the doctrine is explicated during the *sazuke*. The central core of this doctrine is related, for example, in the following terms:

> …all things in the world are the concern of the Lord, and there is not a single thing that can be accomplished by the power of the mortal alone. Hence there is not a single thing that could be called 'mortal.' All belongs to the Lord.
>
> Thus all things, beginning with the corporeal and extending infinitely, all things except the heart are borrowed and used day by day. If we were to identify the reason for this borrowing, it would be the heart.
>
> Thus, the heart alone belongs to us.
>
> Therefore, because the corporeal is protected by the Lord in his benevolence, we may leave things corporeal to the Lord and pass the days without care, but because the heart belongs to each of us, we must

hear the teaching and repent, hear and repent, day by day and day by day, gradually we must repent, and constantly perfect ourselves – this is how we must live (Moroi 1953: 154).

The idea of 'perfecting' the heart is, naturally enough, something that is expressed in daily life in terms of suppression of desire and in taking care in our various dealings with others:

That which we call *makoto* or *shinjitsu* (truth) is not a matter of merely being honest and looking out after oneself. If we do not practice the truth every day, if this practice is not there, then we cannot call it 'truth.' Most important is acting together and mutual cooperation, and hence to be even a little virtuous, even a little happy, even a little helpful, we must move our hearts. If we do, then the eight kinds of dust[1] will not only not afflict our own hearts, but they will not be allowed to cling, even in small particles, to the hearts of those around us.

Examples of this:

If you wish to keep the dust of greed from clinging to the hearts of people, divide up your own belongings and give them away; if you divide one thing in half, that will keep the dust of greed from clinging…If we look at something with regret, then others will undoubtedly feel regret, so quickly return even those things that have been forgotten; again, if it is something we have received from Heaven and which Heaven has protected, even if it is but a bit of cloth or a single piece of grain, do not allow it to fall into disuse, but use all things, wasting nothing (both passages from Moroi 1953: 157–58).

This, according to Tenrikyō, is how one should move one's heart.

The passages quoted here were written at about the end of the nineteenth century. They provide us both with a clear impression of the formative period of the Tenri church and also indicate the general ethos of modern Japanese popular religionists. The 'popular morality' based on rules of personal conduct are here tied to a devout faith. Because it is underlain with a layer of religious humility, it escapes rigorism and utilitarianism, and becomes something that incorporates a kind of warmth. This warmth is not unrelated to the feelings received through the magical/religious experiences in such events as, for example, the *tsutome* and the *sazuke*.

I believe that the above examples show that the magico-religious factor is inextricably interwoven with those elements that brought about the popular ethical reform. Of course, this does not mean that I believe that the religious consciousness that supported this popular ethical reform was completely unrelated to the dethroning of emotion and magic. There was, certainly, a dethroning of emotion and magic. This was not, however, accomplished through an expulsion of magic and emotion by rational elements; it was, rather, based on a drawing out of these magical and emotional elements, of giving them concrete shape and hence of sublimating them. The magical and emotional elements were perforce preserved (in a changed form) within the new religious consciousness and for this very reason the new religious consciousness provided an easy outlet for the non-rational feelings of the people.

The meaning of vitalism: Another modern doctrine

Vitalism in the new religions

In this section I would like to back up and deal with what in the previous section I called the 'magico-religious factor' in the new religions from the perspective of its structure as an element of popular thought based on 'popular morality.' It is easy enough, for example, to see that the Tenrikyō doctrine quoted above has a considerably different character from the 'philosophy of the heart' espoused by Yasumaru. In the 'philosophy of the heart,' the human heart is held to be omnipotent. While it is certainly true that the 'heart' is given an important role in the Tenrikyō doctrine, that which is omnipotent (at least, that which is omnipotent from the idea of actual salvation) is the deity; the 'heart' is said to be able to accomplish anything only insofar as it gives a 'body' to the omnipotent deity. Even though we call the deity omnipotent, however, he is certainly not considered to have a completely supernatural existence or to be separated entirely from the mortal world. The bulk of his will he divides among humans and his is an existence that functions together with, or perhaps in the midst of, humans. This type of thinking can be seen as an expression of the idea of 'vitalism' common to many of the new religions (see Tsushima et al., 1979).

In vitalistic religious thought the Buddha, *kami* and other such religious objects of worship are portrayed as the source of life, and humans and other forms of life are thought to have been born from this fundamental life power and caused to live through a sharing of their existences with it. Thus the true form of humanity is both to be completely merged in the natural internal life function and to be in a state of harmony with nature and other creatures, all of which share the same life existence. Belief in *kami* or in Buddha is to also believe in the connections between human beings and in the interconnected nature of the common life shared by human beings and all other things; such a belief is even a recovery of this state of interconnectedness. I think that one of the most important characteristics of the new religions is that their thought features a strong manifestation, in the purest possible form, of the connections between human and human, and those between humans and other things.

Vitalistic thought appears most typically in the new religions, but it is not limited to them. It is not especially difficult to read vitalistic elements in much of the thought that has developed in modern Japan, such as the concepts of heaven (*ten*), essence (*ki*) and nature (*sei*), or Buddha and Buddha-nature, as well as deity (*kami*) and spirit (*rei*). Vitalistic elements are particularly conspicuous in popular thought. For example, the idea of 'knowing the heart' of Ishida Baigan can be understood more completely if it is seen as an idea that has uncovered the vitalistic elements in the human ego that bring the individual into harmony with others and with nature than it can be understood if it is thought of as an example of spiritualism (*yuishinron*). This is perhaps a somewhat hasty speculation, but it does seem to me that vitalistic thought has played the role of guide in bringing about the popular ethical reform of the nineteenth and twentieth centuries.

A weakness of vitalism, and a response

Incidentally, it has frequently been noted that the thought in the background of the formation of a self based on 'popular morality' contains a conspicuous weakness. This can also be said of what I am calling vitalistic thought. The difficulty of avoiding social struggle caused by power structures, for example, is overlooked by vitalism. Yasumaru Yoshio touches on this point: 'The empirical cognitive power of the various forms of popular thought, while it may have great validity within the narrow confines of inter-personal relationships, lacks objective analytical power when applied to society as a whole' (Yasumaru 1974: 45). In Weberian terms, vitalistic thought reaches strong limits when it attempts to rationalize the actual world. Maruyama Masao would probably call this 'associative ideas' similar to 'Neo-Confucian thought patterns,' characterized by pre-modernistic elements and stagnation (Maruyama 1952). Even more people would probably worry about the dangers of religion being subordinated to political authorities.

There is something to all of these observations, but I would like to touch here on a point generally overlooked by those who make them. This is, namely, that even though it may be true that vitalistic thought is immature as a form of modern social thought, it is certain that it was able to play a positive role in helping people adapt to modern social relationships, and in that sense it presumably includes elements that were able to form the foundation for modern and post-modern social thought.

The modernization process dissolved traditional communal social bonds. In the process, people began searching anew for a clear intellectual symbol of the ties between themselves and others, and between themselves and nature; these were ties that had been evident until that time. Such symbols became one type of support for people who were adapting to modern social relationships. This precedes questions such as wholistic, rationalistic interpretations of the world, or of social order or ways of implementing social justice, and can be identified as an intellectual question existing at the most fundamental level of human life. Japanese vitalistic thought, of which the populace was the principal bearer, attempted to answer this most fundamental intellectual problem of the people who were in direct confrontation with modernization.

It is obviously not the case that this problem of finding a symbol of the ties between the self and others and between the self and nature was not dealt with by the thought of historical religions, philosophy or the social sciences. These thought systems, on the contrary, gave precedence to traditional thought patterns and to the ideas of the intellectual classes, and hence treated such questions as wholistic rationalistic interpretations of the world, or of social order or ways of implementing social justice as their primary concerns, dealing but briefly with the problem of intellectual symbols of the relationships between mortals and others, or between mortals and nature, as questions that had already been resolved. Japanese popular thought, including that of the new religions, themselves born of a folk religion base, began from the perspective of a basic lack of concern over such problems as wholistic, rationalistic interpretations of the world, or of social order or ways of implementing social justice, and were thus able to concentrate all their attention on this most fundamental problem of daily life. In this sense vitalistic thought can be called a thought system that has been able to deal forcefully, if naively, with this one aspect of the modern social experience.

Summary

I have attempted in this essay to present a rough outline of a thesis concerning the relationships between modernization and religion that differs from Weber's views. While Weber sees the meaning of Calvinism in the West as being an 'inner isolation' and an 'elimination of magic,' and hence as an attempt to liberate people from the bonds that tied human to human, and human to the world and to nature, I have interpreted the significance of the vitalism centering primarily around the new religions of Japan as an attempt to recover these bonds tying human to human, and human to the world and to nature. These, I believe, might be called the two patterns of interconnection between modern popular ethical reform and religion.

It was, of course, the Western world that most powerfully ushered in modernization, and the significance of Calvinistic thought as a precursor of modernization greatly eclipses that of vitalism. One cannot say, however, that vitalism has therefore made no contribution to modernization, or that religion in this sense did not provide one of the supports for modernization. This, I believe, supports a call for a reexamination of post-Weberian social-religious theories of modern religion.

3 On Contemporary Salvation Religion

What is salvation religion?

Among terms useful for categorizing the various phenomenon of religion, there is the term 'salvation religion': that is, a religion that holds the promise and pursuit of 'salvation' as its central tenet. Salvation religion played a critical role in the history of humankind, especially following the 'axial age,'[1] and continues to play a significant role in the lives of people throughout the world. In society before modernity, there was a relationship of mutual support between salvation religion, which held monopolistic authority over the spiritual realm, and the hierarchic political order, based on status distinctions. Cultures prior to the modern era were, for the most part, under the sway of salvation religion. As modernization progresses, and as society transforms into one characterized by post-modernity, with advanced democratization and pluralism of values, what is the fate of salvation religions? This chapter will attempt to map a general outline, with Japan as its primary focus.

The concept of 'salvation' assumes that human beings exist in a state of suffering, and thus are in need of salvation. Salvation religion focuses upon the nature of human suffering; differences among religions can be found in the various characterizations of suffering. Buddhism portrays suffering as 'a cycle of birth, age, illness, and death' and 'non-constancy,' while in Christianity we find the concept of 'sin.' There are limits that humans cannot overcome, and eventually those limits must be faced and succumbed to. While not apparent in the quotidian concerns of daily life in general, there is a reality of existence that comes to the fore when crisis situations occurs. These also provide the occasion for the emergence of the fundamental aspect of the human spirit, concealed in everyday life. Salvation religion encourages the human person to make a decisive choice in the midst of such existential crisis.

Karl Jaspers' concept of 'limit conditions (boundary situations)' may be seen as an attempt to render philosophically the thought of salvation religion.[2] Among the examples of limit conditions given by Jaspers are coincidence, conflict, death, and debt. For instance, in their pursuit of a better life, human beings inevitably face situations where they come in conflict with others, where they harm and are harmed by others. Also, while forgotten in daily life, human beings eventually must face their own death. A parent who has undergone the death of a child or some other excruciating pain may feel as if their very life had been taken away. Illness presents in a visible form such a threat to human life. In such moments of crisis, salvation religion shows the way to transcend the limits of human life in this-worldly existence, and frames humanity as a whole and the world as a whole within the context of the eternal.

A person who constantly reflects upon the limited condition of human life may appear as too serious and difficult to relate to. Salvation religion as a systematic thought may also appear to have such seriousness. It has a tendency to regard human limits and human suffering with more gravity than usually accorded these problems. However, at the same time, salvation religion presents the possibility of overcoming suffering and an optimistic hope of bliss beyond such sufferings. Beyond these difficult-to-overcome sufferings waits a miraculous, joyful bliss. While salvation religion emphasizes the limits of the human situation, it also provides the dramatic possibility of overcoming these limits. Religion in general promises to fundamentally renew human life through such experiences as ecstasy, union, and catharsis. In the case of salvation religion, ecstasy, union, and catharsis are experienced as moments of glory in achieving, or in expectation of, salvation over suffering. In this way, a powerful contrast between pessimism and optimism that far exceeds the joys and misfortunes of daily life appears before one's view. And thus the possibility for reflection in joy and freedom beyond the cycle of daily joy and misfortune arises.

Salvation religion provides a solid foundation for human thought. It lends a framework to understand human limitation and a means to overcome it; salvation religion also supplies the polar categories of suffering and hope, and other various bases for human thought that enables people to face precarious situations as they emerge. It provides for a 'foundation' that allows for an absolute standard for all things – for instance, in Tenrikyō, *moto no ri,* or *moto hajimari no hanashi* ('truth of origin,' or 'story of the origin'), a myth regarding the process human creation until the moment of revelation, provides a foundation of faith. This way of thinking, grounded in the mythical, is developed through systematic forms of ritual and thought, and functions to support social order as well as everyday life. For this reason, salvation religion was able both to lend support to the hierarchy of a status-based society as well as become the focal point of a new quotidian order in opposition to the established dominant order. Whether it functions in conservative or revolutionary mode, salvation religion is a powerful ingredient for the making of social structure.

However, this institutional order is not created only through abstract ideas or principles. Rather, it is established in the personal manifestation of a founder figure and an ideal human model that is expressed through story. The opposition of suffering and salvation is projected upon the founder-as-model, and is deeply ingrained in the minds of the faithful. An individual's life changes dramatically upon experiencing this model. Similarly, the history of humankind is divided into that before and after the emergence of the founder. A history of salvation is developed where the possibility of human salvation becomes attainable after the appearance of the founder. Through the indwelling within the human spirit of a supra-human figure representing the axis of human history, the human person is able to approach the possibility of salvation and become a decision making 'subject.'[3]

The human being whose shell was broken through cognizance of suffering and of the possibility for salvation begins to see others in a different light. No longer distant strangers, others, whose lives are separated from oneself in the order of daily life, his or her peers are now viewed as those who share the potential of breaking out of the shell of the same troubled existence. Others become comrades with whom one can face sufferings and seek joyful salvation. Seen from the point of view of common sense, salvation religion proclaims a rather extreme hope, that is, a hope that all people are capable of sharing the bond of friendship.

However, this 'ethics of religious camaraderie'[4] includes a peculiar contradiction. There is the possibility of discrimination and hostility between those who have awoken to salvation and those who subscribe to other faiths, or to none at all. When reflection on the limited condition of the human person predominates, then this ethic encourages the attitude of compassion and the sharing of suffering rather than hostility to those who have not yet seen the truth. However, as a group with a mission to spread the truth of one's salvation, there is also always the possibility of exclusion or even attack on non-believers. As long as salvation religion has as its foundation the unconscious separation of the world into those who share one's belief and those who do not, there is always the possibility for the formation of new groups among those who are unsatisfied with the status quo. As long as there are no political constraints, competition among various religions and sects is inevitable. This is because the devoted faithful always believe that their truth is the final, all-encompassing truth.

The overstatement of human suffering and limitations is linked to an unending power struggle and an unbalanced distribution of power. Nature and the universe, overshadowing petty human conflicts, lead to the realization of something sacred and add to the self-realization of the limitations of human power. However, while based on respect and awe towards the mystery and might of nature and the universe, salvation religion simultaneously offers a way to confront conflict among human beings. Religion has been viewed as rooted in a socialized means of self defense by a humankind suffering from various uncertainties and aggression, as well as violence of its own making (Durkheim 1915, Freud 1912–13, Girard 1972).[5] There is some measure of truth in interpretations that link religion to class society and resentment among the oppressed, such as those proposed by Marx and Nietzsche.[6]

It is theoretically possible to voice dissent to distributions of power (wealth, position, status, fulfillment of ability, aesthetic pleasure), and to forego this implies acceptance of suffering. Salvation religion can become a means of pressing an unjust situation on those who do not share in power by urging acceptance of the suffering that accompanies class domination. At the same time salvation religion has the possibility to become a means to voice dissent, through providing an ideal of human life and the ethics of camaraderie. However, in either case, a secondary social order, distinct from the political order and framed within the bounds of class society, emerges through the union of intellectuals who have given up direct political power and from those who were distanced from power. If culture could not relativize political order, the world as it is would be suffocatingly constrictive. While seemingly strict on its own, salvation religion also offers a systematic and institutionalized place of escape.

From the perspective of the suffocating situation of modern society, I want to emphasize that salvation religion functioned to encourage self-reflection against the bound and tragic nature of human beings leading to self-restraint, and it acted as a cultural reserve providing ideals of altruistic love for the other and for one's fellow human being.

Salvation religion, thereby, contributed to endowing society with a moral sense by providing high ideals. Salvation religion was not to merely act to provide meaning to the individual in order to overcome personal suffering. Through such religion the dignity of the human spirit came to be accepted as a goal for people of all social classes. As democracy and social equality advanced, and conflict between individuals was acknowledged as an inevitable reality, the individual pursuit of one's own goals was accepted as a self-evident premise of human life, salvation religion was no longer tenable.

A society where labor, service, and self-sacrifice are deemed worthless and where self-realization and self-improvement are relentlessly pursued presents its own oppressiveness, different from that where labor, service, and self-sacrifice are demanded. Exaggerated demands for meritocratic values and independence from others not only take away spiritual freedom (if this were the only problem, psychological methods may provide a cure), but also cloud the irreplaceable values of deep self-reflection, friendship, and virtuosity. 'Affluent society,'[7] a consumer society with abundant goods (which threatens to destroy the limited resources of the planet), driven by impatience even seems to have a grudge against salvation religion. Why were people in the past ever attracted to salvation religion, with its teachings of subservience and subordination? Why do people today depend so foolishly upon religious figures and organizations? The values of democracy and salvation religion naturally incompatible, aren't they? The contemporary Japanese view of salvation religion alternates ambivalently between these doubts and a traditional sense of awe and respect toward salvation religion (Shimazono 1987).

Historic religion and new religions

'Historic religion' is a term that Robert N. Bellah, a sociologist of religion, used in his article, "Religious Evolution" (1970). Bellah argued that, as human civilization progressed and social structure became more sophisticated, the form of religion transformed from primitive religion to archaic religion, historic religion, early modern religion, and modern religion. In this series, the biggest leap lies between archaic religion and historic religion.

The representative historic religions are Buddhism, Christianity, and Islam, while Judaism, Greek philosophy, Confucianism, and Taoism are also counted among the historic religions. In primitive and archaic religion, there is no fundamental gap between the human and sacred realms. Although distanced from the sacred, human beings are readily able to return to the sacred through participation in ritual. This is a monistic view of the cosmos. However, in historic religion, there is an irreversible gap between the sacred and human. Life in the profane world is cut off from the foundation of values; human life is characterized as immersed in suffering and agony. At its polar opposite, there is a state of absolute existence and happiness. Religious doctrine mediates these two poles in this dualistic worldview, and is something that an individual chooses to adopt on one's own. Through positing a transcendental framework, religion achieves an order independent from political order. Historic religion offers a possibility of a critique of politics from the basis of a religious principle.

While there are many problems with Bellah's ideas of historic, early modern, and modern religion, I want to focus on his idea that Buddhism, Christianity, and Islam are the representative historic religions. In societies prior to the modern age, salvation religion took the form of historic religion and could be found throughout the world. In contrast, in the years following the coming of the modern period, in some parts of the world, new religions took the place of historic religion as the salvation religion, and slowly began to infiltrate the domain of the historic religions. Japan is a typical case of this process, and there was something similar in the United States, while the same could be found in somewhat abbreviated form in other parts of the world (Stark and Bainbridge 1985). Salvation religion takes the forms of historic religion and (modern) new religion, and during and after the modern period, there was a partial transition from historic religion to new religion (Bellah's 'early modern' and 'modern religion' refer to Protestant and contemporary American religious thought, but these can be replaced by new religion and the new spirituality movements, usually called 'New Age' in the West, as noted below).

Historic religion was institutionalized in societies with large gaps between the urban and rural areas and between the elites and the masses, with most of the people belonging to the latter. Orthodox religious tradition was passed down through literate intellectuals who were in the minority, yet had international connections. This is the 'great tradition' as noted by anthropologist, Robert Redfield (1956). 'Folk society,' Redfield argues, inherited the little tradition based on oral transmission. There is a religious, inherited little tradition, but it differs significantly from those of the orthodox traditions, such as Buddhism, Christianity, and Islam. Religious functionaries mediate between the great and little traditions, in order to extend the authority of the great traditions. Encroachment by the populace upon the fountain of religious truth or its framework would threaten the authority of the religious functionaries and therefore was not permitted.[8]

These divisions of great and little traditions were blunted in the process of modernization. With changes in the industrial structure of society, large segments of the population moved from the rural village to the cities. As a consequence, the monopoly of literacy by the elite was lost. Print technology, and later electronic media, coupled with mandatory education, as well as advanced education, fundamentally changed the distribution of knowledge within society. In place of a dual culture divided between city and countryside, elite and masses, there is now a (seemingly) single national culture, and eventually a single (but also extremely diverse) global culture. Through the popularization and democratization of society, there is a drastic restructuring of culture (Anderson 1983). The extent of this transformation cannot but influence the sphere of religion. Historic religion, of course, adapted to these changes and continues to exist. On the other hand, in some areas of the world, as culture transformed into mass culture, the new religions began to take the place of historic religion as the religion of the masses.

New religion can be characterized as the salvation religion that appears after the advent of modernity. As noted above, it may emerge through the changes taking place in the structure of society and of the distribution of knowledge; however, there is also another condition for its possible emergence. This is the extent of the tolerance within society for religious groups based on the initiative of the masses. This relates to the tolerance that a nation and the culture of the region displays toward popular religion, and also to legal guarantees based on freedom of worship. Such a situation also reveals a loss of authority among the established religions. Despite the fact of religious persecution in prewar Japan, Japan was an extremely 'progressive' nation in that regard. Defeat in the war and the introduction of American-style democracy further advanced this tendency.

New religions inherit much from historic religion and folk religion (the little tradition, as well as the mixture of the little tradition and the great tradition) of the pre-modern era. Elements common to salvation religion are passed on, including the notion of human beings as being in a state of suffering and in need of salvation, demands for individual self-abnegation, the call for an existential decision based on individual self-abnegation, mutual assistance among people in such a state of suffering, and a community of humble individuals willing to submit to a higher ideal and authority. However, there are also large differences between historic religion and new religions. In regard to the idea of salvation, this difference can be summed up in the difference between this-worldly salvation and other-worldly salvation (Tsushima 1979).

A pessimistic worldview, based on the ideas that there is a fundamental limit to human life in this world and that suffering and sadness are inevitable, was a point of departure for salvation religion. However, they also held out the possibility for happiness. So the question then occurs as to where and when happiness will be achieved. Historic religion locates the possibility for happiness in another world detached from our current world but continuous with this one. Typically the contrast is between salvation after death or salvation in this lifetime, but there are various images of salvation lying between these two poles. There is, for example, the idea that when one is devoted to salvation in the next world one can come closer to happiness in this world through abandoning attachments to things of this world (as seen in the Pure Land tradition). There are also faiths that teach that although happiness cannot be attained in this life it will occur upon one's reincarnation in this world, or perhaps for one's descendants. In a millenarian worldview where the ideal world is to appear in this world, there are varying degrees of distance between such an ideal world and the current one. However, historic religion tends to aspire to other-worldly salvation, while new religion tends to aspire to salvation in this world.

In most historic religions, the celibate life of religious specialists and monks, along with the other ascetic disciplines demanded of them, are manifestations of historic religion's radical rejection of the current world. The very existence of ascetic monks indicates that life in this world has little relevance. In societies prior to the modern age, one's life seemed determined from the moment of one's birth. In historic religions, the way to salvation is a life that shows no regard for what little change could take place in one's current situation. In contrast, new religions place great stress on the daily concerns of this world, and seriously seek to affect changes in one's current life. Social conditions that make change based on personal decision possible constitutes the background to the view of this-worldly salvation found in the new religions. In a society where there is little change and where most people live similar lives, an image of happiness in this world cannot be easily formed. In contrast, if happiness and rewards, or misery and poverty, are seen as the result of personal decision, then high expectations regarding a good life in the present world become reasonable.

Analogous to the opposition between this-worldly salvation and other-worldly salvation, another contrast can be noted between seeking salvation either through one's own power or through the power of the other. If salvation religion emphasizes the limitations of human existence, it is difficult to conceive of salvation based only on one's own efforts. However, even among faiths that express dependence upon the power of a transcendent existence or principle, there is still a demand for some effort on the part of the human. Early Buddhism, Theravada Buddhism found in Thailand and Sri Lanka, and even Mahayana and Zen Buddhism all place emphasis on the power of the self. In Christianity as well there is strong element of self-dependence in the mystic tradition. However, historic religion as accepted by the common people generally leaned towards salvation through power of the other.

In new religions, great weight is attached to faith in a divine figure with transcendent powers. Some groups also see prayers to the divine as an important method for salvation. However, great demands are made for training and discipline on the part of the faithful as well, and these demands increase over time. Japanese new religions particularly emphasize the 'transformation of the heart,' that is, the daily practice of ethical conduct and an improvement in one's outlook. In extreme cases, there are those that argue for a completely causal relationship, where happiness or misery is decided completely by the extent of the transformation of the heart (Shimazono 1992d). In addition to the transformation of the heart, occasionally other intellectual and bodily training are also demanded. This-worldly salvation is achieved through an interplay of one's own training and cultivation and the power of the transcendent other.

Healing and miraculous experiences also play a large role in new religions. Salvation is typically experienced through an act of healing. Healing and other miracles are occasions for direct contact between the human being and the sacred. Through emphasis on the direct experiences of the sacred, less weight is placed on indirect contact with the sacred. Intellectual pursuit of sacred truth and formalistic ritual – both emphasized in historic religion – become secondary for the attainment of salvation. Intellectual elites who had wielded authority through demonstrating the truth in intellectual systems no longer command authority in the world of the new religions. Emphasis on experience and actual proof, which seek to solidify the grounds for faith through actual examples of healing and miracles, is a crucial element of new religions (Shimazono 1988). The tendency to eliminate subservience to traditional and intellectual authorities is a manifestation of the orientation towards self-reliance and the democratic nature of new religions.

The orientation towards self-reliance and the democratic nature of these groups also lead to a stress on one's abilities and merits. The world of the new religions renders no privilege to birth or educational accomplishments; rather, it rewards those who produce results based on standards provided by the group itself. In historic religion, individuals are promoted on the basis of their formal training and education; new religions recognize actual results achieved in missionary work, or one's capacity for organizational leadership or organizational management (or, in certain cases, one's financial background). It even appears that new religions have incorporated the principle of competition in answer to that found in capitalist society. Missionary work, formerly for the sake of helping those in need, often appears to be the result of an intensive effort towards organizational maintenance, or enlargement. In salvation religion, the principle of mutual assistance among those in need was always fraught with the danger of surrendering to the principle of competition for survival of the fittest; in the case of the new religions, this danger appears in the form of an incorporation of capitalism's competitive dimension.

The above summary takes new religions in Japan as its subject, but similar trends can be found in the Protestant denominations of the United States. This-worldly salvation, an orientation towards self-reliance, a democratic nature, an emphasis on experience, and the principle of free competition are all characteristics that can be seen in Protestant – especially popular Protestant – movements in the United States during the 19th and 20th centuries. These movements grew in the form of sects and revivalism; some of them can be seen as part of the American version of new religions (Wilson 1970).[9]

Salvation religion in contemporary society

In societies prior to the modern period, historic religion's worldview was the orthodox worldview that stood at the center of society's framework of knowledge. Modernization disseminated scientific knowledge and undermined historic religion's dominance in the framework of knowledge. Science and, concomitantly, a secular worldview (Enlightenment rationalism) commanded authority. New religions and sects, which replaced or inherited from historic religion, could not claim a central role in the framework of knowledge.

Inevitably, these groups constituted a minority at the periphery of society, communities of believers with a framework of principles that differed from those of society at large.

Historic religion, which continued to uphold a traditional worldview, could place itself closer to the center of society than could the new religions. However, in the face of science and a rationalist worldview, it eventually had to relegate itself to the periphery. Anxiety over this development led to trends toward fundamentalism, a further indication that previously dominant historic religions have been forced to act as if they were peripheral sects. In such a way, science and a rationalist worldview became the orthodox worldview in modern society, and worldview of salvation religion became peripheral. The opposition of materialistic science and salvation religion became identified with the opposition of science and religion in general, and many believed that the progress of civilization made the eventual victory of science, and consequent defeat of religion, inevitable.

The revival of religion seen in various parts of the world since the 1970s has led to a rethinking of such a polarized point of view. There is increasingly a call for emendations and change in views setting science against religion. On the one hand, there is a tendency on the part of science to recognize the appropriateness of religious worldviews. This is a utopic view espoused by so-called New Age science. For example, what happens when material is divided into its smallest molecular fragment? Is it adequate to still call it material? Can materialistic explanations based on cause and effect account for the development and evolution of life? Does the management of data in reaction to the stimulus upon the individual's brain by the five senses account for all of reality experienced by the human mind? Rather, is there not an entity in the universe that resembles the spirits and mystical powers taught by religion? Is there not a teleological existence underlying the world that integrates and organizes the whole, overcoming the causal relations of the parts? May not notions of divine will and cosmic rules, intuitively believed by humankind, be now explained using the terms of science?[10]

New Age science is closely related to religious movements called New Age movement or new spirituality movements – that is, religious movements that seek to overcome the perceived crisis in the progress of human culture through a transformation in one's consciousness (Melton 1990). New age science is a new scientific worldview and also a manifestation of a religious worldview shared by popular religious movements that I call the new spirituality movements and culture.

This indicates the emergence of a new system of thought that attempts to be both science and religion at the same time. Ways of thinking that were rendered invisible by the polar opposition of science and religion – that is, knowledge and technology found in the daily life of the masses (the world of folk knowledge),[11] and certain aspects of environmental principles and cosmic principles (the tradition of nature religion and nature theology)[12] – are beginning to resurface. In place of the two opposing worldviews of materialistic science and salvation religion, there is a new triangular opposition between the rationalist worldview, a worldview intermixing science and religion, and a salvation religion worldview.

How does the mixture of the religious and scientific worldviews of the new spirituality movements and culture relate to the worldview found in salvation religion? The new spirituality movements and culture consider some elements of salvation religion acceptable and some unacceptable. While affirming faith in a spiritual entity existing within the cosmos, they reject faith in a personalized deity transcending the world. While accepting beliefs that are seen as being continuous to rational knowledge, they reject the concept of faith in an ultimate reality that lies beyond rational knowledge. In particular, they are critical of orthodox doctrine found in monotheistic religions such as Christianity, Judaism, and Islam. One of the reasons for such criticism is the observation that a personalized deity implies the abandonment of individual autonomy, and subservience accompanied by a shift of responsibility to others. If the model of salvation in salvation religion is based on the idea that human beings be aware of their limitations and thereby subordinate themselves to a personalized deity or founder figure, the new spiritual movements and culture would find such a model objectionable.

However, is there an irrevocable distance between the worldviews of the new spirituality movements and culture and that of salvation religion? Or, is there a possibility for some mediating position? Eastern religion and science provides a rich resource for thinking about this issue. Buddhism includes both worship of a personal deity in the form of the Buddha and a meditative practice offering intellectual and mystical insights into the world. New religions in Japan teach absolute subordination to a founder figure or a spiritual entity as the source of life in the universe; yet, they also include doctrines concerning the principles of the universe and the laws of the cosmos and nature.[13] Eastern religion has the tradition of salvation religion including a worldview that is religious/scientific, as well as a religious/scientific worldview that includes salvation religion. Not only Eastern religion, but in Christianity as well such an integrative dimension must have existed. With the emergence of a new religious/scientific worldview, there is the possibility to overcome the modern gap between rationalism and salvation religion.

However, when attention is focused on the shifts in dominance within the religious worldview, one can observe that the religious/scientific worldview of the new spirituality movements and culture (or New Age) in contemporary Japan and the United States has challenged salvation religion, with the latter in slow but steady retreat. The first reason for this trend is the accelerating pace of what had been a general trend since the modern period, that is, the loss of authority of the mythical worldview. This acceleration can partly be attributed to increases in available information and an awareness of pluralistic culture. For those who are exposed to education and the mass media, the myths of salvation religion become difficult to believe literally. On the other hand, control over nature has increased, and the trust placed on rationality and human technology has increased; an acute realization of the limits of human capacity has begun to diminish. Moreover, communities have broken down and there are less reasons for long-term involvement with others, whether in conflict or solidarity; thus, it has become difficult to comprehend the contrasts of selfishness and compassion, or of guilt and love. There is less awareness of each other as human beings sharing in suffering and the need to help one another.

These are all transformations of religion within the context of a shift from group to individual and an increase in self-control, rather than control over the natural and social environment by the individual. I have noted earlier that the new religions place emphasis on self-reliance and a democratic nature, and that these relate to the increased independence of the masses and the stress on meritocracy found in modernization. As the orientation towards self-reliance and a democratic nature increases, there may no longer be a need for a stable community providing mutual assistance. When new religions begin to stress individuality to such an extent, they exceed the realm of salvation religion. At that point, they begin to resemble the new spirituality movements and culture. New spirituality movements and culture dislike creating organizations that bind individuals, and rather stress a network of autonomous individuals. From historic religions to new religions to new spirituality movements and culture, there is increasing emphasis placed on the view that individuals are empowered to approach the sacred as individuals; there is a transformation from salvation religion to a religion that no longer resembles salvation religion, but rather resembles Marxism to the extent that it is utopian and offers an intellectual systematic philosophy. From the perspective of an educated intellectual in a developed nation with sympathies for new spirituality movements and culture, such a progression is a 'necessity of history' – the term 'New Age,' for example, reveals an optimistic view of the progress of history.

The shift from salvation religion to new spirituality movements and culture is a reflection of a radical individualism that is necessitated by the affluence and information-oriented nature of contemporary society. The proponents of new spirituality movements and culture argue that, through the rejection of religious organizations, they seek to construct a non-authoritarian spiritual movement that offers true individual realization. During the transition from historical civilization to modernity, the authority of the transmission through written materials was overly respected, and religion stood on the side of a strict anti-individualistic order. With modernity and the strengthening of individual autonomy, and with the post-modern liberation of the emotive dimension of life, there is now an opportunity at the level of mass religion to overcome the dependence on community and authority. New spirituality movements and culture hope that a great transformation of society will emerge from these developments. This hope is not an unrealistic delusion, but is rather grounded in the reality of the new social structure.

However, shared political action that seeks to actually introduce reforms in society can only come about through ongoing efforts at the base level to create a consensus in groups. New spirituality movements and culture dislike stable communities and prefer a loose organization based on networks; yet, in reality, they are often dependent on the mass media, which does not offer the depth of communication available through the interaction of human beings who share a common existence. The dislike for community among the new spirituality movements and culture is related to the enlargement of bureaucracy and the weakening of human ties that are characteristic of contemporary society.[14]

As noted earlier, salvation religion, on the one hand, reinforced hierarchical order in society and, on the other hand, acted to provide cultural resources for reflecting upon the limits and tragedy of human life and the concomitant self-restraint, as well as an ideal for unselfish love for the other. In a society lacking self-reflection and the unselfish desire to live for the sake of the other there is a lingering sense of void underneath the veneer of a comfortable life. The mass media tries to provide escape from stress through a forced cheerfulness and surface pleasantry, and individuals seem uninhibited in pursuing their own 'self-realization.' However, these are qualitatively different from the sense of fulfillment found in communal life with shared goals; at times, people might feel lost in isolation, uneasiness, and lethargy. It is said that the Japanese people, having acquired material affluence, are now in need of an affluence of the heart. However, precisely because of having acquired material affluence, the basis for ties with others has been lost and there is a keenly felt pain in the poverty of the heart. There is no reason to be optimistic that movements such as the new spirituality movements and culture will succeed in their pursuit of the fount of the sacred within the individual.

Societies in contemporary developed nations continue to marginalize salvation religions. However, in the functions performed by salvation religion in the past and partly in the present, there is something that led to close human ties full of relief and fulfillment (however repressive it may be). This is something that cannot be replaced by a rationalism based on materialistic science or the humanistic worldview, nor by the religious/scientific worldview of the new spirituality movements and culture. Thus, no matter how antiquated and marginal salvation religion may seem in the developed nations where intellectual and expressive ties between individuals are privileged over deep relationships among humans, salvation religion continues to thrive, rooted deeply within the masses throughout the world, especially in third world nations where there remains overwhelming poverty and conflict.

Part II:
Popular Buddhist Movements and Nationalism

4 Crisis of Authority and the Lotus Sutra-Based New Religions

The place of Lotus Sutra-based new religions in modern Japan

Japan's religious scene has drastically changed since the mid-nineteenth century. Of prime importance among these various changes is the growth of many new religions whose influence is now as great as, or rather greater than the power of all the established Buddhist sects. With respect to religious authority, there has been a great change in Japanese society during these hundred and some tens of years.

Religious groups that can be called new religions had already emerged in the early nineteenth century, but it was in the 1860s that several groups started to grow rapidly almost at the same time. The history of the new religions since then can be broken down into the following five periods (Table 4.1). The groups listed are those with a large following that grew rapidly in each period.

In each period new groups appeared and grew, and then co-existed with other groups that had already experienced their initial period of growth. Because only a small number of groups disappear, there are more and more groups as time has gone by. As to the numbers of the groups and of the followers of all the groups, we have neither exact data nor any reliable scholarly estimate. One author guesses the number of the groups to be 'two to three thousand or even more' (Matsuno 1984: i). My own rough estimate is that the total number of the followers of all the new religions is between ten to twenty percent of the whole population.[1]

Table 4.2 shows the sixteen groups that have the largest self-reported following at the end of 1985.

The sum of the number of these sixteen groups is about 43.2 million, more than 36 percent of the total population. This is because the self-reported membership of each group far exceeds the actual number of their followers.

Table 4.1: Historical periods of new religions and the main groups from each period

Period	Main groups with remarkable growth in the period
(1) 1800–1890	Tenrikyō, Konkokyō, Honmon Butsuryūshū, ōruyamakyō
(2) 1890–1920	Omotokyō
(3a) 1920 – 1945	Hitonomichi Kyōdan (developed into Perfect Liberty Kyōdan), Reiyūkai, Seichōno Ie.
(3b) 1945–1970	Sekai Kyūseikyō, Nenpōshinkyō, Risshō Kōseikai, Sōka Gakkai, Bussho Gonenkai, Myōchikai, Zenrinkai, Byakkō Shinkōkai
(4) 1970–	Shinnyoen, Reihanohikari Kyōkai, Oyamanezunomikoto Shinjikyōkai, Sukyō Mahikari

Table 4.2: Self-reported membership of large new religions

Groups		Self-reported membership
(1)	Sōka Gakkai	17,209,159
(2)	Risshō Kōseikai	6,201,629
(3)	Seichō no Ie	3,009,558
(4)	Reiyūkai	2,998,000
(5)	Perfect Liberty Kyōdan	2,438,594
(6)	Shinnyoen	2,079,954
(7)	Bussho Gonenkai Kyōdan	1,988,628
(8)	Tenrikyō	1,792,061
(9)	Sekai Kykseikyō	835,756
(10)	Nenposhinkyō	807,486
(11)	Myōchikai kyōdan	767,363
(12)	Reihanohikari Kyōkai	755,874
(13)	Oyamanezunomikoto Shinjikyōkai	672,242
(14)	Zenrinkai	612,006
(15)	Byakkō Shinkōkai	500,000
(16)	Honmon Butsuryūshū	466,456

Source: Bunkachō, ed. (1987), Shūkyō Nenkan (Religions Yearbook). Tokyo: Gyōsei.

There is great variety of beliefs and practices among the new religions, but the simplest classification may be to break the groups down into three categories: syncretic Shintoist, Lotus Sutra-based or Nichirenist, and others. Syncretic Shintoist groups worship the supreme deity universalized from indigenous deities. The greater part of their belief system is inherited from various folk religions. The belief system of Lotus Sutra-based new religions is derived mainly from the tradition of the Lotus Sutra, one of the most popular Mahayana Buddhist sutras, and from the Nichiren tradition that revitalized the Lotus Sutra tradition. The third category, 'others,' includes groups inheriting items from Christianity, Buddhist traditions other than the Lotus Sutra, and various other religious and philosophical traditions. This chapter will focus on Lotus Sutra-based new religions and explore how they have responded to the crisis of authority in modern Japan.

Of the sixteen groups listed in Table 4.2 six groups, Sōka Gakkai, Risshō Kōseikai, Reiyūkai, Bussho Gonenkai Kyōdan, Myōchikai Kyōdan, and Honmon Butsuryūshū, belong to Lotus Sutra category. The sum of the self-reported followers of these six groups is about 29.6 million, 68.5 percent of the total for all sixteen groups. The percentage of followers of all new religions that belong to this category is perhaps not very far from this percentage. Among all the established religious traditions, the Lotus Sutra has had the greatest influence on the new religions. This is not because the Lotus Sutra or Nichiren tradition had been the dominant one in the past. The power of the traditional Buddhist sects can be estimated fairly accurately by the number of temples affiliated with each sect. According to statistics as of 1985, of the total 74,600 temples belonging to the various Buddhist sects, 6834 temples, about 9.2 percent, are Nichiren (Bunkacho 1987, p.60). Even if we add the 4311 temples belonging to the Tendai sect, which represents the Lotus Sutra tradition in a wider sense, they comprise only 14.9 percent. This means that the Lotus Sutra or Nichiren tradition, which had not been very large before Japan's modernization, became the most influential tradition when inherited and revitalized by the new religions.

When did the Lotus Sutra-based new religions enjoy their greatest growth? Only Honmon Butsuryūshū had its initial growth in the first

Table 4.3: Change of the composition of working population

	Type of industry	Number ('000)	Percent
1920	primary industry	14,672	53.8
	secondary industry	5,598	20.5
	tertiary industry	6,464	23.7
1970	primary industry	10,075	19.3
	secondary industry	17,827	34.1
	tertiary industry	24,293	46.5

(The statistics for1920 include unclassifiable labor.)

Source: Zaidan hojin Yano Tsuneta kinenkai, ed. (1981), p.34

period. All the other Lotus Sutra-based groups were started and grew rapidly in the third period, that is between 1920 and 1970. It is true that in this period new religions as a whole grew rapidly. However, in contrast to the syncretic Shintoist groups, some of which grew rapidly in the first and second periods, and the 'other' groups that grew quickly in the fifth period, the growth of the Lotus Sutra-based groups is concentrated in the third period.

Between 1920 and 1970 Japanese society experienced great change. During these fifty years the national population jumped from fifty-six million to one hundred and four million. As the Table 4.3 shows, the composition of the working population also changed drastically.

With industrialization and urbanization people became more and more involved in organizations such as the state, companies, the army, schools, unions, and so forth. Although traditional customs and authorities still provided norms of life for many people, sometimes people felt that they had to fight against or ignore these traditional norms in order to improve their situation. The traditional worldview, which had been accepted as self-evident, was now put into question. People were faced with a plurality of ideas and faiths. On many occasions they were asked to judge for themselves and to act on their own will. Politically, class-based friction between capitalists and laborers, land owners and tenants, became increasingly grave. Ideological conflicts concerning democratic reform, socialist revolution, or national identity were intense. Many Japanese were deeply dismayed by the fact that those who held different positions or who had different opinions had to face down others as if they were one's enemies.

On the other hand, tension with foreign countries was always strong during these fifty years. The war with China started in 1931 and escalated into one with the United States and all the Allied Powers in 1941. In these domestic and international difficulties, national unity was sought in fascism, and people were taught to believe that Japan was a divine country and that the Emperor was the living representation of the ancient gods. Although this extreme Shintoist nationalism was rejected in 1945 with the end of the Second World War, there was still present a strong tendency towards nationalism of the kind that sought to recover national pride, and that carried the hope of being included among the world's first-rate countries. All through these fifty years the Japanese people were deeply involved in the vicissitudes of the state, and were more or less committed to the political and ideological struggles at the national level. This crisis of traditional authority and national identity was the background to the rise of Lotus Sutra-based new religions.

Lotus Sutra, Nichiren traditions and their modern manifestation in the new religions

The Lotus Sutra was compiled in India in the first and second centuries, and has been one of the most popular sutras in Mahayana Buddhism. There is such a wide variety of sutras in Mahayana Buddhism that sometimes it is hard to discern the essential ideas among different trends of thoughts and to determine what is more authentic and what is less. One of the outstanding features of the Lotus Sutra is that the sutra itself sets out how to interpret this variety within Mahayana Buddhism and provides a means to find order in the various sutras.

According to the Lotus Sutra, various sutras represent the teachings of the Buddha in the various periods of his fifty-year-long life after his enlightenment. Of course, the Buddha after enlightenment always knew the supreme truth, but he changed his teaching in accordance with his followers' ability to understand the truth. Before the Lotus Sutra, the supreme truth had not been revealed. All the sutras proclaimed before the Lotus Sutra represent provisional teachings skillfully devised by Buddha in his great mercy for all suffering creatures. The supreme truth is finally revealed in this sutra. Thus, the Lotus Sutra is the highest of all sutras, and all other sutras are of secondary importance. People must adore, chant, copy and propagate this sutra. The Lotus Sutra has great power that leads people to emancipation and that can deliver people from various sufferings, including physical suffering. The sutra neither requires hard ascetic discipline nor does it develop a complicated and difficult teaching. Again and again people are urged simply to have faith in the sutra and to believe in the deliverance given by the sutra.

Thus the Lotus Sutra is based on the assumption that there are already a variety of different religious ideas and practices. It then stresses its own supremacy and exhorts people to have simple faith in the sutra itself. Mahayana Buddhism as a whole can be seen as a protest movement against the formalized and established Buddhist tradition that had lost contact with the life of ordinary people. The Lotus Sutra represents this aspect of Mahayana Buddhism perhaps most clearly. The Lotus Sutra seems to have much relevance to modernity in the sense that it teaches how to deal with the ambiguity of authority in a pluralistic situation, and that it struggles against the established authority of the religious elites by advocating a simple faith.

Since the late sixth century when Buddhism was first introduced to Japan, the Lotus Sutra had always attracted the faith of many priests and laymen. *Sankyo Gisho*, which was believed to have been written by Shotoku Taishi (574–622), the highly respected prince popularly regarded as the founder of Japanese Buddhism, includes a commentary on the Lotus Sutra along with two other shorter sutras. When *Kokubunji* and *Kokubun niji* were set up in each of the sixty-two districts of the nation in the eighth century, the *Kokubunn niji* were also called *hokke metsuzai no tera*, and the chanting of the Lotus Sutra was an important rite at these temples. In the early ninth century Saichō, intending to renew the stagnant established Buddhism of the time, introduced to Japan the Tendai sect, which places the Lotus Sutra at the top of all the sutras. From the ninth century through the thirteenth century, however, the Lotus Sutra did not enjoy evident popularity. During these centuries there were more and more adherents to other trends of Mahayana Buddhism, Esoteric Buddhism, Pure Land Buddhism, Zen Buddhism and Vinaya (Precepts) sects, so that the relative importance of the Lotus Sutra in Japanese Buddhism declined somewhat at this time.

It was under these circumstances that Nichiren (1222–1282) appeared on the scene and revitalized the Lotus Sutra tradition. Thirteenth century Japan was marked by turmoil both in politics and religion. With the decline of the aristocrats' power, warriors now began to rule, but the warrior regime was not yet firmly established. Moreover the threat of a Mongolian invasion was on the horizon. Buddhists were divided into various sects whose teachings were very diverse. Nichiren were deeply annoyed by this political and religious situation. He prophesied the coming of disasters, engaged in fierce criticism of the other sects thriving at the time, and advocated the religious unity of the nation under Lotus Sutra faith. On the other hand, Nichiren advanced the simplicity of Lotus Sutra faith a step further so that ordinary people could practice it even more easily. He insisted that one does not necessarily have to read and understand the Lotus Sutra oneself. Rather, the repeated chanting of the short phrase '*namu myōhō rengekyō,*' called the *daimoku*, is sufficient for expressing sincere faith in the Lotus Sutra. The practice of the *daimoku* is similar to that of the *nenbutsu*, a practice widespread in Pure Land Buddhism. The idea that this simple practice is the way to salvation was based on a view of history widely accepted at the time.

After 1052, two millennia since the Buddha's death, it was believed that human history had entered the age of *mappō* (the Latter Days), in which people cannot be saved by traditional complicated beliefs and practices. According to Nichiren, the common people of this difficult age can be saved only by the Lotus Sutra, whose power is called forth by the simple and easy practice of chanting the *daimoku*. Along this same line of thought he established an object of worship called the *honzon*, a calligraphical symbolization of the essence of the Lotus Sutra.

Thus Nichiren revitalized Lotus Sutra belief, with an emphasis on certain aspects of the tradition and by developing it a step further. First, inheriting Lotus Sutra belief regarding the sutra's supremacy over other Buddhist teachings, he extended this thought in the direction of a national religion or an ideological unity. Second, the exhortation to simple faith found in the Lotus Sutra was stressed, but with the addition of the idea that this simple faith was uniquely necessary in the new age of *mappō*. These points offer some explanation as to why the Lotus Sutra faith revitalized by Nichiren had much appeal for the common people in the modern period. Although some parts of the Nichiren sect were occasionally persecuted because of their radical claims, the sect as a whole grew gradually and was counted as one of the eight main sects of Japanese Buddhism when Japan entered the modern period.

Buddhist temples and priests had spread all over the country by the seventeenth century. The Tokugawa Shogunate, established in 1603, forced all the people to belong to a temple, making the temples an organ of state control of religions and beliefs. In a sense, Buddhist sects were given favor by the government, but at the same time they themselves were kept under strict control. During the Tokugawa period (1603–1867) they lost their vitality and fell into ritualism, the main task of the priests being the performance of funeral and ancestral services. The Nichiren sect was not an exception to this. Lotus Sutra-based new religions, dissatisfied with the established Nichiren sect governed by the priests, started their movements outside of these established groups.

There are three clusters of Lotus Sutra-based new religions. The first is Honmon Butsuryūshū, founded in 1857 by Nagamatsu Nissen(1817–1890).[3] He was born into a wealthy merchant family in Kyoto. His mother was a devout believer of Nichiren and, being intelligent and well-educated, he was very well versed in Nichiren theology while he was still young. At first he intended to become a priest, but he was not accepted because of his radical view. He then organized laymen to form a new group. His teachings were not very much different from the frame of the traditional Nichiren doctrinal system. What was new in his teachings was that, paying little respect to the priests, he put much stress on the importance of lay activities, and also on healing and other improvements in one's personal fate in this world by the power of the *daimoku*. Honmon Butsuryūshū was successful in propagating itself in big cities such as Kyoto and Tokyo, but it was before the industrial revolution really got under way that the group's foundation was made.

The second cluster is Reiyūkai and the groups that separated from it. Reiyūkai inherited a great deal of its teachings from a small group called Bussho Gonenkai (not the one listed in Tables 1 and 2), which was founded by Nishida Toshizo (1850–1918).[4] Reiyūkai was founded in 1925 by Kubo Kakutarō (1892–1944) and Kotani Kimi (1901–1971). More than two dozen groups, including Risshō Kōseikai, Bussho Gonenkai, and Myōchikai, can be counted as offshoots from Reiyūkai. The teachings and the practices of these groups are now quite diverse, but there is a common core of beliefs that was established in the early days of Reiyūkai, around 1930. Reiyūkai's uniqueness lies in the combination of Lotus Sutra faith and ancestor worship. People are suffering and the nation is in conflict, because, they believe, correct ancestor veneration is not being performed. Those spirits, which should receive ancestor veneration and would protect the people and the nation, are not yet saved. Since they are not yet saved they cannot protect the people and the nation, allowing devils and demons to attack. Now the time has come for the laity to practice ancestor veneration themselves, instead of relying on priests, most of whom are corrupt. Thus Reiyūkai invented a new mode of ancestor veneration that the laity can practice at home everyday. In traditional ancestor veneration, it is the household head and his wife in each generation, along with others who have died in the household, who are the object of prayer. This means that in most cases the wives' ancestors are not venerated. In Reiyūkai, however, it is taught that every lay couple should venerate all the dead relatives of both the husband and the wife, and together with them even non-relatives who are more-or-less related to the family. Moreover, even those who have just converted are strongly exhorted to engage in *omichibiki*, or proselytization, for it widens the circle of ancestor worship and will bring happiness back to the proselytizers themselves.

The third cluster is groups that originated in Nichiren Shōshū, a sect within the Nichiren tradition. In this group are included Sōka Gakkai and a much smaller group, Kenshōkai. Here we will deal only with Sōka Gakkai.[5] Nichiren Shōshū is a group with a doctrine very distinctive from other Nichiren groups and is highly exclusivistic, strongly emphasizing its own supremacy. It believes that the *honzon* (*daigohonzon*, the great *honzon*, as it is called) found at Taisekiji (the head temple of Nichiren Shōshū), located at the foot of Mt. Fuji, is the supreme and absolutely unparalleled object of worship that was established as such by Nichiren himself. This *daigohonzon* is the highest manifestation of the supreme truth contained in the Lotus Sutra, and every human wish is fulfilled by praying to it. It was with this old sect as the basis that Makiguchi Tsunesaburō (1871–1944) and Toda Jōsei (1900–1958), adding the modern pragmatic thought of sociology and pedagogy, founded Sōka Gakkai, a new religion with emphasis on practical reform of everyday life.

Makiguchi lived most of his life as a teacher of elementary schools. Out of his experience as a school teacher he was convinced that educational thought and practice must be reformed. He enthusiastically wrote and published several books on this subject. In his fifties, after the death of his three sons, he converted to Nichiren Shōshū. This brought about a unique combination of a new educational movement and an old sectarian religion. Makiguchi denounced the old method of education in which pupils only learn from teachers passively, and proposed a new one in which pupils, realizing concrete purposes related to their lives, actively learn themselves. This is value-creating (*sōka*) education. In order to create values systematically you must know the highest value, which can only be known by the faith of Nichiren Shōshū. Toda was Makiguchi's close disciple, but more of a businessman than an educator. His contribution was to make a movement that had been largely focused on educational reform into a movement involving a much wider range of people. Under his leadership Sōka Gakkai started political activities that developed into a political party, Kōmeitō or Clean Government Party, the third largest in the present Japanese Diet.

In the following, our attention is focused on the second and third clusters of Lotus Sutra-based new religions that prospered in the third period (1920–1970), Sōka Gakkai, Reiyūkai, and offshoot groups from Reiyūkai, and the question of how they are related to the crises of authority is addressed.

Nationalism in Lotus Sutra-based new religions

During the period from 1920 to 1970 Japan was threatened by a continuing stream of internal and external problems that forced many people to become involved in harsh ideological and political conflicts. Most of the people felt that the nation was in severe difficulty, and sought to find a vision under which the people could be united and fight to overcome this difficulty. Among the visions proposed were ones that pursued international solidarity, but the more powerful ones were nationalistic. During the period of war with China, the United States, and other countries from 1931 to 1945, the dominant ideology was the extremist Shintoist nationalism that believed that Tennō, the Emperor, was a lineal descendant from the supreme god Amaterasu, and that Japan was a divine country protected by gods and given a special mission to unite the world. Before 1931 and after 1945 this kind of extremist Shintoist nationalism was not that influential, but there was among the people a strong desire to be nationally united under some religious symbolism. Nichiren tradition had enough elements that could respond to this desire. In Nichiren's thought the religious unity proposed by the Lotus Sutra was turned into a more concrete idea of national unity of religion or ideology. Some modern intellectuals, such as Takayama Chogyu who advocated *Nihonshugi* (Japanism), had already been attracted by Nichiren's thought.[6] Lotus Sutra-based or Nichirenist new religions can be seen as popularizing this trend of modern Nichirenist thought that had a strong nationalistic overtone.

The nationalism contained in Lotus Sutra-based new religions, however, was not in complete accord with the trends of the time. Until 1945 Shintoist nationalism had gained a more and more exclusive position as the official ideology, so that other nationalistic ideologies were oppressed and even prohibited. After 1945 freedom of religion was established by the new Constitution, according to which the idea of national unity under the Lotus Sutra might be regarded as a dangerous thought. Thus all through the period from 1920 to 1970 the nationalism of Lotus Sutra-based new religions could seen as heretical or antisocial and could be open to oppression. In fact, Sōka Gakkai was oppressed by the government in 1943 and assailed by journalism around 1970, while Reiyūkai was under official scrutiny and suffered severe public criticism in 1950 and 1953.

In the case of Reiyūkai, from the time of Nishida Toshizo's Bussho Gonenkai to the early days of Reiyūkai itself around 1930, national mission as well as deliverance of the nation from its present plight was given as much emphasis as personal salvation.[7] The present age, they claimed, when Western material culture has prevailed and most of the people are able to read, is the very age within which the truth of the Lotus Sutra must be realized. Now Japan is facing an unprecedented national crisis. Both domestic and international difficulties are caused because proper ancestor veneration is not widely performed. If the government does not adopt Lotus Sutra belief as the basis of national policy, a terrible disaster will befall the country, as if it had fallen into hell. The adoption of the Lotus Sutra is not only for Japan, rather Japan has the mission to establish a new civilization based on the Lotus Sutra and propagate it to the whole world. They insisted that these beliefs do not contradict their allegiance to the Shintoist regime. Japan is divine and the Imperial House is sacred because of Japan's unique *kokutai* (national polity based on Shinto myths) conform to the truth of the Lotus Sutra. Above all ancestor veneration is the fundamental principle of the Meiji Emperor's *Kyōiku Chokugo* (Imperial Rescript on Education, which school children were forced to learn by heart), and at the same time the essence of Lotus Sutra faith.

However, around 1934 when the group's periodical, *Dainippon Reiyūkaihō*, was first published, they had ceased to openly claim that Japan could be saved only by adopting the Lotus Sutra as the official religion. Still they believed that Japan was in the utmost difficulty and that the Lotus Sutra could be useful in overcoming the difficulty. But their denunciation of priests was toned down, as was their claim that ancestor veneration using the Lotus Sutra should be the national religion. They were still concerned about the nation's crisis but their enthusiasm for establishing a state based on the Lotus Sutra was greatly reduced. This diluted nationalism was further diluted after 1945. Among the groups that parted from Reiyūkai there are some variations on this point, but as a whole Reiyūkai-related groups have preserved their nationalism, though in somewhat diluted forms.

Let us turn to Sōka Gakkai.[8] Sōka Gakkai (then, Sōka Kyōiku Gakkai) was oppressed by the government in 1943, and many members including Makiguchi and Toda were arrested, and Makiguchi died in jail the following year. The reason of the attack was that they refused to worship the *taima* (a small tablet inscribed with a god's name) of Ise Shrine, that is of Amaterasu, the Emperor's ancestor and the highest deity of nationalistic Shinto (State Shinto). While most Japanese conformed to State Shinto, Sōka Gakkai resisted such conformity. Sōka Gakkai literature from 1932 to 1943 rarely referred to such topics as the nation's deliverance from its difficulties and the special mission of the state. Of course, they had hoped to guide the state to Lotus Sutra faith. It was at least part of Nichiren Shōshū's ultimate goal to establish the *honmon no kaidan* – the National Platform for the Precept Ceremony (*jukaishiki*) on the basis of the Nichirenist doctrine – at Taisekiji on the state's authority. But before 1945 Sōka Gakkai did not raise this openly as a goal of their activities. Their main aim was, by changing each person's thought, to bring personal happiness and greater vitality to life. Only in connection with educational policy was social reformation proposed.

After the Second World War, however, when Sōka Gakkai was rehabilitated under Toda Jōsei's leadership, much emphasis was laid on Japan's national deliverance and national mission. Japan was, they pointed out, suffering various hardships: humiliating occupation by the United States resulting from defeat in the war, conflict and crime in every sphere of life, fires, floods, famines, and so forth. They believed that they were living in a time of national crisis, in which Nichiren's warning about the danger of internal rebellion and foreign invasion had become reality. It was precisely at such a time as this that the country must be saved by the propagation of Nichiren Buddhism. Moreover Japan has the mission to propagate true Buddhism all over the world. Buddhism was brought from India through China to Japan, that is, from west to east. But in the time of *mappō*, the latter days, true Buddhism appeared in Japan, and, after spreading throughout the country, will be propagated to other Eastern countries, that is, from east (far-east) to west. This, they believed, is what Nichiren prophesied.

These ideas about Japan's national relief from the crisis and about its special mission constituted the main motive for Sōka Gakkai's political activities when they were initiated in 1955. At that time Sōka Gakkai openly proclaimed that the aim of their political activities was to establish the National Platform for the Precept Ceremony (*kokuritsu kaidan*) at Taisekiji on the state's authority. Since they believed that the National Platform could only be established when Japan was unified under Nichiren Shōshū faith, it became the symbol of their concern for the nation's crisis and mission. However, this concern for the nation's destiny was gradually diluted. At the end of 1969, Sōka Gakki was severely criticized by the public for its interference with the selling of books critical of the group. The criticism extended to Sōka Gakki's political activities, which were suspected of contradicting the principle of the separation of religion and state prescribed by the Constitution. In response to this criticism Sōka Gakkai had to proclaim that it is not the goal of the Clean Government Party, Sōka

Gakkai's political organization, to establish the National Platform for the Precept Ceremony, or even to lead the nation to Nichiren Shōshū faith. This development might also be related to the fact that at this time Sōka Gakkai was growing rapidly overseas. From around this time on Sōka Gakkai's perspective has become internationalized and the concern for the nation's crisis and mission has become more and more implicit and realistic.

In sum, during the period from 1920 to 1970 Lotus Sutra-based new religions were for a while highly concerned with the nation's crisis and special mission. At that time the Japanese people in general found ideas regarding nationalistic concerns attractive. The rapid growth of Lotus Sutra-based new religions during that period can be partly explained by the fact that their teachings had nationalistic elements envisioning a national spiritual unity with which to overcome the crisis of authority. However, their nationalism based on the Nichiren tradition was not altogether acceptable to the political regime of the time. Its open manifestation could and did invite governmental oppression or public criticism. Thus their nationalism was, at times, more or less reduced or made implicit.

It should be added that Lotus Sutra-based new religions did not have to change the essentials of their faith when nationalistic elements was downplayed. Fundamentally, Lotus Sutra-based new religions proclaimed salvation for every individual, regardless of his or her race, nationality, gender or class, was possible by the power of the Lotus Sutra. Nationalistic concerns can be seen as having been added temporarily to these essential beliefs in the special situation of the time. This is different from many of the new religions of the syncretic Shintoist type.

Popularism in Lotus Sutra-based new religions

Another factor that greatly contributed to the rapid growth of Lotus Sutra-based new religions during this period is what I would call the popularism that they inherited from the Lotus Sutra and Nichirenite tradition, and that they reconstructed and enlarged in their unique ways adding some modern ideas. Popularism is defined here as a thought and attitude that urges active participation by ordinary people – people without much wealth, higher education, or high social status – demanding that they make their own judgments and make their own decisions regarding action, aiming to improve the situation by cooperative behavior. During the period from 1920 to

1970, this type of popularism spread progressively in various fields of life. When traditional institutions and customs are less and less coercive and obedience to traditional authority means stagnation and timidity, many people will choose to act on their own judgment and to obey new, more democratic and participatory authority. In the fields of politics and economics, as well as arts and education, such thoughts and attitudes became more and more common. The Second World War, a total war, requiring people from all the classes to be mobilized equally in battle and production, contributed very much to the advancement of popularism. In the field of religion, new religions generally have a highly democratic tendency, but among them, popularism in the Lotus Sutra-based new religions is particularly advanced.

The Lotus Sutra taught that the final truth is in fact simple and can be understood directly by everybody, at a time when it was generally believed that the truth is complicated and is hard to be understood by ordinary people. In this sense the Lotus Sutra originally contained the seeds of the concept of popularism we are addressing here. Nichiren advanced Lotus Sutra popularism even further. Believing that even the traditional Lotus Sutra faith is still too complicated in the age of *mappō*, he advocated the simplest of practices, the chanting of the *daimoku*. In both Lotus Sutra and Nichiren faith, however, the difference between priests and laity (*shukke* and *zaike*) was taken for granted. The fundamental Buddhist premise that priests and monks who keep special precepts and endure ascetic life are much closer to final truth and enlightenment was not challenged. It is true that other traditions in Mahayana Buddhism, like *The Teaching of Vimalakirti* (*Yuimakyō*), challenge this assumption. There it is argued that the laity are no less close to truth and enlightenment, or that they may even be closer to this reality than priests. However, *The Teaching of Vimalakirti* refers only to one wealthy layperson, and not the ordinary people. In the Lotus Sutra-based new religions that grew between 1920 and 1970, the premise of clerical superiority was not only denied, but new democratic systems of practice and organization were initiated.

The term 'laicism' (*zaikeshugi*) is part of the essential teachings of Reiyūkai.[9] At the time of Nichiren, they assert, most of the people were illiterate and so laicism was impossible. It is only in the present age, with the spread of civilization, that most people can read, making laicism realizable, and thus, it is only now that the ideal of the Lotus Sutra is within our grasp. This is seen in the form of ancestor veneration using the Lotus Sutra. While in Japan's traditional Buddhism ancestral rites are left to the priests, Reiyūkai advocates the performance of ancestor veneration by the laity themselves. Reiyūkai inherited a new system of ancestor veneration invented by Nishida Toshizo: every home should be equipped with a *butsudan* (Buddha altar) even when traditionally it was unnecessary; and every morning and evening the people of the household, sitting in front of the altar, should chant a small sutra excerpted and edited by Nishida mainly from the Lotus Sutra. Moreover this practice is not to be done in isolation. Proselytization, or *omichibiki*, is part of every believer's obligation. Even though one has just been initiated into the faith and has only a minimum knowledge of it, the believer has to draw others to the group. For, they believe, by spreading ancestor veneration the believer's own happiness will be promoted. Those who bring others to the faith will soon become the leader of a small group (*hōza*), holding regular home meetings (*hōza*, in another sense). One can rather quickly become the leader of a group by participating in simple religious practices and active communication that can be performed by anyone in daily life.

This 'laicism' is closely related to what I would call 'experiential-ism.' According to this way of thought, fundamental religious truth cannot be grasped by passively listening to the preaching of learned priests or by learning from books as fixed knowledge. It can only be grasped through one's own personal experience, which will be brought about by simple practices such as chanting the sutra and *daimoku*, pouring cold water upon oneself as an ascetic practice, and proselytization. One must not depend on others but must seek the truth and deepen one's faith through one's own efforts. In the Reiyūkai of the 1930s through the 1960s, little effort was made to compose doctrinal literature. In their meetings and periodicals doctrines were rarely taught except in fragmentary references. Systematic and intellectual discourse, they believed, would block believers' spontaneous practices and experiences. Instead experience stories (*taikendan*), or testimonies, are quite often used in meetings and written periodicals. In present-day Reiyūkai, in large gatherings that last two hours, an hour is spent in chanting of the sutra, forty-five minutes are for experience stories, and no preaching is presented. Each experience story is about fifteen minutes long. Many believers are skilled in storytelling, not in preaching, and the audience is often moved deeply by the stories. The main part of Reiyūkai's periodicals is also devoted to experience stories. Small group discussion is quite common in Reiyūkai and its offshoot groups. There, too, the main topics are personal experiences.

This experientialism was established as the norm by Reiyūkai's two founders, Kubo Kakutarō and Kotani Kimi. Because of poverty Kotani was unable to finish her elementary school education. With the guidance of Kubo she became acquainted with Reiyūkai's belief system through reflection on her own personal experiences. When she guided followers, she rarely explained doctrines systematically. Rather she used to order them to practice first and to realize the truth by themselves. Kubo was much more oriented to intellectual culture, but he believed that ordinary people without much education should be convinced of their faith by their own experience.

As for Sōka Gakkai's two founders, Makiguchi Tsunesaburō and Toda Jōsei, even though their social status was not so high, as school teachers their intellectual ability was quite high.[10] But they were not satisfied with the traditional way of teaching in which teachers give knowledge to passive pupils. They aimed at a new method in which pupils, realizing the purpose and usefulness of what they learn, would actively study by their own will. Born into poor families, they knew that people will be diligent in learning when they know the practical value of the subject. Makiguchi's book *The System of Value Creating Pedagogy* (*Sōka kyōikugaku taikei*) and the group based on it, the Value Creating Educational Academy or Sōka Kyōiku Gakkai, the former name of Sōka Gakkai, was based on this ideal of pragmatic and participatory education. Sōka Gakkai was at first a movement combining this educational philosophy with traditional Nichiren Shōshū faith. The first members were teachers who were attracted by Makiguchi's ideas and who tried to put them into practice in their educational activities. The movement can be called democratic in the sense that they aimed at a method that everyone could understand and practice, and that members were attracted by its practical value, from their own experience. Makiguchi and Toda also shared anti-authoritarianism in that they had little respect for established political and academic authorities that are separated from people's practical concerns.

As in Reiyūkai, experientialism is also clearly found in Sōka Gakkai. Makiguchi often used the term 'experiment and demonstrate' (*jikken shōmei*). We cannot find ultimate value through passively acquired knowledge. We can find it mainly by practicing it and finding that it bears the best result. Experience is essential to be convinced of the supremacy of Nichiren Buddhism and of the power of the *daigohonzon*. In the Nichiren tradition *genshō*, or factual evidence, is held to be of primary importance. Experience stories also play an important part in Sōka Gakkai's meetings. In each local organizational unit they have regular home meetings called *zadankai*, or discussion meetings, in which talking about personal experiences is the central element. In contrast to Reiyūkai, in Sōka Gakkai believers are to study doctrines diligently. They must read Nichiren's writings and even take examinations to get qualifications. Not only priests but all the believers should learn doctrines themselves.

Sōka Gakkai also exhorts even the just converted to actively join in proselytization. Moreover the typical form of proselytization is *shakubuku*, meaning aggressive persuasion. Believers are advised to challenge others who may be relying on some established authority. Challenge and participation rather than fear and hesitation are the norms. Sōka Gakkai testifies to the fact that the exclusivism of the Lotus Sutra and Nichiren tradition has much relevance to the active and challenging attitude of modernity. Another characteristic of Sōka Gakkai is that their energetic activities are not restricted to the specifically religious area, but spread to various fields of life. This is because they believe Nichiren Buddhism is beyond all the authorities and can be applied in every field of life. The first field of application was education. Later on, economics, politics, labor unions, medicine, art and culture – in all these fields where people's spontaneous participation is possible, the uniquely Sōka Gakkai way and organization were projected.

This popularism is supported by their view of history. Makiguchi believed in the progress of civilization, assuming that education's role is to spread civilization to the people. After the Second World War their identification as a people's movement was strengthened, as seen in the coining of the term *Buppō Minshushugi*, or 'Buddhist Democracy.' They believe that history is heading for the age of the people. Now it is believed that *mappō* is not the age of decline but that of the ascent of the common people, and Sōka Gakkai is the Buddhism of these ascending people.

In sum, Lotus Sutra-based new religions that grew from 1920 to 1970 developed a strong sense of popularism and practices based on that sense. Both Reiyūkai and Sōka Gakkai, regarding the established religious and other social authorities as not worthy of trust and sometimes severely criticizing them, constructed new movements in which ordinary people are to be the masters. In the Lotus Sutra and Nichirenite traditions there is the idea that the ultimate truth is simple and can be practiced by anyone. This formed the basis for the popularism of Lotus Sutra-based new religions. Reiyūkai and Sōka Gakkai in their turn added new ideas like laicism and experientialism. According to them the most important truth is grasped by ordinary people in their daily life, and knowledge given by priests and academics is at most of secondary importance. Moreover, they defined our age to be the age of the ordinary people and reinterpreted Lotus Sutra and Nichirenite faith as illustrating this age's unique meaning. Popularism is also found in some syncretic Shintoist new religions. But in Lotus Sutra-based new religions more pronounced is the spirit of challenge to established authorities and the appeal for people's active participation and initiative. The Lotus Sutra and Nichirenite traditions originally contained a spirit of challenge to authorities that were perceived as loosing their credibility. In the period from 1920 to 1970 people were so disturbed by the crisis of authority that they were willing to enthusiastically embrace, reformulate, and revitalize these traditions in a significant way.

Crisis of authority and Lotus Sutra-based new religions

During the period from 1920 to 1970 social institutions were still largely based on traditional hierarchical relationships, but the validity of the authorities that were to support these relationships was often questioned. In many areas of life established authorities were challenged and desacralized. People were increasingly less able to rely on established authorities. One response to this crisis of authority was to reestablish a new authoritative order at the national level. Thus, for many people the state was a focus of their sense of order. With rapid social change under the state's initiative since the Meiji Restoration in 1868, people increasingly felt that their own fortune was being determined by the political and economic changes initiated at the state level. Moreover, because of the continuing international tension and wars, the state was thought to be one community sharing the same fate. The crisis of authority was often interpreted as the crisis of the state or the nation.

Lotus Sutra-based new religions grew rapidly under these circumstances. One reason for their rapid growth is that they inherited much from the Lotus Sutra and Nichirenite traditions, which support the reestablishment of firm order and authority when these are shaken. Part of the central messages of both the Lotus Sutra and Nichiren is the assertion that one supreme religious authority must be established in a period of general confusion and conflict between differing faiths and ideologies. Reiyūkai and Sōka Gakkai added various ideas and practices that are appropriate to the modern situation. One was nationalism, and the other popularism. They both contain new prescriptions to overcome the crisis of authority. The former prescription, nationalism, was for some time effective, but not in the long run. A major reason for this is that the modern political regime of Japan was not compatible with their visions of religious and ideological unity in Lotus Sutra or Nichiren Buddhism. The latter prescription, popularism, seems to have had a more lasting validity. It was effective not only in the democratic political regime that emerged after the Second World War, but also in the fascist era.

Around 1970, however, the domestic growth of Lotus Sutra-based new religions slowed dramatically, and then came to a complete stop. Some groups included in the syncretic Shintoist or 'others' categories have shown conspicuous growth, while Lotus Sutra-based groups have only been able to maintain their numbers. Various reasons can be mentioned for this change. Mystical experience, magic, and meditation rather than simple faith in the ultimate being or teaching seem to be more attractive in the 1970s and 1980s.[11] Exotic religious traditions from India, Europe, and other areas of the world are also more fascinating to them than the familiar Japanese religious tradition, of which the Lotus Sutra is a part. The relevance of the nationalism and popularism of Lotus Sutra-based new religions to the New Age is something that still needs to be examined. It is evident that their nationalism is not very popular now, for with internationalization and globalization international tensions and the importance of national identity has diminished. Also, the attainment of a prosperous society has reduced the sense of solidarity among the people that they are battling the same difficulties. Popularism, on the other hand, was still relevant in 1970s and 1980s, but less than before. People enjoy a wealth of material things and an abundance of information. They are less and less oriented towards the future and towards improvement than they are to the enjoyment of what has been given. Naturally they do not feel obliged to challenge established authority. They are more and more concerned with a stable life and the satisfactory exercise of personal abilities, rather than cooperative group activities aimed at common goals. It is true that social order is still supported by various authorities, but they are assumed to be neither intrinsically reliable nor worthy of sincere protest. Rather, people are inclined to set up something like authority intentionally, without the sense of awe or reverence that leads to the conclusion that essential social order must be preserved. Japanese society after 1970 may be called in the age of fictitious authority or utilitarian authority, rather than crisis of authority.

5 Popularism Derived from the Lotus Sutra Tradition

Reiyūkai and experientialism

Among the groups responsible for the enormous growth of new religions in postwar Japan, the various groups drawing on the current of Buddhism based on the Lotus Sutra (Skt. *Saddharmapupdarika-sūtra*, Jpn. *Hokkekyō*) have played a major role. While about half of the phenomenal growth of these groups is attributable to Sōka Gakkai, the remaining half has been due to groups derived in large part from Reiyūkai (Society of Companions of the Spirits).[1] That being so, what then are the philosophical characteristics of these Reiyūkai-derived groups? And what new religious ideas, differing from those of traditional Lotus Sutra Buddhism and the Nichiren sect, have Reiyūkai and related groups introduced to the history of religious thought in Japan?

It has often been argued that the tenets of the Reiyūkai and related groups are far removed from intellectual discipline requiring complex knowledge of the written word, and have instead inherited elements of Japan's traditional folk religion such as shamanism and ancestor worship, to which they have done nothing more than add a somewhat contemporary veneer. But if one turns one's attention to the aspect of experientialism, it is also possible to view their thought as a decidedly self-conscious philosophy of which an important element has been the encouragement of a modern brand of self-reliance and independence, and which embraces a view of history that seeks to ascribe a positive meaning to the present age (Shimazono 1988).

Religious experientialism refers to a current of thought that seeks the core content and primary basis of religious beliefs in an individual's experiences of salvation, conversion, the witnessing of mystical phenomena, sublime states of body and mind, and so forth. Notwithstanding the designation 'experientialism,' it does not look for all religious knowledge in experience, for it also relies to a certain degree on traditional or rational knowledge, but, relatively speaking, it attaches considerable importance to experiential knowledge. It should also be pointed out that the 'experiences' of experientialism differ from the 'mystical experiences' of historically renowned thinkers and practitioners of mysticism, and are instead closely associated with everyday life and characterized by a mass appeal such that they can be readily attained by individuals among the masses.

This final point is closely related to the fact that experientialism has developed against the historical background of modern society, which has seen the advance of mass popularization. A focus on this point enables one to realize that experientialism is not an idea that can evolve in total isolation. In the case of Reiyūkai, it is underpinned by laicism, a philosophy of independence and self-help, and a view of history that stresses the importance of the masses. By clarifying these ideas, it should become easier to understand the experientialism of Reiyūkai and the overall structure of its thought, of which this experientialism forms one part.

The aim of this chapter, then, is to shed light on a number of philosophical ideas related to experientialism in order to clarify the structure of Reiyūkai's thought, evolving as it did against the background of mass popularization. On the basis of these inquiries, I then suggest in the final section the use of the term 'religious (mass) popularism' (or simply 'popularism') to facilitate a comprehensive grasp of experientialism and its associated ideas.

Reiyūkai's view of history and its background

In a previous work (Shimazono 1988), I attempted to approach the experientialist thought of early Reiyūkai chiefly through the writings of Kotani Kimi (1901–1971), the first president of Reiyūkai. The writings in question were *Watakushi no shugyō seikatsu sanjūgonen* (My thirty-five years of living a life of religious practice, Reiyūkai Kyōdan, 1958) and *Kotani Kimi shō: Ten no ongaku* (Selections from the sayings of Kotani Kimi: Celestial music, Hotoke no Sekai Sha, 1972), both of which present teachings that Kotani Kimi received from Kubo Kakutarō (1892–1944) in the early stages of the establishment of the Reiyūkai, and they are without doubt an excellent source of material for acquainting oneself with the experientialist thought studied and transmitted by ordinary members of the Reiyūkai.

But it turned out that Kubo Kakutarō had himself recorded in writing teachings that were more systematic and had a higher degree of intellectual content than the writings of Kotani. These are found in three booklets entitled *Hotoke no daiji daihi to unmei* (Destiny and the Buddha's great benevolence and great compassion, 1928), *Shōwa no Hokkekyō to Jōfukyō bosatsu* (The Lotus Sutra in the Showa era and the bodhisattva Never-Disparaging, 1928), and *Hotoke wa messhitamawazu* (The Buddha never dies, 1929), which were all published under the name of Bekki Sadao, an early collaborator of Kubo's. Fortunately these publications are included in Vol. 3 of the four-volume *Reiyūkai shi shiryō 1*, published in 1988, and as a result they have become widely accessible to researchers (Reiyūkai shi shiryo hensan iinkai ed. 1988).[2]

There is, however, a possibility that these booklets are interspersed with elements of Bekki Sadao's own ideas, differing from the thought of Kubo himself, for prior to his contact with Kubo and his introduction to the doctrines of the *Lotus Sutra* and the Nichiren sect Bekki had been in contact with Ōmotokyō. These booklets contain direct references to Ōmotokyō, and it is even stated that 'the founder of Ōmotokyō heralded the construction of the wondrous empire' (*Reiyūkai shi shiryō 1*, Vol. 3: 231). There are also references to 'a great rebuilding,' 'the missions of East and West,' and 'material civilization and spiritual civilization,' as well as passages alluding to Christianity. These should perhaps be regarded as fragments of ideas that Bekki brought with him from Ōmotokyō. Nonetheless, it is clear that the essential framework of the ideas expressed in these booklets has its basis in the Nichiren sect and can be safely attributed to Kubo, who had been deeply involved in the Bussho Gonenkai of Nishida Mugaku and was well-versed in the thought of the Lotus Sutra and Nichiren sect.

A comparison of these three booklets reveals that it is *Shōwa no Hokkekyō to Jōfukyō bosatsu* in which the author's doctrinal knowledge of the *Lotus Sutra* and the Nichiren sect is set forth in the greatest detail, while *Hotoke wa messhitamawazu* is the least detailed in this regard. It could be considered that *Shōwa no Hokekyō to Jōfukyō bosatsu* reflects most faithfully Kubo's own thought and that there is a gradual deviation from Kubo's authentic voice in *Hotoke no daiji daihi to unmei* and then *Hotoke wa messhitamawazu*. But it is a moot point whether or not passages outlining current nationalistic and socialist thought or passages presenting a popular understanding of natural science, world history and the contemporary global situation should be considered to reflect Kubo's own thought. There are, however, no fundamental differences in the basic content of these booklets, and even if they do include some borrowings from Ōmotokyō, these may be regarded as insignificant.

In point of fact, there are virtually no inconsistencies in the ideas propounded in these three booklets, nor are there any great discrepancies with what was related by Kotani Kimi in later years. All in all, they may be regarded as systematic accounts of the teachings and doctrines of early Reiyūkai. To the upper right of the title on the cover of each of these booklets are inscribed the words *Myōhō renge. Kyō bosatsu hō. Busshogonen. Senpu* (Lotus Flower of the Wondrous Dharma; Teaching the Bodhisattva-Dharma; Protected by the Buddha; Dissemination). Below the title of *Shōwa no Hokkekyō to Jōfukyō bosatsu* is written 'Part Two' (*dainihen*), while above the title of *Hotoke wa messhitamawazu* we find 'In "The Lotus Sutra in the Showa era"' (*Shōwa no Hokekyō no naka*) and below it 'Part Four' (*daiyonhen*). In addition, the introduction to *Hotoke wa messhitamawazu* ends with the following statement: 'The publication of Part Three, which ought to precede this volume, is to be deferred for the present because the time for its publication is not yet ripe.' It is to be surmised that Kubo considered these booklets to constitute part of a work to be entitled *Shōwa no Hokkekyō* (The Lotus Sutra in the Showa era) and set out to expound therein the essence of the doctrines in which he believed.

The term 'experience' (*taiken*) does not appear very often in these booklets. Experientialist thought would have been given clearer expression when instructing Kotani Kimi and other believers with little education or intellectual training than in these booklets, the aim of which was to provide a systematic presentation of Kubo's doctrines. It would not have been easy for Kotani and other ordinary believers like herself to comprehend the overall thought contained in these booklets, and in the initial stages, when they were still in the process of acquiring their faith, the main emphasis would have been on experientialism. It is to be surmised, therefore, that experientialist thought would have exerted a greater degree of influence on the life and thinking of Kotani and other believers than of Kubo himself. However, these booklets describe in great detail the philosophy of the independence and self-help of the masses, which underpins experientialism, and a view of history that gives credence to this philosophy. If experientialist thought is seen as a type of philosophy of history, then these booklets become extremely important sources of material. In my earlier work I was able to touch only briefly on the view of history underlying experientialist thought, but now it is possible to give a more detailed account.

1. Ever since Buddhism was established by Sakyamuni, it has on the one hand degenerated and society has fallen into disorder, while on the other hand the original teachings of Buddhism have

gradually been revealed. Just as one proceeds from elementary school to a specialist or professional school, so too do the teachings successively advance from the age of expedient means and preparation to 'the true goal of the specialist real Dharma,' and they are 'devised to guide people by revealing the profound and wondrous teachings' (*Reiyūkai shi shiryo 1*,Vol. 3: 151). Times change, passing through the one thousand years of the true Dharma, the one thousand years of the imitative Dharma, and the ten thousand years of the latter-day Dharma, and in human terms the age of the true Dharma corresponds to the age of three or four to seven or eight years, the age of the imitative Dharma corresponds to elementary school, and the age of the latter-day Dharma corresponds to the time after leaving elementary school. As human wisdom unfolds, it advances towards 'the realization of the Buddha's decrees': 'The Buddha Sakyamuni left the Lotus Sutra to be used during the age of civilization. Therefore, the period of the dissemination of the Lotus Sutra coincides with the formation of civilization.' (Ibid.: 215)

2. With the advent of the latter-day Dharma, the stage is reached when sentient beings must live by their own moral standards. Nichiren now appeared, and the Lotus Sutra was presented as a form of secondary education. It was clearly explained that when all the doctrines and scriptures of Buddhism are reduced to their essentials, there is none other than the Lotus Sutra by which the peace and happiness of sentient beings can be achieved. But even though the Lotus Sutra may be theoretically superior, there is no clear distinction between it and other teachings with regard to the merits that may accrue, and in many respects the true meaning of the Lotus Sutra has still not been clarified. In addition, the teachings and practices of Buddhism remain in the hands of monks, although this is only provisionally so since many people are still illiterate. Thus, although the Lotus Sutra has been revealed, it is still an age of expedient means and preparatory education.

3. Several hundred years after Nichiren's death the age of the latter-day Dharma enters the period of higher preparatory education, corresponding to the period from the Meiji through to Showa eras. Human wisdom develops, civilization advances, and it becomes a time of 'peaceful practices' in which practitioners of the Lotus Sutra are no longer persecuted. But at the same time the truth of the Lotus Sutra is no longer understood, and the world

becomes ever more evil and defiled. The first five hundred years of the age of the latter-day Dharma, a time of conflict in which the benefits of the Dharma are evident, have elapsed and there begins a period in which the true teachings disappear and there is no practice of the Dharma nor proof of its efficacy. People no longer pay any attention to gods, Buddhas or ancestors. This state of affairs is not confined to Buddhism, but is an indication of 'a turning point for the reform of religions throughout the world.' It is at this juncture that spiritual leaders such as the founders of Tenrikyō and Ōmotokyō appear as messengers from the celestial realms and as 'harbingers of the implementation of the wondrous Dharma in which heaven and the four seas all take refuge' (ibid.: 222). Thereafter the ultimate teachings of the Lotus Sutra, that is, the truth and practices for purifying sinful sentient beings and leading them to enlightenment, are revealed.

4. This revelation of the ultimate teachings of the Lotus Sutra is first carried out by Nishida Mugaku, who was dispatched from the Buddhas' realm as the bodhisattva Sadaparibhūta (Jpn. *Jōfukyō*: Never-Disparaging), just as is foretold in the Lotus Sutra. Nishida Mugaku (i.e., the bodhisattva Sadaparibhūta) presents the teachings and practices for 'protection by the Buddha,' whereby lay believers correctly worship and placate the spirits of their ancestors. Next, Kubo himself reveals the 'teaching of the Bodhisattva-Dharma,' which represents the teachings of repentance and expiation of sins for the purification of living people. By means of these teachings the existence of the spirit world is confirmed, the existence of gods and Buddhas and the will of the soul are demonstrated, and it becomes possible to predict the future. In addition, benefits are gained in this world, the destiny of each person is steadily improved, and the eternal peace of the nation and humanity is achieved.

> How grand are the practices for protection by the Buddha and how great is the teaching of the Bodhisattva-Dharma! Both having obtained the majestic and divine might of Samantabhadra (Jpn. *Fugen*: Universally Good), they are about to flower and bear fruit, and with these seeds a new world will be created. The first step in the golden age of the Buddha-Dharma, for a Pure Land in which the truth will be revealed, has been planted by us on this earth. The premise for the world as a single Buddha-land – the wondrous Dharma of great joy in which heaven, earth and people

join in bright harmony and sentient beings gather together – this is,
namely, the Lotus Sutra of the Great Showa era. (Ibid.: 172)

5. Until now the Buddha had deliberately not revealed the ultimate
teachings and had left people to their own devices. This was to
allow for the development of human wisdom through trial and
experience. But because people had understood Buddhism in an
abstract fashion and had contented themselves with teachings
removed from reality, Buddhism now faced a crisis. At a stage
when human wisdom had not yet developed and many people
were illiterate, reading the scriptures and understanding the
teachings were left to monks, and the masses were unable to
practice Buddhism for themselves. But now that civilization
and enlightenment have evolved and the masses are all able to
read, it is time for the 'great undifferentiating wisdom' (*byōdō
no daie*: lit. 'great wisdom of equality/sameness') of the Lotus
Sutra to be translated into reality. This is, moreover, a teaching
and practice whereby definite benefits are obtained and one's
destiny is changed. 'Great undifferentiating wisdom' does not
mean that everything is equalized; it means that the masses are
all able to open up their own destiny. The 'great practices for the
masses' (ibid.: 221) of 'protection by the Buddha' and 'teaching
of the Bodhisattva-Dharma' and the corresponding teachings of
the 'Showa Lotus Sutra' constitute the real content of Buddhism
encapsulated in this 'great undifferentiating wisdom.'

> Rituals and practices have until now been in the hands of monks,
> but now these teachings are about to leave the hands of monks and
> the true Buddha-Dharma is about to be made manifest through the
> general laity. That time has now arrived. (Ibid.: 171)

> The great undifferentiating wisdom that has been propounded
> until now was great undifferentiating wisdom only in speech and
> writing. Therefore, sentient beings had no way of knowing the
> reality and truth of it. Now is the time, long-awaited for thousands
> of years, for the manifestation of great undifferentiating wisdom.
> (Ibid.: 187)

6. It is the mission of Japan to embody the truth of the Lotus Sutra
and become the leader in the salvation of the world. Japan's
imperial household has since times of yore been practicing

the two rituals of veneration of ancestors and expiation of sins, representing the quintessence of the Lotus Sutra, and this is the reason for the majesty of Japan's national polity. In the future it behooves Japan to advance boldly as a 'Mahayanist country' and 'wondrous empire,' for otherwise it will face a grave national crisis. Without relying in accordance with proper Buddhism on the might of the gods of the spirit world, there will be little hope of victory in the coming war.

As is evident from the above, Kubo Kakutarō held a consistent and systematic view of history. On the one hand, it showed a pessimistic perception of the present age as a time of crisis in which the defiled world of the latter-day Dharma had plumbed its depths. But on the other hand it also offered the optimistic view that the time was now approaching when the masses themselves would become the true upholders of Buddhism and the salvation that had been promised since the time of Sakyamuni would become a reality. This bipolar sense of history, which sees a turning point in the fate of humanity in the present point in time and attaches to it a decisively important significance, is widely found in millennialist religious thought.[3] Kubo's view of history could be seen on the one hand as drawing on a crisis-inspired sense of history characteristic of the Nichiren sect, while on the other hand also being strongly influenced by the nationalistic millennialism prevalent in Japan at this time. But the distinctive feature of Kubo's stance was his progressive sense of history that emphasized civilization and enlightenment, as well as the independence of the masses, and it was this that lay behind the solid experientialist thought of early Reiyūkai. Let us now consider this point in a little more detail.

Properly speaking, the Lotus Sutra does not contain any millenarian elements. But it does embody a sense of time that attaches importance to the passage of time and regards the present as the decisive moment in the manifestation of the sacred. It also maintains that although the Buddha expounded many different teachings, these were all provisional expedients and the ultimate truth was revealed for the first time in the Lotus Sutra. This means that the Buddhist teachings include relative elements that change with time, and that at a certain point in time there occurs a decisive event in which the truth is revealed. This sense of time contributed to the development of a dynamic view of history that did not regard past truths as being necessarily immutable and considered changes in doctrine to be quite natural. In actual fact, this reflects the diversification and relativization of Buddhist doctrine within Mahayana Buddhism.[4] The fluidity of doctrine in Mahayana

Buddhism led to the emphasis in the Lotus Sutra on the 'now' in which truth is revealed, and the classifications of Buddhist doctrine (*chiao-hsiang p'an-shih*) that played such an important role in the development of Buddhist thought in China served to further entrench a way of thinking that recognized gradual changes in doctrinal content and the need to organize diverse teachings under some unifying principle.

But for later Buddhists the decisive point in time intimated in the Lotus Sutra remained in the past, when Sakyamuni was still alive, and it did not imply any major changes in the present or future. Nichiren (1222–1282) made the Lotus Sutra the mainstay of his faith, but at the same time he was also strongly influenced by the idea of the latter days of the Dharma (*mappō*) that was widely accepted at that time in Japanese Buddhism, especially in the Tendai sect. In Japan, the year 1052 was regarded as the first year of the latter-day Dharma, and Buddhist movements from around this time through to the Kamakura period became dominated by a concern for how to survive this present age of the latter-day Dharma. Since, moreover, Nichiren lived at a time of national crisis brought about by the Mongol invasions, his writings came to be strongly permeated by a sense of time that viewed the present age as a decisive time of crisis. In addition, Nichiren also had a strong interest in the current state of the nation, and there is no doubt that some of his writings contain eschatological and millenarian elements.[5] Such elements are in the forefront especially when he entrusts the construction of the 'ordination platform for the true teachings' (*honmon no kaidan*) to future generations and links to this the future realization of a utopian state.

However, once the start of the age of the latter-day Dharma had receded into the distant past, there no longer existed for the Nichiren sect a specific point in history, either in the near past or in the future, about which it could feel overly concerned. Neither millenarian motifs nor elements based on a particular view of history played any important role in the Nichiren sect during the Muromachi and Edo periods (form fourteenth to nineteenth centuries). But during the Meiji era power relationships between nations became visible driving forces that were seen to be having a decisive influence on history, and once again the fate of the nation became a focus of people's interests just as it had at the time of the earlier Mongol invasions. As a result, the millenarian elements and historical awareness of the Nichiren sect took on a renewed appeal and attractiveness. One person who quickly took cognizance of these developments and made a major contribution to the revival of the Nichiren sect's dynamic view of history was

Tanaka Chigaku (1861–1939), the most important leader of Nichirenist movements in modern times.

Already in his *Shūmon no ishin* (The renovation of our sect, 1901), Tanaka predicted that Japan would achieve religious unity in the near future under the Nichiren sect and become the world's leader, and he also set out concrete methods for attaining this goal.[6] Then in *Sekai tōitsu no tengyō* (The heavenly enterprise of world unification, 1904) he incorporated elements of State Shinto and came to look upon Nichirenism and emperor ideology as being mutually concordant.[7] This could be seen as an aberration from the original ideas of Buddhism as based on the Lotus Sutra, but insofar that Tanaka believed in national salvation through the Lotus Sutra there can be no doubt that he drew on Nichiren's millenarian thought. He also had a powerful desire to discover a form of Buddhism suited to the modern age. It is well-known that his religious sense of history exerted considerable influence on the revolutionary ideas of people like Ishiwara Kanji (1889–1949), and it is to be surmised that Nishida Mugaku and Kubo Kakutarō were also influenced by Tanaka's thought, either directly or indirectly. For example, there is a passage in *Hotoke wa messhitamawazu* analyzing the character *kō* (emperor/imperial), in which the element *ō* (king) is interpreted as 'a symbol of the harmonization of heaven, earth and man' (*Reiyūkai shi shiryō 1*, Vol. 3: 186), and this tallies with the explanation found in Tanaka's *Sekai tōitsu no tengyō*.

However, a marked difference between the historical awareness of Kubo Kakutarō and that of Tanaka Chigaku may be seen in the importance that Kubo attached to the self-awareness and praxis of the masses themselves. In my earlier work I dealt in some detail with the fact that the advocacy of the self-reliance and self-help of the masses represented one of the mainstays of early Reiyūkai's thought. This characteristic is also evident in section 5 of the above summarization of Kubo's thought, and in the following I wish to supplement what I was unable to state clearly in the earlier article, based as it was on the utterances of Kotani Kimi.

In the first place, Kubo's self-help philosophy was strongly influenced by the vocabulary and ideas of modern self-independence (or individualism) that were first introduced to Japan via Samuel Smiles's *Self Help* (translated by Nakamura Masanao as *Saigoku risshi hen* in 1871) and Fukuzawa Yukichi's *Gakumon no susume* (An encouragement to learning, 1872–1876) and began to spread widely among the general populace from around the time of the founding of the magazine *Seikō* (Success) in 1902.[8] The experientialist thought of early

Reiyūkai was situated within the broad current of self-independent thought in modern Japan, which urged people to help themselves as independent individuals for the sake of the independent nation of Japan. Let us compare a passage from the publisher's message in the inaugural issue of *Seikō* (Success) with a passage from *Hotoke wa messhitamawazu*.

The people required for today's society are not the so-called modish men about town who receive others with fine words and smoothness of manner but have no personal integrity, nor are they the so-called Oriental stalwarts with unkempt hair who are uncivil and use bombastic language but lack in sincerity; they are rather people who simply help themselves, respect themselves, occupy themselves, exert themselves, and create their own destiny through their own ingenuity. If one considers the matter carefully, a nation arises on account of the existence of such people, and it falls into decline on account of a lack of such people (Takeuchi 1978: 114).

You have not yet developed the wisdom to embody the will of the Gods and Buddhas. Therefore, there have been provided as intermediaries of their will people whose task it is to serve the Gods and Buddhas. They are proxies who accumulate your merit until you yourselves are able to embody the will of the Gods and Buddhas, and they are instruments. Make worship! If these instruments exert themselves for the sake of the world, then yours will be the good deed of acting as their assistants. Even the illiterate can perform this good deed. Make worship! Make donations! For the sake of your own merit: *this is* the intent of the Gods and Buddhas *with regard to worship*...[new paragraph]...What about now? If you reflect upon yourselves, it should become clear of its own accord. [new paragraph] Civilization knows the truth that heaven helps those who help themselves. Because leaving things to others goes against this truth, worship also goes against reason. If you shift to practices based on the Buddha's decrees and then worship, the Gods and Buddhas will accept it as a gift, but otherwise it will remain empty worship without any effect whatsoever. (*Reiyūkai shi shiryō 1*, Vol. 3: 224–25)

The second point to be noted is that Kubo's thinking was based on the affirmation of the expansive energy of the 'masses' as a collective and physical entity. It is clear that Kubo viewed society in terms of a schema that pitted the elite, wealthy and powerful against the masses and that he positioned himself on the side of the masses. Moreover, it is to these masses that terms such as 'freedom' and 'equality,' as well as other related affirmative concepts, appertain. The sense of physical and material unclosedness that M. Bakhtin identified as an important factor in the view of the world espoused by the general populace is also included among these affirmative elements (Bakhtin 1984). It could be said that the reason that the term 'great undifferentiating wisdom' (lit. great wisdom of equality) was singled out from the Lotus Sutra was to give expression to this popular, affirmative worldview.

The austerities and asceticism of former times were provisional practices and were not the real thing. If it is impossible to demonstrate its efficacy without the practice of austerities and asceticism, then it does not deserve to be respected and revered as the Buddha-Dharma. Not only that, but claiming to save all sentient beings would be the height of folly. If it is not a method that even a child of seven or eight can practice, then even human beings will not easily be saved, and advocating 'great undifferentiating wisdom' and so forth would be no more than a grand delusion. But since this practice was accomplished with ease by Sadaparibhūta in accordance with the words of the Buddha, it is finally time for the real thing. From now on ordinary people will have their own way. (*Reiyūkai shi shiryō 1*, Vol. 3: 168)

The actions of the Buddha are infallible. It was determined that with the advent of civilization the cover would be removed and the entrances and exits be opened so that all people might be enabled to savor [the true teaching] and take a seat. That is what great compassion is. Up until now the entrances and exits had been deliberately closed and the cover had remained in place so that people could not ingest [the true teaching] and not take a seat. [new paragraph] Saint Nichiren was a forerunner, a crier, a person with the task of summoning people together, a solicitor of customers. He was a commander in charge of making the arrangements for regaling them with great undifferentiating wisdom. (Ibid.: 215–16)

Poverty is not necessarily everlasting. Illness is also not necessarily everlasting. By eradicating bad karma, the root cause of their occurrence, they are both eliminated. [new paragraph] That is the prerogative of man, the lord of all creatures, and the freedom and equality of the human world. (Ibid.: 217–18)

Behind the scenes preparations were steadily being made to hand over the assets of the Buddha-Dharma. He had withdrawn for these reasons. This was a great practice for the masses, representing the path expressive of great benevolence and great compassion for entering great undifferentiating wisdom. (Ibid.: 221)

Then, what about now? All of you, celebrate! sing! dance for joy!

'The great time when one succeeds in purifying the sense-organs (the elimination of the impurities of the six sense-organs of eyes, ears, nose, tongue, body and mind, which are the causes of karma) and eliminating sins without eschewing the five desires' has arrived.

The time has come when there is no need whatsoever for the abstinence called for by the dictum that 'the root cause of all suffering is avarice.' Just think how the father-like Buddha admonished monks, his children, in order to enable you, the masses, to arrive at this practice! He imposed upon them abstinence difficult to endure and austerities difficult to practice, forcing them to do it, and not just for a day, but for thousands of years. Moreover, because the time did not come when you, the masses, might practice together with his children who resolutely performed these austerities and this abstinence, you were not granted those important teachings, nor were you informed of them.

What is this if not great undifferentiating wisdom? What is it but mass-oriented? What is it if not great benevolence and great compassion? (Ibid.: 226)

Thirdly, Kubo was fully cognizant of socialist ideas of reform, and although opposed to them, he was also critical of the 'wealthy and powerful.' Though there is no denying the existence of distinctions of social rank due to individual karma caused by actions in past lives, if the upper classes indulge in pleasures on account of selfish greed, this will naturally cause rebellion. This rebellious 'mass movement' has meaning as an expedient for admonishing the upper classes for their arrogance and awakening the lower classes to their rights and duties. But if such movements go too far, they result in undesirable social phenomena, and the only way to avoid this is to follow the will of the spirit world. According to Kubo, this too is part of the evolutionary process foreseen by the Buddha.

It is only natural that there should exist in the world social distinctions of rank and differences in wealth, for these are aspects of natural society and natural laws. These distinctions and differences are the result of reflections of one's own karma, and they represent a natural judgment of equitable recompense in which there is neither contradiction nor tyranny...

That being so, since this status and rank are dictated by the justice of Nature, one must submit to the Buddha-Dharma, representing the justice of Nature, and begin to act in accordance with Nature. One must share one's good fortune with the needy and mutually act for the maintenance of great compassion. But unable to do this, there are some who lavish their vast wealth on their own pleasures without taking any notice of the fact that in the same human world there are people unable to make a satisfactory living, and they tie a rope around the necks of these unfortunate people and try to make them work without eating. If they should complain, they are immediately hanged with that rope.

Since they thus do not tread the path of repaying the compassion of the Gods and Buddhas and rebel against the justice of Nature, there is disapproval of them in the spirit world too. A rebel suited to them is appointed and sent into the world in an attempt to seek their awakening and bring about harmony between the high and the low, and in this manner a display of divine punishment is avoided if at all possible.

This is what that red-colored mass movement, so popular now, is all about. It is an envoy from Heaven that has been sanctioned as the substitute for a display of divine punishment. But there is no need to fear. Heaven is not fond of doing this, but has arranged things in this manner so as to make you human beings undertake the maintenance of compassion; it has caused this movement to arise so as to make the human world a better place of happiness.

This is, namely, a device in the evolution of the Buddha-Dharma. It is the acme of the mystery of Providence. (Ibid.: 202–3)

It should be noted with regard to this third point that there is a possibility that it includes some of Bekki Sadao's own ideas.

In the above we have considered Kubo Kakutarō's view of history on the basis of three booklets published in 1928–1929. This view of history was based on a dynamic sense of time that had been taken from the Lotus Sutra by the Nichiren sect. An historical sense of national crisis and salvation, inherited by Tanaka Chigaku from Nichiren, also occupied an important position in his thought. But in the modern Nichirenism of Tanaka and others the traditions of the Nichiren sect, grounded in the idea of the latter days of the Dharma, which implied that history was following a downward course, were transmuted into expectations of the realization of their ideals in the near future. Optimism about modern civilization and human progress and hopes for the establishment of a modern state fused with the Nichiren sect's concept of an 'ordination platform for the true teachings' to mould and develop a new religious view of history.

The foundations of these ideas were laid by Tanaka Chigaku in the Meiji era, followed in the Taisho and early Showa eras by further developments in various directions, and they exerted considerable influence politically too. There is no doubt that Reiyūkai's view of history also falls within the overall confines of this modern movement of Nichirenism. But its distinguishing feature lies in its emphasis on the self-help and independence of the masses and its assertion that a form of Buddhism able to be practiced by the masses had now been revealed. It was this assertion that was encapsulated in its use of the term 'laicism,' and it was this sense of history that underlay its experientialist thought.

Popularism and experientialism

Ever since its establishment, Reiyūkai has defined the keynote of its thought as 'laicism.' Many traditional historical religions, such as Catholicism, Theravada Buddhism and many sects of Mahayana Buddhism stress the qualitative differences between the clergy and the laity and take the view that only clerics are able to act as intermediaries between the sacred and humanity. In contrast to this clericalism, laicism in a general sense rejects this distinction between the clergy and the laity and asserts that through study and practice lay people are themselves able to approach ultimate truth. The bodhisattva thought of Mahayana Buddhism has points in common with this type of laicism, and such ideas are especially pronounced in scriptures such as the *Lotus Sutra* and *Vimalakirtinirdesa-sutra* (Jpn. *Yuimakyō*).[9]

In the traditions of Japan's Mahayana Buddhism the distinguishing signs of monks or clerics have, in practical terms, been the taking of the tonsure, a life of abstinence involving celibacy and so forth, non-engagement in secular occupations and secular life, and special knowledge and the ability to officiate at religious ceremonies. But doubts about the significance of a life of abstinence grounded in celibacy were raised already by Shinran (1173–1262) and followers of Shugendo (mountain asceticism), and their views could be regarded as an early form of laicism. Partly because of the influence of people such as these, the authority of monks in Japan began to decline from an early stage. Then during the Meiji era marriage by monks came to be openly sanctioned, and as secular knowledge began to take precedence and the influence of the doctrinal knowledge of Buddhist sects weakened, monks gradually lost their positions of dominance. It was under such circumstances that there developed movements led by people who had become disaffected with the clergy whose authority was declining, and were cultivating their own faith as lay people without becoming clerics. Among the new religions and Buddhist movements that arose in the late Edo and Restoration period there were few that emphasized the importance of being a cleric. In this sense it could be said that laicist thought is to be widely observed in Japan's new religions and modern Buddhist movements.

The point that distinguishes Reiyūkai among these various laicist movements of the modern period is that it explicitly rejected the idea of clerical dominance. Whereas there were many groups that were in reality practicing laicism, Reiyūkai itself actively advocated laicism and made it an important basis of its identity. The laicism of Reiyūkai could be described as a form of laicism that was consciously espoused and self-assertively advocated.

Laicism was without question one of the distinguishing features of early Reiyūkai. But it can, I believe, be more readily understood if one regards it as part of a broader current of thought that I propose to call 'religious (mass) popularism' (or simply 'popularism'). Religious popularism holds that ultimate truth is accessible to all people and can be readily approached by anyone. It also places a high value on the self-motivated participation of the general masses, far removed from positions of power or a high level of knowledge based on the written word, and it actively approaches them in order to prompt their self-motivated participation.

Religious popularism is premised on a broad distinction between the elite and the general masses, and it encourages the self-motivated participation of the latter. Laicism, on the other hand, is premised on a distinction between the clergy and the laity, which represents one mode of differentiation of the elite and the general masses. In addition, whereas religious popularism aspires to overcome an ill-defined discrimination between the elite and the general masses, in the case of laicism there is an emphasis on overcoming a clear-cut institutional discrimination between the clergy and the laity. In short, religious popularism is premised on a vague sense of discrimination and aims to overcome such wide-ranging discrimination, while laicism focuses on institutional discrimination between the clergy and the laity. Wherever there exists discrimination between the elite and the general masses, either on a religious level or on a cultural level, there is always a possibility that religious popularism will arise. Laicism, on the other hand, will occur only in a situation where there exist clerical institutions that have, moreover, become merely formalistic. Therefore, laicism may be described as one mode or facet of the broad-ranging philosophy or stance of religious popularism.

In the context of Buddhist history, Mahayana Buddhism, which evolved as a community of bodhisattvas emphasizing contact with the laity in contrast to the traditional monastic order (*sangha*) centered on monks, possessed from the very outset the characteristics of religious popularism. The Lotus Sutra in particular is strongly tinged with popularism. Within Mahayana Buddhism, Japanese Buddhism of the Kamakura period, which under the influence of the idea of the latter days of the Dharma taught salvation by means of simple practices accessible to ordinary people, could be said to have pushed this popularist tendency even further to the fore, and this tendency was especially pronounced in the Pure Land sects and the Nichiren sect. The majority of new religions in modern Japan are characterized by popularism, but this is particularly so in the case of new religions derived from the Lotus Sutra, which are also distinguished by the fact that they consciously advocate popularism.

One advantage of using the term 'religious popularism' is that it enables one to clarify the relationship between experientialism and laicism, for experientialism may also be described as a manifestation of popularism. As was pointed out earlier in this chapter, a distinctive feature of the 'experiences' emphasized by experientialism is their mass accessibility. Experientialism places considerable weight on the experiences of the masses as important opportunities for approaching ultimate truth. Since it encourages, in this manner, the participation of the general masses from below, experientialism may be regarded as one expression of popularism, although modes of popularism that do not assume the form of experientialism are of course also conceivable. These would correspond to cases in which the performance of religious practices and rites and the intellectual study of doctrine by ordinary believers are stressed and little emphasis is placed on religious or other experiences. Nonetheless, religious popularism is susceptible to the incorporation of experientialism, for the masses have a natural tendency to set greater value on knowledge closely associated with everyday life than on refined ritual and intellectual understanding. Both laicism and experientialism may thus be regarded as different manifestations of popularism.

One further advantage of using the term 'religious popularism' is that it becomes easier to turn one's attention to its relationship with the moves towards popularization and democratization in society as a whole. During the course of modernization there was a steady rise in the economic and political status of the general population, and at the same time there also evolved a newly stratified social order befitting this new political and economic order. The popularism of the new religions can be seen as an expression of their responses to and protest against this reorganization of stratified order accompanying social change.

In one respect, the popularism of Reiyūkai may be regarded as an expression of the confidence and self-assertion that accompanied the betterment of the social status of the general populace. But at the same time in another respect it may be seen as an expression of protest against the establishment of a new stratified order. It was, in other words, a protest against social stratification based on economic power and academic credentials. Popularism involves protesting against the rule of the elite, but in the case of the Reiyūkai this elite was not in fact the clergy, rather it would appear to have been the people who on the basis of their academic credentials gained high positions in both the government bureaucracy and private enterprise. The experientialism of Reiyūkai may thus be understood to have been partly intended as a protest against the rule of a new elite that was seeking to base its authority on knowledge acquired through a school education.

6 Sōka Gakkai and the Modern Reformation of Buddhism

In a world of rapid change, progressively urbanized and information-intensive, what transformations are taking place in Buddhist practice and in the community of practitioners that make up Buddhist congregations? In pursuing this question, one is instinctively drawn toward those Buddhist movements that have won popular acceptance and shown a rugged vitality over the past fifty years, while many traditional Buddhist groups appear to have fallen into decline. Esoteric Tibetan Buddhism and Zen attract an enthusiastic following in the United States, Europe, and Taiwan. The urban masses of Thailand flock to Thammakai and Santi Asoke (Fukushima 1989). Among Japan's new religions, Buddhist movements like Shinnyoen and those derived from Reiyūkai stand out for their dynamic appeal, but the most successful of all is Nichiren Shōshū/Sōka Gakkai, which has spread beyond Japan to attract a large number of followers worldwide.[1]

In the modern world of East Asia, the most significant change that has occurred in praxis-oriented groups within the Mahayana Buddhist tradition has been the rise of popular Lotus Sutra (or Nichiren)-based Buddhist groups. In contrast to the widespread recession and fossilization of established temples and sects, these groups have completely altered the distribution of power and influence in the region. Here again, Sōka Gakkai, the largest active Buddhist group since the end of the war, stands out as representing the dramatic transformation taking place within Mahayana Buddhism in the twentieth century.

Without wishing to minimize the kinds of changes that have gone on in faith-praxis, group activity, and organization, I would like to focus my remarks here on the doctrinal side of these movements, which – at least in the case of Japan – can be characterized as religions of 'this-worldly salvation.'[2] In particular, I will try to account for the emergence of this notion in Sōka Gakkai's second president, Toda Jōsei, and his 'theory of life-force.'[3]

In Sōka Gakkai today, as the following excerpts attest, 'life-force' is understood as the foundation of faith and practice:

The greatness of the Buddhist teaching is that in trying to provide for the happiness of the human person, the subject of human life and society, it gets right to the root of the problem, namely *life-force*, and through scientific analysis emerges with a principle that can be practiced by ordinary people.

Nichiren...systematized the principle of life-force into a practical method to provide happiness for the masses. (Sōka Gakkai Kyōgakubu, 1971: 77)

Faith is firm belief in the universe and the life-force...Only a person of sublime faith can live a good and vigorous life...

Buddhist doctrine is a philosophy that has human life as its ultimate object, and our Human Revolution Movement is an act of reform aimed at opening up the inner universe, the creative life-force within each individual, and leading to human freedom. The Movement sees humanity poised on the summit of a new idea of life-force, surveying the twenty-first century and ready to build the future. (Seikyō Shinbunsha 1980: 109, 112)

Originally formed as a lay organization within Nichiren Shōshū, Sōka Gakkai assumed the doctrine of the sect by and large intact. But the idea of 'life-force,' not to mention what Sōka Gakkai has made of it, is not apparent in traditional Nichiren Shōshū.

The foundational ideas of Sōka Gakkai are found in Makiguchi Tsunesaburō's 1930 book, *Sōka kyōikugaku taikei*. Makiguchi himself does not speak so much of life-force as of 'value theory' and 'the life of great virtue.' Toward the end of his life he also proposed a theory of dharmic retribution.[4] It was only after Makiguchi's death that the term came into ascendancy with Toda Jōsei, who was responsible for rebuilding the movement, giving it the name Sōka Gakkai, and overseeing its rapid growth in the postwar period. The opening chapter of *Shakubuku kyōten* (1951), the doctrinal compendium that Toda edited and that was the mainstay of the movement during these years, was entitled "The Doctrine of Life-Force." In terms of the doctrinal history of Sōka Gakkai, the idea of life-force marks a move away from Makiguchi's thought towards that of Toda.[5] What is of more interest to us here, however, is how this idea reshaped the traditional teachings of Nichiren Shōshū in the direction of a belief in this-worldly salvation that is typical of popular Buddhist movements in East Asia in the modern period.

Toda Josei's doctrine of life-force

Toda's reflections on life-force go back to the experience of being imprisoned in 1943, along with Makiguchi, on a charge of *lese majeste* for having refused to display a talisman from the Ise Shrine. Immersed in the study of Buddhist scriptures and teachings, Toda came to a firm conviction of belief within his prison cell. He seems to have had visions of the word *seimei* (life-force) flashing before his eyes and of himself seated among the assembly in the presence of the Buddha (Seikyō Shinbunsha 1972b, vol. 2: 235–55). Years later, in response to a question from a Sōka Gakkai believer as to the meaning of *Namu myōhō rengekyō*, the chanted phrase popularized by Nichiren, Toda recalls:

> Ten years ago, absorbed in the search for who the Buddha was and whether he was real or not, I looked for help in books about Buddhism, but they were of no help. In the end, I came upon the *Muryōgikyō*, where I read: 'Body neither is nor is not…It is neither red nor purple, nor any other color.' Reflecting on these words, it dawned on me, 'The Buddha is life-force.' After agonizing over the relation of the Buddha to the *namu myōhō rengekyō* in light of the theory of the ten worlds, I realized that life-force is the name of the Buddha, and that this is the fundamental force in the universe, the *Kuon gansho*, which has the power to change the fate of every person. After that I was able to read and understand all the Buddhist scriptures.[10]

For Toda, this life-force, the essence of humanity and the universe, is an omnipresent, creative power emanating from the Buddha. The root of this universal, vital life-force is the 'True *Honzon*,' inscribed with the words *namu myōhō rengekyō*. To receive the *honzon* and to chant the *daimoku* is to release that power. This is the source of happiness and ultimately leads to the attainment of Buddhahood. Hence the goal of the human person is to attain happiness personally and then to spread this happiness to others.

To break this down in further detail, we may single out six elements, referring to Toda's own words as much as possible.

The eternal nature of human life

Human life is more than this present existence: it includes life in its past, present, and future existences. This is not the same as saying that one's 'spirit' survives through time in the form of great accomplishments or things passed on to one's descendants:

> Just as in life nothing can come between one sadness and another, one joy and another; or just as in sleep the mind does not go anywhere, so, too, at death the life-force is taken up in the Great Life-Force of the universe. No matter where you look for it, it is not something you can find.
>
> When you wake up in the morning you remember the activities of the day before and pick up where you left off. In the same way, new life receives the karmic causes from past existences and continues to live their effects in the present existence. (Toda Jōsei 1960: 17, 19–20)

Toda traces this doctrine of the 'eternal nature of life' back to Sakyamuni Buddha, but claims that Nichiren has taken it still further, to its 'true form and origin' (Toda Jōsei 1960: 50, 52–53), namely, the *Gohonzon*.

The universe is the life-force

'Life coexists with the universe. It does not precede the universe, neither does it come later by accident or as someone's creation.' The universe is life even before biological life appears. 'If the universe itself is life, then primary life forms can appear wherever conditions allow' (Toda Jōsei 1960: 13–14). In effect, for Toda all of existence, including non-life forms, participates in life.

At times Toda sets up a mutual self-identity of universe, life-force, and Buddha, but his arguments tend to be mystical and hard to follow. The 'true reality of life-force' is equated with the Tathagata (*nyorai*), who at each moment 'comes forth from its own suchness':

> Every moment of this man Toda is the essence of life. When you stop to think about it, every moment of every single thing must be a *nyorai*. This is the meaning of the fundamental doctrine that all things in the universe are the activity of life itself.
>
> For us, too, every second of life is true reality, and in the true reality

of this moment past life for all eternity is included, giving birth in turn to future life on into eternity...This moment is the activity of the universe Itself as well as the life and essence of the individual. This moment-to-moment activity of the universe is expressed as the ever-changing phenomena that make up the totality of all things in flux. (Toda Jōsei 1960: 450–52)

In this idiom of 'life-force' and 'universe' we see reflected the doctrine of *ichinen sanzen* (three thousand existences contained in one thought) and *kanjin* (introspection into one's mind-essence) that Nichiren took over from Tendai Buddhism.

Becoming one with the life-force of the gohonzon through faith

The Three Great Esoteric Methods of Practice (*sandaihihō*) that Nichiren taught to sentient beings in the age of *mappō* – that is, the *Daimoku* of the *Honmon* section of the Lotus Sutra (*Honmon no daimoku*), the *Honzon* of the *Honmon* (*Honmon no honzon*), and the *Kaidan* of the *Honmon* (*Honmon no* kaidan) – can all be summarized in the *gohonzon* (or Great Mandala), which is the origin of the life-force of the universe.

> The enlightenment of Nichiren, the true Buddha, and the life-force live continuously in the Great Mandala.
> By embracing the life-force, everything is enjoyed, nothing is suffered. This is called liberation (*gedatsu*)...and it is attained through faith in the *gohonzon*...Therefore, when you sit before the *gohonzon* and believe that there is no distinction among the *gohonzon*, Nichiren, and you yourself, when you allow this great blessing to permeate your heart and offer thanksgiving, when you chant the *daimoku* fervently, you enter into harmony with the rhythm of the universe: the great life-force of the universe becomes your own life-force and gushes forth. (Toda Jōsei 1960: 339, 171–72)

Nichiren's awakening to the truth of the universal life-force (*ichinen sanzen*), is thus directly embodied in the *gohonzon*. In contrast to the 'ideal *ichinen sanzen*' taught by Sakyamuni in the first half (*shakumon*) of the Lotus Sutra, Nichiren's Three Great Esoteric Methods of Practice represent the 'practical *ichinen sanzen*' (*jigyō no ichinen sanzen*) that can be learned by ordinary people just as they are.

Varieties of manifestation of life-force in daily life

Good fortune and bad can also be explained as states of the life-force:

> Two laws of cleansing (*senjō nihō*) exist in our lives. A life of pure innocence (*kiyorakana seimei*) accepts everything from the outside world meekly and in harmonious rhythm with the universe; for this reason, its transmigration is completely natural. Such a life manifests a tremendous life-force, and is thus able to enjoy existence. But in the course of its many transmigrations, life becomes tainted by the mistakes of daily life and falls into vice of all sorts. This is why we speak of a cleansing (*senpō*) of life…that has fallen out of harmony with the rhythm of the universe and whose life-force has faded away. (Toda Jōsei 1960: 36)

In the doctrine of *ichinen sanzen*, these fallen states are summarized as the 'life of the ten realms' (*jikkai*) in accord with the *Kanjin honzonshō*. The following ten realms can be identified in our own life-force as well as in the Great Life-Force of the universe:

> Anger (a life of affliction): hell
> Covetousness (a life of desire for things): the realm of the hungry spirits
> Foolishness (a life of being attracted to what is before one's eyes and losing sight of the overall meaning): the realm of animals
> Flattery (a life of anger): the realm *asuras* (demigods)
> Tranquility (a human life): the realm of human beings
> Joy (a life full of joy, but limited in time): the realm of heavenly beings
> Impermanence (the person who has realized that nothing is permanent in this world and seeks peace of mind in contemplation): the realms *srāvakas* and *pratyekabuddhas* (disciples of Buddha or Hinayana sages)
> Virtue (virtuous human life): the realm of bodhisattvas
> Faith (a life of belief in the *Namu myōhō rengekyō* of the Three Great Esoteric Methods of Practice): the realm of buddhas. (Toda Jōsei Zenshū Shuppan Iinkai 1982, vol. 7: 117)

Each of these life states, in turn, represents one of the 'ten suchness aspects' (*jūnyoze*) of reality, which works its own effects on them. For example, people in the *asura* realm 'are incited to more and more anger,' whereas people in the state of the bodhisattva 'are filled with the desire to help those who have fallen and an awesome energy wells up to support them in their effort' (Toda Jōsei 1960: 266–67).

Happiness and the attainment of Buddhahood as manifestations of the universal life-force

Happiness, for Toda, 'springs forth from the relationship between our own life-force and the external world' and 'an affirmation of inner truth.' Religion, in particular Nichiren Shōshū, teaches this internal truth and leads humanity to happiness. Again, we let Toda speak in his own words:

> Through belief in this great religion, life harmonizes with the rhythm of the universe and one feels completely the happiness of life...But if the energy of the life-force energy is applied only to problems in the home, then the home will be taken care of, but what about problems in the neighborhood or in the city?...
>
> The attainment of buddhahood is a state of absolute happiness. No one can attack you, there is nothing to fear, and each moment of life is like the clear blue ocean or the cloudless sky.
>
> And what is the attainment of buddhahood? Impossible as it is for ordinary people like us to explain such things, I will try – realizing that it may amount to no more than one millionth of the insight of faith all of you have: It means the attainment of eternal happiness. Our life is not limited to this existence...The attainment of buddhahood means being born full of vital life-force energy, accepting the mission given you at birth and acting freely in accord with that mission, achieving the task set out for you from birth, and possessing a happiness that no one can destroy. If one can enjoy such a life tens of times, hundreds of times, even thousands or millions of times, does that not make happiness all the greater? To forsake the search for such happiness for the greedy pursuit of lesser pleasures can only be called pitiful. (Toda Jōsei 1960: 38–39, 351, 177–78)

Compassion and life-force

'Compassion is the characteristic of the Buddha, and Nichiren was compassion itself.' Believers are called on to imitate this compassion:

If you would possess even one millionth of the compassion of Nichiren, you must be diligent in chanting the *daimoku* day and night…You must engrave it on your heart, color your life with it; you must strive for the faith to change all of your daily actions into expressions of compassion.

All of the universe is in essence the Buddha, and all things without exception are the activity of compassion. Therefore, compassion is the innate form of the universe…If the universe is the *myōhō rengekyō* itself, the *myōhō rengekyō* is none other than the original Buddha. And if, therefore, the universe is the form of the Buddha, the universe must also be the activity of compassion itself.

If the universe itself is compassion, it follows that our daily activities are acts of that same compassion. But since they are set in motion by the life-force unique to human life, the human being cannot remain at the level of common animals and plants. A higher level of activity is required of the true servant of the Buddha. As I said before, since the practice proper to the latter stage of the law (*mappō*) is the practice of Nichiren, we must chant the *daimoku* as he taught us to do;…we must encourage others to chant, and thus help to produce more people whose actions are filled naturally with compassion.

Although in the age of *mappō* wicked people abound, which makes works of compassion absolutely essential, there is a great lack of compassion in the actual world. (Toda Jōsei 1960: 44–45, 54–56, 48)

Only through the wisdom of the Buddha is true compassion put into action, and 'only through faith can this wisdom be gained.' Accordingly, 'the implanting of pure life-force' through *shakubuku* is described as a particularly important concrete expression of compassion, while almsgiving is dismissed as less than true compassion. (Toda Jōsei 1960: 46–48)

Such are the major elements in Toda's idea of life-force as he presented it when talking about his own faith or giving direction to others. Obviously he believed he was passing on the essence of the Buddhist teaching as he inherited it through Nichiren Shōshū. At the same time, he introduced innovations of his own, as will become apparent when we turn to a more traditional exposition of Nichiren Shōshū doctrine.

The Transformation of Nichiren Shōshū doctrine

Nichiren Shōshū is the branch of Nichiren Buddhism that follows in the tradition of Nikkō (1246–1333), a disciple of Nichiren. Its center is located on Mt. Fuji at Taisekiji.[11] Nikkō was one of the 'Six Elder Monks' (*rokurōsō*) named by Nichiren before he died to take over the control of the order. Following a clash with the other five elders, Nikkō left Mt. Minobu for Taisekiji to pursue his own path. The resulting branch of Nichiren Buddhism constructed a distinct doctrine based on books of teachings purportedly passed on to Nikkō by Nichiren – among them the *Honinmyōshō*, *Hyakurokkosōjō*, *Juryōbonmonteidaiji*, and *Ongikuden* – as well as on works written by Nikkō himself. Various schools of doctrine developed within the branch, for example, around Nishiyama Honmonji, Omosu Honmonji, and Yōhōji in Kyoto; but the school associated with Taisekiji, organized around the systematization of doctrine by Nikkan (1665–1726), predominated. In 1900 the sect was reorganized under the name Nichirenshū Fuji-ha, and in 1912 the name was changed again to Nichiren Shōshū. It was the doctrine of this Nichiren Shōshū, as formulated by Nikkan, that Makiguchi and Toda followed.

Nichiren Shōshū teaching revolves around the Three Great Esoteric Methods of Practice: the *Mandala Honzon* (*dai gohonzon*) presented by Nichiren as the ultimate Buddhist teaching or the ultimate reality needed for salvation; the *kaidan* where the *Mandala Honzon* is enshrined; and the *daimoku*, or chant of *namu myōhō rengekyō*. This forms the core of Buddhist faith in the age of *mappō* (Last Dharma). Taisekiji is believed to be the true *kaidan* and the *Mandala Honzon* enshrined there (the *Ita Mandala* thought to have been inscribed in 1279) is regarded as the supreme presence.

The value set on Nichiren's *honzon* reflects the fact that Nichiren and his teaching are held in far higher regard than Sakyamuni Buddha and the message he preached in India so many centuries ago. In particular, the teaching of Nichiren is believed to surpass that of even the Lotus Sutra, the supreme teaching of Sakyamuni. As a result, Nichiren is revered as *Nichiren Honbutsuron*, the rebirth of the ultimate Buddha (*Musa no honbutsu*) who is superior to Sakyamuni. Behind these claims lies a reading of history at odds with that normally held by Lotus Sutra tradition of Buddhism, to which we may now turn our attention. In doing so, I should like to avoid as far as possible the doctrinal terminology particular to Nichiren Buddhism.[12]

Nichiren Shōshū's Buddhological history

In the sixteenth chapter of the Lotus Sutra, the *Juryōbon* (The lifespan of the Tathagata), Sakyamuni, who was previously considered to be the highest enlightened being, is revealed to be merely one finite manifestation of a more universal Buddha. This universal Buddha is called the 'True Attainment of the Remotest Past' (*kuon jitsujō no shakuson*), while *Jōgyō* and other bodhisattvas who spring out of the earth in chapter fifteen of the sutra (*jūji yujutsubon*) are presented as figures taught by various Buddhas in the past. In Nichiren Shōshū, however, while *kuon jitsujō* is held to have achieved buddhahood in the eternal past, belief is focused on a supreme being that has existed from the beginning of the universe (*kuon gansho*). This being reveals itself as the Dharma in the mantra *namu myōhō rengekyō*, and as a person in the *musa no honbutsu*. Nichiren is the rebirth of this latter. The period prior to the appearance of the *kuon jitsujō* Buddha is described as the age of the true Buddha, when people who bear some relationship to the Buddha follow the law and can attain the state of Buddhahood.

Following the appearance of *kuon jitsujō*, Sakyamuni Buddha makes his own appearance several centuries B.C.E., and the periods of *shōbō* (True Dharma) and *zōhō* (Semblance Dharma) – periods before the revelation of the true *honzon* and the *daimoku* – are described as a time of provisional teaching. The *Lotus Sutra* itself is held to be a provisional teaching, and the people who were able to attain enlightenment through the sutra are those who had in fact previously been implanted with the 'seed' to become Buddha by *kuon jitsujō*. The material in the first fourteen chapters of the sutra, the *shakumon*, 'ripened' the state of these people, and the latter fourteen chapters, the *honmon*, brought them to liberation. However, for the 'wild common person' (*arabonpu*) of the *mappō* period, such a teaching of ripening and liberation is not sufficient; a new 'seed' for becoming a buddha must be revealed. This was where Nichiren enters history, in Japan at the beginning of the age of *mappō*. The very *musa no honbutsu* who existed from the beginning of the universe and who appeared previously during the life of Sakyamuni as Jōgyō Bosatsu, has come again as savior for the age of *mappō*.

This reading of history is said to be present in Nichiren's writings and intimated in the Lotus Sutra – absent from the text but hidden in the deeper meanings of the *Juryōbon*.[13] The doctrinal reinterpretation of the sutra resulted in a hierarchical ordering of increased value from sutras that preceded the *Lotus Sutra*, through the first fourteen chapters of the *Lotus Sutra*, to the latter half of the sutra.

Nichiren Shōshū teaches that in addition to the apparent *honmon* (*monjō no honmon*) there exists a deeper *honmon* (*montei no honmon*), with the most important elements of Sakyamuni's teaching being contained in the latter. It is there that the presentation of the *gohonzon*, *namu myōhō rengekyō*, and the *musa no honbutsu* (that is, Nichiren) is foreshadowed; and it is because of this foreshadowing that the Lotus Sutra maintains its relevance for the understanding of the *gohonzon* and Nichiren's teaching. At the same time, the claim is made that this sutra was previously proclaimed for the sake of those who could benefit from 'ripening' and liberation, and is no longer suited to ordinary men and women in the age of *mappō* who seek a new 'sowing.'

Kanjinron in Nichiren Shōshū

Although there are the two aspects of Dharma and person in the true original Buddha (*kuon gansho*), it is the Dharma, namely the *daimoku* (*namu myōhō rengekyō*), that is of greater importance. This is the ultimate existence that is contained in the *gohonzon*, and it is through the 'reception' (*juji*) of this ultimate reality, that is, through belief in the *gohonzon* and chanting of the *daimoku*, that the common masses living in the age of *mappō* can achieve buddhahood. Concentration on the *gohonzon* as the object of faith gives profound significance to that act of 'reception.'

This view is expounded in Nichiren's *Kanjin honzonshō*. Basing his argument on the *ichinen sanzen* Tendai doctrine of Chigi (Chinese: Chih-i, 538–597), Nichiren seeks to demonstrate that belief in the *honzon* and the chanting of the *daimoku* constitute the means to attaining buddhahood. The explanation of *ichinen sanzen* found here comes to occupy a central place in Nichiren Shōshū. Following the *Kaimokushō*, both Nichiren Shōshū and Sōka Gakkai consider this doctrine to be the ultimate teaching hidden in the depths of the *Juryōbon* of the *Lotus Sutra* and the heart of Buddhist teaching. A quick look at the contents of the *Shakubuku kyōten* and *Sōka Gakkai nyūmon* make this plain. Chigi's *Makashikan* (C. *Mo ho chih kuan*), based on the doctrine of the *Lotus Sutra* as the most sublime sutra, lays forth both the theory and practice of meditation (*shikan, zazen, kanjin*). An explanation of *ichinen sanzen* is presented here in the section where *kanjin* is described as a 'mysterious state' in which 'all spirit is possessed in one spirit.' *Sanzen* refers to all living creatures and everything in existence, and it is explained in terms of the concepts of *jikkai, jūnyoze*, and *sanseken* (the three categories of realm). *Jikkai* refers to the ten modalities of existence of all sentient beings (hell, realms of hungry spirits, animals, *asuras*, human beings, heavenly beings, *srāvakas, pratyekabuddhas, bodhisattvas*, and buddhas). These realms are not isolated aspects of being, but each incorporates all of the others as potential existences. This state is called *jikkai gogu*, which confirms the reality of one hundred aspects of existence. Of these relationships, those of the realm of buddhas with the other nine realms are central: while humanity finds itself under the aspect of the other nine realms it is at the same time incorporated in the realm of the buddhas; and conversely, the Buddha is also incorporated in the other nine aspects of existence.

When these realms are multiplied by the *jūnyoze* (form, nature or quality, substance, function, action or motion, cause, indirect cause or condition, effect, reward or retribution, ultimate non-differentiation) and the *sanseken* (the realm of sentient beings, the realm of non-sentient beings, the realm of the five aggregates) that results in the *sanzen seken* or three thousand worlds. Just what the *jūnyoze* and *sanseken* refer to is not as easy to grasp as the concept of *jikkai*, which doubtless leaves many believers with only the vaguest impression of having understood it. Suffice it to say here that *sanzen seken* indicates the pluralistic modality and 'complex totality' of existence, in particular of living beings. The state in which this totality is completely grasped at a single moment is *ichinen sanzen* and culminates in the realization that the Buddha is present within one's own spirit.

The realization by the masses of ordinary people that they are, each of them and within this present life, Buddha is captured in the phrase *sokushin jōbutsu*. In the *hongaku shisō* of Japanese Tendai Buddhism, where all sentient beings are taught to exist in the state of enlightenment in their present life, the link between *ichinen sanzen* and *sokushin jōbutsu* is dominant. Nichiren, too, presupposes this position in the *Kanjin honzonshō* and elsewhere. The influence of *hongaku shisō* on Nichiren Shōshū was even greater after Nichiren's death, which in turn reinforced the orientation towards *sokushin jōbutsu*.

In the development from Nichiren's *Kanjin honzonshō* to Nichiren Shōshū's doctrine, the *honzon* and *daimoku* are stressed as concretizations of *ichinen sanzen*, as is the conviction that *shokushin jōbutsu* can be realized through the practice of chanting the *daimoku* rather than meditation. This 'experience of *ichinen sanzen*' contrasts with the 'principle of *ichinen sanzen*' of Chigi. Differences between Nichiren Shōshū and the other sects of Nichiren Buddhism revolve about whether this 'experience of *ichinen sanzen*' as attained through the *honzon* that embodies the *kuon jitsujō* Buddha from the latter half of the *Lotus Sutra* is followed, or whether the accent is rather placed on the *honzon* that embodies the original Dharma-Buddha hidden in the sutra.

In other words, for Nichiren Shōshū, belief in the *gohonzon* and chanting of the *daimoku* are themselves considered to be the realization of *sokushin jōbutsu*, and this is called *juji soku kanjin* (reception as meditation). This doctrine is offered to the masses in the age of *mappō* as an easy practice. But since ultimately it requires that one experience oneself as existing in the state of the Buddha, more is involved than a mere notional assent. Not only a small number of monks and doctrinal experts, but the masses of ordinary people also need to be convinced of the reality of the proposition. This is the problem that faced Toda in his prison cell, and that the concept of Buddha as life-force helped him solve.

Toda Jōsei's innovation

Toda's life-force theory reshapes Nichiren Shōshū doctrine by providing a vitalistic interpretation of the *sokushih jōbutsu* attained in chanting *namu myōhō rengekyō*. To single out the main elements: (1) Buddha and humanity, as well as (2) Buddha and the various beings of this world – since they share in the essential life-force – (3) can become one with the life-force of the *gohonzon* through faith; (4) the fortune or misfortune concretized in the life-force activity of everyday life (5) can be transformed into a state of achievement of buddhahood characterized by absolute happiness overflowing with life-force energy; (6) furthermore, it is the life that takes as its mission spreading this happiness to others that can be called a truly Buddhist life.

Understanding the life of faith and its purpose in this way, three possibilities emerge.[14]

Buddhism can be conceived as the fervent pursuit of a way of life in the present world

The *gohonzon*-as-Buddha is the source of life-force energy and provider of this-worldly benefits. The attainment of buddhahood that Buddhism teaches to be the final goal of life remains absolute. But even if particular benefits are not considered to be the realization of that ultimate goal, they can be seen as a first step towards its achievement. One can see in these benefits indications of that ultimate goal. Thus one may link the easily understood goal of happiness in this life with the ultimate goal of Buddhism. Since happiness is the overflowing of life-force, it is in itself a manifestation of the Dharma and the Buddha (*gohonzon*), the origin of life, and not something vulgar or base. Conversely, the attainment of buddhahood does not imply a separation from life, as indicated by the word nirvana, nor does it necessitate taking leave of this world. It is to be realized in this world, since life's ultimate purpose can only be achieved in the continuous rebirths into life in this world.

The relationship with ultimate reality is perceived as pertaining to this-worldly existence, and hence is both practical and concrete

Life-force and its energy are realities that can be touched and affirmed through the senses, and the Buddha (Dharma) shares in the same substance of life in this world. No discontinuity between bodily sense experience and the experience of a connection with ultimate reality is emphasized. Rather the two are seen as continuous. Belief and the chanting of the *daimoku* are thought of in the same way as attempts to influence this-worldly existence or power. The *gohonzon* is often compared to a machine – a machine for manufacturing happiness – and the mutual relationship with the *gohonzon* is perceived as a process for drawing out energy that can be confirmed by the senses through physical activity. Thus faith and secular knowledge are not separate but are seen as overlapping domains. Just as ordinary knowledge of life is deepened through science, so, too, must it be deepened through religion. Through the mediation of life-force, science and religion are joined as mutually complementary undertakings.

Personal religious transformation is perceived as inseparable from an active stance towards the present world, which is positively promoted

The achievement of buddhahood is not an inner event that involves temporary separation from everyday life; nor is it something to be experienced after death in some other world (*jōdo*). Rather, it is experienced in the very midst of daily life as a transformation of that life. This follows from the belief that life-force is manifested in the everyday just as the various states of *jikkai* are. The reception of the *gohonzon*, through belief and chanting of the *daimoku*, might be perceived as somehow other-worldly and distant from daily life. But insofar as it has to do with life-force, it involves daily life. Faith that does not effect progress towards greater happiness is regarded as imperfect. Nor is the advance of happiness restricted to one's own personal life; it must be extended to include others as well. In more immediate terms, this implies activity aimed at increasing the ranks of believers and also a reform of collective life.

The three points enumerated above are not to be found in the doctrine of traditional Nichiren Shōshū, except perhaps in germ. Strictly speaking, the reformulation of traditional doctrine does not follow from Toda's revelation that 'Buddha is Life-Force,' but it does allow for the incorporation of truly modern ideas and religious attitudes into that doctrine. It also affects the structure of the Japanese Buddhist idea of salvation. The reformation of religious ideas through the establishment of a this-worldly idea of salvation, conceived in vitalistic terms – as seen in new religious movements based on folk-religious or syncretic beliefs, as well as in Buddhist groups such as Honmon Butsuryūkō and Reiyūkai – has borne new fruit in Toda's transformation of Nichiren Shōshū doctrine.

Reformation of the conception of salvation

A host of new religious movements has emerged in Japanese society since the beginning of the nineteenth century. These movements have been stimulated by a wide variety of religious and intellectual sources, among them the various sects of Buddhism, Shintoism, the National Learning School, Confucianism, Christianity, folk religion – especially as it pertains to *shinbutsu* syncretism, modern sciences, and even nationalism. Despite this wide variety of influences, a certain commonality emerges in the basic structure of their concept of salvation. Recent scholars have dubbed this structure a 'Vitalistic Conception of Salvation' and singled out a number of claims that undergird it (Tsushima 1979):

1. The essence of the cosmos. The cosmos is perceived as a living body or life-force possessed of everlasting, inexhaustible fertility. In human terms, this means that we are given life through nature and that the universe is the source of unlimited benefit for humanity.
2. Primary religious being. The new religions posit a central holy figure such as God or Buddha as the reality that unifies the universe. Conceived of as the primary religious being, it is symbolized as the 'Source of Life' who gives birth to all beings and provides tender nurture to all.

3. Human nature. The human being is also thought to have an existence born of and nurtured by the Source of Life. Not only that, human beings are regarded as tributaries of the Life Source, possessing a divine, unpolluted nature that is able to return to or unite with this source. Furthermore, in this way all human beings participate in the same life-force and are therefore all brothers and sisters.

4. Life and death. Due to the positive evaluation given life in this world, concepts of other-worldly salvation in a post-death existence are rare. Salvation is presented as the growth and efflorescence of life in this world, and rebirth as a return to this world is endowed with a positive meaning.

5. Evil and sin. If ties between the self and Life Source, or with others and one's environment, are severed, the harmonious development of life is hampered and life-force dries up. It is the attachment to self and selfish desires that causes this evil.

6. Means of salvation. One must restore harmony between the Life Source on the one hand, and oneself, others, and the environment on the other in order to overcome the state of evil. In addition to repentance and the recovery of the harmonious spirit, various practices are prompted to restore bonds to the Life Source.

7. The saved state. Salvation is defined as the state where the bonds with the Life Source have been restored and one is filled with the fertile life-force, a state of unity – or peace and harmony – between humanity and God, the living of a life suffused with joy. The image is this-worldly, sensate, even sensual. Although this is related to individual this-worldly benefits, it is represented as the total efflorescence of a life-force that transcends these partial benefits.

8. Founders. Founders are not merely regarded as instructors of ultimate truth but are represented as those within whom the Life Source resides, those from whom the Life Source flows, the ultimate mediators of this Life Source to humanity.

Toda Jōsei's life-force doctrine is typical of this 'Vitalistic Conception of Salvation.' Although it varies somewhat from the pattern in that there is little emphasis placed on a 'harmonious spirit,' and the *gohonzon* and Nichiren himself become the objects of veneration rather than a founder figure, in terms of overall structure it corresponds closely to the conceptual model. In commenting on the eight points listed above, the authors describe the vitalistic concept of salvation as 'a this-worldly centered concept of salvation' in contrast to the pessimistic worldly view of liberative or other-worldly concepts of salvation. Furthermore, it is argued that this view rejects both the dualistic thought that sets up some ideal religious world cut off from the present reality and the logic of world-renunciation that preaches a total overcoming of the world and the separation of oneself from the world.

To say that the view of salvation presented by the New Religions is this-worldly, however, does not go far enough in describing the unique development that the idea of salvation has undergone in these groups. Other religions, such as Shinto or animistic folk beliefs, as well as the *hongaku shisō* characteristic of Japanese Buddhism, also take a positive attitude towards the present reality. But these differ from the concept of this-worldly salvation found in the new religious movements.

For example, the concept of 'salvation' is rather weak in Shinto and animistic thought. Since *hongaku shisō* presents a typical case of premodern religious thought that is both this-worldly and directed towards salvation, it offers a more promising topic for comparison, especially given the fact that the basis of Sōka Gakkai's religious thought, Nichiren Shōshū, was strongly influenced by *hongaku shisō*. The various sects of Kamakura Buddhism exhibit the influence of *hongaku shisō* in their core beliefs, though this influence is more marked in Shinran, Ippen, and Nichiren than in Hōnen or Dōgen (Tamura 1987). The influence of *hongaku shisō* is especially clear in arguments concerning the significance of the *honzon* in Nichiren's *Kanjin honzonshō*, and Nichiren Shōshū – among the branch sects of Nichiren Buddhism, the one where the *honzon* is venerated and the *Kanjin honzonshō* is considered authoritative to a greater degree – is especially close to *hongaku shisō*. Many valued texts of Nichiren Shōshū once attributed to Nichiren but now held to be of questionable authorship were also influenced by later *hongaku shisō*. It is therefore safe to conclude that Sōka Gakkai has transformed the *hongaku shisō* conception of salvation into the vitalistic concept found in the new religions.

The Iwanami *Buddhist Dictionary* defines *hongaku shisō* as an inquiry into the undivided, absolute world that transcends the dualistic relativity of reality, and then returns to reality in order to affirm the varieties of dualistic relativity as expressions of the undivided *hongaku* (Nakamura 1989). In terms of the achievement of buddhahood, it constitutes a rejection of the dualistic way of thinking that opposes the Buddha and common humanity, and sees humans attaining buddhahood by rejecting their common nature. *Hongaku* is an absolute that transcends such a dualistic relativity. It is the true mode of being of the Buddha that returns one to the real world, thus demonstrating the enlightened insight that the lost masses are already the undivided unity of the Buddha and common humanity. 'Evil passions are themselves enlightenment' (*bonnō soku bodai*) and 'endurance is itself tranquil light' (*shaba soku jakkō*) are expressions of this affirmation of reality.

In its extreme application *hongaku shisō* affirms wandering from the path of virtue and completely rejects the importance of religious practice (*shugyō*), landing it in a view that can hardly be called Buddhism any longer. Tamura argues that when Japanese Buddhism was being swept along in this direction of affirming an absolute monism, Kamakura Buddhism countered by reinforcing the dualistic element (Tamura 1987). Hōnen's opposition of Amida to common humanity and the overcoming of reality through birth (*ōjō*) in the Pure Land is a classic example of this development. At the same time, as Tamura notes, *hohgaku shisō* was the fountainhead of the Kamakura reform, and with Shinran and Nichiren regained its prominence.

In the doctrine of Nichiren Shōshū, common humanity already possesses within itself the realm of the Buddha, and through the reception of the *gohonzon* humanity immediately achieves buddhahood. Within Nichiren's thought one also finds the idea of *ōkei shisō*, which holds that after death one is reborn in the Pure Land and there achieves buddhahood. This is closer to a dualistic salvation theory that presents the overcoming of this deviant reality on the other side, rather than the manifestation of buddhahood in our present state. Some scholars argue that this dualistic *ōkei shisō* was emphasized in Nichiren's latter years, when confrontation with society deepened (Mochizuki 1958, Tamura 1987: 601—11). No trace of *ōkei shisō*, however is to be found in Nichiren Shōshū, where the monistic salvation theory of the attainment of buddhahood through the reception of the *gohonzon* – within the framework *shaba soku jakkō* and *bonnō soku bodai* – dominates.

Nichiren Shōshū's doctrine of salvation, emphasizing as it did the immediate attainment of buddhahood, was clearly this-worldly or world-affirming. But it did not encourage engagement with the world and the transformation of present reality. Salvation was not seen to entail participation in the transformation of reality. It remained rather at the level of an internal transformation of the self unaffected by everyday life. Despite a strong desire for reform in the national religion, tied to the ideals of Nichren's *Risshō Ankokuron*, the idea of a practical reform of one's own life extending to reforms on behalf of others was rather weak.

For Toda Jōsei, who had learned the importance of the practical transformation of daily life from Makiguchi Tsunesaburō, such a this-worldly, world-affirming concept of salvation was not easy to swallow. His idea of 'life-force' gave him an alternative: the immediate attainment of buddhahood means salvation through engagement in the realities of daily life, through attaining benefits and happiness that involve all of life, and through extending this happiness to others. While affirming present reality, this idea of salvation does not simply accept reality as it is. It retains the hope that reality can be changed and may therefore better be described as reality-transformative. The transformation in question does not necessarily imply the reform of social structures or a dramatic change in communal life, as found in the *yonaoshi* concept. At certain times such a transformation may be advocated; at other times, not. What remains constant is the aspiration to transform the self and life around oneself, and the belief that these efforts have to do with salvation. As befits a faith community centered on the laity and teaching participation in reality, this contrasts sharply with the low esteem accorded present reality in historical religions centered on religious specialists and preaching separation from the world.

Part III:
Perspectives on Religious and Spiritual Movements

7 Millennialism

If a new religious movement is seen to have millennialistic ideas,[1] one or both of the following conditions must be met: (1) traditions of millennialistic ideas must already exist or be imported; and (2) a millennialistic worldview must be created. The first condition can be broken down into various levels. On the least systematized level, vague and amorphous images of catastrophes or ideal states of affairs exist, such as a big flood or an abundant harvest. They are found in folklore and are called *yonaori* (world renewal) in Japan.[2] At the opposite pole, there are highly refined and systematized traditions concerning the ultimate state of the world, based on articulated views of history and mankind. The millennialistic ideas of new religious movements are largely derived from these highly systematized millennialistic traditions. However, when these traditions do not exist or are weak, what is the source and salience of millennialism in new religious movements? They seem to inherit vague and amorphous millennialistic images from folklore, thus fulfilling the second condition for the formation of millennialism, that is, a millennialistic worldview. In large part, this worldview directly or indirectly reflects rapid social change.

Among Japan's new religions dating from the middle of the nineteenth century, we can find several groups whose beliefs have a millennialistic inclination. Well-known examples are Tenrikyō, Maruyamakyō, Ōmoto, Sōka Gakkai and Honmichi, a schism from Tenrikyō. The millennialistic ideas of these groups are heterogeneous and, generally speaking, unorganized.[3] This is because there is no firm tradition of systematic millennialism in Japan. Among earlier movements such as Tenrikyō and Maruyamakyō in particular, millennialism is vague and amorphous, largely reflecting their perception of changing situations. In these groups, moreover, there is no messianism, and the founder or foundress is worshipped merely as a living *kami* (god), not as a divine king or queen. But the circumstances of the later movements are different. Traditions of millennialistic ideas preceded them even though they had not been articulated in the forms previously developed by other new religions. The millennialism of the new movements was nevertheless based on these foundations. In some cases systematic millennialistic ideas were eventually formed, as happened in Honmichi. This is a rare case in which an indigenous messianism was also created. In this chapter I shall investigate how amorphous millennialism developed into systematic millennialism in conjunction with messianism in the course of the development of Honmichi as a splinter group from Tenrikyō.[4]

An important condition for the formation of millennialism is a millennialistic worldview, which can be seen in part as a reaction to rapid social change. Before millennialism is established as a system of thought, millennialistic ideas depend largely on this type of worldview. In order to elucidate the contents of millennialistic ideas in Tenrikyō and early Honmichi, it is therefore necessary to analyze how these ideas reflected believers' worldviews at different historical junctures. I shall describe the believers' worldviews in the following three ways:

1. Perception of the total society, that is, how they perceive the society with which they believe they share a common destiny (humankind, nation, tribe, etc.). This will be called 'perception of the societal situation.' For example, when the societal situation is perceived as dangerous, believers expect some supernatural power to overcome the crisis, and millennialism is likely to develop with this expectation.

2. Perception of the movement itself, that is, how they perceive the situation of their own movement or group, which is believed to embody the earthly manifestation of supernatural power. This will be called 'perception of the group's situation.' For example, when a movement spreads very fast, and various miracles are believed to be changing the destiny of many believers, it is likely that members will also expect transformations of the whole society.

3. Perception of the relationship between a movement and the wider society (government, police, mass media, established religions, etc.). This will be called 'perception of the relational position.' For example, when a movement is persecuted, the persecution is recognized as a symptom of the confrontation between God and some evil power, and there is an expectation of an imminent catastrophe as a result.

In the following sections, the histories of Tenrikyō and Honmichi in their early phases are first sketched, and then the processes whereby the millennialistic ideas in each group were formed and transformed are analysed.[5]

The formation of Tenrikyō

Tenrikyō was founded by Nakayama Miki (1798–1887), the wife of a farmer in Yamato province.[6] She was born in Sanmaiden village (now part of Tenri City), the daughter of a rich farmer. At the age of 13 she was married to Nakayama Zenbei, the first son of a rich farmer in Shōyashiki village (now another part of Tenri City).[7] Miki's religious career began when she was 40 years old. In the autumn of 1837 her only son Shūji, then 17, developed a severe pain in his leg when working in the fields and could not work any more. Miki, very anxious about her son's illness, asked a *yamabushi* (mountain ascetic) called Nakano Ichibei to offer prayers for Shūji. This seems to have been effective initially, and Miki eventually became a devout believer of Ichibei's cult. However, Shūji's pain recurred again and again, and it became evident that the disease could not be cured easily. A year after the onset of the illness, Ichibei was invited to the Nakayamas' house, and a shamanistic ritual was performed to cure Shūji's recurrent problem. It was during this ritual that Miki claimed that she was possessed by the original and genuine God (*moto no kami, jitsu no kami*), later called Tenri-Ō-no-Mikoto, God the Parent, or Tsuki-Hi (Moon and Sun). After three days of violent and continuous possession, Miki believed that she had become the 'Shrine of God' with a great mission to save humankind.

According to Tenrikyō doctrine, the last day of her possession was the beginning of the new religion, Tenrikyō. Members believe that from that day on the Creator came to earth and revealed His will directly to humankind. In fact, however, Miki's belief was not recognized by anybody for more than ten years and was regarded as a kind of madness that would lead the family to ruin. It was not until 1862, when Miki was 65 years old, that a group of believers began to form.

As the number of members increased, the group gradually became an organized body with its own identity. First, a system called *sazuke* was initiated. This was a system for giving devout believers the capacity to reveal God's will or perform magical prayers. Only a few people were ever qualified to reveal God's will, and after about 1870 only the latter qualification was bestowed. Eventually the term *sazuke* came to mean the magical prayers themselves.

Between 1866 and 1867 the first scripture in a 'counting song' style, *Mikagura-uta*, was composed. In a mild and pleasant tone reflecting the folk songs of those days, the believers were instructed in daily practices and attitudes. Then a ritual called *tsutome*, which consists of dances, gestures and the chanting of *Mikagura-uta*, was developed. Later, *tsutome* became the central practice of the religion. Moreover, some people called *toritsugi* began to take on the role of giving instruction to those who visited Miki for the first time. Their teachings formed a set of doctrines which later became the practical part of Tenrikyō's doctrinal system.

The contents of these initial doctrines are as follows. Human beings are children of God the Parent for they were created by Him (or Her). The world is the body of God, and human bodies are lent to men and women by God. Only the mind belongs to each person, and when he or she uses it incorrectly, *hokori* (dust) piles up around it. This dust is the cause of disease and of other misfortunes. Dust, or misuse of the mind, is of eight kinds: miserliness, covetousness, hatred, self-love, enmity, anger, avarice and arrogance. People can stop piling up dust by turning their minds to God and getting rid of the dust that has already collected by reflecting on themselves (*sange*), by practicing *tsutome* and service work (*hinokishin*), and by proselytizing (*nioigake*). It was taught that diseases would then be cured and other misfortunes would vanish. People do not experience life on earth only once, but are reborn again and again. Thus, dust piled up in one lifetime influences the next life. This connection is called *innen* (cause and effect). If diseases or misfortunes afflict a life lived in virtue, it is because of the *innen* from a previous life (or lives). One should, and can, get rid of this by more self-reflection and religious practice than is strictly necessary for removing the dust accumulated in one's present life.

Beginning in 1869, the second year of the Meiji Restoration, Miki started writing a new scripture called *Ofudesaki* and she continued writing it intermittently until 1882. It is written in *tanka* (a traditional Japanese poem of 31 syllables) style. Because Miki wrote these verses when possessed by God, the scripture is full of God's words expressed in the first person and is not a systematic statement of doctrine; rather, it reveals God's will concerning concrete problems of the present moment. It is often difficult to know what is meant, however, for the expression tends to be vague and allusive.

One type of situation that is covered in *Ofudesaki* is when the movement was oppressed and faced interference from the outside. Oppression and interference directed towards the community of believers surrounding Miki gradually increased as the group grew larger and as the administrative system of the Meiji government became firmly established. In 1874 the Nara prefectural government and the Nara Middle Teaching Academy (the local office for propagating Tennoist and Shintoist ideology through all the religious bodies) interfered in Tenri's activities. The following year the police also began to interfere. Miki was arrested nine times before her death. Miki's God spoke with fierce indignation against this interference and oppression.

Meanwhile, Shūji and other leading believers sought approval for their activities from the authorities by getting a license for a public bath, registering as a suborganization of a traditional Buddhist temple, and so on. Miki, regarding these efforts as unfaithful compromises, issued strong warnings against them. Nor was this the only instance of such warnings, for she also warned throughout most of the *Ofudesaki* against the irreligious actions and attitudes of those around her. In her opinion, the followers were motivated too much by worldly concerns and too little by faith in God. She suggested that there was great hope for the future and implored them to mend their ways and deepen their faith.

Miki believed that the most fundamental doctrine of her religion was the story of the creation and the growth of humankind (it can be called the 'Heilsgeschichte' of Tenrikyō). Although part of it is also alluded to briefly in the *Ofudesaki*, she created another scripture called the *Kōki*, or the *Doroumi-kōki*, in order systematically to state the myth in full detail. She told the story to some educated believers and dictated it to them several times between 1881 and 1887, leaving several variations. The outline of the story is as follows. 'Originally, this world was an immense expanse of muddy waters. Tsuki-Hi, God the Parent, found this chaotic condition unbearably tasteless and thought of creating human beings so that He might share their joy by seeing their *yōkigurashi* (joyous life)' (Tenrikyō Church Headquarters, 1972a: 25). He therefore chose nine aquatic animals as materials for creating human beings. From these materials 999,999 (or 900,099,999) human fetuses were created and delivered to the place where the house of the Nakayama family stood. Eight of those nine aquatic animals were also gods, and so the original God was simultaneously conceived of in three ways: as one, God the Parent; as two, Tsuki-Hi (Moon and Sun); and as ten, two plus eight. The ten gods each protect various functions of the human body, representing the sun, the moon and the stars, and they are also the substance of popular gods, buddhas and bodhisattvas.

The fetuses were then born in various places that had not yet been formed as land in the Yamato area and throughout Japan. At first they grew to only three inches in height and then died. But as they were reborn several times they grew to five feet in height. Meanwhile, the whole world – heaven and earth, land and sea – was formed, and humankind began to dwell on land. Those who were originally born in Yamato lived in Japan, while others lived elsewhere. By this time 990,000 (or 900,090,000) years had passed. During the further period of 9,999 years God indirectly gave humankind various cultures. Following this period of preparatory education, in accordance with the original promise, God descended to earth and started Tenrikyō. It was believed that the *kanrodai* (nectar stand) would be built at the place of human creation, and that, by taking the nectar (*kanro*) which would fall on it, people could live their full span of life, that is, up to 115 years.

The *kanrodai* was to be made of 13 hexagonal stones piled up about eight feet high. A first model of the *kanrodai* was constructed in 1873, and the location of the true *kanrodai* was determined in 1875, when Miki walked around the garden of her house, and her feet stopped, as if attracted by the earth. At this spot she believed she had found the place of human creation. In 1881 the bottom two pieces of the genuine *kanrodai* were made and erected, but the next year the local police removed and confiscated them. After that incident Miki did not order the making of the genuine *kanrodai*. Following her death another wooden model was constructed, and now the third one stands at the center of the shrine of the Tenrikyō Church Headquarters. Every month a mask dance symbolizing human creation (*kagura zutome*) is performed around this model *kanrodai*.

As the group grew larger, Miki came to be worshipped as the sole 'Living God,' who represented God's will on earth (see Shimazono, 1979, 1981). The members believed that all important problems should be resolved in accordance with her divine will. There were also occasions, however, when someone substituted for her in relating God's will to the believers. For a while Miki's fifth daughter Kokan played this role most frequently, but in Miki's last years Iburi Izō (1833–1907), one of her earliest followers, monopolized the role. After Miki's death in 1887, this role became very important, and Izō became the spiritual leader of the whole group. As *tenkeisha* (the revealed one), he was the sole person to mediate God's will to humankind. He also monopolized the role of conferring *sazuke* on the believers and was called *honseki* (the true seat). On the other hand, the leader of the group's secular aspects was called *shimbashira* (the central pillar) or *kanchō* (superintendent). Nakayama Shin'nosuke (1866–1944), a son of Miki's third daughter, who had been adopted into Miki's family, performed this role. Thus there were two complementary leaders in Tenrikyō at this time. During Izō's 20-year period as the *honseki* the group grew so rapidly that, according to one source, the number of believers reached about 1,242,000 by 1907 (Tenrikyō Dōyūsha, 1929).

Izō's revelations were collected by others and called the *Osashizu*. The *Osashizu* are of two kinds: '*sashizu* for questions,' giving answers to concrete questions about troubles with the authorities, permission for opening branch churches and so on; and '*sashizu* of the fixed time,' delivered at a special hour of the night, giving general directions about what the faithful should believe and how they should act. Like the *Ofudesaki*, the *Osashizu* does not give a systematic presentation of the doctrine and is for the most part vague and allusive, although some passages touch on fundamental problems of doctrine. One such important problem is how to explain the death of the Foundress. Miki died when she was 90 years old, although she herself had forecast that she would live to be 115. There had to be an explanation, therefore, for her premature death. Izō's answer in the *Osashizu* is in two parts: (1) she died early because she loved her 'children' (humankind), and (2) she would live in her 'house,' that is, in the Headquarters' shrine, and continue to work in the world. This doctrine is called 'the doctrine of the Foundress's further life' (*zonmei no ri*). Though it did not answer the question completely, it did greatly mitigate the shock caused to the believers by her death.

One of the consequences of this answer was that the role of Izō himself was limited to a certain extent; for, according to this doctrine, it was still the Foundress who mediates God's power and will on earth, and Izō was only her proxy. Since the organizational management of the Church was basically in the hands of the superintendent and other leading believers, Izō's role was confined to correcting their decisions from the spiritual viewpoint. 'The doctrine of the Foundress's further life' and this limitation on Izō's power are closely related to each other.

Izō played his corrective role most effectively in connection with the problem of how to cope with public authorities. There had been, as we saw earlier, a lot of oppression and interference by public authorities during Miki's lifetime. In 1888, a year after her death, the group received official approval as Shintō Tenri Kyōkai, albeit in the unsatisfactory form of being assigned to Shintō Honkyoku, one of the Shinto sects (*kyōha shintō*) embracing miscellaneous religious groups. Oppression and interference did not stop, however, and as the organization spread rapidly throughout the whole country, the government in 1896 issued an order limiting Tenrikyō's activities (the so called 'secret official order of the Ministry of Home Affairs'), which caused local Tenrikyō organizations considerable trouble. The leading believers took various measures to stop or mitigate the problem, and from 1899 onwards their efforts were concentrated on getting official approval as an independent Shinto sect. The way to gain approval often involved doctrinal changes and restrictions on activities. Izō handled such measures from the spiritual viewpoint, but when tension arose between secular logic and religious logic, Miki stuck to religious logic and did not permit compromises. Izō, on the other hand, suggesting religious logic, sometimes did permit compromises. The *Ofudesaki* was filled with the sense of tension between God's will and humanity's worldly thinking, but in the *Osashizu*, even though the tension was still a lingering tone, its character was somewhat softened.

Izō died in 1907, and the status of *honseki* was handed over to Ueda Naraito (1863–1937). But she could not live up to her leadership role in the Church as 'the revealed one,' and in 1918 even the role of conferring *sazuke* was transferred to Nakayama Shin'nosuke's wife Tamae. Since then, the position of the highest authority of the Church has been monopolized by the head of the Nakayama family. Meanwhile the government gave official approval to Tenrikyō as an independent sect in 1908, and the tension between the group and the wider society was greatly reduced (Tenrikyō Dōyūsha, 1929).[8]

The formation of Honmichi

Honmichi was founded by a Tenrikyō missionary, Ōnishi Aijirō (1881–1958).[9] Aijirō was the third son of Kishioka, a farmer in Uda village in Nara Prefecture. The Kishioka family had been rich farmers of high standing in the Tokugawa period, but by the time Aijirō was born they had lost a lot of their land and had sunk to the status of middle-class farmers. Since the third son could not inherit the family's lands, and since Aijirō had a talent for learning, he became an elementary school teacher. In 1899, when he was 19 years old, he entered the Nara Prefecture Normal School in order to gain a higher qualification while living in Nara City as a boarding student.

About this time the Kishioka family fell victim to some unfortunate events. In 1897, after the second son's serious hypochondria, the first son, Sentarō, developed an eye disorder and soon lost his sight. In 1898 their mother, Kisa, began to suffer severe pain from a tumor in the womb, and from then on the pain was recurrent. Out of the agony of his disease Sentarō developed faith in Tenrikyō and exhorted Aijirō to have faith as well. During the summer vacation of Aijirō's first year in the Normal School, Kisa's condition became grave. Aijirō began to have deep faith in Tenrikyō as a result of an experience in which his mother's pain was alleviated by his prayer; but Kisa died shortly afterwards. Aijirō thought that her death revealed that the Kishioka family had bad karma (*innen*) and that consequently he had to devote his life to Tenrikyō and eliminate bad karma.

After official approval of the Tenrikyō movement in 1888, proselytization has been conducted through its churches. Every follower belongs to a church and is required to increase the members of the church through proselytization. When a believer (or, rather, a missionary) converts a certain number of people and gains the qualification of a priest (*kyōshi*), he can then start a new church and become its head (*kyōkaichō*). Thus, a 'child' church is born from a 'parent' church. Because a child church is a suborganization under the guidance of a parent church, the creation of a new church by a successful missionary does not jeopardize the parent church's prosperity. It is the ideal of a missionary to devote all of his or her life to the propagation of the church, donating all property and abandoning any profession; to establish a new church by his or her efforts; and to 'give birth' to as many child churches as possible. To attain this, a missionary often goes to a distant place by him- or herself, or with only their immediate family, and in extreme poverty looks for new converts.

Aijirō belonged to the Nara Shikyōkai (branch church) in Nara City, but he left the Normal School in December 1900 and began traveling for the purpose of proselytization without telling his father anything about it. He went to Annaka, a town in Gunma Prefecture, and made a few converts. In late 1903 he came back to Nara in order to be married to a member of Nara Shikyōkai, Ōnishi Toh, thereby becoming a member of the Ōnishi family. (Hereafter Aijirō will be called Ōnishi.) Then he was ordered by the head of Nara Shikyōkai to do more proselytization in and around Yamaguchi City. There were already some members in Yamaguchi City, and in 1895 Yamaguchi Fukyōjo (propagation office) was established. He was appointed the head of Yamaguchi Fukyōjo but later went to Hanaoka (now in Kudamatsu City) with his wife and mother-in-law to start 'solitary proselytization' again.

Ōnishi had to come back to Yamaguchi Fukyōjo in 1907 after about two years of proselytization because of the Yamaguchi prefectural government's new policy of religious regulation. He then proselytized in Yamaguchi City for seven years while working for four years as an officer of the Tenrikyō Church Association in the Chūgoku District. This work took up a lot of time and money and did not help the task of proselytization. As a missionary, Ōnishi was unlucky because, for reasons beyond his control, he had to move several times and could not devote his time to proselytization. Since he was not a successful missionary, and members of Yamaguchi Fukyōjo were far fewer than was expected by the Nara Shikyōkai, he must have felt alienated from the Nara Shikyōkai.

It was against this background that in 1913, when he was 33 years old, Ōnishi believed that he received a revelation from God, which gave him an understanding of fundamental truth. This happened at a time when he had confined himself to his house for six months and had been reflecting on himself and on the seemingly incurable diseases of some members of his church. He came to believe that he himself was the 'revealed one' (*tenkeisha*) who should reign over the whole Tenrikyō organization. On 15 August, wearing nothing, Ōnishi and his wife began walking around and around in one room, bearing their children on their backs. After several hours Ōnishi's feet came to a halt as if attracted by the floor. He believed that it was God's affirmation that he himself was the *kanrodai*. Present-day Honmichi members celebrate this event annually on 15 August as the foundation day of their religion.

As we saw earlier, the *kanrodai* in Tenrikyō is a stone stand that is meant to be set on the place of human creation. But Ōnishi believed that there must also be a human *kanrodai* (*nin no kanrodai*) along with the stone *kanrodai*, and that, since he himself was the human *kanrodai*, he should become the spiritual leader of Tenrikyō. Moreover, his revelation held that, because the Foundress was to have lived on earth only until she was 115 years old, or in other words until 1912, and not eternally, as Tenrikyō doctrine taught, there should be another revealed leader after 1912 and that it was he himself. Although these ideas were quite strange and heretical from the viewpoint of orthodox Tenrikyō doctrines, Ōnishi believed that many passages in the *Ofudesaki* and the *Osashizu* predicted the advent of a human *kanrodai*.

Following his revelation, it was not Ōnishi's intention to challenge the Tenrikyō Church. Until 1922, in fact, he merely sent *tankas* (short poems named *Kanrodai-kōki*) expressing his new ideas to the leaders of the church. However, the established Tenrikyō organization, naturally, could not tolerate keeping a missionary with such ideas. Ōnishi accepted Nara Shikyōkai's proposal in 1914 that he should resign as head of the Yamaguchi Senkyōjo (propagation office) and leave the church. The Ōnishi family lost contact with members of the Church and fell into extreme poverty. With virtually no belongings, they went back to Nara Prefecture where their relatives and acquaintances lived, and eked out a living in a small hut at Tsuji in Makimuku village until 1917. After the birth of their fourth child, Ōnishi found a job in a hospital and then in a taxation office, and in 1920 he became an elementary school teacher in Iwaki village, Takenouchi, and was assured of a stable livelihood.

In June 1920, a Tenrikyō missionary who had read the *tankas* that Ōnishi had sent to the local churches came to join him. At last, here was a sympathizer from outside his family; and from that time on, more and more Tenrikyō missionaries and believers, hearing of his revelation, came to him. In 1923 four followers were sent to Tenri city (then Tanbaichi Town) to visit the headquarters of Tenrikyō and the homes of church staff in order to persuade them that Ōnishi should become the leader of the Church. In 1924 he resigned from the school to devote himself again full-time to religious activities after a lapse of 11 years.

By 1925, with the number of Ōnishi's followers exceeding several hundred, a new religious organization was rapidly taking shape. The group was called Tenri Kenkyūkai (Tenri Study Association), and was not intended to be an independent religious organization outside Tenrikyō but, rather, to be a study group for Tenrikyō's scriptures, especially the *Osashizu*, and to spread their correct interpretation within the Tenrikyō organization. However, because Tenrikyō dismissed the priests and excluded from its churches those followers who joined in Tenri Kenkyūkai's activities, it became de facto an organization independent from Tenrikyō.

Meanwhile, Ōnishi began to believe that the great remaking of the whole world was imminent. The apparent reason for this idea was the development in 1925 of a serious mental disorder in his first son, Yoshinobu, who was then 18 years old. Ōnishi thought that this disease was God's message that the catastrophe hinted at in the *Ofudesaki* and the *Osashizu* was approaching. At the end of 1925 he therefore left Takenouchi for Ujiyamada (now Ise City) with his wife and a few upper-level staff on a mission connected with the anticipated catastrophe. For more than a year, he wrote *tankas* called *Iwato-Kōki* and sent them to Takenouchi, one after another. Most of these *tankas* were precepts for the believers' daily life, but in some there are words hinting at the imminence of some grave events.

From September to December 1927, Ōnishi worked on a pamphlet called *Kenkyū shiryō* (Study Data) with Nakai Ginjirō and Nakagawa Kiroku, both of whom were retired naval officers and the most important leaders of the group at the time. Expecting a detailed investigation by the police in the immediate future, they intended the pamphlet to inform the public authorities of their ideas about the future. The pamphlet, details of which will be discussed below, criticized the Tennō regime and warned people about a massive transformation of Japan and the world that was believed to be imminent according to their interpretation of the *Ofudesaki* and the *Osashizu*.

In early 1928 Ōnishi moved with his wife and Nakai from Ujiyamada to a follower's house in Nagoya and concealed their whereabouts, perhaps so that his arrest would be postponed for as long as possible. Meanwhile, Yoshinobu's illness became more serious, and Ōnishi was more and more convinced that the catastrophe was about to occur. On 12 March Ōnishi sent the *Kenkyū shiryō* to Takenouchi, and as soon as Yoshinobu saw it he gave orders for it to be taken to the Nara prefectural government. On 22 March the staff in Takenouchi took a copy to the neighboring Takada police and legations in Tokyo. This action was later called the *uchidashi* (campaign).

As the government was drawing up stringent regulations concerning anti-government movements (for example, the enactment of the Law for the Maintenance of Public Peace in 1925), it naturally took strict measures against Ōnishi's whole organization. On the legal grounds that delivery of the pamphlet was an act of *lese majeste*, 467 believers were arrested, of whom 180 were prosecuted alongside Ōnishi and his wife. All the activities of Tenri Kenkyūkai were temporarily prohibited in what has come to be called the 'Tenri Kenkyūkai Incident.' Tenri Kenkyūkai argued in court that they did not intend to overturn the state but simply to foretell and warn against future events. In the first and the second trials Ōnishi was found guilty and sentenced to four years of penal servitude, but the Supreme Court decided in 1930, on the evidence of a mental examination, that Ōnishi was not guilty by reason of diminished capacity for judgment. Devout followers took this decision as proof that their beliefs and actions were correct.

As a result of this incident, the Tenri Kenkyūkai organization at first suffered serious damage, not only because so many followers were arrested, but also because activities in Takenouchi were brought to a halt, and newspapers attacked the group in sensational articles reporting the incident. But soon after the Supreme Court's acquittal, the organization recovered and became active again. The headquarters was shifted to Osaka and facilities were rapidly expanded there, as well as in other places.

In this process the group became more like an independent religious body, and by 1934 it claimed 10,000 followers. It was probably about this time that a short doctrinal book, *Kyōgi ippan* (An Outline of the Doctrine), written by Ōnishi himself, began to be used as the text for the introductory lecture course. The first three and the last sections teach the basic doctrines of Tenrikyō such as creation and the protection of human beings by God; the eight dusts and *innen* (karma). The fourth and fifth sections, entitled 'Three Steps of the Way' and 'Solely for Kanrodai,' teach Ōnishi's original doctrines. In the 'Solely for Kanrodai' section it is asserted that there is not only the stone *kanrodai* but also a human *kanrodai*, and that this human *kanrodai* will accomplish the 'Way.' It is also hinted that the human *kanrodai* is Ōnishi himself. 'Three Steps of the Way' explains the process of the Way as initiated by Nakayama Miki and completed by Ōnishi in three stages. The first step, occurring from the Foundress's first possession until her death, was the 'Way of the prototype,' a state full of difficulties representing a model for the true way. The second step, the 25-year period from the Foundress's death to Ōnishi's revelation, is called the 'Way of Reason,' a provisional stage of compromising with the world and preparing for the next step. The third step, beginning with Ōnishi's revelation, was the *honmichi* (True Way), namely, the genuine Way in which the goals of humankind will be attained. Based on this idea, the name of the group was changed from Tenri Kenkyūkai to Tenri Honmichi.

However, this period of attracting converts and giving instruction in doctrines did not last long. In 1936 Ōnishi's wife Toh developed a kidney disease, and in 1937, when her body became paralyzed on one side, the group's activities again turned to the outside. A new propagation campaign was launched in June 1937, and in September three leading believers moved to Tenri City for about a year, visiting Tenrikyō Headquarters and trying to convert its leaders. In early 1938 Toh's disease took a serious turn that made Ōnishi all the more convinced that a catastrophe was imminent. Ōnishi and other leaders therefore planned a second public campaign, and from July to September seven pamphlets entitled *Shoshin* (Letters) were written by Iwata Gen'emon, Koura Yoshio and Ōnishi Aiko (Ōnishi's daughter). About 9 million copies were printed and were delivered to police stations, military police offices, politicians, and prominent men of the time. In addition, when Toh's condition became critical on 3 August, Koura wrote a pamphlet entitled *Yūkoku no shi ni tsugu* (An Announcement for the Patriots) and sent copies to two leading newspapers in Osaka.

These pamphlets claim to explain the events of 1928 and to correct the public's misunderstandings. Although it is true that they refer to these events, the main contents are a repetition of the *Study Data*. 'The Fifth Letter' and 'The Sixth Letter' are, respectively, concerned with Ōnishi's detailed autobiography and *An Outline of the Doctrine*. The history of Tenrikyō and the relationship between Tenrikyō and Honmichi are described and explained in 'The Second Letter' and 'The Seventh Letter.' As a whole, however, the style of the pamphlets is more objective and the argument is clearer than in the *Kenkyū shiryō*.

The government, which had just crushed two big new religions, Ōmoto and Hito no Michi in 1936 and 1937, used the publication of these pamphlets as a pretext for taking strong repressive measures against Honmichi. On 21 November 1938, 346 leading believers and Ōnishi himself were arrested, and 237 were prosecuted for violating the Law for the Maintenance of Public Peace and on the grounds of *lese majeste*. The Ministry of Home Affairs prohibited all activities of Tenri Honmichi and ordered its dissolution in September 1939 in what has come to be known as the 'Tenri Honmichi Incident.' The result was that Honmichi was unable to conduct any religious activities for about six years. In the first and second trials of Ōnishi and a few leading believers, all were found guilty and Ōnishi was sentenced to penal servitude for life. But while they were on trial in the Supreme Court, the Second World War ended.

Along with many prisoners previously accused of political crimes and thought 'dangerous' to the state, Ōnishi was released in September 1945. He and other believers were finally acquitted in March 1946, and a few days before that, in accordance with the new Religious Corporation Ordinance, the group received official recognition for the first time as a religious corporation. Following the Tenri Honmichi Incident the government had ordered the disposal of the group's properties, and the Ōnishi family had moved to Hagoromo Town in the southern part of Osaka Prefecture, which became the location of the group's new headquarters. Membership increased steadily, reaching about 230,000 members in 1954 and about 300,000 members in 1980.

I shall not describe the history of Honmichi in the postwar period, but one point needs to be raised: namely, the problem of the succession of 'charisma,' in the Weberian sense. As early as 1932, when his first son Yoshinobu died, Ōnishi told some of the leading believers about his death and about his successors. He said he would not live to be 100 years old, he would be born again and again eternally in the Ōnishi family as the human *kanrodai*, and until the reborn *kanrodai* reached maturity, proxies (*tegawari*) designated by him should take his place. After release from jail he designated his first daughter Aiko and his second son Masanori respectively, as *kyōshu* (teaching head) and *kanshu* (superintendent) and as two proxies. Ōnishi himself retired from major activities soon after his release. By the time he died in November 1958 Aiko and Masanori were already venerated by the followers. When Aiko and Masanori died in 1966 and 1971, they were succeeded by Masanori's first and second sons, Motooki and Masataka. Meanwhile, in 1962, in the headquarters at Hagoromo, a group called Mirokukai developed in support of Ōnishi's second daughter, Tama, who claimed that she was the reborn Foundress and that she should be the successor of the human *kanrodai*. The governing body, rejecting her claim, expelled the group, which then formed a new religious body named Honbushin (True Construction). Soon after this 'Mirokukai Incident' the leaders of Honmichi announced that the *kanrodai* had already been reborn as one of Masanori's sons, and they later revealed that this reborn *kanrodai* is Masanori's sixth son, Yasuhiko, who was born in 1960. At present, followers of Honmichi are looking forward to the day when the reborn *kanrodai* will receive his revelation from God.

Millennialism in Tenrikyō

Three periods can be discerned in the development of millennialism in Tenrikyō: (1) the period represented by the *Mikagura-uta*, the earliest stage in the formation of the group; (2) the period represented by the *Ofudesaki* and the *Kōki*, the stage when the group's identity was established; and (3) the period represented by the *Osashizu*, about twenty years after the Foundress's death. The periods after the *Osashizu* will not be discussed, for there was no literature with millennialistic ideas to guide the whole group, and no activity connected with millennialism was undertaken by most of the group.

Mikagura-uta

In the *Mikagura-uta*, millennialism is still very vague and amorphous. It is true that there are words predicting the coming of the ideal world by God's power.

> Tong! Tong! Tong! The beginning of the dancing at New Year: How delightful it is!
> Second, This marvelous construction once it is started: How lively it is!
> Third, Nourishment will be put on you.
> Fourth, The World will change to prosperity,
> Fifth, If all come and follow Me,
> Sixth, I will cut off the root of rebellion.
> Seventh, If you help others who are suffering,
> Eighth, I will cut off the root of illness.
> Ninth, If you keep your mind determined,
> Tenth, Peace shall reign everywhere.[10]   (Chapter II)

Though it does not indicate clearly when the ideal world will come, it seems that the shift to the ideal world is already under way and the goal near at hand. However, the coming of this ideal world is not conceived as accompanying a fundamental change in the present order of the world. The shift is smooth, and the ideal world is the extension of present village life. The 'joyous life' consists of such images as abundant harvests, sound health and the end of social disorders. It is not completely different from the present state.

This vagueness in their millennialism is inherited from the folkloric concept of *yonaori* (world renewal). In fact, the manner in which *Mikagura-uta* is sung to the accompaniment of various simple instruments with slow dances and gestures is reminiscent of rural folk festivals.

How, then, did this vague and amorphous millennialism reflect the contemporary worldview? The societal situation is perceived quite optimistically, but the political trends are not grasped or clearly represented. There is just a vague, optimistic expectation for the future of village life in the Yamato district:

Third, Keep the mind of a three-year-old child!
Fourth, Then, a rich harvest.
Fifth, The providences shall come forth.
Sixth, Unlimited abundance everywhere.
Seventh, If you grow and reap whatever you wish,
Eighth, Yamato will be blessed with a rich harvest
Ninth, Now come hither and follow Me!
Tenth, Then the full harvest will become fixed.   (Chapter I)

The *Mikagura-uta* was composed at a time when rapid social change was just beginning. The political change known as the Meiji Restoration was anticipated, but wars, social disorders and economic suppression had not yet severely affected the farmers' lives. Most of the people were still living a quiet and orderly village life. They hoped for a better life, but not for a world greatly different from the contemporary one. In 1867 people's hope for change exploded in the form of mass pilgrimages to the Ise shrine from all over the country (*Eejanaika*). The *Mikagura-uta* reflects the kind of hopeful perception of the societal situation that was shared by a wide range of people.

Tenrikyō itself had just started. People who had not been acquainted with each other formed a new community and voluntarily worked together to build a shrine (*tsutome-basho*). The community was expanding rapidly, and the members were experiencing miracles one after another. The future of the community was full of possibilities, and the *Mikagura-uta* expresses a bright perception of the group's situation:

Second, This marvelous place for the Service,
    Though I ask no one to build,
Third, All gathering together from the world,
    The construction has been accomplished.
    How miraculous it is!
Fourth, With much effort, you have followed Me thus far;
    True salvation will begin from now.   (Chapter III)

Following Nakayama Miki's possession by God in 1838, her faith was accepted at first only by a few people around her. But in the late 1860s, when she was invariably surrounded by her followers, including influential farmers from neighboring villages, she did not

feel so isolated. It is true that in certain passages a sense of tension
with the external world is expressed:

> First, Whatever others may say;
>> God is watching, so be at ease!
> Third, All of you close to Me,
>> Watch whatever God acts and works!
> Fourth, Night and day, dong! chang! we perform the service;
>> The neighbors may feel it noisy and annoying.
> Fifth, As I am always in haste to save you,
>> Quickly become joyful and come to Me!
> Sixth, Villagers I wish to save at once,
>> But they do not understand My heart.   (Chapter IV)

On the whole, however, there are not many passages with such a tone
of tension. Moreover these passages are not closely connected with
ideas concerning millennialism.

Thus, *Mikagura-uta* reflects a bright outlook on all three levels, and
this is in a sense conducive to the formation of millennialism. But, at
the same time, an important component of millennialism is lacking:
namely, the sense of crisis. This is partly why millennialism in the
Mikagura-uta is very vague and amorphous.

The Ofudesaki and the Kōki

The vague and amorphous expectations characteristic of the *Mikagura-
uta* can still be found in the first part of the *Ofudesaki*, but the optimistic
tone of the *Ofudesaki* gradually fades away. There are more and more
phrases expressing a keen awareness of the distance between the ideal
state of affairs and the actual one, which is filled with various evils.
There are also many phrases forecasting a drastic turn from the
present bad state of affairs to a good one. As we have already seen,
the *Ofudesaki* was written in order to show God's will concerning the
concrete problems of the moment; and the more critical the situation,
the more drastic and the more total the impending change was thought
to be. Thus, millennialism is better articulated in the *Ofudesaki* than
in the *Mikagura-uta*.

For example, the verses referring to the construction of the *kanrodai*
predict the coming of the ideal world, a world fundamentally different
from the contemporary one:

If only you have finished the sweeping of your mental dust, I will work remarkable salvation. 98[11]

You shall be saved according to the true sincerity of your mind. You shall not fall ill, die or become weakened. 99

By this salvation I, God, intend single-heartedly to fill the natural term of human life at one hundred and fifteen years. 100   (Part III)

I set up the *Kanrodai* as the evidence that I created human beings at this place. 9

If only this Stand is completed, and every Prayer shall be heard. 10

Before that time the sweeping of the dust of human hearts must be accomplished throughout the whole world. 11   (Part XVIII)

These words correspond to the actual construction of the *kanrodai*. Some followers believed that they really watched nectar falling to earth, and Miki herself, at least for a period, believed that the *kanrodai* would be completed and that the ideal world would be ushered in during her lifetime.

Phrases predicting the great change and, in turn, demanding faithfulness are found not only in passages related to the *kanrodai* but almost everywhere in the *Ofudesaki* (see Shimazono, 1981). The composition of *Kōki* and the performance of the *tsutome* (service) are also referred to as preconditions for the coming of the ideal world. Words like 'until now' and 'henceforth' appear many times, showing that the present was considered an important point of change.

It may be asked, however, whether all the changes referred to in the *Ofudesaki* represent millennialistic ideas. Some predictions are concerned too narrowly with the future of the Nakayama family to be called millennialistic, and, on the whole, phrases expressing the nature of the change are vague and fragmentary. One typically vague expression is the metaphor of the 'way' (or road):

Do not despair of your present way, whatever kind of way it may be! Look forward with delight to the main road [true way] ahead of you! 37   (Part III)

Moreover, the timing of the ultimate change is not clearly and consistently stated. Sometimes the change is pictured as occurring in the remote future, an interpretation adopted by Tenrikyō today for most of the verses concerning change. However, we can say that all predictions of change found in the *Ofudesaki* arise from a more or less millennialistic mood. How then is this millennialistic mood related to the perception of the contemporary situation?

Two pair-concepts, foreigners vs. Japanese and the high mountain vs. the bottom of the valleys, are used to express the perception of the societal situation. It was, according to the *Ofudesaki*, against God's will that the 'foreigners' and the 'high mountain' dominated the 'Japanese' and the 'bottom of the valleys':

> Until now the foreigners have managed the Japanese[12] as they please. The sorrow of God was so severe that I could not find any way to clear it away. 86
> Henceforth the Japanese will lead the foreigners. All of you, be aware and expect it! 87
> They are the root and branches of the same tree. Branches may be broken, yet the root will grow prosperous. 88
> Until now the foreigners have been said to be great; henceforth they shall only be broken. 89 (Part III)

> Although until now those who are on the high mountains have done whatever they pleased, scolding noisily, 57
> Henceforth, however high their position may be, those who are on the high mountains shall never be able to do as they please to those who are at the bottom of the valleys. 58 (Part XV)

'The high mountains' refer to political and religious rulers who are regarded as being heavily influenced by 'the foreigners.' Contemporary politics is considered bad because of the foreigners' influence. The right people are in powerless positions, and this bad state of affairs must change – these ideas represent the perception of the societal situation in the *Ofudesaki*. They imply criticism of the political reforms and economic instabilities around the time of the Meiji Restoration that made farmers' lives desperate. Rapid social change was beginning, and many farmers lost their land and had to leave their villages. Because the main cause of these undesirable changes was believed to be, and in a sense really was, pressure from Western countries, criticism of the societal situation takes the form of chauvinism.

The combination of millennialism and chauvinism is also very evident in Maruyamakyō and Ōmoto and is one of the common components of millennialism in Japan's new religions before the end of the Second World War. In the case of Tenrikyō, the chauvinism was vague and general, for there is neither criticism of Western customs nor references to specific policies.

As the perception of the societal situation became more pessimistic, the perception of the group's own situation was hardly brimming with optimistic expectation. Even though the believers' community was still expanding rapidly, and God's presence was strongly felt, a trend contrary to God's will was observed in the obviously conciliatory attitudes of the leading believers towards oppression and interference. Miki thought that those around her did not have true faith and that this was both the cause and the result of the fact that God was not exercising his power fully.

> Make haste in high spirits! Do you not know the expectation of Tsukihi? 49
> I, Tsukihi, truly have a single-hearted desire to exhibit my omnipotence at once. 50
> Although I, Tsukihi, care with so much true sincerity, the minds of you close to Me are yet as common as those of the world. 51   (Part VII)

Among those 'close to' Miki, she was most concerned for her son Shūji. Although, as the head of the Nakayama family, he naturally played an important role in the group's management, Miki doubted whether he had much faith in her God. One reason was that Shūji's leg pain, which had inspired Miki to create a new religion in the first place, had not been cured. For Miki, his misery was also a part of God's will, and human will, she thought, struggles against God's will. This situation had to change fundamentally:

> I, Tsukihi, made you lame, though you had to that time no bodily defect at all. This has given you much trouble. 118
> Therefore you are doubting whatever words I, Tsukihi, may say. But, it is natural. 120
> This time I am preparing to clear up your innermost heart. This is the prime matter. 121
> My regret which has piled up to the present is not slight, so it cannot be expressed by word of mouth. 126
> Until now I have been passing through a mountainous regret. If only I can clear it all away this time, 127
> Thereafter I will save you from any and every kind of disease or trouble, however serious it may be. 128   (Part XII)

The perception of the group's situation to the effect that God's benevolent power, though active in life on earth, is not yet fully revealed, leads to the formation of millennialist ideas.

The criticism of the upper stratum of society referred to above is related not only to the perception of the societal situation but also to that of the relationship between the religious movement and the rest of society. Typical expressions of the tension between the believers' community and society are 'regret', 'anger' and the 'return' of God. They appear again and again in verses written when the Nara Middle Teaching Academy ordered God's name to be changed and ritual properties were confiscated in 1874; and when the police removed two pieces of the stone *kanrodai* in 1882:

> They rejected the name given by Tsukihi. What do you think of this deep regret of Mine? 70
> Understand that the true anger and regret of Tsukihi is not slight! 71
> Until now those who are on the high mountains have been rampant and managing everything as they please. 72   (Part VI)

> But from now on, in their place I, Tsukihi, will reign as I intend. Copy whatever I, Tsukihi, will work. 41   (Part XVII)

Beginning with the perception that some external force is blocking the full realization of God's power, there is a swelling expectation of a great change that will get rid of the obstacle.

In the *Ofudesaki*, we can observe millennialistic ideas that are somewhat clearer than those in the *Mikagura-uta*. This means that there is a keen perception of the situation conducive to the formation of millennialism. These millennialistic ideas, however, were so heavily dependent on the perception of the situation that they could not be integrated into one system and so are expressed without a close, logical connection among them. Thus, this scripture does not form one organized millennialistic doctrine, but rather expresses in general nothing more than a millennialistic mood.

This will become clearer when comparing it with the *Kōki,* which was written at the same time as the *Ofudesaki*.[13] The *Kōki* refers, though only briefly, to the future of humankind when the *kanrodai* is set up and the ideal world arrives, allowing people to live to be 115 years old. But it does not say that the coming of the ideal world is imminent, or that it will follow a catastrophic event. Moreover, it is difficult to draw the conclusion from what is written about the past in the *Kōki* that there will be a massive change in the near future. This scripture, mainly telling stories about human creation and God's intentions for it, as well as about God's protection of people's bodily functions, aims at confirming the harmonious relationship and oneness between God and humanity. Consequently, it says nothing about the tension or antagonism between the two. Thus, the millennialistic mood of the *Ofudesaki* and the *Kōki*'s guiding ideas fall into two different categories. This is evidence that Miki's ideas of millennialism and her basic view of humankind and of human history were not integrated into one system of thought.

The Osashizu

The *Osashizu* is so voluminous that it is very difficult to analyze it thoroughly. I shall give only a rough outline for future study. There are, no doubt, expressions that can be called millennialistic, but, like those in the *Ofudesaki*, they are not systematic. Here, too, various ideas reflect different perceptions of the situation. The *Osashizu* has the same structure as that of the *Ofudesaki* in that it expresses God's will concerning the specific problems of the situation. The *Osashizu* basically imitates the *Ofudesaki*'s style.

Generally speaking, however, the tension between God and humanity is less severe, and patience rather than resolution is exhorted in the *Osashizu*. In the perception of the societal situation and of relationships between the movement and society, the tendency is to regard the crises as manageable; for, while Japan's industrial revolution was in progress and the two wars with China and Russia were being fought, Izō and others did not think that they were very dangerous. The catastrophe and the coming of the ideal world are conceived of as occurring in the distant future, and the process of change is seen as slow. But the difference between the *Ofudesaki* and the *Osashizu* is most conspicuous in the perception of the group's own situation. According to 'the doctrine of the Foundress's further life,' the Foundress, who is the incarnation of supernatural power, though still alive and on earth, has hidden herself. Here is a latent awareness that supernatural power has ceased to be very active. Although the rapid increase of members is taken as evidence that the process initiated by the Foundress is on the way to its completion, there is also another conception of time: namely, that the greatest period of history lay in the past. Since the ideal world will be brought about only by the highest supernatural power, the *Osashizu* does not consider that it will occur in the near future.

Thus, although the *Osashizu* inherited millennialism from the *Ofudesaki*, the perception of the situation on various levels was not conducive to its further development. Consequently, millennialism in the *Osashizu* is no more refined than in the *Ofudesaki*.

Millennialism in Honmichi

As in the case of Tenrikyō, we can discern three periods in the development of millennialism in Honmichi: (1) from 1913, when Ōnishi came to believe that he himself was the human *kanrodai*, to 1923, when Ōnishi's belief was first propagated in Tenri City; (2) from 1923 to 1945, the period of the two 'campaigns' and the suppressions that immediately followed; and (3) from 1945, when the suppressed group was reorganized, to the present.

1913–1923

Although we do not have enough information for this period and must to some extent depend on conjecture, we can safely say that millennialism was only latent. Ōnishi's main concern was that he himself was the human *kanrodai* and that he should be the leader of Tenrikyō. According to the *Ofudesaki*, the *kanrodai* will be established at the coming of the ideal world, so we may infer that the human *kanrodai* will be the leader of the coming ideal world. Here is messianism, although not clearly expressed, and it is true that in the *Ofudesaki*, too, we can find messianism in its embryonic form:

> This time, purifying the water, I desire to take in quickly the Shimbashira (central pillar), who is to control the internal affairs. 56
> The central pillar of those who are on the high mountains is a foreigner. This is the prime cause of the anger of God. 57   (Part III)

In these verses Miki expresses, even if only vaguely, her wish to establish a male leader for her group and also to make him the leader of Japan or perhaps the world. However, this idea appears only in fragments. The Shimbashira was conceived mostly as the leader of the group and not as a messianic leader of the whole world. On the other hand, Ōnishi's belief that he himself was the *kanrodai* was quite likely to develop into messianism, for the image of the *kanrodai* cannot be separated from the notion of the ideal world. Messianism is not common in Japan's new religions; for, although founders and foundresses are worshipped as living gods (see Shimazono, 1981), they are not regarded as kings or queens of a coming ideal world. As a sacred king there is already the Tennō, the Emperor of Japan, a figure who is not easy to compete with (see Miyata, 1980). This lack of messianism is closely connected with the fact that millennialism in Japan was vague and unsystematic, yet Ōnishi's belief that he himself was the *kanrodai* was capable of breaking through this limitation.

Ōnishi's outlook in this period, however, was so narrowly restricted to the framework of Tenrikyō that the human *kanrodai* was conceived only as the leader of the religion. Furthermore, the idea that the transformation of the world was imminent was not yet clearly developed. Of course, as an eager reader of the *Ofudesaki* and the *Osashizu*, he might have taken special notice of millennialistic passages in them, but he did not give expression to millennialistic ideas in his own words or actions at this time. This indicates that his own perception of the situation on any level was not likely to lead to the formation of millennialism.

In this period, while rapid industrialization and imperialistic diplomacy were continuously causing both internal and international political tension, it seems that Ōnishi, at least in the first part of the period, paid little attention to the societal situation. Since he was almost entirely preoccupied with the doctrinal system of Tenrikyō, he was not very concerned with ideological problems concerning the future course of the state and society. In the latter part of the period, however, when he was working in a tax office and an elementary school and had contact with many believers from various districts, he might have paid closer attention to political affairs.

As early as 1913, he held the idea that he himself was the highest embodiment of the supernatural on earth. But it was only an abstract idea. Until about 1920, in the absence of a community of believers, he was most unlikely to have had a strong awareness of any substantial activity of supernatural power in the world at large. Only when a believers' community rapidly formed around him must he have perceived that a momentous change was imminent.

After his revelation in 1913, he was extremely isolated in Tenrikyō. It might be the case that he regarded this isolation as a symptom of some grave crisis. However, there are no writings by him or stories about him which prove that this was how he saw the situation.

In sum, Ōnishi in this period took one step forward from the vague millennialism of the *Ofudesaki* towards a more systematic one in the sense that a messianic idea was constructed. However, because the millennialistic outlook was weak, a new millennialism, yet to find expression, remained merely latent.

1923–1945

This is the period when a fairly clear belief in millennialism was established, becoming the central component in the belief system of the whole group. The millennialism of this period was expressed mainly in three documents – *Study Data*, *Letters,* and *An Announcement for the Patriots* – as well as in the group's actions during the two 'campaigns'. The millennialistic ideas that crystallized around 1928 and those from around 1938 are basically the same, although slight differences can be found. In *An Announcement for the Patriots*, the contents of the *Study Data* are skillfully summarized and itemized. I shall introduce the millennialistic ideas of Honmichi at this period by further summarizing them.[14]

1. 'The central concern of this Way': this Way is not merely a religion, but the Way to the destiny of the whole world.
2. 'The records of the Divine Age': the so-called Divine Age described in the *Kojiki* and *Nihon Shoki*, two ancient mythological texts, is not a story about the past, but prophecies. For example, Amaterasu Ōmikami, the sun goddess who governs the world and who is considered the ancestor of the Tennō family, is in fact the Foundress Nakayama Miki; '*Iwato-gakure*,' a story in which Amaterasu hid from anger in a stone cave, is in fact the prophecy of the death of the Foundress; and the descent of the goddess's grandson, a story in which an ancestor of Tennō, Ninigi, descended to earth to reign over Japan or the world, is in fact a prophecy about the succession from Miki to Ōnishi, who will become the leader of the world. In the same way, the Paradise and the advent of Christ in Christianity, as well as the Land of Happiness and the advent of Maitreya in Buddhism, are all in fact prophecies about the impending divine world of the *kanrodai*.
3. 'Our Tennō has no heavenly virtue': Tennō has no heavenly virtue to rule the country, the Emperor's insistence on divine origin is false, a mistake based on misinterpreting prophecies about the future as a story about his family in the past. People, realizing this, will not obey him in the future. Moreover, he must accept the return of God to earth and what it entails, for (the former) Tennō, opposing God's will, persecuted the Foundress.

4. 'God's regret': the Foundress sacrificed herself in this world full of selfishness to save humankind, but she was persecuted and had to shorten her own life from 115 to 90 years. This is the cause of God's great regret, and rulers who are responsible for it must accept God's return to earth, that is, natural calamities and wars. In order to be saved, people should believe in, and rely on, God, who wishes to save people from these disasters.

5. 'A great war will occur in the near future, and Japan will be placed in the ultimate predicament': when Japan is in the ultimate predicament, the human *kanrodai*, Ōnishi, will save her, for through him people can know God's will. Then, as the divine country (*shinkoku*), Japan will reign over the whole world.

6. 'The Diet will not be able to govern the country': people's eternal peace can be attained only by divine rule.

7. 'The construction of the *kanrodai*': this means the construction of paradise in this world under the rule of the human *kanrodai* with all the people in the world united as one. This is the purpose for which God made humankind.

The *Study Data* also predicts that the year 1928 is the 'year of grace' when the great event will happen and all the people will then become equal.[15] And *Letters* maintains that the group's claims in the *Study Data* were proved correct by the acquittal pronounced by the Supreme Court. However, there is no reference in *Letters* to whether the prophecy of the great event in 1928 turned out to be true or not and, if not, why.

The two 'campaigns' were conceived to inform and warn rulers of the coming catastrophe, and the proselytization directed towards Tenrikyō had the same purpose. These were the collective actions of the whole group motivated by millennialism. With these actions and the three documents discussed above, a tradition of millennialistic ideas dating from the *Mikagura-uta* became a clear doctrine for the first time. Messianism, which was latent in the period 1913–1923, became clear with the belief that the human *kanrodai* is the divine king of the impending ideal world. This concept occupies a unique position in Japan's history of ideas in that it boldly challenges the divine authority of Tennō.

The maturation of millennialistic ideas in this period was brought about by the keen critical perception of the situation shared by Ōnishi and others. The most important element was the perception of the societal situation, in which Japan was, internationally, in a very difficult position. Of course, this perception reflected the international situation and the political ideology dominant at that time. After the First World War Japan's international position was elevated, and the tension with the United States and other western countries became more and more serious. On the other hand, the aggressive policy against China was gradually escalated, turning into outright belligerency after 1931. In this position of international isolation, the government intensified internal control of the country. This policy was supported by the ideology that, in order to protect Japan from foreign countries, the people must become united under the reign of Tennō. Honmichi of this period modified this idea and incorporated it into its own set of teachings. In the process of modification and incorporation, a few leading believers played an important role as advisers to Ōnishi, for they had a great deal of knowledge about the political situation and about ideological problems as well as the ability to state their opinions about them in theoretical terms. Such ideas as the crisis of Japan and the illegitimacy of Tennō's reign were probably incorporated not by Ōnishi but by these believers. Without them, Honmichi might not have established a clear concept of millennialism.

The perception of the societal situation that was incorporated primarily by these believers and expressed in the three pamphlets, however, was not very wide in its scope. Although they asserted that the present ruler had no ability to rule, they said little about the consequences of this inability, that is, how people were suffering, how the society was changing for the worse and so forth. A short reference to the selfishness of ordinary people can be found, but only as an introduction to praising the great mercy of the Foundress. There is an indifference to social evils that is characteristic of Tenrikyō thinking after the *Mikagura-uta*. This is in sharp contrast to the perception of the societal situation in Ōmoto with its strong stance against social evils.

The perception of the group's own situation, too, has much to do with the establishment of millennialism, although not as much as the perception of the societal situation. The rapid growth of the group after 1920 must have caused the believers to feel that a supernatural power was taking the world in hand. But it was the serious diseases of Ōnishi's son Yoshinobu, and his wife Toh, that sparked the launching of the two 'campaigns.' For Ōnishi and his followers, these diseases meant that some evil power or tendency had obstructed God's benevolent power. It was believed that this evil, which must have been conceived, at least unconsciously, as the cause of the long adversities of the Ōnishi family before 1920, would lead to catastrophe and would then disappear. As in the *Ofudesaki*, the perception that a benevolent supernatural power was very active in the world but not effective in the very center of the group enhanced the idea that massive change was imminent.

The relationship between millennialism and oppression of the group is not directly expressed in the three pamphlets. There are no references to the government's blocking of God's will or to prophecies that God will remove obstacles hindering the group. But we can surmise that, in fact, there was such a strong sense of tension between the group and the wider society that it motivated the articulation of millennialistic ideas. The two 'campaigns' were planned with the expectation that sooner or later there would be oppression, which was explicitly thought to be a chance to inform the public authorities of the group's teachings rather than the operation of some evil power or tendency. Yet behind such a thought there was a strong awareness of the coming crisis that would be caused by this oppression. It was this awareness that forced Ōnishi to go into hiding in 1927. Moreover, it is clearly stated that the persecution of the Foundress was an important cause of God's regret and retaliation. This means that the believers had a firm idea that the persecutors or the authorities represented evil.

Thus, the perception of the situation in Honmichi at this time was such as to precipitate the formation and the articulation of millennialism. Through this perception the vague millennialistic ideas that had crystallized since the *Ofudesaki* turned into a fairly clear concept with links to messianism. But it did not become an independent systematic idea at that time; that is, its contents still depended largely on the current worldviews, especially on the perception of the societal situation. In other words, the realization that Japan was in a crisis and Honmichi's central doctrine that Ōnishi was the human *kanrodai* are only contingently related, not integrated into one all-encompassing theoretical system. There is no fundamental explanation of why the crisis was deepening or why the final event was imminent. As was discussed earlier, we cannot conclude from the 'Heilsgeschichte' in the *Kōki* that a catastrophic change is imminent, because it says nothing about why and how the tension between God and humankind began and grew. In this respect Honmichi of this period added very little: it had neither a view of human beings nor a view of history that could become a basis for the development of millennialism, and the current millennialistic ideas, though fairly clear, did not evolve into systematic thought.

1945–present

There have been no dramatic events or drastic changes in doctrine in Honmichi during this period; yet, of course, there have been developments in various aspects, including doctrines. Indeed, much progress has been made in the systematization of the doctrines based on the scriptures from Tenrikyō and of ideas arising in the early days of Honmichi. The result of this systematization is presented in *An Outline of Honmichi*, published in 1972, where Honmichi's millennialistic ideas are stated in a logically consistent way. The basic contents of the prophecies and the assertions, however, do not differ from those of their predecessors. In the near future, a world war will occur and humankind will suffer a grave crisis; but by prayer (*muhon zutome*) performed around the human *kanrodai* at the place of human creation, the war will be ended, and those who follow the human *kanrodai* will be saved. As to the nature of future events, the main change is the disappearance of chauvinism and nationalism. A few new ideas that do not greatly affect the whole structure of millennialism are added concerning Honmichi's own history: that the two 'campaigns' were necessary in order to inform society of Honmichi and were preparatory actions for future events; that Japan's defeat in the Second World War and the democratic reforms following surrender were fulfillments of prophecies in the scriptures; and so forth.

The most important characteristic of the millennialism in this period, however, is that it is firmly founded on the dualism of 'the unique Way of God' and 'the worldly and rational way,' that is, on the antagonism between Honmichi itself and the wider society. The two main incidents of oppression are seen in the light of dualism. The 1928 incident, regarded as the result of the 'misunderstanding' of *Letters*, is now considered the inevitable consequence of profound antagonism between the two spheres. Just as the Foundress, according to Honmichi, was persecuted again and again, those who follow God are naturally persecuted by those rulers who oppose God. On the basis of this idea, harsh criticisms are directed against Tenrikyō, which, they assume, has taken a compromising line with society since the Foundress's death. By withdrawing the *Kōki* and other scriptures, requesting governmental approval and providing various aid for the wars, Tenrikyō, they argue, has run counter to the 'Way of God' and degenerated into the 'way of humanity.'

Moreover, this dualism of 'the unique Way of God' and 'the worldly and rational way' is believed to have its basis in human nature. God gave human beings free will when creating them, and although He furnished the path for people's maturation, they abused this freedom of will and ran counter to the will of God. The impending catastrophe, in which people will be placed in a situation of grave danger, is the result of this abuse. Until people developed maturity, God permitted them, His children, to run counter to Him. But now that humankind has reached maturity, God will no longer permit people to commit profane actions. Furthermore, despite the fact that ultimate truth was revealed through the Foundress and the human *kanrodai*, humanity responded to it by committing acts of persecution. This heightened God's regret. All these abuses by humankind will result in the coming catastrophe. Here the whole history of humankind is viewed from the perspective of the tension between God and humanity, and it is this perspective that has enabled millennialism to become a logically coherent system for the first time in a tradition dating from the *Mikagura-uta*.

On the other hand, actions based on millennialistic ideas are not extraordinary and one-off things but, rather, are embodied in daily activities. The construction of big shrines (*shinhaiden*) by service work (*hinokishin*), regarded as preparations for the coming catastrophe and the ideal world, have been the group's central activities in postwar Honmichi. The big shrines are, it is believed, places where people will be saved from the catastrophe and where believers will start to construct the ideal world. This routinization of millennialistic action, as well as the systematization of millennialistic thought, is closely connected with the institutionalization of the movement, whereby the group's situation and its relations with its social environment have become stabilized. Thus, both millennialistic ideas and actions tend to be independent of the current perception of the situation. In fact, although the perception of the societal situation has to some extent been conducive to the development of millennialism because of the chronic international tension between the Western and Eastern blocs, the perception of the group's own situation in postwar Honmichi is not such as to elicit millennialism. This is because God's direct and immediate involvement in the world's affairs is felt to be weaker since Ōnishi's retirement and death. The tension between the movement and the external world has been lowered by the legal establishment of the freedom of religion. Yet, in spite of a situation unfavorable to millennialism, Honmichi has stuck firmly to it, chiefly because millennialistic ideas have become a systematized doctrine, and millennialistic actions have been routinized.

Conclusions

There is no influential tradition of systematic millennialism in Japan, but among new religions there are quite a few groups that display elements of millennialism, even if they are vague. The history of Tenrikyō and Honmichi shows how systematic millennialistic doctrine can develop out of amorphous ideas. In Tenrikyō and Honmichi before the end of the Second World War, as in most of the other new religions with elements of millennialism, millennialistic ideas were vague and largely dependent on the current worldview. Basically, their millennialism was simply the expression of a millennialistic perception of the situation and not a systematic doctrine.

We have not yet discussed why Nakayama Miki and Ōnishi Aijirō and those who followed them had a more acute perception of the situation than did others. Limitations of space prevent me from giving more than a single clue to the solution of this problem. Miki and Ōnishi tended to place great emphasis on the appearance both of God's power and of evil power or the tendency to obstruct God's power. This emphasis on the contrast between God's power and evil is due, at least partly, to their experience of long isolation at an early stage of their religious life. At the basis of all three aspects of their millennialistic worldviews, there is a keen sense of tension between their belief and the values of the wider society. But as long as this sense of tension could not be related to a firm view of humankind and history, millennialism remained vague.

In postwar Honmichi, however, millennialistic thought advanced beyond this limit, and a systematic millennialism was established. This unique process was accomplished, I assume, by the combination of the following three factors. (1) In the 1920s and the 1930s, when Honmichi grew rapidly and the basis of its doctrine was laid down, Japan's international relations were in a state of utmost tension. The dominant ideology at the time was itself millennialistic. Honmichi absorbed a great deal of the atmosphere of the age. (2) Honmichi was a schism from Tenrikyō, and most of its followers had been members of Tenrikyō. They were loyal to most of the Tenrikyō doctrines, opposing it only on one particular point. Thus, Honmichi could elaborate and refine Tenrikyō doctrines from one clear perspective, the problem of the divine leader. (3) For more than thirty years after Ōnishi had received his revelation, he and his religion were in continuous tension with society. Consequently, awareness of the severe tension with society became an essential part of Honmichi's thinking and helped the systematization of its millennialistic ideas.

Millennialism can be the expression of any traditional or imported view of humankind and history that puts an emphasis on the limitations and evils of human beings. But there are cases where such a view of humankind and history is formed only as a result of the work of millennialistic movements. Honmichi is an example of the latter. By further study of such cases, we shall be able to develop a deeper understanding of the structure and evolution of millennialistic thinking.

8 Spirit-Belief

In this chapter I would like to consider the vitality of new religious movements within modern societies under the process of rationalization, and to do so in terms of the relationship between elite and popular culture in matters related to religion.[1] In pre-modernized societies, historic religions were bound to the culture of the elite and took the form of an unshakeable tradition of elite religion that enjoyed hegemony in the religious culture of those societies. The process of elite religion's rejection of the religion of the masses and expansion of its own influence progressed but slowly there. We might rather say that the two forms of religion complemented one another symbiotically, so that the religion of the masses was able to maintain strong roots and continue carrying on its tradition.

The growth of market economies, national governments, and the cultural milieu of urban centers brought about the collapse of this balanced relationship of peaceful coexistence. The course that the history of religion took depended greatly on whether the religion of the elite maintained a position of superiority or whether the religion of the masses succeeded in breaking free of the framework of the religion of the elite. Where elite religion kept a firm grip on its hegemony, the energy was drained from popular religion and secularization was able to seep into the private lives of the masses (as happened in France, Germany, and northern Europe). But where the religion of the elite lost sway, salvific religious movements came to life from out of the religion of the masses and assumed a posture of rebellion against the elite culture that was bolstering the process of secularization (as happened in the United States, Korea, and Japan). New religious movements can thus be seen as developmental modes of popular religion liberating itself from bondage to elite culture and adjusting to modern environments.

Popular culture and popular salvific religious movements

Before discussing new religious movements, let me lay out in broad outline what I understand by the relationship between popular culture and popular salvific religious movements (or more simply, popular religious movements). Generally speaking, popular salvific religious movements grow out of the soil of traditional popular culture. Insofar as a movement is able to transform the distinctive quality of traditional popular culture at the same time as it continues to preserve it, it may be seen as an attempt to cope with changing new conditions. In what follows I will focus attention on this interplay of preservation and transformation by distinguishing between forms of social cohesion and forms of mythical worldview.

Let us begin with the question of social cohesion. Here we may distinguish between a sense of morality and solidarity. In terms of the former, the strong sense of the norm present in popular culture – that is, the consciousness of a moral norm – is something sacred, so that an offense against the norm is believed to incur the punishment of divine will and sacred powers. However, this sense of the norm is preserved not as a self-evident fact that has been absorbed into the customs of life, but as something that each individual must be taught and must choose as an autonomous subject, on occasion even assuming a critical posture against traditional morality. On this point it differs from what we find in traditional popular culture.

Along with the moral sense, popular cultures preserve a strong sense of solidarity wherein peers sharing a common faith are to assist one another and cooperate in all areas of life. However, this sense of solidarity does not obtain among all the members of a life community, but only among those who have awakened to faith and chosen a particular lifestyle. Those who fall outside of this group are counted as persons who have yet to awaken to faith – those in whom conversion remains latent – but who remain outside the primary community. On this point it differs from the sense of solidarity found in traditional popular culture.

Next we come to the nature of the mythical worldview, where we may distinguish between mythical language and the view of divine spirits. In terms of the former, just as we find with myths and legends in traditional popular culture, mythical stories that tell of the origins of the community or things associated with the community are treated seriously as something at the very core of life. However, the religious language of religious movements is usually tied to historical consciousness as well as to the rational statements found in dogma and the like. On this point religious language differs from traditional popular culture.

In terms of the idea of divine spirits, just as we find in traditional popular culture, a strong conviction persists that the fate of the community and the members that make it up depends on the will and the power of divine spirits. However, the view of divine spirits found in popular religious movements, which stress the working of ethical savior gods and the like, introduce a fair share of rationalization into the picture. On this point it can be distinguished from traditional popular culture.

In actual historical societies, because the influence of salvation religions or 'historic' religions extends more or less to society as a whole, actual popular culture is not only referred to as traditional popular culture, but commonly exhibits a great deal of the nature of popular salvific religious movements.

The distinctive quality of modern popular religious movements (new religious movements)

That having been said, what I wish to consider in the present chapter is the nature of mass religious movements, particularly in modern times. In Japan, popular religious movements since the nineteenth century are referred to as 'new religions;' while in Europe those since around the 1960s are called 'new religious movements,' here I shall adopt this latter designation to refer broadly to mass religious movements active in the context of the rapidly progressing urbanization that marks the modern period in general.

With the advance of modernization, village communities and labor guild communities were dissolved, which led in turn to an undermining of the foundations of traditional popular culture. On the other hand, along with the diffusion of literary culture has gone a rise in the cultural competency of the masses and a patently vigorous new popular culture based on urban life and mass media. This new popular culture differs considerably from its traditional counterparts, and the quality of 'popular' elements in new religious movements – which mirror this transformation of popular culture as a whole – also demonstrate dissimilarities with popular religious movements of the past.

To begin with, the solid moral norms and sense of tight-knit solidarity have already suffered considerable erosion in supposedly foundational popular culture under the pressures of modernization and urbanization. New religious movements reflect this transformation of popular culture and show two tendencies. First there is a tendency towards utilitarianism whereby the movements seek to compensate for the weakening of social cohesion by laying stress on personal benefits and happiness as a response to the changing situation. Second we see a tendency to what we might call communitarianism, which seeks a continued revival of social cohesion and responds to the changing situation by rebelling against it.

Mythical worldviews have also been affected at the level of supposedly foundational popular culture, where modernization and urbanization have greatly weakened the role of mythical language and belief in the existence of divine spirits. Here, too, the responses of new religious movements take two directions. First there is a tendency to respond to the changing times by promoting demythologization and rationalistic interpretations of divine spirits. A second tendency resists the changes, seeking rather to resurrect the myths and to stress a simple, unsophisticated procession towards divine spirits possessed of personal will.

Reactionary tendencies that lay the stress on social cohesion and mythical worldviews run counter to the deterioration of the foundations of popular culture and in this sense can be viewed as attempts to revive and revitalize popular culture anew. But insofar as the concrete execution of these tendencies takes place against a backdrop of progressing modernization and urbanization, it is to be expected that the very popular culture that is thereby revived and revitalized will in turn reflect that backdrop.

The new religions of Japan provide suitable case material for trying to pin down the relationship between new religious movements and popular culture described above to concrete facts. With the Meiji restoration and the end of the Tokugawa shogunate, there was a proliferation of popular religious movements in Japan that captured the minds and hearts of large numbers of people. Looking at these movements in terms of the degree to which they preserved popular religion and the degree to which they transformed it, the picture is extremely variegated and complex. Here I should like to focus on the belief in spirits (animism), one important facet of belief in divine spirits in general.

Since around 1970 a number of new religious groups underwent a period of rapid growth. These groups have since come to be known as the 'new new religions' (Nishiyama 1985). One of the special traits of these religious groups is their stress on belief in spirits. Belief in spirits is accorded a similarly prominent role in the so-called phenomenon of a return to religion that has taken place in recent years. Reflection on the currents of belief in spirits within the new religions may help provide clues for understanding the relationship between the return to religion in contemporary Japan and popular culture.

The 'rebirth' of belief in spirits in the new religions

The new religious groups treated here represent two clusters of religious groups from different periods. First, there are religious bodies like Tenrikyō and Konkōkyō that came to birth and took shape in rural villages around the time of the Meiji restoration. Second, there are the groups like Ōmotokyō, Reiyūkai, and Seichō no Ie that were formed in the cities during the Taisho and Showa periods. Both types of religious bodies occupy a major position in the mainstream of the new religions, and the latter, especially in matters concerning belief in spirits, has exercised a decisive influence on mass religious culture in modern Japan. It is on these latter groups that I should like to focus in particular.

We may begin with the rural form of new religions emerging in the post-feudalistic Meiji period. Despite the fact that these groups rose up out of a cultural soil rich in spirit belief, they are markedly lacking in such beliefs. The founders of these groups had dealings with various divine spirits during the time of their youth, but in the course of disturbing middle-age experiences they experienced salvation through a parent deity that subsequently became the focus of a monotheistic faith. The revolutionary quality of their faith consists in the fact that the world thereby ceases to be a disorganized arena in which all sorts of gods and spirits can function according to their own whims, and becomes a thoroughly coherent locus unified by the will of the parent god (Shimazono 1979). This is not to say that in their religious bodies belief in the existence of ancestral spirits was entirely rejected, but only that the place they were accorded within the system of belief was not very great.

In contrast, among some of the main representatives of the urban form of religious bodies that flourished quickly in the Taisho and Showa eras, such as those mentioned previously, belief in spirits was a very important element. The matter merits a closer look.

First of all, stress is laid on the reality of the 'spirit world' and the entities that populate it. This 'spirit world,' unlike the life to come and other world of Buddhism and Christianity, is an other world that is near at hand. Just as in folk belief, the borderlines that separate the other world from this world are not fixed, so that traffic and communications between the two worlds can take place easily. Yet insofar as it is called a 'spirit world,' it represented an abstracted, generalized belief different from what is found in folk belief. The concept of a 'spirit world' arises from rationalizations of folk religious views of the other world. The spirit world is inhabited by gods and buddhas, guardian deities, ancestors, malevolent spirits, and so forth, whose real existence is emphasized. But the strongest accent falls more on at-hand spiritual entities like ancestors and malevolent spirits that have not been rationalized, more than on gods and buddhas.

The second point is that spirits are depicted mainly as bearers of unhappiness. In a large number of new religious groups, the primary source of unhappiness and disaster in the real world is believed to lie in the state of mind of human beings. Furthermore, a large number of religious groups posit causal affinities carried over from previous lives. In contrast, Ōmoto, Reiyūkai, and Seichō no Ie speak of hindrances of ancestral spirits and other malevolent spirits, and at times even stress these latter more than one's state of mind. Particularly where ancestral spirits figure predominantly, it is not that these spirits bear ill will towards people in this world, but simply that because they are not enlightened they cannot exercise protective powers and hence are depicted as beings who must depend on the people of this world.

The third point is the practice of contact with spirits through magical salvific rituals. A first type of such contact is possession. In Ōmoto this is called *chinkon kishin*, 'quelling the soul and returning to the divine.' One sits opposite a leader called the *saniwa* (discerner of spirits), hands joined, and begins to chant '*hito, futā, mī, yō…*(one, two. three,…, ten)' until entrancement sets in. Sometimes a good spirit (*seishugojin*, 'main-guardian god') appears and at other times an evil spirit (*fukushugojin*, 'vice-guardian god') appears. It is one of the functions of the *saniwa* to discern the spirit. In Reiyūkai, there is a practice of entrancement for novices known as *innen o toru* (removing karmic affinities) and another known as *kage no junjo o toru* (the miracle method) in which leaders become spirit-possessed and in that state respond to questions. In Seichō no Ie there is no formalized practice of possession by spirits, but in a practice during which the words *jissō enman kanzen* (ultimate reality, full and complete) are repeated over and over for a long time, entrancement is frequently experienced. In many cases these practices are connected to healings. Through the practice of spirit-possession the unhappiness wrought by spirits is driven away, or it is believed that the means to do so are attained.

The second type of contact with spirits takes place through *kuyō* (veneration or Buddhist services). The practice of intoning sacred texts to spirits twice a day, morning and evening, or on the occasion of community rituals is of great importance. The *kuyō* service itself is of course a Buddhist ritual that has been in practice since ancient times. But in the case of Reiyūkai and Seichō no Ie, ancestral spirits are depicted in particularly vivid terms as beings depending on beings in this world, and the *kuyō* is taken seriously as a means of removing unhappiness from life. In these groups special scriptures are composed that believers are expected to chant daily and *kuyō* to be performed to the spirits is ranked alongside – if not above – prayers to the gods and buddhas. This *kuyō* does not rely on a religious clergy or special functionaries, but is to be performed by individual believers on their own.

In the foregoing I spoke of Ōmoto, Reiyūkai, and Seichō no Ie, but there are, of course, numerous points of difference among the three. In particular, the role of spirit belief, which is not very predominant in Ōmoto, is accorded much more attention in the other two. Originally Ōmoto had a strong belief in a saving deity. Belief in spirits was connected mainly to the practice of *chinkon kishin* and seems for a time to have carried great weight. But this practice, as a technique for becoming aware of the actual reality of the spirit world, came to take on the character of a rite of initiation. Once one is convinced of the reality of the spirit world, there is no longer any pressing reason for performing *chinkon kishin*. In addition, the suppression of the occultist practice by the government helped the practice of spirit-possession through *chinkon kishin* to gradually fall out of use. Accordingly, the role played of spirit belief is decreasing and belief in the saving deity becoming central. For Reiyūkai and Seichō no Ie, the expulsion of spirits in connection with the rooting out and dissolving of unhappiness stands alongside, or even above, the goal of becoming aware of the reality of the spirit world.

Summing up what has been said so far about Japan's new religions, there was a conspicuous shift from the form of belief that marked the rural-based new religions that arose around the Meiji restoration to the urban-based new religions of the Taisho and Showa eras. The trend towards belief in a saving god has weakened and belief in spirits has gained in strength. Even in the case of Ōmotokyō, which we may place in a period beginning around the late Taisho and early Showa era, or perhaps the end of the Meiji period, belief in a saving god was nevertheless rather strong. This trend accords with the gradual shift in the principal living environment of the Japanese from a rural to an urban setting. That is to say, we witness an increase in belief in spirits among the new religious movements coinciding with the advance of modernization and urbanization. Since the 1970 spirit belief in groups like GLA, Mahikari, Agonshū and other 'new new religions' also seems to belong to this more widespread current.

Taking Japanese society as a whole, Reiyūkai and Seichō no Ie may seem typical of this trend of maintaining a firm foothold in the spirit-belief of the masses dating from before modernization, while rural-based religious movements of the early post-feudal period such as Tenrikyō and Konkōkyō stand out rather as exceptions. But at least in the middle classes, it is also the case that there has been a strong trend away from belief in spirits. This can be seen as a consequence of the downward spread of the elitist cultural worldview. Post-feudal rural new religions reflected this continuing deterioration of belief in spirits. However, from around the end of the Meiji period there has also been a countercurrent of vigorous revivalism of belief in spirits, which may be considered a response to changes in lifestyle induced by urbanization.

Such being the case, to what may we attribute the revival of belief in spirits within modern urban society? In answering this question, the distinctive quality of this new belief in spirits should become clearer.

Belief in spirits and modern urban society

We may approach the question of the reasons for the revival of belief in spirits by considering first the predominance of belief in spirits vis-à-vis other forms of belief and worldviews. As a change to new beliefs and worldviews taking place on a mass scale, we may presume that the revival of belief in spirits represents the choice of a worldview suited to an urban setting. There are three important worldviews that compete with the new belief in spirits: traditional belief in spirits, belief in saving gods, and rationalism. Let us consider how the new belief in spirits measures up to each of these three as a response to urban life.

From traditional belief in spirits to urban belief in spirits

To begin with, urban belief in spirits may be thought to arise as an alternative to traditional ancestor veneration. This is the approach of Morioka Kiyomi and Kōmoto Mitsugi, and is also the most influential view on the nature of spirit belief in urban-based new religions (Kōmoto 1978, Morioka 1984). Belief directed towards ancestors as household gods, they argue, represents the core of traditional Japanese folk belief. This veneration of the ancestors is in turn bound inextricably to the system of the *ie* (household). Modernization and urbanization have led gradually to the disintegration of the *ie* as a social system transmitted generation after generation from elders to their offspring. Focusing principally on mobile urban residents, large numbers of people have appeared who have been crowded out of the order of the *ie* and who no longer possess the sense of the unity of the *ie*. Take for example the second or the third son and their spouses who migrate to the city. People like this are still deeply concerned with the nearby spirits of the dead and are desirous of religious communication with them. Ōmotokyō, Reiyūkai and Seichō no Ie are attempts to respond to this demand of the masses.

To be sure, traditional belief in spirits was not directed only towards ancestors as protective gods of the house. Belief directed to lost souls and vengeful souls also formed an important element in folk belief. But *kuyō* performed for evil spirits of this sort tended to be entrusted to clerical functionaries. In contrast, the religious observances of these religious bodies passed through the mediation of monk and other religious specialists to formalized practices for individual believers. In modern urban societies that require spontaneous, positive action of the masses, it was the spirit-belief of these religious bodies that revolutionized traditional belief in spirits to make it suitable for the changed conditions.

From belief in saving gods to belief in spirits

A second force which compete with spirit-belief is belief in saving gods. Among the masses of Japan, there was a strong tradition of faith in Pure Land Buddhism's Amida Buddha and personalistic saving gods (Buddhas) like the parent gods of Tenrikyō and Konkōkyō. Here the role of belief in spirits was not very great and at times was altogether dispensed with. This belief in salvific gods belongs to the mainstream in soteriological traditions such as those that speak forcefully of human limits and their deliverance. The urban-style new religions that appeared in Taisho and the early part of the Showa period were of course also salvific religions that held to traditional belief in a saving god. At the same time, spirit-belief took an important place in those religious bodies, and to that extent belief in saving gods became diluted.

Why did this sort of change take place with modernization and urbanization? A first reason lies in the diffusion of technological thought and manipulative attitudes. Belief in saving gods implies a strong tendency to seek the will of God behind all the phenomenon of the world. Human beings at all times and places, it is held, are supposed to turn to God. The I-Thou relationship with God is seen as the fundamental posture of a human being.[2] In contrast, the technological mind-set and manipulative approach of the modern world sees the various phenomena of the world as links in a chain of cause-and-effect, and concentrates attention on organizing and controlling the environment based on knowledge of those cause-effect relationships. Here the relationship between the ego and the things of the world represents the fundamental posture of the human being. Belief in saving gods was not able to complement this attitude.

One aspect of spirit-belief, however, is that it was indeed able to complement the technological-manipulative frame of mind. Spirits are not universal beings related to all phenomena, but simply one of many causal elements at work in the environment, so it is possible to organize them technologically and dominate them manipulatively.

A second reason why belief in spirits can be thought more advantageous than belief in salvation within a modern urban setting is that it renders the image of the world more complex and intensifies uncertainty. The image of the world underlying belief in saving gods is that of a single whole whose parts represent a comparatively pure symbol of the relationship between the divine and the human. What makes this image acceptable is not so much that it is confirmed in experience as that it is firmly rooted in a self-evident mythical image of the world that was accepted in the past and passed down to the present. Through the dissemination of scientific knowledge and rationalistic attitudes, modern urban societies everywhere foster a critical attitude to mythical images of the world with the result that the number of people who do not believe in myths has risen. What is more, to survive in the modern city one is obliged to acquire a complex and ever-changing body of knowledge like that expressed in science. People are continually brought face to face with uncertainty and forced to make do with the understanding requisite to each situation. Such conditions do not complement the view of the world as a simple totality that marks belief in saving gods.

It is quite another thing with belief in spirits. Not only is such belief able to coexist with a complex image of the world and with uncertainty, but it can even serve to ameliorate and temper the psychological oppression accompanying uncertainty. The functions of spirits do not relate to the world as a whole but only to particular realms of phenomena. Even had Edward B. Tylor not been around to point it out, the existence of spirits would have been suggested by the presence of various kinds of phenomena. That is to say, spirit-belief can be tied to experiential and inductive laws of thought, whence it is able to grant a strong sense of certitude.

From rationalism to belief in spirits

A third force competing against belief in spirits is rationalism. Obviously the spread of rationalistic thought and attitudes throughout society as a whole goes hand in hand with the process of modernization. This may be considered the primary moving force behind the continuing erosion of belief in spirits. Modern rationalism is bound to a materialistic view of the world and it rejects the style of thinking that assumes the existence of spirits without sound logical inference.

Two assumptions within the modernizing process underlie the spread of rationalistic thought and attitudes throughout society as a whole and the debilitation of belief in spirits. First, elite culture takes a firm initiative and tends to oppress popular culture, in particular folk belief and popular religious movements. Rationalism first takes shape within elite culture and then is passed down to popular culture, whereas the rationalistic elite cultures of modern times take the position of enlightenment in aiming at the education of the masses. This position lays the ground work for the oppression of popular culture – particularly in its religious aspects – and the ostracizing of things like belief in spirits.

A second assumption resides in the presence of an ascetical ethos. When rationalism seeps down to the masses, it carries with it the ascetical ideal of hard work and frugality. In order to survive within the mercantile economy of capitalism, one needs to succumb to the ascetical ethos, systematizing the things of life and investing energy in highly efficient economic activities. The ascetical ethos stimulates a level-headed awareness of the relationship between means and ends, and rejects the expenditure of energies on sentimental behavior and emotional satisfaction. Things like belief in spirits are dispensed with as literally worthless (Weber 1958).

With the advance of modernization and urbanization, however, these two presuppositions were undermined, and a general countertrend against rationalism itself began to take shape. To begin with, the progress of modernization and urbanization accorded popular culture wider means to make itself heard. Modernity not only led to an increase of sociopolitical rights, but through the dissemination of literacy and the enlargement of urban space the power of expression was also amplified. The mass media unified the channels and the amplification of the cultural expression of the masses, and not infrequently served as an advocate for the masses. Concomitant with this process, a large segment of the elite and quasi-elite (intelligentsia) aligned their sympathies with popular culture. In lieu of the rationalism that the elite strata had theretofore represented, a preferential option for popular culture, including belief in spirits, has come about.

A second basic force promoting the trend from rationalism to belief in spirits was the decline of the ascetical ethos. When capitalist economies achieve a certain level, consumer activities above and beyond the work of production come to be seen as good and the tendency to affirm one's own desires gains strength. In addition, the interplay of human relationships becomes the key to economic success and concern gathers with expressing one's wishes and one's feelings proficiently. In this way the ascetic ethos wanes and the tendency to evaluate non-rational, feeling-toned modes of behavior in a positive way is enhanced. This shift favors the development of belief in spirits. Compared with the enhancement of cultural expression for the masses, this latter development tends to show up later.

The same can be said of a third causal element in the shift away from rationalism, the reaction against rationalism itself. The fact that the reaction against rationalism has gained ascendancy among the masses is related to the very recent heightened awareness of problems related to the environment, natural resources, population, and the like. But doubts raised against the identification of progress with an increase of rationalistic control over the environment have been around much longer. Already early on there was a chorus of voices raised against the varieties of pollution engendered by the urban environment and advocating the ideal of a communal life within nature. Among the leaders of modern popular religious movements, not a few harbored sympathies for these ideas.

Summing up

In the foregoing I have offered some suggestions as to why belief in spirits has revived in the modern urban setting. Based on those remarks, I would like to conclude by considering briefly to what extent the revival of spirit-belief in the new religions can be referred to both as a preservation as well as revival of popular culture itself, and to what extent what can be said of the new religions of Japan also applies to religious phenomena in other places.

The first and third causal elements singled out to explain the revival of belief in spirits show that spirit-belief in the new religions lends support to the basic ingredients of popular culture. The appearance of movements rooted in traditional animistic images of the world and revolting against modern rationalistic elite culture can be seen as the spirit-belief of the new religions. In contrast, the second causal element, the shift away from the ascetical ideal, shows that spirit-belief in the new religions represents an attempt at a suitable response to conditions of modernization and urbanization. In other word, behind the actual belief in spirits itself rests a submission to the technological mind-set and the manipulative attitude, above and beyond which a clever strategy is posited for attaining certainty within an ever more complex image of the world. The fact that such belief in spirits was able to earn the support of large numbers of people in Japan seems to reflect a gradual loss of important constitutive elements of traditional popular culture within Japanese society.

The deliberate attempt to simplify matters by viewing Japan's modern religious history in terms of elite culture and popular culture allows us to speak of a process in which the hegemony of elite religion is collapsing while the religion of the masses is gaining self-assertiveness. But as heirs of a tradition of popular religion, the new religions have generated a religious culture different in nature from that of older popular cultures. This is surely not something that can be confined within the explanatory framework of a simple interplay between elite and popular culture.

The social influence of the new religious culture that the new religions represent, as became apparent at the time of the suffrage movements, has battened and grown strong in the last quarter of the 20th century. We are speaking of something that is nipping at the heels of the rationalistic elite who up until a few years ago stood confidently as the leaders of social progress. Looked at this way, one is tempted to compare the new religions of Japan with the forces of religious revival in other countries.

Peter Berger and others consider the emergence of neo-evangelicalism in American Protestantism as an attempt by traditional Protestantism to rebel against the modern world even as they seek to adjust to it, while the rationalistic, liberal elite 'new class' signals the rise of a new form of class conflict.[3] In the American case, one seems justified in seeing traditional Protestantism as pointing to the popular Protestantism represented in sects and revival movements. While there are marked differences in beliefs and political orientation that distinguish the new religions of Japan from American evangelical groups, the two are quite similar in the sense that both are heirs of popular religious tradition that have grown into powerful socio-political forces. In both we can speak of a modern developmental mode of popular religion that has broken free from the bondage of elite culture. When elite culture loses confidence in rationalism, the power of popular religion, which has been preserved, though transformed, becomes widely recognized.

9 Conversion Stories

The study of conversion is one of the central tasks of religious studies. It has been taken up in all branches of religious studies, in psychology of religion, sociology of religion, and the history of religious thought. However, surprisingly few efforts have been made to approach this question in terms of conversion stories, i.e., from the perspective of religious language. Modern Japanese conversion stories, with their appeal to the general public, are an everyday occurrence. They frequently take the form of testimonies about personal experience in the new religious movements. The topic of this present essay is the characteristics and functions of religious language as manifested in conversion stories, especially testimonies.[1]

The scope of conversion stories

Conversion stories are stories told by persons about their subjective experience of acquiring and deepening religious faith, or stories based on such narrations but related by another party. Needless to say, conversion is a phenomenon that occurs within the hearts of individuals. Unless it is reported by those who have experienced it, there is no way we might know what it means. There are, of course, some indirect indications that aid our understanding, such as the observable changes in the behavior of the converted, witness by others, or utterances by the converted about matters not immediately related to their conversion. The content of a study of conversion depends greatly on whether or not such 'reference data' can be obtained. One cannot deny, however, that the 'primary data' are the statements and descriptions of the converts themselves, i.e., their conversion stories.

The term 'conversion' is here used in a broad sense to indicate not only the once-and-for-all leap from unbelief to belief, but also the acquisition and growth of faith over a long period of time, passing through several stages. The classical studies of conversion, as represented by E. D. Starbuck and W. James, focused initially on cases which emphasized the experience of the acquisition of faith as a once-in-a-lifetime event. Religious persons stress the discontinuity between unbelief and belief. One might expect that when we look at conversion stories, those that relate once-in-a-lifetime conversions will easily catch the eye.

On the other hand, the acquisition and growth of faith may pass through several stages in accordance with specific religious traditions. The observer can most often detect several stages even in the case of a once-in-a-lifetime experience: the awakening of faith, its establishment, and the further strengthening of beliefs. As sociology and depth psychology have clarified, changes in religious beliefs go hand in hand with changes in social life as a whole and in one's relationships with other people. It is, moreover, a common fact that these changes proceed gradually over a long span of time. Whatever the converts themselves might relate about their experience, we must recognize the possibility that the process of change of religious beliefs probably requires a long time.

Let us then establish two poles, which we might call 'sudden conversion' and 'gradual conversion.' Conversion stories are stories about phenomena occurring somewhere along a line between these two poles.

Persons who relate a conversion story do not necessarily do so self-consciously and they themselves may not always have a very clear notion of just what conversion is. Yet, those believers with a strong sense of self-awareness can be supposed to have at least some general idea about how they acquired their faith and how they deepened it. When asked, they can tell about these matters either at length or briefly. However, it remains difficult at times to determine the peripheral and essential elements of conversions in such stories.

If the story is told in a time sequence, where does the conversion story begin and where does it end? One must distinguish stories which deal with conversion as a singular event separated from the context of the convert's life, and stories which take that conversion event within the continuum of the convert's life. In the former the story constitutes a whole and is completed by the narration of the conversion event from its beginning to its end. The convert might add a brief description of his or her personal history, but this is simply an appendix and easily removed from the story. Such reports of conversion events are the shortest type of stories in the sense that they cover the smallest time span.

What about conversion stories that cover a long period of time? Since this type of story has been infrequently treated, I will deal with it in some detail by using as a concrete example the account Akazawa Bunji

(Konkō Daijin, 1814–1883), the founder of Konkōkyō, provided about his own faith in *Konkō Daijin's Memoirs* (See Murakami 1971a).

Changes in Akazawa Bunji's faith were most prominent in the period between his thirty-seventh and forty-sixth year of age. The account of the events that occurred at that time covers one hundred pages in Japanese script, more than forty percent of the entire *Memoirs*. It is also their most lively part. Especially dramatic is the description of his encounter with the *kami* when he suffered a serious illness at the age of forty-two, an account that provides insight into Bunji's inner state and thus constitutes a most valuable source for the study of conversion. We may with reason see this period of his life as a conversion story reported in this central part of the *Memoirs*.

However, this is only a part of the whole story. The book opens as follows:

> Today, a message from Tenchi-kane-no-kami who told me: 'Write down your place of birth and other things of the past of the living kami Konkō Daijin.' I, Konkō Daijin, was born in the village of Urami in the same county where I live now, as the grandson of Kandori Sennosuke and the second son of my father Jūhei, on the festival day of the local deity Ōmiya-daimyōjin, before 6 p.m. My father, of the year of the fowl, was thirty-eight years of age and my mother, of the year of the rabbit, was thirty-two. It was the sixteenth day of the eighth month of the seventh year of Bunka (1814), year of the dog. I was named Kandori Genshichi. My mother was Oshimo, daughter of Tokuhachi from Masuzaka village.

This text shows how, following the command of the *kami*, Bunji will reflect on his whole life and that the story starts from the moment of his birth. All the events of his life are recorded year by year until the end of his writing at age sixty-three. The account is not, however, a disorganized enumeration of facts. Bunji traces back his relationship with the *kami*. The intent of elucidating his present state of faith pervades the entire book. This seems to be why he mentioned that his birth occurred on the festival of the tutelary deity. Although there are only a few lines for the period between his twentieth and twenty-fifth years which were devoted to an enlargement of his house, they had a deep significance for his life of faith. *Konkō Daijin's Memoirs* is a religious autobiography in which Akazawa Bunji constantly looks back at his whole life 'from the time of [his] birth until the present.'

Although the central part of this autobiography is a series of conversion experiences, they cannot be separated from the wider

*Figure 9.1:   Mutual relationship between the notion of conversion
and conversion stories in terms of 'length'*

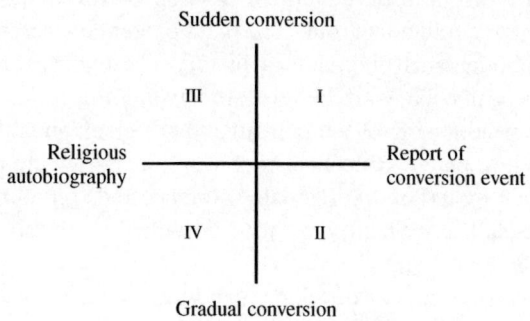

context in which they occurred. In other words, we must consider the
entire religious autobiography with both the conversion experiences
and the context as one, single conversion story, so that these reflections
on his faith 'from birth until the present' really constitute what was
identified above as the 'extended' type of story.

Conversion stories have various time-frames and their content
ranges from reports on conversion events to 'religious autobiographies.'
Differences in the time framework are related to differences in the
understanding of conversion as either a sudden change in beliefs or
as a more gradual process (see Figure 9.1). One who holds to the
notion of conversion as a sudden, once-in-a-lifetime event would
tend to talk about it in the form of a 'report on the conversion event,'
a Type I Conversion Story. On the other hand, one who regards
conversion as a gradually occurring event would take up the form of
a 'religious biography,' Type IV. To round out the picture, in Type III
one's whole religious life is told as the clarifying background for a
sudden conversion event and in Type II the event is told as a synthesis
illustrating a conversion that has been gradually building up over an
extended time period. Conversion stories contain all of these four
quadrants.

Conversion stories as one type of religious story

The characteristics of conversion stories are clarified by comparing
them with other types of religious stories. A clue can be found by

comparing mythological history (salvation history and mythology) with miracle stories and legends.

Mythological history can be represented as stories that tell the origin of the world or of the human race, or stories that explain the beginnings of a religious group. The main content of sacred writings usually embodies such mythological history. These stories are deemed official accounts. They are believed to have an important meaning for the community life of the faithful and are given an authoritative status binding on all. By contrast, conversion stories are private in nature. Their material is individual experience and their purpose is to convey the 'subjective reality' of those individuals. They elicit interest through personal sympathy.

Conversion stories can develop into mythological history, as in the case of the autobiographies of religious founders. For example, the *kami* possession of Nakayama Miki (1798–1887), which took place on the occasion of the leg pain of her eldest son, is the climax of the biography of the foundress of Tenrikyō (see Shimazono 1977). During the twenty years or so that it took to build a group of believers, this event was of central concern only to Nakayama Miki herself and to the small number of her family members. It remained a private conversion story about how she came to speak the words revealed to her by the deity. As the group of believers became established and Miki's personality itself became an object of faith, the same event became gradually mythologized by Miki herself and by the believers around her. They began to regard the divine indwelling in her as the source for their religious group. This did not mean that the event completely lost its character as a conversion story. Its nature as such a story is seen in the felt difficulty of why Miki, supposedly deified, several times thereafter still considered suicide.

A conversion story is one in which the self of the converted person is deeply engraved and in which the telling of the story is to a great extent left to that person's freedom. Opportunities for such free expression of personal religious experiences were extremely limited in the pre-modern world. As will be treated later, it is only in modern times that this became a general, popular phenomenon.

It is striking that such popularization of conversion stories, originally expressing individual experience, often became standardized and uniform. Typical examples of this are testimonies or the stories of personal experience, such as those told at the meetings of the new religions or as appear in their journals or newspapers. In these, many people repeat stories of conversion which closely resemble one another. To talk about one's own experience becomes a training ground for imitating and internalizing the original model.

The popular conversion story is of a different type, however, than the miracle story or legend. For example, the following story can hardly be called a conversion story.

> I am employed in the building industry, but after the oil shock work rapidly dwindled and I gradually sunk into poverty. Through an acquaintance I was introduced to the *sensei* ('teacher' or 'leader') who advised me to pray for the repose of my aborted baby on the thirteenth anniversary of its death. I immediately started praying for spiritual purification (*jōrei-kigan*). Since then, my business, which had been quite sluggish, has recovered smoothly. At present the number of workers has also increased and profits are double those of the past. I am humbly grateful for what the *sensei* did for me (From a newspaper insert provided by a diviner in March 1981).

Here it is difficult to judge whether a conversion has occurred or not. This story does not try to relate a conversion but a miracle and a spiritual experience. In this sense the story corresponds to the legends collected by Yanagita Kunio in his *Tōno monogatari* (Tales of Tōno). In contrast, the following story of an experience in a new religion is one that we can include among conversion stories.

> For a long time I could not sleep because of severe lumbar pains. My older sister worried about me and advised me to become a member of the Reiyūkai. At first I tried not to listen to her. But one night I saw in a dream an emaciated baby. Why did this happen? All of a sudden I realized. I had aborted two babies. Is it then right that I think only about the happiness of my living son and daughter who are in good health and fail to pray for the repose of those aborted children? While pondering this, one day a young Buddhist, beating a hand drum and chanting *namu myōhō-renge-kyō*, appeared at the entrance to my house. He asked me to let him in to take a short rest. He entered the house, looked at me, and said: 'You were bad to two of your children, weren't you? And now you are suffering from lumbar pains. What a pity! I would like you to have a longer life.' I felt as if a long nail was suddenly driven through my heart. The priest left without saying anything further, but when I talked about this occurrence with my husband big tears welled up in his eyes. I thought, 'I don't want to die. For the sake of my husband and children, I cannot die young.' I started appealing to all kinds of ascetic practitioners and faith healers, asking them how I could be

saved. But to no avail! Finally I went to the house of my older sister who is a believer of Reiyūkai. She welcomed me warmly. In 1964 I myself became a member. A short time thereafter, one morning when I was praying for the souls of the deceased, the name of a house in the vicinity kept popping into my mind. I went to visit that house and a lady told me in a tearful voice that her husband had died several years before and that recently she had not even opened the doors of the Buddhist home altar to pray for him. She also became a member. When I awoke the next morning, I called out for joy. Incredibly, the lumbar pains I had suffered for four years were completely gone (See Reiyūkai 1976: 202).

The above story was written down from the oral account of the person involved, but one can detect in it the personal touch of the lady who told it. While telling about the miracle and spiritual experience, it also relates a conversion, viz., the growth of a religious self in the concerned individual. This religious self is formed in the daily activities of the religious group through dialogue and training. The typology of conversion story reflects that of the religious self as presented originally in systematic thinking on doctrine and practice. While they belong to an identifiable type, they do not lose their character as expressing individual personality.

The milieu of the formation of conversion stories

Conversion stories are based on 'reality,' but they also are limited by the various elements proper to the milieu in which they are recounted. Therefore, in interpreting such stories, one has to take into due consideration the nature of the milieu in which they have been formed and in which they are actually told.

In order to be told, conversion stories presuppose a religious self. In the establishing of this self, dialogue with a religious group plays an important role. Conversion stories take on their specific form through such dialogue. This does not mean that their form is unalterable. New forms do occur in accord with the personal and doctrinal interests and wishes of the listeners. In being retold, the interests of the narrator tend to be inserted in the story. Let us examine a typical case.

The following conversion story of a shamanistic practitioner (*gomiso*) has been partly excerpted and summarized by a psychiatrist who heard the story from the person in question, but used it for a treatise on what *kami* possession means.

Case No. 18 – Male – 35 year old

At the age of twenty the patient lost his job and suffered poverty. Finding it strange that his father, who was a diviner, was doing well in his profession, and wholeheartedly wishing to ascertain for himself the existence of *kami*, he started ascetic practices at Mount Iwaki. On the night of the eighth day, while sitting alone on a rock in prayer, he was attacked by a violent feeling of numbness and then induced into a state of drowsiness. All of a sudden the beautiful landscape of a spring field opened up before his eyes and on the far shore of a small river he saw the figure of a goddess stretching out her hand which held a beautiful jewel. Although he thought this a strange thing to see in the midst of the mountains, he submitted himself to this state of rapture. Soon he returned to reality 'as if awakening from a dream,' and he interpreted the event to mean that he himself had become a disciple of the *kami* who had showered him with immense grace and loved him as 'the apple of her eye.' Again he was submerged into a feeling of supreme bliss (see Sasaki 1981: 111).

In the case of charismatic religious figures such as a *gomiso*, the formation of a conversion story can be said to occur in a process of solitary introspection. When they become regular believers, they further build this up in dialogue with other believers. If someone with scholarly interests, like a psychiatrist, comes and asks direct questions, then the conversion story takes on a new form of expression. The scholar then develops this into a treatise appropriate to scholarly discussion.

The most important element in the limiting milieu is the nature of the relationship between the one who tells the story and those who listen to it. Based on this relationship we can distinguish three different ideal types of stories; (1) the introspective type, (2) the group type, and (3) the listener type.

Conversion stories of the introspective type are written down by the narrator to ascertain his or her own faith. They are usually stories that the convert relates by looking back in solitary introspection to his or her own past without any intention to convey this experience to other persons. In this type, the initiative for the formation of the story comes totally from the narrator and such stories are therefore often overflowing with individuality. The examples William James gives in his *The Varieties of Religious Experience* belong almost without exception to this type. The above mentioned *Konkō Daijin's Memoirs* can also be classified under this type.

The group type occurs in cases in which the narrator and the listeners share a common faith and jointly compose the story of the conversion. Typical examples are the stories about religious experiences found in many of the new religions. Prior to the self-reflection of the convert a request is made for an account of his or her conversion experience. The way to tell that story is then taught by the leaders and the older believers and the story is formed along the model of other similar stories. The initiative for its formation comes from the group to which both narrator and audience belong. As a result, these stories tend to be very similarly patterned.

In the listener type, the stories are related as heard from the convert by a listener, particularly someone with scholarly interest, not in order to share faith but to obtain needed information for oneself. A pure type is when a believer, who still has but shallow religious self-awareness and who has not yet composed his story, for the first time in response to the research questions of a listener (or questionnaire) composes a consistent account. Here there is a strong tendency for the stories to become eclectic, containing a mixture of images that the convert holds about his or her own faith and conversion and of the scholarly concepts of the listener about conversion.

Most conversion stories, however, are not pure types, but share in all three types. They are then to be located within a triangle (see Figure 9.2) with three ideal types as angles. For example, the case of the *gomiso* is originally formed as an introspective type of conversion story. But through the process of scholarly research and its transmutation into treatise form, it is gradually transformed into the listener type.

Conversion stories as fiction

Although varying in degree, the basic content of all the above mentioned types of stories depends on the testimony of the convert. From a research perspective, the question urges itself as to what extent the 'story' actually reflects the 'reality' of the conversion.

Sociology and depth psychology have made it clear that one should not accept the converts' stories at face value, but reconsider them critically in the light of other material. That material also comes for the most part from the converts, but goes beyond their explicit intentions. Information from other sources, persons, or writings are

Figure 9.2: Ideal types of conversion stories according to milieu

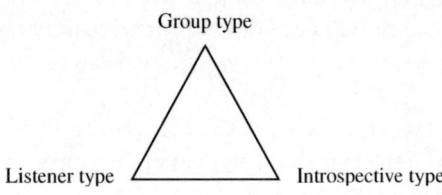

certainly significant. In the case of Akazawa Bunji, the reference material provided by the *Onoke monjo* (Documents of the Ono Family), which are records written by the village headman about life in the village where Bunji lived (see e.g., Seto 1974), open up new possibilities of interpreting the conversion process as related in *Konkō Daijin's Memoirs.*

By combining such materials with the conversion stories themselves, one often discovers unexpected insights, often including facts that may differ from the descriptions given by the converts themselves. By considering why such discrepancies occur, hidden meanings of the conversion story may come to light. Much progress in the study of religious biographies has been made by the discovery of such hidden meanings.

There are more likely to be fictional elements in autobiographies than in ordinary biographies. Conversion stories are particularly subject to such a possibility, for they are often written with a strong motivation to reassert and strengthen religious faith. One can easily understand that accounts of religious experiences benefit and strengthen the faith of practicing believers. A clear example of one's personal process from unbelief to belief further establishes one's self-identity as a believer. It is easy to imagine the rather extreme case of new believers, who do not yet have a firm awareness of whether they have faith or not, coming for the first time to firm faith precisely because they are given the opportunity to relate their experiences. In other words, it is possible that the very formation of the conversion story is an important aspect of the conversion process itself.

The fictional character of the conversion story appears more strongly in the selection of the elements included than in the fabrication of particular facts. Therefore, one must consider what has not been related in the story. Omitted facts may either have been excluded on purpose or unconsciously overlooked and forgotten. In either event, such omissions may have important relevance to the life of the convert. In interviews the researcher not infrequently stumbles into matters that he/she needs to know, but which the convert does not like to discuss.

If one can ascertain what is untold, one can acquire a deeper understanding of the expressed content of the conversion experience. These 'other matters' refer precisely to things the converts themselves do not want to talk about. There are clear limitations in ascertaining them. In many instances the interviewer is limited to hearing what the convert wants to say. In most cases this results in 'shelving' the different interests between the researcher and the convert. If a researcher tries to touch upon matters the convert does not wish to speak about, this diversity of interests becomes apparent, possibly jeopardizing the very premises necessary for a fruitful interview.

Such may perhaps not be the case with research methods other than the direct interview. In using written conversion stories one might be able to research the private life of the convert to know things not included in the written material. Yet even here, if the researcher is to gain the respect of the convert and of those close to him, he must refrain from making public material that would debunk the conversion story.

Such limitations are part and parcel of research into conversion accounts, dependent as it is on what the convert wants to relate. Even if the interpreter can to some extent read the story in a different light, the main themes cannot but rely on the testimony of the converts themselves.

The popularization of conversion stories

As mentioned above, in present-day Japanese society conversion stories are widely found in the daily activities of the new religions. They are prime sources for insight into the characteristics of contemporary religious language. Of course, stories about religious experiences do exist in all religions everywhere. Such testimonies are expressed in the language of popular or mass religion. But the greater part of these are simple stories about miracles or the like. They seldom refer to the inner self of the narrator, focusing attention solely on specific events or manifestations of the sacred. By contrast, conversion story testimonies deal with an experience within the context of an individual person's life. They tell about a conviction of being saved and of personal change. Thus they characterize a single person's inner self and are naturally limited in number. It was the exception that such things were related in a society in which the rural population constituted the majority. When we study the biographies of famous religious persons from the past, we find only meager data about their conversion and faith-formation. This certainly does not make our task any easier. Even in the case of those who preached often and wrote much on religious themes, only a few have made their religious experiences public. In a word, it was not generally accepted that talking about one's personal inner feelings could be a form of expressing a sublime religious truth.

This remains the case for believers in general. It is not that they have no experience of conversion or no interest in what moves the heart of others. Rather, since religious communities in the past reflected the same background and similar life-histories, without waiting for verbal expression, people could naturally understand each other's feelings. Moreover, ordinary believers were regarded not as suppliers of a religious message, but recipients.[2]

In the Catholic Church confession has been an important element in the life of faith. The words of confession lay bare the inner feelings of the individual and, just as in the testimonies about religious experiences in the new religions, they have a cathartic function (see Turner 1975 and Shimada 1980). Perhaps one can see in confession a type of religious experience story that can be termed a 'liability or sin story.' However, confession is made in an enclosed space from one person to another under the total guidance of the confessor and does not by itself promote the establishment of individuality in the penitent. There has traditionally been little possibility for the penitent to locate their experience within the context of their whole life or to construct a story relating to fundamental changes in their hearts.

With the advent of modern times, awareness of individuality and self has increasingly strengthened, and ideas of the value of personal experience have gained importance. Concurrently, the number of persons who relate and write down their conversion stories has grown. In Japan this idea of grounding one's search for truth in one's own experience of conversion and of telling each other about that conversion can be found as early as Ishida Baigan (1685–1744) and his monthly *tsukinami* meetings. In both the West and in Japan the golden age of confessional literature (the I-novels) clearly reflects the centrality of seeking ultimate truth in individual experience. In the case of Japan, an aversion for abstract thinking and a pragmatic tradition of adopting a plurality of ideas have, it would seem, spurred on this proliferation of stories about experiences and conversions.

The testimonies in the new religions are one result of this trend to diffuse and popularize such conversion stories. The very act of expressing one's individual feelings in a personal way and of presenting one's religious self to the general public became increasingly popular. However, this was not done in terms of personal freedom in conflict with religious group activities, but instead was performed within these activities. In other words, the conversion stories came about as a common religious language of the masses.

Religious truth in testimonies

Not all testimonies in the new religions are conversion stories. Quite a few deal simply with miracles or with a reconfirmation of faith. Here the focus is upon those popularized stories which do treat one's own inner experience and which deal exclusively with conversion.

What then are the characteristics of such popularized conversion stories as a language for expressing religious truth? How are they different from traditional religious language? The remainder of this essay addresses these questions in four points from the perspective of the religious language used by people and for people (See also Takagi 1958: 194–201, Takagi 1959: 142–48, and Saki 1960: 196–203).

Uniqueness in time

Stories about conversion experiences are unique in time, limited to one particular occasion in the sense that they seldom linger on in common memories. They stress unique, dramatic inner changes of particular individuals that do not occur every day. Except in small, tightly knit groups, most testimonies are not meant to be permanent records. Most frequently they are slowly forgotten after having 'stirred up' faith when recounted. It seldom happens that they are preserved as common memories or further discussed on subsequent occasions.

The topic of these testimonies tends to be seen as new and relevant, much as in newspaper articles or TV news programs. In large or middle-size groups it is not considered proper to talk too much about long past experiences, however important such might have been. The narrator has to show concretely how a sacred power has appeared now, how one individual person has been enlightened now and now stirred into action. Testimony seems to be restricted by the present time in this double sense.

Doctrinal talks and sermons often contain similar references to the concrete present as an aid to memory. Thus they might also be thought to be restricted to the present. But at base level they express some truth proposition, and their use of concrete language and examples related in the present-tense surround this core of unchanging truth. By contrast, the concrete references in testimonies are the prime reality without any necessary appeal to unchangeable truth.

This is the salient difference between popularized conversion stories and religious autobiographies. Conversion stories in the form of testimonies seldom develop into extensive religious auto-biographies. The inner, personal religious understanding of a believer is in a continuous process of development. Such a slow and gradual growth, however, is rarely mentioned in testimonies. The focus is on the occurrence of a new, dramatic event, from which one may only occasionally look back and interpret the past.

Practicality

Stories of conversion experiences are practical in the sense that they express teachings as being in touch with the concrete life of the people and in the sense that they can directly aid in the practice of faith and religious self-understanding. This is one reason why they are so popular. They concretely address the problems people face daily and bring to speech hitherto unspoken feelings from the depth of one's heart. The reality of sacred power is shown as bringing salvation from the depths of suffering. Short passwords of the specific faith are provided as a means for finding one's way. In such words and phrases a concise guide is expressed for 'rebuilding the heart,' i.e., for changing one's heart and life.

The use of examples to illustrate doctrine is of course not restricted to testimonies. The language used in the *toritsugi* 'mediation' in Konkōkyō with their face-to-face dialogue between the religious leader and the believer emphasizes concrete descriptions of felt problems. Many doctrinal sermons with their ready examples have a practicality closely resembling that of testimonies. Indeed, when they treat important events in the life of the preacher, they take on the character of conversion stories. Nevertheless, the aim in these cases is always to present teaching, and the concrete examples remain peripheral. The salient feature of testimonies is that one can enter into, participate, and 'live out' their exampled world.

Activity

The language of conversion stories is active in the sense that their main protagonists articulate their own problems and present themselves before others as overcoming these problems. The method of these stories is not passively to accept the words of a teaching, simply to convey them to others, or silently to put them into practice. The one engaged in practice is the one who gives the sermon wherein he or she presents a personal faith to others. Here the distinction between teacher and disciple, between giver and recipient, is bracketed and people from all levels participate in dialogue on an equal basis (at least in principle). All are qualified to participate simply as believers and all present their personal, individual experiences before the others.

This does not mean that all testimonies are indiscriminately accepted. They are in fact subjected to the critique and appraisal of the community. The leaders naturally take the initiative for these critiques and appraisals, but the overall group of believers is given a chance to express opinions and the comments of the leaders take into account the reactions of the community. In the presentation of the stories, the extent to which the narrator has understood doctrine becomes apparent. Stories that move the heart, whether coming from the leaders or from ordinary believers, are heard by the audience on an equal basis. Because most of the audience will become narrators themselves once in a while, they are being trained in their daily faith activity in telling about their own experiences and in critically regarding such stories. In a word, the audience can participate as 'authors' and 'critics' in constructing the story itself.

Solidarity

Conversion stories establish a strong sense of solidarity among people who seldom come into contact in their ordinary lives. They are oriented to and evoke this solidarity by assimilating people into common values.

All the participants share in the story 'time' and participate in the feelings expressed in the telling of the story. Furthermore, feelings of solidarity and fellowship arise from the 'naked' face-to-face encounters of the participants. A sense of oneness with the narrator is brought about by the sympathy elicited in the hearers. The listeners can and do feel that they should share in others' stories, for the religious attainments described therein relate directly to their own concerns. This sharing in a common endeavor engenders solidarity, whether expressed by hand clapping or other signs of approval. Without compulsion all are drawn into the group values and unconsciously learn group forms of expression, further solidifying their fellowship.[3] Needless to say, such fellowship is more permanent than the contrived togetherness of TV group programs or rock concerts. It draws the participants into group activities and their accompanying lifestyle.

When stories are told in large gatherings, the entire audience often becomes totally engrossed in the narrative. For example, in salvation stories about how grave troubles suddenly turn into great happiness, or in stories about repentance, in which the narrator repeatedly apologizes with a heartfelt sorrow, both narrator and audience easily share in a deep sense of unity. Stories of salvation instantly take away the fear of evil powers that threaten one's fate or make one lonely. Repentance stories instantly remove the walls of enmity and guilt that separate one from the others. Such feelings of unity resemble those elicited among the spectators of the Christian passion plays. In the case of testimonies it is not so much the power of traditional symbols or artistic refinement that evoke those emotions. It is rather the fact that those who underwent the experience are themselves recounting it and the fact that the content of such stories reflects common experiences. In traditional religious language, assimilation into the sustaining and unifying values of the group is accomplished through the stereotyped language of myth and doctrine, ritual and practice, or through the acquisition of specific religious conduct. This is an extended process and involves many gradations. By contrast, in conversion stories a quiet and deep assimilation occurs through the demonstration and sharing of subjective experience in everyday language.

It goes without saying that the above description does not exhaust all the characteristics of popularized conversion experience stories exemplified in Japan's new religions. I would like to leave further systematic investigation of them, together with an attempt to trace the development of testimonies in other parts of the world, for a later occasion.

10 Alternative Knowledge

In what follows, I shall discuss a religiosity that does not belong to any specific world religion. It is a kind of religiosity that can be found in many parts of the world, especially where the world religions have not penetrated people's lives and thinking. This religiosity has a variety of names, such as folk religion, nature religion, and animistic mentality.

This naturalistic religiosity differs from major world religions in its way of regulating body and nature. Contrary to the rationalization and secularization theory derived from the Weberian sociological tradition, this naturalistic religiosity has not been excluded from the life of industrial society. Rather, it has been preserved through the process of modernization, and perhaps we are now witnessing a resurgence of this religiosity in advanced countries, in the form I like to call new spirituality movements and culture, or in the West is called the New Age movement.

I attempt in this paper to show how naturalistic religiosity has been preserved through modernization, by discussing a Japanese example of an alternative agricultural or farming movement. This example will help us to understand one way in which religions are concerned with food production and nourishment. It will also elucidate the complicated patterns in which religions function in regulating or coordinating body and nature.

Before describing in detail the alternative farming movement in Japan, the concept of an 'alternative knowledge movement' (AKM) will be proposed in order to locate this kind of religiosity in modern and contemporary religious and cultural history.

Formation of alternative knowledge movements and religion

Transformation of the knowledge system in modern times

When a society undergoes the process of modernization, great changes occur in the knowledge system of the people of that society. In place of the knowledge conveyed mainly orally through daily life, or that accumulated by a literary tradition centering around sacred texts, modern scientific knowledge, and knowledge required for modern institutions such as law and bureaucracy, is accumulated and absorbed by the people. Modern knowledge becomes dominant over folk knowledge and knowledge carried over from previous civilizations. School education has played the greatest role in spreading this modern knowledge.

The knowledge system built up by the literary tradition was established long before modern times, and the school system as a channel for transmitting knowledge through the generations has a long history. However, until modern times, systematic knowledge based on literacy and the school system as an imparting channel was available only to a privileged minority. The majority of the population lived in a world of orally transmitted folk knowledge. Because of this, the range of influence of literacy-based systematic knowledge was limited within the day-to-day life of the general population. One of the differences between modern and traditional schools (the latter taught mainly writing and simple arithmetic) is that the former attempt to inculcate systematic written knowledge in the great majority of the population. As a consequence, systematic written knowledge in the form of modern knowledge rapidly penetrates the sphere of daily-life knowledge that had developed spontaneously among the people.

Reacting against this penetration, traditional religious organizations that maintained their own systematic doctrine and written traditions began to reorganize their structures so as to allow the general public to acquire their religious knowledge; in other words, the popularization of traditional, written religious knowledge began. Protestantism within Christianity and what is called Islamic fundamentalism can be seen as typical examples of such religious popularization. On the other hand, there were other attempts, from those who valued knowledge closely associated with daily life, to retain some aspects of daily-life knowledge and adapt them to the modern social system and knowledge system. These are defined here as 'alternative knowledge movements' (AKMs); or they could have been named 'alternative technique movements' because of the alternative knowledge in turn is used to adapt practical techniques.

Alternative medicine in the United States

A typical example of an AKM is found in the field of medicine in the United States.[1] From the late 18th century, orthodox medicine gradually gained authority there. Medical doctors were considered to be those who had acquired systematic knowledge based on modern science with which they were able to cure diseases. They were awarded official qualifications upon completing medical school, which was considered to be the sole institution to impart accurate knowledge about the human body's structure and functions. They also formed a strong professional association with governmental authorization.

The view of the human body and health in modern science is based on a reductionist scientific methodology and a dualistic worldview of body and mind. It stresses analytical knowledge of various component organs and their functions, and has a high regard for surgical treatments and the administration of chemically synthesized drugs. A hospital combining modern medicine and a bureaucratic organization represents a social institution based on modern knowledge.

While orthodox medicine was taking the path of progress, various alternative medicines emerged seeking authority in knowledge other than modern medicine. Thomsonianism (using herbal medicine), hydropathy (employing the healing effects of water), Grahamism (maintaining health by regulating one's meat intake) and chiropractic medicine and osteopathy to reposition distorted bones and joints are some examples. The efficacy or the reason for these therapies cannot be verified fully by scientific methods. Therefore, the knowledge cherished by the users of these therapies has not yet been incorporated into modern science. Among the general public, however, many believe in their efficacy, and place great expectations on these therapies.

AKMs and religion

As seen in medicine, AKMs evolve in parallel to prevalent modern knowledge, as an antithesis or a supplement to modern knowledge.[2] There may be an underlying discontent with modern knowledge, or awareness of its faults. Those who are negatively affected by modernization often consider modern knowledge to be the source of a power that destroys the traditional order of life. Modern knowledge causes emotional anxiety and leads to fierce opposition. The discontented may insist on a return to tradition, or they may find their outlet in religious or spiritual movements that emphasize relief experiences. Another strategy to resist modern knowledge, or to supplement it on the practical level of daily life, is the AKM.

The religious movement and the AKM in modern or contemporary society can be classified into different categories. However, the border between the two is ambiguous; there is a wide overlapping area. Some religious movements are found to have the nature of AKMs while some AKMs are seen to have the characteristics of religious movements, or some AKMs have philosophies with strong religious overtones. The 'religion' that overlaps with AKMs is more deeply associated with the religious concepts and practices of common people than with the orthodox doctrine and rituals of traditional religions. The AKM has much in common with popular religions such as syncretic folk cults and new religious movements. It is the world of culture and knowledge linked with practices in community living.[3]

Before modern times, such a world existed in relative stability, retaining a certain autonomy despite being affected by orthodox religions. It was the world of oral transmission termed 'small tradition' by Redfield (1956), and the world of folk knowledge and folk religion that folklore scholarship of Japan has been exploring. However, with the progress of modernization, the world of folk knowledge and folk religions has undergone an extensive interaction with written knowledge. The written knowledge of traditional and orthodox religions has also intervened in the world of folk knowledge and religions. Both AKMs and religious movements, including modern new religious movementss and syncretic folk cults, appear to be developing from the interaction of three kinds of knowledge: (1) the folk tradition of community life practices; (2) orthodox religious knowledge; and (3) new written knowledge influenced by modern knowledge.

Alternative knowledge and modern knowledge

As previously stated, religions and AKMs in modern Japan share a feeling of discontent with modern society. But it is not sufficient to see in such emotional discontent the motivation behind AKMs. Alternative knowledge is based on an intuitive insight into misgivings regarding modern knowledge, resulting in strong popular support for alternative movements. Modern knowledge advocates universal reason that is free from context (knowledge applicable to any time, opportunity and person), and tends to emphasize systematization, certainty and rigidity. In order to ensure these elements, specialization tends to occur in modern knowledge. Although impartiality is the goal, in reality modern knowledge is often used to serve the needs of modern states and industries, and above all, economic efficiency. AKMs can also be defined as those movements that criticize the shortcomings of modern knowledge, and that try to adapt intuitive knowledge developed through daily community life to a new modern living environment.

An important difference between modern knowledge and alternative knowledge is that the latter values usefulness in community life. For reasons of practicality and utility, perception of the delicate balance and harmony between objects, between humans and objects, and between humans is considered important. The total, sustained experiences of a person acquired through the activities of the whole body and mind are highly valued. Holistic perception achieved by contextual and participatory attitudes, by sense perception such as 'inspiration' and by cultivated skill, are preferred to non-contextual, universal rationality and the systematic and rigorous accumulation of segmented knowledge. As such, perception cannot be formulated clearly in written form, it is recommended that one should participate and learn it experientially. This concept of holistic knowledge that is acquired empirically and that is applicable to daily experiences in the community is often lacking in modern knowledge.

Certain common tendencies are to be noted in the worldviews of many AKMs. A noticeable feature is that they challenge both the modern dualistic view of seeing spirit and nature, and mind and body as separate entities, and the mechanistic view of nature and body. Against such a dualistic, mechanistic view of nature and body, AKMs present a worldview that stresses organic relations between various elements, and the harmony of all; in other words, a world view that leads to monism and holism. They consider human beings not as outside nature but as a part of nature that must live in harmony with it.

In the sphere of society and morality, AKMs are distinctive in highlighting utility, and the need for interdependence and mutual care as opposed to modern individualism and social and moral ideas that are based on a transcendental norm. They advocate a social and moral worldview with a high respect for harmony with others and the whole. In short, a tendency widely observed in the thought systems presented by AKMs in their views of nature and morality is the concept of interdependence, a holistic harmony among living things.

AKMs in modern Japan

In modern Japan, a number of AKMs have been initiated and receive popular support. In comparison with the United States and European countries, Japan has many more AKMs with large numbers of participants and sympathizers. Another distinct feature of Japanese movements is that many of them have religious orientations. What explains these features?

One reason is that in Japan modern knowledge was seen as imported knowledge and, therefore, originally alien to the people. It was regarded as knowledge of Western origin, unfamiliar to the culture. Hence, from the early period of modernization, there was a strong tendency to foster knowledge suitable to Japanese tradition. The worldviews of Buddhism, Confucianism, Shinto and folk religions incline to non-dualist and non-mechanical thinking. A great portion of the nation shared the idea that they should develop methodologies of medicine, health promotion, diet, farming, education, management and so on of their own that were to be different from Western knowledge, while maintaining the generally recognized 'Eastern' or 'Japanese' traditions.[4] Although 'Western' knowledge was dominant in social life, there were times, such as during the Second World War, when 'overcoming modernity' was part of the mainstream thought of the nation.

The second reason is the characteristic of Japanese religious culture that admits pluralism in concept and practice, instead of one authorized religion prevailing among the population. This characteristic enables people-led religions and cultural organizations to be formed quite easily. In societies dominated by Catholicism and Islam, movements advocating folk knowledge that is different from the knowledge system of the traditional, organized religions are considered to be heterodox and dangerous. In such societies, folk religious groups can scarcely be formed outside the orthodox religions in the process of rationalization of society. People's knowledge movements, if any, are either incorporated into the orthodox system, or suppressed as being anti- or non-orthodox.

In contrast, there exists no dominant orthodox religious organization in Japan. Since early in Japan's history, diverse religions, sects and syncretic religious groups have coexisted. From this multi-religious climate, a number of religious groups founded and supported by common people, such as new religious movements, have emerged in modern times.[5] These popular religions full of folk cultural elements share a monistic and holistic cosmic view closer to nature religion, rather than the dualistic view of the historic religions. The degree of interrelatedness between religious knowledge and daily-life knowledge is high. AKMs are likely to gain popular support in environments receptive to popular religions. As a syncretic culture closely related to day-to-day knowledge is dominant in such an environment, AKMs could easily grow along with the development of new religious movements and other popular religions.

Alternative agriculture and its Japanese version

Alternative knowledge in production and nourishment

AKMs are often based on people's concern about the 'usefulness' of placing an importance on the mutual dependence of all living beings. The most familiar activity closest to each individual's consciousness is the working of one's own body. In this sense, it is natural that alternative knowledge has developed with the greatest diversity in the field of the human body, notably in medicine and health. Health, food and nourishment are closely related. Thus, AKMs have often shown an interest in food, and developed knowledge about what is good nourishment. Natural food movements and vegetarian movements occupy important positions in AKMs. Concerns about food and nourishment lead as a matter of course to concern about food production. Among food production industries, agriculture in a wider sense, including livestock breeding, is questioned. Hence, agriculture has been the focus of interest for many AKMs.

However, it is not only because agriculture is closely related to health that alternative movements have developed in the field of agriculture. Another important reason is that agriculture is an activity carried out upon animals and plants in the natural environment. In agriculture, human beings are required to nourish the life of animals and plants with their hands, and to intervene with and control their delicate life processes. Agriculture is an act of intervention into the interdependent life system of the earth, and for this reason, it is a sphere of production activity in which the limits of modern knowledge are revealed most distinctively.

Optimum nourishment is a requirement for the health of humans to grow and maintain their lives; on the other hand, it is a requirement for production to breed and maintain the life of animals and plants in order to have them serve the needs of humans. Furthermore, it is related to environmental conservation to sustain the ecology of the earth embracing humans, animals and plants. Agriculture as a nourishing activity involves nourishing the environment as a whole in addition to nourishing humans, animals and plants. Because it touches the life process at various phases, agriculture has become a proper arena for the development of alternative knowledge.

Development of alternative agriculture in the world

Alternative agriculture aims to produce good quality food with high productivity, yet without using agricultural chemicals and chemical fertilizers, which are the products of modern knowledge. This method has been advocated since the 1920s and 1930s when the use of chemical fertilizers and agricultural chemicals spread rapidly in Europe and North America after the First World War, and when soil erosion was recognized as a serious problem in the United States.[6]

An early example of alternative agriculture movements in Europe is the Bio-Dynamic Farming of Rudolf Steiner in the 1920s. Steiner's alternative agriculture movement is based on his mystical religious philosophy. In this sense, it has points in common with many Japanese alternative agriculture movements. There are a few more examples of alternative agriculture with religious inclinations in Europe. In Britain and France, however, alternative agriculture movements based on rational knowledge are dominant.

It was the educational activities of Albert Howard after the 1930s that strongly influenced the spread of alternative agriculture movements based on rational knowledge. Brought up in a farming family, Howard became a plant pathologist. While engaged in plant pathological research, he became skeptical of modern 'conventional agriculture' that used a great deal of chemical fertilizers and agricultural chemicals. He observed agricultural production in India and the Caribbean islands and recognized the importance of nourishing the soil. After his long-term field survey in Indore, India, he devised the 'Indore Process,' which aimed to raise productivity by maintaining the fertility of the soil using compost and barnyard manure and doing away with chemical fertilizers and agricultural chemicals. *Agricultural Testament*, which he published in 1940, exerted an impact on many people throughout the world. Inspired by this book, J. I. Rodale published his own work on organic agriculture in 1945, and since then, has been engaged in spreading this alternative agricultural process in the United States (Howard 1940, Rodale 1945).

Howard and other advocates of alternative agriculture have been critical of agricultural research based on modern science. According to them, modern scientific agricultural researchers are looking at agriculture from a narrow, specialized viewpoint without an eye to the whole picture, and their research has no relevance to actual farming practices. They see that such an agricultural process would result in damaging the health of both humans and the natural environment.

Howard gave the name 'natural agriculture' to the way wild animals and plants nourish each other in forests, and showed, in a practical manner, that his agricultural process to maintain soil fertility would do minimum damage to the 'wheel of life.' In his process, interdependence of life and holistic thinking are stressed, but there are no religious overtones. Howard is critical of Steiner who pushes forward religious thought and proposes an organic agricultural process on weak rational grounds.

Alternative agriculture in Japan

Alternative agriculture had already been attempted in the 1930s in Japan by some people, probably influenced by reports from Europe and the United States about alternative agriculture movements or criticisms of modern agriculture (Kume 1983, Fukuoka 1983). There were few examples of alternative agriculture movements such as that of Howard, based on academic, rational knowledge, but some movements with strong religious elements did develop. Since the early 1970s, when the issue of environmental conservation attracted public attention, rational alternative agriculture has been gaining strength, but religious agricultural movements still exert most influence. Before the 1970s, religiously oriented movements were in the mainstream of alternative agriculture in Japan.

Two major streams existed in the religious alternative agriculture movement in Japan before 1945. One is 'no-fertilizer agriculture,' later renamed 'natural agriculture,' advocated by Okada Mokichi, the founder of Sekai Kyūseikyō (the Church of World Messianity) (Sekai Kyūseikyo Inc., 1981). Sekai Kyūseikyō criticizes modern Western medicine, and medication in particular; healing by raising a hand above the affected parts of the body is the main pillar of belief. Therefore, this religious organization is also seen as an alternative medicine movement believing in the natural healing function of the body. In the same way as it vetoed the use of medication, this group began advocating and practicing farming methods that respect the function of the soil, nourishing life using only compost, and no agricultural chemicals or chemical fertilizers.

Another movement, 'enzymatic agriculture,' tries to fertilize soil by the action of enzymes secreted by germs under the ground (Shimamoto Kakuya 1984). This method was promoted during the Second World War by Shibata Kinshi, born of a brewer's family, who tried to apply the action of enzymes in food processing to farming. Shibata was a religious person who saw divinity in enzymes and worshipped them, calling each 'My Venerable Enzyme.' But it was only after a follower of Ōmoto, a new religion, became fascinated with this process that enzymatic agriculture became a more sustainable process. This follower, Shimamoto Kakuya (1899–1974), called the enzymatic farming process by another name, 'microbiological agriculture,' and established it as an effective alternative agriculture after long years of research and practice. His work is now continued by his son, Shimamoto Kunihiko (1928–), who is energetically extending the method to wider areas both in Japan and elsewhere. In the following section we turn to a discussion of the microbiological agriculture promoted by Shimamoto Kakuya.

A case study of alternative agriculture in Japan: Shimamoto Kakuya and microbiological agriculture

Shimamoto Kakuya's grandfather, Benji, was a warrior (samurai) serving the Minakuchi Clan in Shiga prefecture. When the warriors' class was abolished at the time of the Meiji Restoration, Benji started as a malted rice supplier taking advantage of his wife Nui's knowledge of brewing, which as a daughter of a brewer she had learned at home.[7] Malted rice is developed by propagating rice mould, which is then applied to rice, wheat and soya beans. It contains various enzymes and is used as a starter to brew Japanese rice wine, soya bean sauce, soya bean paste and many other food materials. In 1899, the Liquor Tax Law was enforced whereby private rice wine production was prohibited and the demand for malted rice dropped drastically, causing Benji to give up his business. The family moved to the large city of Nagoya, where they started a tofu (soya bean curd) shop. Kakuya himself grew up in Nagoya and worked for a while in a doll-making workshop, later becoming a successful confectionery company owner. In the process, he acquired artisan skills in tofu making, glasswork and confectionery. As a confectioner he developed his knowledge about the enzymes contained in saliva.

Kakuya developed a greater interest in religion after he suffered a major injury. He became affiliated to a Shintoist group, Dai Nippon Hokokai, led by Mizuno Mau'nen, and devoted himself to reading the *Kojiki*, the mythological story about the history of ancient Japan. In 1940, he converted to Shinto from Buddhism. In 1945, he met one of the founders of Ōmoto, Deguchi Onisaburō (1871–1948), the Sacred Master (*Seishi*). Fascinated by him, he became a member of the organization. Onisaburō emphasized the importance of agriculture. Partially influenced by Onisaburō, Kakuya returned to the family home in Minakuchi in Shiga prefecture and began farming after the end of the Second World War. There, he developed an interest in Shibata's enzymatic agriculture, to which Onisaburō had referred many times, and attempted to put the process into practice.

Enzymatic agriculture involves the nurturing of rich compost and using the enzymes secreted by micro-organisms in the compost to fertilize the soil, and, whenever possible, avoiding the use of chemical fertilizers and other agricultural chemicals to grow crops. Advocates of this method consider the soil to be a living thing and believe that by enriching its fertility, they can harvest tasty products that are free from harmful materials. In order to nurture the soil and to give it vitality, farmers should learn both the theory and the practice of how to grow effective micro-organisms in the ground. In addition to scientific experiments and analyses, the accumulation of knowledge through on-the-farm experience is essential. For a long period of time, the Shimamoto father and son undertook research and trials to devise theories and techniques to fertilize soil until they established what is called Shimamoto Microbiologic Agriculture.

This farming method was developed and extended through Aizen Mizuhokai, a group of farmers organized by Ōmoto followers. Later, the group was separated from the parent religious body, and a corporate body, Kōso no Sekaisha (The World of Enzymes, Inc.) was founded with Shimamoto Kakuya himself as its president. The organization devotes itself to technical development and its dissemination. Many of the members from farmers' groups in their local areas are making concerted efforts to increase productivity under the leadership of Shimamoto Kakuya's son Kunihiko and other outreach workers. Seminars held at the headquarters in Minakuchi provide the members with the opportunity of learning newly developed knowledge and techniques. Its monthly journal *Kōso no Sekai* (The World of Enzymes) serves as an information and communication network uniting the 3500 members.

The knowledge and techniques of this farming method are quite complicated and require a lot of time to learn. As research is always progressing, it is not enough for a farmer to depend on any one technique once mastered. In order to adapt techniques properly to various soil conditions, climates and the marketing and distribution systems, mutual information exchanges and teaching and learning among farmers are necessary. This is one reason why this microbiological agriculture movement is organized under a strong leadership.

Applications of microbiological agricultural techniques and food processing technologies

The main feature of Shimamoto Kakuya's microbiological agriculture is the development of nutrient-rich soil that fosters the growth of plants by activating the work of the micro-organisms in the soil, thereby ensuring that those nutrients that plants and animals take from the soil are effectively renewed. In other words, it tries to achieve a high yield of crops by making and applying fertile compost and barnyard manure from organic materials such as crop residue to farmland. The group excels in the technique of making compost by using sawdust, and is able to mass-produce compost at low cost.

The main points of the knowledge and techniques the group develops and adopts are how micro-organisms are cultivated, and to what and how they are applied. Members study soil chemistry and microbiology so as to apply their knowledge to practical farming. Therefore, scientific knowledge and techniques based on modern science are further important components of Shimamoto's agriculture. On the other hand, the knowledge and techniques of traditional processing techniques to make good food using micro-organisms such as rice mould and yeast as starters of fermentation are also valued.

Shimamoto considered the fact that techniques to process rice wine, soya bean paste, and soya bean sauce by applying rice mould and yeast to rice and soya beans and other raw materials were using the action of enzymes secreted by micro-organisms. Enzymes also play important roles in digesting food within the human body. Therefore, enzymes were considered to be key elements in the process of production and intake of food. Enzymes work when organic materials nourish other creatures and help them maintain and activate their life. In the early days of his movement, Shimamoto said 'Enzymes nurture the life of all living things in the universe. It is love that nurtures, and love leads to the good and truth. This is "the Way of enzyme" and not "a method of enzyme"' (Shimamoto Kakuya 1949: 5).

Shimamoto aimed to encourage enzymes to work in soil just as they act in food processing and in the human body. Just as rice mould is applied to rice and soya beans to cause fermentation in order to make food, he tried to activate the work of enzymes by applying mould to the organic residues of plants and animals and also to soil. He produced a fermentation starter called an 'enzyme breeder' and applied this to sawdust to prepare compost. In addition, he processed many other materials and applied them to the soil and fallen leaves, believing that by so doing the fertility of the soil was maintained and even enhanced by preventing the increase of harmful insects and ensuring that good crops are harvested. He also made enzyme products to be eaten as food. According to his philosophy, micro-organisms and enzymes intervene at all stages to sustain and nourish life, and work as an important element in (food) production activities.

The Shimamoto worldview: Setting a high value on soil and agriculture

Many farmers maintain membership in Kōso no Sekai, Inc. partially for the purpose of learning complicated and elaborate knowledge and techniques. But it is not the only reason. Kōso no Sekai, Inc. has another side to it as a spiritual or religious movement. On the front page of *Kōso no Sekai*, slogans are printed under the heading 'The cause of true agriculture': 'If the root is not nourished well, the extremities will never prosper. Realize that it is soil preparation and root cultivation that constitute the basic foundation for plant growth'; 'Agriculture is the root of a nation, and the greatest authority for all humankind. When agriculture is controlled well, the nation prospers, and when food is properly given, people can live in peace.' This religiosity of the corporation is deeply related to the belief in Ōmoto of Shimamoto Kakuya and Kunihiko. Ōmoto teaches people to see divinity in soil and to respect it as one of the three elements of the universe together with fire and water. Shimamoto Kakuya was taught by Deguchi Onisaburō's wife Sumi (1883–1952), the Second Matriarch of Ōmoto. Sumi insisted on the need to venerate the soil. In Kakuya's biography (Shimamoto Kunihiko 1984), Sumi's poems are quoted: 'Even if you are grateful to heaven, if you fail to thank soil, it is as though you have forgotten your own mother'; 'All living things in the world are born from soil'; 'Every person is born from soil, lives on soil, receives benefits from soil, and hides themselves in soil.'

Shimamoto Kakuya placed a special emphasis on the veneration of soil in the faith of Ōmoto, and preached this in relation to the significance of agriculture:

Soil is the mother of the life of all. Soil is in possession of power to cause all things in the universe to live and grow. Soil is God, God is soil. Soil has self-contained properties and ever-generating and developing properties. Soil has power to raise all things, and it is always active with minerals, organic matters, micro-organisms, and enzymes within. The elements for its activity are sunshine, carbon, oxygen, hydrogen and nitrogen...In other words, sunshine, carbon, hydrogen and water nurture the mould that feeds micro-organisms in the soil, and they make soil foster the growth of all plants – soil helps all things to grow and it produces all things. That is, human beings are able to live, thanks to soil. Here, we may see the truth of the statement 'Thank the moon, the sun and soil; soil is the mother of all life.' Agriculture is respected because it has its base in soil. Agriculture is a vocation to harmonize with nature, to love soil, get friendly with soil, nourish soil and cultivate soil. This should be the aim of agriculture. Agriculture that goes against the law of generation and development of nature will, quite simply, perish. Prudent application of science to the law of generation and development of nature is the right course to follow. Observe this truth, follow this rule, and certain happiness awaits us. (Shimamoto Kakuya 1975: 161–63)

Shimamoto Kakuya's moral and religious thought

Ōmoto is a new religious movement founded in 1899, inheriting the traditions of Shinto and folk religion. Shimamoto joined the organization, studied the Ōmoto doctrine and was strongly influenced by it. However, in his books and writings in the magazine *Kōso no Sekai*, he states his own moral view and religious view in his own words, although they are not far from the Ōmoto doctrine. They describe the spiritual atmosphere in which his alternative agriculture has been extended. They can be summarized as follows:[8]

Good agriculture means to nourish the source of life, that is, soil; therefore, it should have its foundation in soil preparation. To prepare good soil, the development of good persons is essential. And to develop a good personality, a good spirit must be developed. To develop a good spirit in a person, morality and religious sentiments must be cultivated.

A person cannot live by him or herself. Everyone has a source of life and is able to live because of this. The source of life for all individuals is our parents and ancestors. If we trace our ancestors far back to their origins, we reach God, the origin of all beings. A person's daily life is also supported by the earth and other gifts of this great nature. It is the law of generation and development of the great universe that regulates the life of nature and humankind. This is the very manifestation of God. We should revere God as the original source of our ancestors and great nature.

Humans must obey the law of nature; we must perform our missions, and endeavor to develop ourselves to be perfect persons. To live a better life according to the law of nature means to coexist with other living things, including other persons. We must not hate and have a grudge against each other, and we must not get angry. We must keep our minds peaceful and pure. If we carry such an attitude through our life, then we can live a happy life. This is not the teaching of a specific religion, but it is the common goal of all religions. Religious self-assertion in favor of one's own God is not desirable.

There is a nationalistic or ethnocentric element in his ideas. Again, the following is my summary of this element.

The above concept and the way of living is a long-cherished Japanese way of life carried over from ancient times. Japan is a country where belief and daily life are kept in harmony and where people live feeling the presence of God in their lives. Japan is a nation with a stronger peace-loving spirit than any other nation of the world. Such a spirit is clearly expressed in the family system respecting the head of the family, and in the ancestor-worship tradition. It has naturally developed through our practices. Being a grain-eating nation whose diet consists mainly of rice and little meat is an indication of peace-loving spirit.

Shimamoto's thought is shared not only by Ōmoto but by many other new religious movements, especially by syncretic Shintoist groups. Nonetheless, not all members of Kōso no Sekai, Inc. are in agreement with this religiosity. In fact, since Shimamoto Kakuya's death, the movement's religious and nationalist aspects have been reduced. But still, as of 1994, about ten percent of the members are estimated to have faith in Ōmoto and it retains a powerful influence within the movement.

AKMs and modern society

AKMs and their interrelations

In this paper, the new concept of 'alternative knowledge movement' has been proposed as a tool for understanding cultural and social movements that aim to oppose modern knowledge or make up for its faults. AKMs cover many aspects of social life, such as productive, reproductive and other activities. Here, agriculture is taken as an example.

Shimamoto's alternative agriculture has points in common with new religious movements, and faith in Ōmoto by the Shimamoto father and son was the driving force that sustained their passionate activity. It must not be forgotten, however, that Shimamoto developed his movement in collaboration with other AKMs. He knew of a natural food movement that had been in existence since the turn of the century, and he was clearly influenced by it. As illustrated by producing and marketing products containing enzymes, his movement is also intended to be a natural food movement. While engaged in the propagation of microbiological agriculture, he co-organized seminars on health and agriculture with Shibata Sumihiro of Nippon Chōseikai (The Japanese Longevity Society), who advocated a spinal correction therapy. Both AKMs can be categorized as movements respecting a Japanese tradition based on a nature-revering religious concept.

Alternative movements are extremely diverse in kind, and some are even in conflict. They criticize and supplement the defects they find in modern knowledge, and develop their knowledge and techniques at the actual sites of practice, the fruits of which often turn out to have common points. In addition, not a few of the movements collaborated in their evolution, for they have some shared views of nature and the world. In Japan, the common ground for these AKMs was provided by traditional religions including Shinto, folk religions, and new religious movements based on the traditional religions.

AKMs and new spirituality movements

After the 1970s, imperfections in modern knowledge were widely recognized in academia and journalism in industrialized countries, and an interest in alternative knowledge grew. In various academic fields, efforts have been made to review the knowledge that was part of alternative knowledge or religious knowledge and to incorporate it into science. Transpersonal psychology and holistic medicine are typical examples. In Japan, the Society for Mind-Body Science was founded in 1991 and has been engaged in 'scientific research' into 'gi-vital energy' (omnipresent in the universe, including the human body, activated by the art of trained abdominal breathing). While asserting their activities to be scientific, a religious concept is also included. Therefore, this society is also understood as an new religious movement, part of the religious culture.

These movements applying science to alternative knowledge can be seen as offshoots of new religious movements or new trends in religious culture. In Europe and the United States, they are known as New Age movement; in Japan, 'Spiritual World' (*Seishin Sekai*). It may be said that a new global religious culture has emerged, but in slightly different forms in different regions. The author has named this global trend the 'new spirituality movements and culture.'[9] In this new religious culture, religious knowledge is not considered to belong to a transcendental dimension away from the perception of nature; rather, it is insisted that divinity can be found in nature, which is the object of scientific perception. It sounds like a revival of nature religion or nature theology.

New spirituality movements often insist that they seek a new kind of knowledge in which religion and science can be in accord with each other. What is called 'new science' or 'New Age science' is an attempt to prove these assertions as concrete scientific achievements. Such assertions and attempts bear similarities to those of AKMs in the recent past. A notable similarity is found in the attempts to seek a perception of nature beyond a modern dualistic and mechanistic view.

In spite of the aspirations of AKMs and New Age science, many of them (recall the example of healing techniques) find difficulty in incorporating alternative knowledge into science as it is. One reason might be that alternative knowledge has elements that do not go well with elements such as accuracy, rigidity and universal validity that modern knowledge aspires. Alternative knowledge tends to depend on a person's holistic intuition of the body and mind, or often it is linked with community life practices. It is difficult to adapt these factors to the rules of modern science. In addition, contemporary science as part of modern knowledge can hardly step outside the framework of the economic and social systems of contemporary society. In particular, knowledge and those techniques that do not respond to the demand for efficiency under a capitalist market economy will not be accepted as orthodox knowledge.

The future for AKMs

Nonetheless, the possibility of alternative knowledge being integrated with the orthodox knowledge system, or replacing modern knowledge, cannot be completely ruled out. Alternative agriculture drew public attention afresh in the 1970s when concerns about environmental issues were heightened. In some European and North American countries, certain support systems for alternative agriculture (organic agriculture) are being created (Nakamura 1992, Fukushi et al. 1992). Agriculture using chemical fertilizers and agricultural chemicals still enjoys the advantage of supplying less expensive food. When problems such as soil erosion and the safety of food become a matter of grave concern, and when soil fertility and food safety are given priority over economic efficiency, then a greater portion of alternative agriculture techniques may be adopted as orthodox agricultural methods.

A similar indication can be found in the field of health. In Japan, for example, health promotion and medical treatment using acupuncture had long been considered incompatible with orthodox medicine and was practiced as a type of alternative medicine. But as its efficacy has been gradually recognized, a few medical institutions are applying it along with modern Western medicine. There may be other examples of alternative knowledge being incorporated into modern knowledge, hence, becoming part of the orthodox knowledge system.

On the other hand, the rise of something like alternative knowledge in contemporary society must also be viewed in terms of commercialization. Knowledge that has developed as alternative knowledge now has more of a chance of being sold as a commercial product. In such a case, alternative knowledge is separated from its source and is made an object of consumerism. A postmodernist view of the world in which science and religion are combined has much to do with the commercialization of new nature-controlling technologies, and mental and physical controlling technologies.

In this chapter, only one case in Japan was briefly examined. Comparative studies of alternative agriculture and other forms of AKMs in various parts of the world will reveal unknown aspects of the views of nature, life, body, morality, production and nourishment harbored by people in the modern and contemporary world.

11 From Religion to Psychotherapy

The concept of psychotherapeutic religion

Although Bryan Wilson's theory of sectarian movements was first established on the basis of examples taken from Western Christianity in the modern period, he has further expanded and applied it beyond these limits to the non-Western and non-Christian world. His book *Magic and the Millennium* (1973) is the fruit of this endeavor. He deals with religious movements in various parts of the world, but his main attention seems focused on movements in relatively simple societies that have experienced external pressures. Japan is not mentioned. This does not mean, however, that Wilson is not interested in the new religious movements of that country. Indeed, in *Religious Sects* (1970), a slightly older work, he devotes quite a few pages to a description of Japan's new religions. As a student of Japan's new religions, I would like to offer a few comments on Wilson's view of sects. It is not my intention, however, to argue about the extent to which his attempts at theorization have succeeded as a whole. I shall deal with only one part of his typology, and, focusing on one specific Japanese example, try to develop Wilson's insights a little further into a more universally applicable theory.

In *Religious Sects* Wilson states that many of Japan's new religions belong either to the thaumaturgical or to the manipulationist type of sect.[1] Although he presents their founders and successors as thaumaturges, these sects are typically closer to the manipulationist type in his opinion. As a preliminary step in my discussion, I shall try to apply his typology of sects to Japan's new religions. According to Wilson, both the manipulationist and the thaumaturgical types of sect are principally concerned with problems of health and other kinds of this worldly benefits.[2] Admittedly, millenarianism, social reform, and utopian community are also objects of attention in Japan's new religions, but healing and other this-worldly benefits constitute the main point of interest. Wilson's view that the majority of Japan's new religions belong to the manipulationist or thaumaturgical types is therefore basically correct. But the problem remains of deciding under which of the two – manipulationist or thaumaturgical – it is appropriate to classify them. I will focus particularly on the concept of manipulationist sects in this chapter; but in order to arrive at a correct understanding of the situation in Japan, I must give some thought to the question of how to modify this concept.

According to Wilson, sects of the manipulationist type seek salvation in the here and now. Salvation is not something to be attained in another world after death, in an afterlife. It does not consist in a transcendental state completely separated from this world's environment and from the present state of body and mind. Ongoing happiness in this world in the form of, for example, good health, prosperity, and success is believed to pass for salvation. Therefore, unlike many other types of sects, manipulationist sects do not think that the present world is essentially evil. Of course, they believe in the existence of evil; but in their view, it is perfectly possible to eliminate evil from this world. The cosmos is intrinsically harmonious, and human beings are expected to live happily in harmony with the cosmos.

Evil derives from people's false thoughts. It is therefore possible to do away with evil and unhappiness by changing people's way of thinking. Indeed, manipulationist sects teach what false thoughts are and how to change them. They offer people not objective moral norms but new modes of thought. They do not want to change the world, but to change the way in which people relate to the world. Although this change, which comes about through faith, is subjective, it is thought that the individual's objective situation also changes for the better as a result. The label 'manipulationist' is given to this type of sect precisely because it wants to change people's fate by means of subjective changes.

Many sects develop in metropolitan centers, where relationships are impersonal and dominated by role performance. Right thinking constitutes a sophisticated mode of thought in manipulationist sects, involving abstract ideas and methods of intellectual analysis considered appropriate for coping with complicated human relationships in modern city life. The adherents of such sects are, characteristically, city dwellers and individualistic. They detest restraints on their freedom, and are not too keen to establish communities of believers.

A typical example of older manipulationst sects is Christian Science, which drew heavily on the Christian tradition. Later on, however, sects of this type became increasingly syncretistic. For example, there were many deviations from orthodox Christianity in New Thought and Positive Thinking, and groups like the Theosophical Society and the

Vedanta Society found much of their inspiration in Asian religion. More recently established manipulationist sects include Scientology, which has adopted much from depth psychology, and groups which show a strong interest in UFOs.

The distinction between the manipulationist and thaumaturgical types depends on whether the emphasis is on intellectual refinement or on an unsophisticated faith in miracles. Thaumaturgical religion is most evident in less developed societies, and is said to be devoid of complicated teachings. Spiritualism is included in the thaumaturgical type, but Christian Science and the Theosophical Society, which developed their respective teachings under the influence of Spiritualism, are considered to be manipulationist.

A number of Japan's new religions fit into Wilson's manipulationist type as summarized above; or at least, they resemble it closely. Such religions include Seichō no Ie and Hito no Michi Kyōdan (which subsequently became PL Kyōdan). However, there are others which differ somewhat from this type, such as Tenrikyō, Ōmoto, and Sōka Gakkai. The question therefore arises of the way in which Japanese new religions that resemble the manipulationist type differ from the other groups.

A further examination shows that while in Japan's new religions some of the characteristics of manipulationist sects are widely evident, others are not so widely present. Generally present are the notion and affirmation of salvation in this world, together with the idea that the cosmos and the relationship between the cosmos and human beings is basically harmonious (Tsushima et al. 1979). If these aspects of the characteristics of such sects are emphasized, we have to admit that almost all of Japan's new religions belong to the manipulationist type. Religions which correspond closely to the movements characterized by Wilson as manipulationist sects are called 'harmonial religions' by Sydney Ahlstrom (1972), and most of Japan's new religions qualify as such.

On the other hand, there are some characteristics of the manipulationist type that are conspicuous in Seichō no Ie and Hito no Michi Kyōdan, but are not so frequently seen in other religious groups, such as changing one's way of thinking, or 'thought switching'.[3] Evil and unhappiness originate from false thinking, according to these groups, and the core of their teaching is that by changing one's thinking, one's fate is also changed and happiness is achieved. Most of Japan's new religions pay considerable attention to changing people's fate in the present world. As a means to this end, some offer magical practices, prayers, and rituals. Others stress ethical behavior in life, missionary work, or public service. However, in Seichō no Ie and Hito no Michi Kyōdan, the emphasis is on changing one's ideas, rather than on other things. Of course, since 'changing one's ideas' is closely connected in many cases with deepening one's faith and with carrying out various practices, it is also to some extent a feature of types of religious groups that differ from Seichō-no-Ie and Hito-no-Michi. Yet, the most important feature of these two new religions is their insistence that changing one's ideas itself brings about a change of fate.

The belief that changing one's ideas can improve one's fate has replaced the traditional religious belief that improvement can come about only through the intervention of a transcendental power. Whereas formerly one prayed for healing through the power of the divine, healing is now to be achieved through thought-switching. This change has come about partly because in the present situation belief in the divine has become increasingly difficult, and partly because the credibility of the claim that changing one's ideas really does have a beneficent impact on life also seems to play a role in this. In the complex relationships that characterize modern society there is a great danger that psychic instability, caused by anxiety and fear of unknown people, will prevent adjustment. In such circumstances, a change of ideas can adroitly regulate the human psyche and thereby change social life for the better. A rationalistic way of thinking and a pragmatic conception of mental processes are widely found in this type of religion. Wilson's argument that manipulationist sects develop in urban society, in which human relationships are complex and impersonal, can be more easily understood when we take into account that this is so because complex and impersonal human relationships require the objectivization and technical manipulation of the mind.

A variety of Japan's new religions display these kinds of characteristics, but the concept of manipulationist sects does not adequately account for this aspect. We could call the missing aspect 'psychotherapeutic,' since, as mentioned above, religions which aim at changing one's ideas try to cope with the problems of the heart in a pragmatic, technical way, and have many features of secular psychotherapy. We could say that, with the spread of psychotherapy and psychological thinking, elements of psychotherapy have gradually been adopted by religion as well. It has become difficult to accept a divine, transcendental commander, so to speak, and absolute ethical norms in modern society. Instead, an ethical attitude that puts a high value on peace of mind and on adjustment to the environment has become predominant. Philip Rieff (1966) and Robert Bellah and associates (1985) have described this attitude as 'therapeutic.'[4] In their view, the modern era reveals an ongoing process whereby the symbol system that solves ethical problems shifts from religion to psychotherapy. Some sects of the manipulationist type manifest this kind of therapeutic attitude to such a degree that it is justifiable to refer to them as 'psychotherapeutic religions.' It may be possible to acquire a deeper insight into some of the phenomena that have occurred in Japan's recent religious history if we use this concept of psychotherapeutic religion instead of that of a manipulationist sect.

In the next section I will introduce a system of thought and practice that was established in Japan around the middle of the twentieth century and that can be located somewhere between religion and psychotherapy. Although it is not generally considered to be a new religious movement, it has close resemblances to such, and is therefore a fitting focus for a study of the relationship between religion and psychotherapy in Japan. By investigating this concrete example, I hope to unearth clues regarding the extent to which various phenomena that we can call 'psychotherapeutic religions' have developed.

Yoshimoto Naikan

The psychotherapeutic method called 'Yoshimoto Naikan' which is operative in present-day Japan has attracted the attention of psychologists and psychiatrists as a practice rooted in Japanese culture. The creator of this method, Yoshimoto Ishin, simply called it *naikan*, or 'method of inner observation.' But since this term is also used to designate other things, the practice in question is now called Yoshimoto Naikan, after the name of its creator, in order to avoid confusion.[5]

This practical method of therapy consists mainly in being confined for a week in a small space of about one square meter, screened off from others by a folding partition, so that one can reflect deeply on one's past relationships with other people. The Naikan client is supposed to sit all day from 5 a.m. until 9 p.m. in this secluded corner, except for meals and visits to the toilet. He or she engages in intensive meditation (*naikan*), and has contact only with the *shidō-sha*, or 'counselor,' who pays regular visits. No special sitting posture is prescribed, so the client is permitted to engage in self-reflection in a relaxed way. Three questions provide the content of the reflection: 'What care have I received?', 'What have I done to repay it?', and 'What troubles have I caused in my relations with particular people?' On average, the first two questions each occupy twenty per cent of the time, while sixty per cent is devoted to the third one. In most cases, reflection starts with the relationship with one's mother. Beginning with the first years of elementary school, one gradually moves on, in periods of three years, to the present time. Once reflection on the relationship with one's mother is complete, one proceeds to the relationship with one's father, and then to that with one's brothers and sisters, superiors, teachers, and friends. Sometimes one is also told to reflect on lies told in the past or thefts committed and to calculate the expenses incurred by one's parents for one's education, or even the total amount of money one has spent on drinking.

The counselor visits every hour and a half or two hours, and asks the client what he or she has recalled during that reflection period. If reflection has not proceeded well, the counselor does not stay, but simply recommends that the client continue further with serious introspection. Otherwise, he acknowledges the client's confession and announces the theme for the next Naikan period. The length of the interview is usually no longer than three to five minutes. During meals and at the hours of rising and going to bed, clients listen to audio tapes on which model clients record their reflections. Moreover, since in a typical situation, several clients are meditating in the same room, separated only by folding screens, the general tone, if not the details of the confession made by each client to the counselor, can be heard by others. When the Naikan proceeds well, the client becomes aware of 'how much care he or she has received,' 'how little he or she has paid in return,' and 'how much more he or she has caused trouble.' The client becomes filled, not only with deep feelings of guilt, but also with a sense of gratitude towards other people and starts weeping. On the last day of the session the clients come together, and participate in a colloquium for about an hour.

As of 1983, there were about twenty special places in Japan where Yoshimoto Naikan therapeutic sessions were held. At the Naikan Center in Yamato Kōriyama in Nara Prefecture, where the creator of the Naikan method, Yoshimoto Ishin, conducted interviews as a counselor, about 1300 people underwent treatment in 1982 alone. There are also many hospitals, prisons, reformatories, high schools, and other institutions all over the country where Naikan practices have been adopted. However, if Naikan is practiced only at the special sessions and in groups, the effects quickly evaporate. In order to maintain the benefit, clients ideally have to engage in Naikan every day in their own homes, a practice called 'daily' or 'diffused' Naikan, as distinct from the 'concentrated' Naikan at the sessions. If 'daily Naikan' constitutes the real goal, then 'concentrated Naikan' is but a process of initiation into this psychotherapeutic method. In reality, however, it seems to be quite difficult to keep up the practice of 'daily Naikan'.

Yoshimoto Ishin's books contain some letters from a woman client who sent him a weekly report on her daily Naikan for twenty-three years without a break. As an example of the self-introspection performed in Naikan, I quote here from one of her letters:

> I have been investigating the attitude I have towards my mother. Among the things I received from her I should first mention that my older brother and sister, after leaving school, went to live and work elsewhere. Also my mother, leaving my younger brother and sister in the care of our grandmother, went out to work. But selfish as I am, I did not like to be with my grandmother and I followed my mother. She did the cooking for many craftsmen, but I think she took me with her while caring very much about people's feelings. I have done nothing to repay her. I caused her many troubles. Also at the place where my mother worked I often wandered far away to amuse myself and did not come back until late. I do not know how much a source of anxiety I was to her. Really, I have no excuse for this. (Yoshimoto 1983: 99–100)

Yoshimoto Naikan has become a matter of interest to many psychologists and psychiatrists. Many scientific papers dealing with it as a psychotherapeutic method have been published, and in 1978 an Academic Association for Naikan was established. There are many people who consider Yoshimoto Naikan to be a therapy or cure for neuroses, mental diseases, and social deviance. Yoshimoto died in 1988, but the practice of his Naikan will certainly be continued, not only by his personal followers but primarily by psychologists and psychiatrists.

The development of Yoshimoto Naikan as psychotherapy

The creator of Yoshimoto Naikan, Yoshimoto Ishin, was born in 1916, the third son of a wealthy family that ran a large farm and sold fertilizers in Yamato Kōriyama in Nara Prefecture. His four-year-old sister died from illness in the second year of elementary school. This led his mother to become a fervent member of a temple of the Pure Land Shin sect of Buddhism, and the young boy often accompanied her to listen to Buddhist sermons and the chanting of sutras. After graduating from the horticultural school of Kōriyama at age 17, Ishin started working as a calligraphy teacher and, through his frequent visits to temples, he also became an enthusiastic student of the teachings of the Shin sect. Two years later he was introduced to Morikawa Kinuko, who was to become his wife. Many members of the Morikawa family were ardent supporters of a group of believers, known in the Shin sect for their special brand of faith, who were centered on the Taikan hermitage in Fuse, Osaka Prefecture. Under their influence, Yoshimoto was led to a religious experience that gave direction to the rest of his life.

The Shin sect is the largest sect of Japanese Buddhism. It follows the tradition of the Pure Land school, which believes in salvation after death through the power of Amida Buddha by rebirth in the Western Paradise. The sect was founded by Shinran (1173–1262), who gave a new orientation to this faith in salvation after death. According to the teachings of Pure Land Buddhism, ordinary people do not possess the capacity for attaining Enlightenment or being saved. Amida Buddha vowed to save these weak and desperate beings. In Amida's all-encompassing mercy, he ordained that whoever performs the simple act of reciting the *nenbutsu*, or sacred formula '*namu amida butsu,*' will be saved and reborn in the Pure Land – that is, the ideal world of the Buddhas. In other words, the Pure Land school teaches that human beings cannot be saved by seeking wisdom or by performing ascetic practices through their own efforts (*jiriki*), but only by relying on the saving power of Amida Buddha (*tariki*). Mahayana Buddhism, especially the Pure Land school, stresses salvation from an external source. It was the most powerful tradition in Japanese Buddhism, and Shinran became one of its most famous leaders. By the sixteenth century, Shinran's Pure Land Shin sect had become the largest group, not only within Japanese Pure Land Buddhism, but also within Japanese Buddhism in general. He gave new depth to the idea of salvation by faith and to the teaching that human beings cannot perform any good deeds by themselves. Even reciting the *nenbutsu* or believing in Amida Buddha does not stem from one's own initiative, but are possible only through the power of Amida Buddha. As such, human beings are immersed in evil, and it is not in their nature to be saved. Only when this has been sufficiently recognized, does faith spring up from the bottom of one's heart that Amida Buddha will grant his salvific power, so that, even in life, one may enter the state of being reborn into the Pure Land paradise.

In the movement's early years, Pure Land believers often had doubts about rebirth in the Pure Land after death. This was also the case in the Shin sect. As a result, groups appeared at various times that, in addition to nurturing a thorough awareness of human sinfulness, performed esoteric ascetic practices in order to confirm by means of mystical experiences that they had been saved by Amida Buddha. In the Edo period, many of these groups were called *kakure nenbutsu*, or 'hidden *nenbutsu* believers,' and were suppressed as heretics. But since the Meiji period, they have to a certain extent acquired the right to exist as subgroups within the recognized sects. The group that gathered at the Taikan hermitage in Fuse, a temple founded by Nishimoto Taikan, was one of those which retained a deep faith that esoteric practices would lead to salvation. A practice called *mishirabe*, or 'self-inspection,' was cultivated by the members of this group. In this practice, believers were confined in a small room and required to look back intensively upon their sins, ponder the inescapability of death, and become aware of the fearfulness of hell. Contact with outsiders was forbidden during this practice. Those who were undergoing it, called *byōnin*, or 'patients,' were placed in extreme circumstances, deprived of food, water, and sleep. Believers who had already attained the consciousness of being saved, called *kaigonin*, or 'enlightened ones,' took turns to visit them and urge them on to deeper self-awareness. Thereby, the patients could also achieve the mystical experience of being convinced of their salvation by Amida Buddha. Through this 'experiencing a concentrated mind' (*ichinen ni au*), the patients were believed to be saved, and convinced that they would be reborn in paradise after death (called *shukuzen kaihotsu*, or 'development of the goodness stored in past lives').

Yoshimoto had apparently seen himself as a respectable believer of the Shin sect, and had taught Buddhism to many people. When he met the believers of the Taikan hermitage, however, he lost his self-confidence, and began to think that he was no more than a believer who had acquired some knowledge of Buddhism, but who still lacked a real religious experience. In 1936, at the age of twenty, he therefore took part in the *mishirabe* for the first time. But, haunted by strong doubts about himself, he was not able to gain the conviction of salvation. Concealing this from his father, who opposed the kind of special faith that puts emphasis on secret practices, and after experiencing a similar frustration two or three times, he married Kinuko, whose relatives were associated with Taikan, and finally came to the enlightenment of salvation more than a year after his first *mishirabe*.

From 1938 on, Yoshimoto, who had opened a wholesale leather clothes business in Osaka, used his free evenings for visiting people and propagating the faith of the Taikan hermitage. Taking care of his shop during the day, he succeeded in making his business very prosperous. Within a few years he had established twelve branch stores, and was employing a large staff. He continued as president of his company after contracting tuberculosis in 1949, but finally stopped working in 1953, claiming that business was not his real task but had only been a temporary means of building up the capital necessary for the propagation of faith. He then opened the Naikan Center in Yamato Kōriyama, living off the income from his capital, and devoted all his energy to the diffusion of Naikan therapy.

In the meantime Yoshimoto had initiated various reforms in the faith of the Taikan hermitage. Opposition had been growing since about 1940 between those believers who took the stance that only one salvation experience was necessary and those who took a position that stressed the substantial depth of self-introspection of *mishirabe* as such. The former invited people to an ecstatic experience, and were successful for a while in attracting many participants. But their faith tended not to last for long. The latter, on the other hand, acknowledged that the experience of real salvation was for only a few, but that their faith was of a more lasting nature. Yoshimoto took the latter position, and strove to reform the *mishirabe* practice still further. After 1943 he made the employees of his company undergo the experience of Naikan, and, from then on, the aspect of ecstatic, esoteric religiosity declined in importance even more. This development subsequently led to psychologists, psychiatrists, and other intellectuals evaluating the Naikan experience positively.

Between religion and psychotherapy

Between 1940 and 1953 the practice of *mishirabe*, which had been based on the faith of the Shin sect of Pure Land Buddhism, gradually developed into a form of self-introspection almost equivalent to present-day Naikan and, consequently, had a strongly psychotherapeutic nature. The reforms that were made in this meditation practice at that time can be summarized as follows (Yoshimoto 1983: 47–62):

1. Emphasis was placed not on a one-off experience of salvation but on the continuity of reflection. Whereas in the beginning one was to continue reflection in an unhurried way while undergoing the experience of *ichinen ni au*, this experience of salvation soon ceased to be the goal. In other words, it was not so much the experience following from reflection as the process

of reflection itself that acquired more and more value. Concretely speaking, concentrated meditation no longer concluded with an experience of salvation, but simply ended after a period of one week. Moreover, whereas previously, there was no requirement of systematic meditation after undergoing the experience, daily meditation was now to be continued after the concentrated meditation.

2. Esoteric elements, ascetic practices, and special religious terms were eliminated from the process of meditation. Meals and adequate sleep were now allowed, and contacts with outside people also became acceptable. Moreover, the meaning of terms became secularized, as *mishirabe* was changed to *naikan*, and *kaigonin* to *shidōsha*, or 'counselor.'

3. In practical terms, this meant that questions about the identity of the people on whom one should reflect, the duration of the reflection, and the kind of things about which one should feel guilty were specified. The process of reflection was systematically ordered, and made more comprehensible. Moreover, the practice of several *kaigonin* taking turns visiting was replaced by having a single counselor visiting on a regular basis.

4. There was a shift of emphasis from a sense of transience to a sense of sin. Formerly, one tried to heighten the hope for salvation by instilling fear of death and hell (by thinking about *mujō* or the transience of all things). Instead, one is now mainly urged to deepen one's awareness of debts towards others. This has had the practical effect of stressing the guilt one feels towards certain persons as a specific topic of reflection.

It is a moot question what Yoshimoto Ishin thought about the relationship between Naikan and religion. It is certain that he himself firmly believed in rebirth in paradise after death through the power of Amida Buddha. He also thought that someone who had attained religious faith was an ideal Naikan client. Around 1950 he qualified as a Buddhist priest and, in 1955, registered his home in Yamato Kōriyama, the site of his Naikan practice, as a religious body in law, called the Naikan Temple. The Naikan Center became a separate institution attached to the temple. On the other hand, he stressed that Naikan was not a religion. This might be related to the fact that he wanted to disseminate Naikan as a meditation practice in detention houses, juvenile reformatories, and high schools, and the Japanese constitution forbids religious groups from propagating their message in prisons and other public institutions. However, when seen as psychotherapy, prison employees can easily use it in their work with the inmates.

The fact that Yoshimoto did not lay too much emphasis on a belief in salvation by Amida Buddha and rebirth in paradise after death may be due to the experience he gained as a manager whose employees were practicing Naikan. The female employees who practiced *mishirabe* (or Naikan) under instructions from their company president became happier than before. They were more grateful to others, stopped making complaints, and human relationships became very smooth. Judging from these practical effects, Yoshimoto apparently came to realize that there was no specific need to stress faith in salvation through Amida Buddha and rebirth in paradise. He was strongly convinced, furthermore, that Naikan should not be confined to a limited number of selected people, but should be widely propagated throughout the world. He thought that it was therefore much better for Naikan not to take the form of religion. In fact, in so far as Naikan has become widely known, this has mainly been through the contribution of psychologists and psychiatrists who look upon it as a form of psychotherapy. Whereas academies and the mass media have generally been critical of new religious movements, they have been very positive regarding Yoshimoto Naikan.[6]

On the other hand, the claim that Yoshimoto Ishin himself considered Naikan to be a form of purely secular psychotherapy is less certain. He called it 'seeing into oneself,' or 'a method of inner observation.' As it was a method of coming to one's deepest reality, he seems to have thought of it as something that transcends the traditional conflicts between religious schools and that universalizes the truths that they contain on another, higher level.[7] Perhaps it is correct to see it as a new type of religion for intellectuals familiar with scientific thinking, one that is respectful of the authority of science. Moreover, I have to add that Naikan has been adopted in various new religious groups.

Yoshimoto Naikan as a psychotherapeutic religion

When we compare Yoshimoto Naikan with new religious groups, we see that there are considerable differences in organization and practices. Taking into account that Naikan does not claim to offer physical healing or to manifest mystical powers, it might be better to refrain from calling it a new religion. It is also difficult to classify it under the head of 'manipulationist sects' in Bryan Wilson's typology.

However, I believe that it can be called a 'psychotherapeutic religion,' in the sense used at the beginning of this chapter.

There are also a number of differences between Yoshimoto Naikan and Seichō no Ie and Hito no Michi, which can lay similar claim to the title of 'therapeutic religion.' Nevertheless, there are reasons for calling it a 'religion' in the broad sense because of the following features: (a) the practice of deep inner reflection, (b) concentration on the fundamental religious problem of awareness of sin, (c) the view that gratitude is essential not only towards other people but also towards something that transcends people, (d) the emphasis on a feeling of emotional liberation very close to an experience of religious conversion, and (e) the implanting of a thought pattern in accordance with a specific practice concerning a person's way of life and ethical conduct. With regard to organization, it is true that people who have experienced concentrated Naikan do not remain in touch with each other afterwards, so in that regard it does indeed bear more resemblance to psychotherapy than to religion. But the number of contemporary new religions that do not emphasize organizations of believers is certainly on the increase. It may be possible, then, to understand it as something close to what Thomas Luckman (1967) called 'invisible religion.'

By contrast with Seichō no Ie and Hito no Michi, Naikan does not promise physical healing or any manifestation of mystical powers. Another big difference is that, whereas the former religious groups display a strong tendency towards a kind of positive thinking that denies worry and fear and urges people to adopt a cheerful state of mind, Yoshimoto Naikan encourages participants to become deeply conscious of their sins. In other words, Yoshimoto Naikan adopts a pessimistic view of human nature. In fact, it is said that care must always be taken, since not a few clients contemplate suicide. The attitude of emphasizing a person's goodness could be said to be the polar opposite of emphasizing their badness.

The difference might be explained as follows. In the case of Seichō no Ie and Hito no Michi, attention is directed towards impersonal human relationships in urban society, and efforts are made to eliminate and liberate people from the overloaded interpersonal conflicts entailed by stressful city life. By contrast, attention is given in Yoshimoto Naikan to the close human relationships that still exist even in urban society, and this is the model on which attempts are made to re-establish attitudes towards other people. Yoshimoto Naikan has this stance in common with many new religions. For example, in the various groups of the Reiyūkai tradition, people are strongly urged to repent of their sins. Similarly, in Seichō no Ie and Hito no Michi, reflection on one's sins and repentance are stressed to some extent. Both consciousness of sin and positive thinking are adopted in many new religions. But it is interesting to note how in Seichō no Ie and Hito no Michi on the one hand and Yoshimoto Naikan on the other, all of which are typical psychotherapeutic religions, there tends to be a strong emphasis on one or the other of these two orientations.

The concept of psychotherapeutic religion is based on the assumption that in urbanized society a shift in thinking has occurred on a broad front, away from religion and towards psychotherapy. If this presupposition is correct, the advance of urbanization makes the development of therapeutic religions possible in various cultural traditions. Wilson's concept of manipulationist sects was established on the basis of concrete examples from the particular cultural traditions of the West. By contrast, I believe that the concept of psychotherapeutic religion possesses a more universal applicability.

Part IV:
Religious and Spiritual Movements after 1970s

12 The Post-1970 Situation

This chapter is intended to be a short recapitulation of the scheme of the whole book , connecting the previous chapters taking up various perspectives on popular religious movements since the mid-nineteenth century until 1960s discussed in Part II and Part III, to the topics which will be discussed in the following four chapters(Chapters 13 to 16) on religious movements and culture after 1970s.

Christianity and new religions

Japanese society entered a period of rapid modernization from the mid-nineteenth century. As in other areas of social activity, religious communities also underwent drastic change. On the one hand, traditional religions and religious institutions rooted in village communities faced decline, and on the other hand, religions with their social base in urban areas increased significantly. Over the past century, a variety of new religious movements have attracted many followers and created many new religious groups.

Christianity also found its place in the context of these new religious groups. By the 1870s Protestant and Catholic missionaries from various Western countries had arrived in Japan and established strong bases for evangelism in places such as Nagasaki, Yokohama, Tokyo, and Sapporo. Since then and in spite of intense efforts, however, the Christian churches have not been able to attract a large number of members. Even today only about one percent of the population claim membership in Christian churches. There are a number of factors related to Christianity's lack of success in Japan. Until the end of the Second World War, educational policies based on State Shinto and nationalistic sentiments inhibited the development of Christian churches. Furthermore, because Christianity was initially accepted by the old samurai (*bushi*) upper class, it was not able to gain a widespread following among the common people.

In contrast to the situation in Korea, where Christianity has become deeply rooted in the religious life of the common people, both Protestant and Catholic forms of Christianity remain alien to the religious life of most Japanese. In addition to these transplanted forms of Christianity, there are also some indigenous Christian organizations or communities founded by so-called 'minor founders' (Mullins 1993). These indigenous movements, along with Christian-related new religions such as the Mormons, Jehovah's Witnesses, and the Unification Church, are movements that deserve serious consideration in this context.

The role that Christianity is playing in Korea has been filled in Japan by the so-called new religions. Already by the end of the Edo Period (early to mid-19th century), Kurozumikyō and Misogikyō had gained a considerable number of followers. At the turn of the century (early Meiji Era) Tenrikyō, Konkōkyō, and Honmon Butsurūshū achieved rapid growth. This is considered the first period of new religious movements. Ōmoto is representative of the second period, from late Meiji through the Taisho eras (early 20th century). The third period (Showa era, around 1926 to the mid-1970s) includes the period of rapid growth for groups such as Hito no Michi (later Perfect Liberty Kyōdan), Reiyūkai, Seichō no Ie, Sekai Kyūseikyō, Risshō Kōseikai, and Sōka Gakkai. Increasing numbers of organizations were founded, particularly in the postwar period, with more and more people joining these groups.

Sōka Gakkai, the largest of these new religious movements, claims a membership of over seventeen million. However, the actual active membership is probably nearer to three to four million. Statistics are not available on the true number of new religious groups, but some scholars have estimated that they number over three thousand. It is also estimated that between ten to twenty percent of the total Japanese population is involved in one or more of the new religions.

The founders of these new religious movements, in many cases, have been men or women without a high social standing, who have experienced many personal hardships and created their own religious faith after involvement in a variety of religious practices and traditions. Since their faith is often syncretistic and eclectic, it is often difficult – not to say misleading – to identify one religious tradition as the only source of their religious inspiration. Another prominent feature of these new religious movements is the great diversity of their teachings, practices, and rituals. The tendency in the Japanese religious world to combine and mix elements from Buddhism, Shinto, folk religion, and various other sources, is reflected in the pluralism of the new religions. In spite of this diversity, it can be said that there are two main sources for most new religious movements. One is the Nichiren tradition based on the Lotus Sutra, represented by such groups as Sōka Gakkai and Risshō Kōseikai. The other is the syncretistic Shinto tradition characterized by the quest for magical healing and salvation.

Characteristics of the new religions

A this-worldly orientation is one of the defining characteristics of the new religions. Rather than rejecting this world and seeking salvation in the world after death, new religions tend to place great value on this current life, and offer the hope of relief from suffering in this world. The strong appeal of new religions lies in the promise of this-worldly benefits, such as deliverance through faith in the gods (*kami*) and/or buddhas from problems that arise due to illness and poverty. Many people have been attracted to them by their promise to cure illness through magical rituals.

It goes without saying that physical 'healing' (*byōki naoshi'*) is not the only goal of the new religions. Many have also been concerned with solving the fundamental problems of Japanese society and creating an ideal society through faith in the power to transform the world (*yonaoshi*). Rooted in this *yonaoshi* faith, Ōmoto and Sōka Gakkai are two new religions that became active in movements for political reform. However, the aspiration to realize religious ideals in this world through political means met with strong opposition from society at large. In time, the ambition to transform the world did not translate into concrete results, and these movements were forced either to find hope in an ideal society in the future, or compromise and take a more realistic position with regard to social reform.

Many of the new religions also have the goal of personal trans-formation, often referred to as 'transforming the heart' or 'mind rect-ification'(*kokoro naoshi*). There are a variety of causes leading to human unhappiness. There are groups, like Mahikari, that place a great emphasis on spirits of the dead (human or animal), while other movements prefer to explain misfortune in connection with the ancestors or previous lives. Even more widespread is the explanation of problems in terms of evil or impure 'hearts.' In this case, the causes of unhappiness are the conditions of the heart, including malice, jealousy, ill-will, or self-centered desires and feelings, rather than human behavior or action. Consequently, in order to be delivered from unhappiness, one's heart must be transformed into a 'good' or 'pure' heart. In concrete terms, *kokoro naoshi* means developing a 'good' heart that avoids conflict and is kind and accepting of others – in short, strives for harmonious human relationships.

The moral norms implied in such ideals are closely related to the group-oriented values of Japanese society. By teaching and encouraging the practice of these moral norms, new religions contribute to the stability and cohesion of the family and other social groupings. At times new religions function in a conservative way to maintain the established social order, but in many cases they serve to provide stability in the face of new social environments and new human relationships. The new religious organizations provide the basis for new and intimate human relationships apart from previously existing social groups. This is one of the roles of Japanese new religions overseas.[1]

A conspicuous feature of the religious activities and social organization of the new religions is large-scale popular participation. The activities of local groups are characterized by close relationships and gatherings of fellow members. Problems of everyday life are understood in religious terms that all the members share and discuss together. Any and all members are expected to actively participate in group activities and the propagation of their faith. No distinction is made between clergy and laity, and one's religious advancement depends on effort and ability rather than on one's social class or background. In fact, the most powerful social group supporting local activities and giving birth to numerous leaders has been middle-aged housewives, who suffer from a relatively low social standing.

The post-1970 situation

Since the 1970s the established new religions entered a difficult period of development. Japanese new religions outside of Japan began to flourish from about this time, but within Japan many established new religions, such as Sōka Gakkai, faced the problem of stagnation. Accompanying the decline of the established new religions has been the development of the so-called 'new new religions' (the fourth period of the new religions).

A variety of groups fall under this category of 'new new religions,' and many are not so different from previous new religions. However, it is possible to identify some new distinguishing features. First of all, it could be said that the strong concern with this-worldly healing has weakened to a certain extent. In its place there is a greater concern with the problem of meaninglessness and the loss of fulfillment in life. Changes in the type of problems faced by the Japanese have brought with them changes in the goals and aspirations offered by the new religions. The concern for a happy family and working life has declined, and in its stead there is an increasing concern with life after death and personal inner fulfillment. Although miracles and mystical techniques and practices are still regarded as important, the emphasis has shifted from their practical application in group life to that of personal experience and individual fulfillment.

Changes in religious group life have accompanied this shift in emphasis. Previously, local religious groups were characterized by members helping each other with the problems of everyday life. Today, however, when these close-knit groups are created there is a tendency to separate from the larger society and create a monastic or separate religious community, as seen in the Unification Church or Aum Shinrikyō. In other cases new new religions use the mass media and sponsor large gatherings and events, and do not rely so much on local groups to maintain religious activities. These types of activities are certainly more appealing to contemporary youth in Japan, and in fact many more members of the younger generation have joined in a new new religion than was the case with the earlier movements.

It could be, however, that the new new religions are not the most representative religious movements of the period since the 1970s. In urban areas in modernized societies around the world, there are growing religious movements that do not create religious organizations nor emphasize participation in group activities. These movements are shaping each other as they develop simultaneously. In the West this is often referred to as the 'New Age' movement, while in Japan it is often referred to in terms of the 'Spiritual World.' These movements can be seen as local manifestations of a single global phenomenon, which I call 'new spirituality movements and cultures.'

From the point of view of these new spirituality movements, earlier religions with their hardened doctrines and institutional forms have restricted individuals and prevented them from realizing their full spiritual potential. What is important is that each individual search and discover their own inner being, develop their own spirituality, and bring about their own spiritual transformation. For such personal purposes, techniques such as meditation, ascetic training, bodywork, and psychotherapy are offered as forms of practice and combined with the study of ancient mysticism, archaic religions and myths and shamanistic rituals, and psychological theories. Followers of these new spirituality movements maintain that the age

Table 12.1: Statistics for major new religions

Organization	Founder	Founded	Number of members		
			1954	1974	1990
1st Period					
Nyorai-kyō	Isson-myorai Kino (1756–1826)	1802	75,480	33,674	27,131
Tenri-kyō	Nakayama Miki (1798–1887)	1838	1,912,208	2,298,420	1,839,009
Kurozumi-kyō	Kurozumi Munetada (1780–1850)	1814	715,650	407,558	295,225
Konkō-kyō	Konkō Daijin (1814–1883)	1859	646,206	500,868	442,584
Honmon Butsuryū-shū	Nagamatsu Nissen (1817–1890)	1857	339,800	515,991	526,337
Maruyama-kyō	Itō Rokurōbei (1829–1894)	1870	92,011	3,200	10,725
2nd Period					
Ōmoto	Deguchi Nao (1837–1918) Deguchi Onisaburō (1871–1948)	1899	73,604	153,397	172,460
Nakayama-Shingoshō-shū	Kihara Matsutarō (1870–1942)	1912	282,650	467,910	382,040
Honmichi	Ōnishi Aijirō (1881–1958)	1913	225,386	288,700	316,825
3rd Period					
En'nō-kyō	Fukada Chiyoko (1887–1925)	1919	71,654	266,782	419,452
Nenpō-shinkyō	Ogura Reigen (1886–1982)	1925	153,846	751,214	807,486
Reiyū-kai	Kubo Kakutarō (1892–1944)	1924	2,284,172	2,477,907	3,202,172
Perfect Liberty Kyōdan	Miki Tokuharu (1871–1938)	(1925)[a]	500,950	2,520,430	1,259,064
	Miki Tokuchika (1900–1983)	1946			
Seichō-no-Ie	Taniguchi Masaharu (1893–1985)	1930	1,461,604	2,375,705	838,496
Sōka Gakkai	Makiguchi Tsunesaburō (1871–1944)	1930	341,146	16,111,375	17,736,757[b]
	Toda Jōsei (1900–1956)				
Sekai Kyūsei-kyō	Okada Mokichi (1882–1955)	1935	373,173	661,263	835,756
Shin'nyoen	Itō Shinjō (1906–1956)	1936	155,500	296,514	679,414
Kōdō Kyōdan	Okano Shōdō (1900–1978)	1936	172,671	417,638	400,720
Risshō Kōsei-kai	Naganuma Myōkō (1889–1957)	1938	1,041,124	4,562,304	6,348,120
	Niwano Nikkyō (1906–)				
Bussho Gonenkai Kyōdan	Sekiguchi Kaichi (1897–1961)	1950	352,170	1,210,227	2,196,813
	Sekiguchi Tomino (1905–)				
Tenshō Kōtai Jingū-kyō	Kitamura Sayo (1900–1967)	1945	89,374	386,062	439,011
Zenrin-kyō	Rikihisa Tatsusai (1906–1977)	1947	404,157	483,239	513,321
Myōchikai Kyōdan	Miyamoto Mitsu (1900–1984)	1950	515,122	673,913	962,611

of doctrinal-type religions is over, and that humanity is entering a new stage in the evolution of consciousness, of which they are the new representatives.

It is not that there were no such individualistic religious movements before the 1970s, but since that time their development has been particularly prominent. One long-term trend over the past century has been the continual decline of traditional religious groups and communities, and the corresponding development of new religions. Since the 1970s, however, the situation has changed significantly. It appears that we have entered a period in which movements that sought to create new religions have declined, while the number of people pursuing an individualistic spiritual quest have increased. It appears that this trend will continue well into the 1990s and after

Table 12.1 gives a list of the major new religions, the names of their founders, and membership figures for representative years. Table 12.2 provides information on representative new new religions.

Table 12.2: Statistics for the new new religions

Organization	Founder	Founded	Number of members 1974	Number of members 1990
4th period				
Ōyama Nezunomikoto Shinji Kyōkai	Inaii Sadao (1906–1988)	1948	59,493	826,022
Byakkō Shinkō-kai	Goi Masahisa (1916–1980)	1951		(1989) 500,000
Agon-shū	Kiriyama Seiyū (1921–)	1954	500	206,606
Reiha-no-Hikari Kyōkai	Hase Yoshio (1915–1984)	1954		761,175
Jōdoshinshū Shinran-kai	Takamori Kentetsu (1934–)	1958		(1984) 100,000ᶜ
Unification Church	Moon Sun Myung (1920–)	1959		–
Sekai Mahikari Bunmei Kyōdan	Okada Kōtama (1901–1974)	1959		97,838
Sūkyō Mahikari		1978		501,328
Honbushin	Ōnishi Tama (1916–1969)	1961		900,000ᶜ
G.L.A. Sōgō Honbu	Takahashi Shinji (1927–1976)	1969		12,981
Shinji Shūmei-kai	Koyama Mihoko (1910–)	1970		(1988) 440,000ᶜ
Nihon Seidō Kyōdan	Iwasaki Shōkō (1934–)	1974		69,450
ESP Kagaku Kenkyūjo	Ishii Katao (1918–)	1975		16,000ᶜ
Hō-no-Hana Sanpōgyō	Fukunaga Hōgen (1945–)	1980		70,000ᶜ
Japanese Raelian Movement	Claude B. Rael (1946–)	1980		3,000ᶜ
Yamato-no-Miya	Ajiki Tenkei (1952–)	1981		5,000ᶜ
Aum Shinri-kyō	Asahara Shōkō (1955–)	1984		
Worldmate	Fukami Seizan (1951–)	1986		30,000ᶜ
Kōfuku-no-Kagaku	Ōkawa Ryūhō (1956–)	1986		(1989) 13,300ᶜ (1991) 1,527,278ᶜ

Notes:

a The (1925) date refers to the Hito-no-Michi Kyōdan, the mother organization of Perfect Liberty Kyōdan.

b Sōka Gakkai has not released figures for 1989 and 1990, so this figure is the membership numbers for 1988.

c Most of the statistics in these charts are from the 1991 edition of the Shūkyō Nenkan (*Religion Yearbook*, Tokyo: Gyōsei). Numbers marked with 'ᶜ' are from other sources reporting the organizations' own membership statistics around 1990.

For religions introduced from abroad, the year of its establishment in Japan is given as the "founding" date.

These are membership statistics for Japan only, and do not include members outside Japan.

13 The Expansion of New Religions Overseas

The beginnings of the expansion of Japan's new religions overseas go back as far as the Meiji period.[1] At first it spread to nearby colonies and among emigrants to new continents. Then war brought an end to propagation in migrant communities, and defeat in the war checked propagation in colonial territories. Most of the new religions at first restricted their postwar propagation activities to Japan. But it was not long before they were renewing their efforts in emigrant communities. Eventually propagation to people of non-Japanese descent 'took off,' using prewar propagation bases in colonial territories and emigrant communities as springboards. Following the economic boom of the 1960s, propagation within Japan eventually approached an upper limit, and there was renewed enthusiasm for overseas expansion. This enthusiasm came just at a time when second and third generations of migrants were assimilating into local societies. The overseas expansion of the new religions entered a new phase from the 1960s on, that of expansion into foreign cultures. As a result of defeat in the war, Japan suffered an almost complete loss of the foundations upon which its imperialistic, authoritarian control overseas rested. Until the 1960s, it also lacked economic reserves for overseas expansion. As a result, the new religions relied on Japanese ethnic communities in North and Latin America. With the exception of the old colonial territories of Taiwan and Korea, until the beginning of the 1960s the spread of Japanese new religions overseas was almost exclusively in Japanese ethnic communities, where Japan's cultural traditions were strongly preserved.[2]

After the 1960s, however, Japan's new religions were slowly accepted by non-Japanese. In North and Latin America, where there were migrant ethnic communities, non-Japanese believers in new religions would increase steadily. This was a period when new migrants were few in number and assimilation of Japanese communities into local societies proceeded apace. The situation in Taiwan and Korea was slightly different. The results of propagation in colonial times were not completely negated by defeat in the war. Churches run by local people carried on religious activities independently of organizations within Japan. Expansion of membership, begun even in the 1950s, became conspicuous in the 1960s and afterwards. And in the 1970s relations with the organizations in Japan tended to be restored, so that, with increased exchanges of personnel and the propping up of operations by organizations in Japan, the amount of energy put into propagation also increased greatly.

The aim of this study is to consider the significance of this spread of new religions to non-Japanese, so conspicuous from the 1960s on. At present Sōka Gakkai and other groups have reached out to virtually every corner of the world through their missionary activity. The teachings and thought of Japan's new religions have been translated into many languages and have been accepted by people of widely different cultural backgrounds. What has made this situation possible is, first and foremost, the rapid improvement in Japan's economic strength; another factor has been the rapid growth in world communication and information distribution. The expansion of Japan's new religions overseas is primarily the result of changes in economic life. This question of the influence of economic change on Japan's new religions is itself a deeply interesting subject for study. The aim of this present study is a little wider. The entrance of new religions into foreign cultures may even provide hints for thinking about what changes are at present occurring in religions around the world, and also about what special position Japan's new religions occupy in the history of world religions.

The present status of expansion

To what extent have Japan's new religions spread among non-Japanese?[3] As of 1990, non-Japanese believers in new religions are decidedly most numerous in Latin America and East and Southeast Asia; next comes North America (including Hawaii). Brazil and Korea far exceed all other countries in membership, with the United States and Asian countries distant seconds. While there are some believers in Europe, Oceania, South Asia, West Asia, and Africa, their numbers are insignificant in comparison with those in the Americas and East and Southeast Asia.

Brazil

Seichō no Ie boasts the largest membership, followed by Sekai

Kyūseikyō, Perfect Liberty Kyōdan (PL), and Sōka Gakkai.[4] Brazil's news weekly, *Veja*, carried an article in its 28 March 1990 issue entitled 'The Gods of the Sun: The Progress of Eastern Religions Promising Heaven on Earth and Prosperity in the Present World.' According to this article, Seichō no Ie had 2,500,000 members, Sekai Kyūseikyō and PL 250,000 each, and Sōka Gakkai 150,000. Not mentioned in the article but growing remarkably in recent years are Sūkyō Mahikari, with several tens of thousands of followers, and Reiyūkai, with 44,000 (as of March 1989; see Inoue et al. 1990: 650). Other groups as well, such as Sekai Mahikari Bunmei Kyōdan, include many non-Japanese believers, as do such groups as Burajiru Kannon Jiin and the Inarikai begun in Brazil by Japanese. There are said to be 800,000 people of Japanese descent in Brazil, and another 300,000 of mixed descent; thus the influence of Japanese new religions goes far beyond Japanese circles. If one accepts the figures given in *Veja*, more than two percent of Brazil's population of 150 million people are members of Japanese new religions.

Those figures are, however, considerably exaggerated. Nakamaki Hirochika has said of PL that, as of 1984, 'active believers are estimated to have peaked in the neighborhood of 30,000 people' (1989: 417); if this is true, then actual membership is about one-eighth that of the figure given in *Veja*. Of course, it is difficult to say exactly what 'active believers' means. In the case of Seichō no Ie, the official overseas membership is 1,257,907 (as of the end of 1989), of whom roughly 1,200,000 are in Latin America. One of the most important religious practices in Seichō no Ie is subscription to their official publications; as of December 1989, 608,000 copies of the two Portuguese-language publications, *Acendedo* and *Pomba Branca*, were printed. No data is available for exact numbers of copies of the Japanese-language publications printed in Brazil, but it is estimated that about ten percent of Brazil's Japanese belong to Seichō no Ie (Matsuda 1989). Of the members of Shirohatokai [White dove society], the women's group, approximately three belong to the Portuguese section for every one who belongs to the Japanese section. Again, there were about 362,000 (as of December 1989) who were paying monthly dues to the Seishimeikai [Holy vocation society], while the same year there were 821,998 Seishimeikai members in Japan. When looking at these comparisons, however, one must take into account that Brazilians tend to feel it odd to pay membership fees to the religious group one believes in, so that canvassing among members of the Seishimeikai is not done as aggressively as it is in Japan.

United States of America

In the United States the NSA (Nichiren Shōshū Sōka Gakkai of America) far surpasses all others in its spread among non-Japanese. According to Sōka Gakkai's own statistics, it had 333,000 adherents in North America as of 1985, very few of whom were Canadians. George Williams (1989) states that the racial makeup of NSA membership in that year was 25.6% Asian, 47.9% white, 20.4% black, and 6.1% others. Since most of the Asians are of Japanese descent, roughly three-fourths can be regarded as of non-Japanese descent.

Aside from NSA, it seems no other new religion has succeeded in going from Japan and gaining several tens of thousands of adherents. There are some Japanese new religions, however, that spread in the United States without initiatives from groups in Japan, such as the Reiki of Usui Mikao and Macrobiotic, founded by Sakurazawa Yukikazu and propagated in the United States by Kushi Michio (see Albanese 1990). *East West Journal*, which Macrobiotic started publishing in 1970, was printing close to 80,000 copies in 1985. Another new religion, the Unification Church (Holy Spirit Association for the Unification of World Christianity) founded in Korea, spread its forces to Japan and then to the United States, where at the end of the 1970s it claimed a membership of approximately 30,000 (Bromley and Shupe 1981).

Asia

In Korea, Sōka Gakkai and Tenrikyō have made the greatest impact. The former group maintains that it has 709,000 adherents in the Asia/ Oceania area (as of 1985); we can safely assume that two-thirds of these are Koreans. Tenrikyō puts the number of its adherents at about 370,000. Similar figures are given in Korean government reports. Still, officials of the religious groups themselves consider actual figures to be far lower. One mark of deepening faith in Tenrikyō is participation in a three-month 'character-building course' at the group's headquarters in Japan. Because people could not travel freely from Korea to Japan, from 1973 several sites were set up in the country where these long training sessions could be carried out. As of April 1990, there were fifty-one churches scattered throughout Korea, with prospects for that number to increase. By February 1990 the total number of people who completed these courses came to 37,000.

In the rest of Asia, there has been a considerable growth among communities of ethnic Chinese in Taiwan, Hong Kong, Singapore, and other countries. Sōka Gakkai has enjoyed far and away the greatest success overall, but in Hong Kong Shinji Shūmeikai has been quite strong, and in Thailand Sekai Kyūseikyō claims over 60,000 adherents.

This summarizes the countries and groups with the largest numbers of adherents, but I would like to conclude this section with a quick look at the range over which some of the groups have extended their propagation activities overseas. Sōka Gakkai and Seichō no Ie are the two groups with the largest number of overseas adherents, with the former's membership scattered all over the world and the latter's heavily concentrated in Brazil. In 1985 Sōka Gakkai was estimated to have 1,262,000 members in 115 countries outside Japan. Another wide-ranging group is Sūkyō Mahikari, with approximately 100,000 adherents spread over 75 countries outside Japan.

Periods of expansion into foreign cultures

Brazil

Expansion into Brazil practically began with the first migrations of Japanese in 1908. Groups of Honmon Butsuryūshū and Tenrikyō adherents were already formed by 1930. Seichō no Ie had also gained a considerable number of followers by the end of the war. But all of these members were restricted to Japanese ethnic communities. The one exception was Ōmoto, which from about 1930 had begun propagation; right from the start it reached out to non-Japanese (Maeyama and Smith 1983). But because of stiff local opposition, the dissolution of its Japanese headquarters due to government suppression, and the death of missionaries, Ōmoto was unable to form a large group of adherents. At the end of the 1960s solid members numbered only a few hundred.

From the early 1960s large-scale penetration into non-Japanese society began. The two groups that took the lead in this regard, PL and Sekai Kyūseikyō, had no bases in the migrant communities prior to this period. Tables 1 and 2 present the number of adherents by group and the proportion of Japanese to non-Japanese in 1967 as reported by Maeyama Takashi (1983, pp. 192–93). At this stage Japanese were still in the majority in the new religions as a whole, though signs of the expansion to non-Japanese were already evident in Sekai Kyūseikyō in particular as well as in PL. From the end of the 1960s Seichō no Ie began an explosive penetration into non-Japanese society. And according to Nakamaki, by 1984 non-Japanese amounted to more than ninety percent of total PL overseas membership (1989: 417). Therefore, the rapid development of Japanese new religions from the late 1960s was clearly a result of the spread of activities to non-Japanese.

In the 1980s Sekai Kyūseikyō and PL membership tended to remain stagnant, but Seichō no Ie continued to grow, and other groups, such as Mahikari, have recently shown conspicuous growth. Overall one can say that diversification and expansion of Japanese new religions has continued.

United States of America

Missionary activity in the United States had an early start through the activities of such groups as Kurozumikyō in Hawaii, in which there is a history of immigration from Japan going back to 1868. From the late 1920s groups such as Tenrikyō and Konkōkyō carried on organized propagation in Hawaii and California. They were followed later by Seichō no Ie, Tenshō Kōtai Jingūkyō, and several others. Propagation, however, was mainly confined to people of Japanese descent (Inoue et al. 1990, Yanagawa and Morioka 1979 and 1981, and Inoue 1985).

As in Brazil, it was Sekai Kyūseikyō and PL that were the first to stress propagation to non-Japanese; they were unable, however, to achieve the same conspicuous penetration of non-Japanese society that they achieved in Brazil. The breakthrough in the United States was made by NSA. The first group of Sōka Gakkai members was formed in 1960.[5] At first the mainstays were women who had married American men and gone to live in America, and other people of Japanese descent. As early as 1964 there were discussion meetings in English, the journal *World Tribune* was being published, and other early efforts were being taken to penetrate non-Japanese society. In the latter half of the 1960s a remarkable number of non-Japanese, especially white youths, joined the new religions, even exceeding the number of Japanese who joined. NSA's most surprising growth took place in the latter half of the 1960s, and the impetus continued on into the first half of the 1970s. Officially the number of adherents is given as 200,000 in 1970, rising to 245,000 by 1975.

After that, however, NSA membership fell rapidly. The number of copies of *World Tribune* printed in 1975 was 60,000; this dropped to 33,000 in 1977, and down to 19,000 in 1980. The drop in membership was not to prove a long-term phenomenon, however, for in the early 1980s there was a resurgence in strength, and by 1985 the number of copies of *World Tribune* printed rose to 94,000. Still, the figure of 333,000 given for North American membership in 1985 does not reflect actual numbers. Also, penetration into non-Japanese society to such an extent that non-Japanese made up three-fourths of the membership had already been realized in the late 1960s. According to NSA's own survey of 1970, members who identified their racial background as Asian were already no more than thirty percent of the total.

Asia

Propagation in this part of the world was begun by Tenrikyō missionaries working in Korea in the 1920s. Along with colonial expansion after the Sino-Japanese and Russo-Japanese wars, many religious groups made inroads into colonial territories; groups such as Tenrikyō, Konkōkyō, the Kokuchūkai, Ōmoto, and Nihonzan Myōhōji had bases established before 1925, while groups such as Hito no Michi and Seichō no Ie achieved rapid growth after 1925. Of all the groups, the inroads made by Tenrikyō were something spectacular: by 1944 they had 211 churches in Korea, 39 in Taiwan, 124 in Manchuria, and 46 in China (Inoue et al. 1990: 644). This expansion of new religions along with imperialistic expansion naturally was aimed not only at Japanese but also at local inhabitants. And these new religions were also accepted by non-Japanese (mainly Koreans) within Japan, people who either moved to Japan or were sent as conscript labor. Prior to 1945, therefore, penetration of new religions into non-Japanese society was evident in many regions of East Asia.

Nearly all of the fruits of imperialistic expansion were lost by defeat in the Second World War. Still, some remained, and Tenrikyō used some of its prewar propagation achievements to renew missionary activity in East Asia after the war. In fact, of all the new religions that were active before the war, it was only Tenrikyō that had some of its churches maintained by local inhabitants. Of the 51 churches it had in Korea as of April 1990, eight were churches that had been founded in the thirty-one years between 1912 and 1943. In Taiwan only one of its churches remained. Up to a certain point in time after the war, these churches all barely managed to survive despite violent anti-Japanese feelings, and it is easy to surmise that open propagation was not easy.[6]

Nevertheless, some brave souls travelled to former colonial territories after the war in order to carry out missionary activity. The most representative of these is Choi Jae-Whan, who established the

Won Nan Seong church in Pusan (Yamamoto 1982). Choi had come to Japan in 1927 at the age of sixteen and joined Tenrikyō in 1947 after suffering from Hansen's disease. Following some time engaged in missionary activity among Koreans living in northern Kyushu and Hiroshima, he smuggled himself into Korea in 1955 and thereafter achieved spectacular results. By the time of his death in 1988, the Won Nan Seong church had given birth to seventeen other churches. Propagation continued after his death through the efforts of other Koreans living in Japan who returned to Korea. It is estimated that there are now more Tenrikyō adherents belonging to churches established by such returnees than members belonging to churches from prewar days. We can safely conclude that Tenrikyō's membership expansion in postwar Korea went hand in hand with the development of Choi's Won Nam Seong church, and hence took place in the 1960s and 1970s. It would seem that Tenrikyō's growth in Taiwan followed a similar timetable, with remarkable growth occurring in the 1980s.

In contrast, the situation has been very different for Sekai Kyūseikyō in Thailand. Prior to 1970 there was almost no penetration by Japanese new religions into Thailand. Sekai Kyūseikyō missionaries had taken up residence in Bangkok in 1968 and begun propagation, but up to the beginning of the 1980s there had been no great progress made. In early 1982, however, rapid growth finally began. By 1990 membership exceeded 60,000, and a yearly increase of over 10,000 members is expected. Tenrikyō also reports remarkable growth recently in Thailand.

At present I do not have available to me data on Sōka Gakkai, which has had the biggest expansion in membership in Asia, so I am unable to say where and when its growth has been most notable. Judging from the above data on Tenrikyō and Seichō no Ie, however, we could conclude that the expansion of Japanese new religions into Asian cultures began with notable progress in Korea, then spread among ethnic Chinese communities, and more recently reached out into Thailand and other countries.

Conditions in receiving societies

Why is it that Japanese new religions succeeded in penetrating foreign cultures at this time? It is a belief of most of the new religious groups that each member of the human race has dignity as a human being, but existence involves suffering, and for this very reason human beings are in need of salvation. Hence they have a strong desire to extend, if possible, their teaching to people of other cultures as well. Besides, new religions are in general extremely keen to expand membership, and not only out of a desire to save people. In a capitalistic competitive society, one's legitimacy is graphically brought home on the basis of success in expanding numbers. What is more, when the following of one's teaching by people of other cultures is felt to be proof of your religion's universal adequacy, missionary activity to people of other cultures overseas can stir up stronger impulses than propagation among one's compatriots.

Still, sometimes propagation does not produce great results, regardless of how strong the desires or how much energy is poured into it. For propagation to succeed, suitable conditions must exist in the receiving society. Also, the religion doing the propagation must have, along with strong desires, certain features making it easily acceptable by people of foreign cultures. In other words, by considering the special features of both the receiving society and the religion being propagated, we shall be better prepared to understand why, in a certain place at a certain time, particular religions succeeded in expanding. In this section, we shall first consider the special features of the receiving societies.

The first condition for expansion is the cultural and political condition, i.e., how generally tolerant the local government and inhabitants are toward a religion derived from another culture, and how favorable and friendly they are toward that culture, especially a Japanese, Oriental culture. In the period of imperialistic expansion, the fact that the religion belonged to the culture of the side exerting authoritative control was in itself a major cause for expansion. Colonial authority is keen to surround local inhabitants with influences of that authority's own culture. This is especially true when assimilation is deliberately pursued. Under such a political, legal, and military aegis, propagation has an extremely high chance of success.

Yet the postwar expansion of the new religions did not take place under this kind of powerful political aegis. On the contrary, by being different from the existing, dominant religions, in many cases they had to expand by overcoming governmental regulation and the opposition of local inhabitants. Also, success would be difficult if the religion were too exotic for the dominant culture, thus becoming an object of antipathy. This is the condition I am referring to when I talk about a degree of political and cultural freedom and tolerance. When the Japanese community has excellent relations with the outside world, as in Brazil, Japanese culture in general naturally enjoys a good reputation. Economic expansion through the export of goods and capital and personnel exchanges, even if they invite antipathy at first, eventually serve to make people feel attracted to the new culture, and they soften people's antipathies.

But it is even more important that cultural freedom be expanded widely in that society and that the authority of the traditional cultural system be seen as relative. In a society where the traditional religion has monopolistic authority – where freedom of religion is not recognized – one cannot expect success in propagation. Progress in industrialization and urbanization, along with progress in a worldwide interchange of personnel and information, are eroding these cultural and political barriers.

In both Brazil and Korea in the 1960s and 1970s, when there was so much expansion of the Japanese new religions, the countries were in the midst of development through rapid industrialization under authoritarian military-rule; it was not a coincidence that military rule in both countries was the result of a process of social breakdown. Thailand in the 1980s, too, was in a state of rapid industrialization and cultural liberalization and relativization. In both Brazil and Thailand, prior to those changes, there was little scope for tolerance of any other religions besides Christianity or Theravada Buddhism. Even in the case of Korea, which had religious diversity, political regulation was strict. Industrialization, however, brought change in its wake. Industrialization requires free accumulation and investment of capital, the formation of a competent middle class, and the creation of a free labor force. For these ends, even though doing so carries the risk of a certain amount of social unrest, it is necessary to recognize freedom of belief and thought. Also, the liberation of people from traditional ways of life linked with the dominant religions must, if anything, be encouraged. Added to this process of liberalization that follows industrialization are the waves of worldwide information exchange and cultural relativization.

In Korea there was fierce opposition from the inhabitants towards Japanese culture. Yet the expansion of general cultural freedom and the increase in everyday contacts with things Japanese as a result of economic expansion to some extent softened the opposition to Japanese culture on the level of everyday life. In the case of the United States, despite the outward facade of freedom of thought and belief, there always existed a strong confidence in the superiority of Christian, Occidental culture, with a corresponding rejection of Oriental culture. This rejection mechanism, and people's confidence in Christian Occidental culture, began to be badly shaken in the 1960s, a tendency that has continued to the present day. One of the striking manifestations of this unrest is the counterculture movement revolving around young middle-class whites. Positive interest in Oriental religions supported the most powerful wing of this counterculture movement. Disappointment with the Christian Occidental culture manifested itself in a yearning for its antithesis, Oriental religion. The expansion of Sōka Gakkai and Sekai Kyūseikyō into the foreign culture of the United States of America was something that accompanied the tide of interest in Oriental religions stemming from this aspect of the counterculture movement (Inoue 1985: 170–73, 204–6).

To sum up, what happened in Brazil, Korea, and the United States of America in the 1960s and in Thailand in the 1980s was greater expansion of capitalism than ever before, accompanied by advances in communication, transportation, information exchange, and the concomitant relativization of culture. In Japan, driven by a desire to catch up with and surpass Western nations, political leaders were quick to try to build a strong nation by aggressive introduction of Western culture, and they were ruthless in destroying the authority of traditional religions such as Confucianism and Buddhism. Defeat in the Second World War and the Allied occupation added further impetus in this direction. What emerged and developed from that experience of cultural relativization were Japan's new religions; they not only emerged under these conditions, they also offered people many cultural resources for coping with these new conditions. On the other hand, countries like Brazil and the United States had absorbed immigrants from all parts of the world, and as a result were more accustomed to cultural diversity than Europe; consequently, they had a tendency to prefer a pragmatic way of thinking that did not insist upon a single tradition.[7] There can be no doubt that in these countries the essential prerequisite of familiarity with cultural diversity encouraged openness to and acceptance of Japanese new religions.

The second condition for expansion is the emergence of a demand for new religions as a result of socioeconomic changes. The various new religions in Japan grew and developed by satisfying the new spiritual yearnings of people living in the midst of modern Japan's socioeconomic changes. One of the common characteristics of the new religions is their response to strongly felt needs of individuals in their daily lives, their solutions to discord in interpersonal relations, their practical teaching that offers concrete solutions for carrying on a stable social life, and their provision, to individuals who have been cut off from traditional communities, of a place for group activities where congenial company and a spirit of mutual support can be found. As capitalistic industrialization and urbanization advance, large numbers of individuals are thrown into new living environments, thus producing conditions that require spiritual support for the individual. Many people have lost the support of their traditional communities and face a situation in which they must get by on their own resources in the midst of the pressures of competition and the dangers of isolation. Those who have overcome such problems no doubt make up the lion's share of the stable middle-class urban population (including the lower stratum of middle-class laborers). Japanese new religions are abundantly equipped with cultural resources that answer the needs of just these people in the process of treading the path towards the urban middle class. The second condition for expansion, therefore, is the existence of socio-economic conditions that nurture a latent demand among people for a religion that gives guidance in daily life.

In Brazil and Korea from the 1960s, and in Thailand in the 1980s, such socio-economic conditions did in fact exist. Let us take a brief look at Brazil. Brazil, whose principal industry was a monocultural agriculture based mostly on coffee, began to tread the path of industrialization in 1934, with the 'Vargas Revolution.' Amidst the trade slump that accompanied worldwide depression, and backed by the military, the new government forced through the domestic production of many industrial products that had been previously imported. This policy of industrialization imposed from above was to bear fruit in the 1960s, after a period of democratization following the Second World War. The military rule that began in 1964 would prove to be a period of large-scale development and high growth. The result was a rapid increase in population coupled with a rapid decrease in the rural population, which had once constituted the greater portion of the nation's population. Between 1940 and 1980 Brazil's total population grew 2.8 times larger, and the ratio of urban to rural population reversed itself from 3:7 to 7:3 (Nakamaki 1989: 421–22). Whereas 54% of workers were engaged in primary industries in 1960, in 1970 this figure was down to 44.3%, and in 1980 down even more, to 29.3%. The rapid economic growth that drew attention to Brazil as one of the Newly Industrialized Countries (NICS) took place from 1968 to 1973, exactly the same time that Seichō no Ie's expansion to foreign cultures was being energetically promoted.

During the course of such industrialization and urbanization the Japanese community occupied a singular position. Japanese immigrants very early purchased small plots of farmland (as compared to the huge plantation-type farms that were the mainstay of Brazilian agriculture) and set out to produce on self-managed farms commodity crops for sale to urban residents. While accumulating wealth through their characteristic industriousness, the majority of people of Japanese descent were extremely keen on giving their children a good education. As a result, Japanese were quick to improve their status to that of the urban middle class along with the industrialization and urbanization of Brazilian society. Japanese stood for the dream of the new industrialized society: individual success through self-reliant effort. From the 1960s on, Japanese new religions took over this idea of individual success, and in addition presented themselves to Brazilian society as the religions of these urban middle-class Japanese, religions that were eager to form congenial communities, that were deserving of respect and affection.

In respect to socio-economic conditions, the situation in the United States of America was somewhat different. There, propagation of the Japanese new religions succeeded in a society where industrialization had already reached a certain stage and society was about to move into a postindustrial period. In the United States of the 1960s there was also a large number of inhabitants who had left rural areas for the big cities, from the South and Midwest as well as from Central and South America, Korea, and other places. Yet it was not necessarily such people that the NSA attracted in its growth period. Rather, it attracted urban residents isolated in an advanced industrial society, represented most often by young whites in California and in large eastern-seaboard cities such as New York (Williams 1989). Offering a pragmatic value system, a congenial community, and an alternative to the individualistic, rationalistic Western civilization became the role of the Japanese new religions in this county. NSA, Sekai Kyūseikyō, and Macrobiotic were accepted because they belonged to a group of new religions that were countercultural, in that they counteracted the existing Christian, utilitarian culture (see Inoue 1985, Yamada 1983, and Albanese 1990).

Some of the Japanese new religions responded to the fact that it was possible to retain their vigor within a post-industrial environment as well as within an industrial one. Most of Japan's new religions developed in response to the religious needs of lower-class in-habitants who had left rural areas for urban areas with the advent of industrialization. Still, between these nuclei of the new religions in their growth periods and upper middle-class people with a higher education there was not a great cultural gap. When in the course of time the living standards of the Japanese people improved overall, the number of well-educated people who joined the new religions also increased. As a result, the cultural resources of the teachings and group management skills that members of the new religions had nurtured so long were available in sufficient amounts to enable those religions to meet the needs of urban middle-class residents isolated in postindustrial society. This phenomenon can be compared with the way the Pentecostal movement, which began in the United States at the beginning of the twentieth century as a movement among the lower middle class, and developed from the 1960s into a movement that involved the whole middle class, including those with a higher education.

In this way, though there are differences in the socioeconomic conditions forming the background to the new religions' expansion into the United States and other places, still, if taken as the formative process of an urban culture common to cities worldwide in the wake of international capitalism, the phenomenon can surely be seen as the product of one and the same socioeconomic condition.[8] In other words, the new religions gained the support of urban residents by offering in the midst of worldwide urbanization the support of congenial communities and cultural resources that deal with things in a practical, realistic way and preserve stable identities in the midst of diverse human relationships.

The features of expanding new religions and their appeal

The preceding section outlined the way new religions as a whole might appeal to inhabitants of a society accepting them, showing the connections with cultural and political conditions and with socioeconomic conditions. In this section I would like to consider the way those new religions that were accepted appealed to local inhabitants. First, I will note which specific groups expanded successfully into foreign cultures and then consider their particular features.

Though there are hundreds of new religions in Japan, only a few have garnered a sizable following in foreign fields. Representative of the successful groups are Sōka Gakkai, Seichō no Ie, Sekai Kyūseikyō, PL, and Sūkyō Mahikari. While Tenrikyō has been successful in Korea and Taiwan, it has not produced notable results in other regions. Two groups representative of new religions whose expansion into foreign cultures has been relatively unsuccessful despite the size of their membership within Japan would be Risshō Kōseikai and Shinnyoen. Lack of success overseas, however, is also greatly affected by accidental circumstances. For example, Seichō no Ie in Brazil was accepted as a religion offering the wartime and postwar Japanese community support for their identity as Japanese. When the Japanese community built up a large foothold in Brazilian society, a foundation for expansion was available to Seichō no Ie without any extra effort on its part.[9]

It is still possible to say that religions that succeed in expansion into other cultures have some inherent features making them deserving of that success. For example, Sōka Gakkai's spirit of aggressive, argumentative proselytization of complete strangers is easily surmised to be effective in circumstances where isolation in urban society has increased and diverse cultures coexist and clash with one another. Here I do not intend, however, to go into the self-evident factor of aggressive proselytization; what I want to do is consider what aspects in the contents of the teachings and beliefs are suited to expansion into foreign cultures.

Straightforward magical practice

Sōka Gakkai, Seichō no Ie, Sekai Kyūseikyō, PL, and Sūkyō Mahikari are, all of them, groups in which straightforward magical practice forms the essence (or at least is one of the things forming the essence) of religious life. In Sōka Gakkai, performing *gongyō* and reciting the *daimoku* before the *gohonzon*; in Seichō no Ie, performing the simple meditation of *shinsōkan* and intonation of the sacred scriptures for the spirits of the ancestors; in Sekai Kyūseikyō and Sūkyō Mahikari, pouring the deity's 'light' into the body through the outstretched palm; and in PL, praying to have one's problems transferred to the instructor together with a vow by means of the *oyashikiri* (magical prayer) – these are the main, or some of the main, religious practices. The belief that such magical practices produce mysterious, miraculous effects needs no explaining, one merely observes the practice and one understands it at once. And one can try it for oneself and see that it works. When this belief is transmitted to people of another culture, it is attended by almost no difficulties in communication. That is because it is something in the physical, experiential sphere, which needs little meaningful articulation on the linguistic level.

Similar types of religious groups did not just happen to form by chance. Except for Sūkyō Mahikari, which can be considered an offshoot of Sekai Kyūseikyō, all these groups were founded between 1910 and 1930 by intellectually gifted founders with large cities for their bases. In the context of the clashes of diverse value systems and the relativization of traditional culture, both keenly experienced in large cities, they all intended to present straightforward magic as the foundation for unswerving faith, and by this means overcome relativism. The expansion into foreign cultures of those religious groups was advanced with the intention of transcending the relativization of culture in places where such relativization was on the increase.

Practical life ethics

Nakamaki (1989) has made a very interesting study of the reasons for PL's success in Brazil. One of the things about PL that is appealing is the belief in miracles based on the magical prayer referred to as the *oyashikiri*. Still, merely a miracle belief based on magical practice is not enough to take hold of large numbers of people. The reason why people make an effort to follow PL over a long period of time is, he says, the appeal of its ethical teachings and guidance. Its ethics are adapted to the concrete situations of daily life. It preaches the mutual support of equal partners in a nuclear, rather than a patriarchal and extended, family; a work ethic that includes not only honesty and industry but also working for society and for one's neighbors, and regards work as a form of self-expression; and an ethic of 'citizenship' that encourages service to the local community. Furthermore, through one-to-one counseling it provides concrete, practical guidelines. All these things were, he says, lacking in the traditional Catholic Church and were features that appealed to Brazil's rapidly growing urban population. Nakamaki also mentions actual cases of people who talked of the appeal of the teaching that responsibility for one's good or bad fortune rests with oneself, or the appeal of the teaching that labor freely and gladly rendered ultimately redounds to one's own happiness. Practical ethics that include the utilitarian idea that service ultimately brings happiness reveals particularly well the characteristic feature of ethics in the new religions (see Shimazono 1991).

Explaining the appeal of PL in terms of its miracle beliefs and practical urban ethics would also apply to most of the other groups that have succeeded in advancing into other cultures. Whether Brazil, or the United States of America, or Korea, or Thailand, cultural resources that were lacking in the traditional religious groups but abundantly available in Japan's new religions appear here in their classic form.

Only, in the case of PL, the manner of presenting the practical ethics is systematic and thoroughgoing, and herein lies the reason why it has had a greater appeal than the other groups. As Nakamaki explains, PL's ethical guidance reaches out into the practical details of living in an exhaustive and minute way. Another feature of its ethical statements, like those of Seichō no Ie, is that they pay careful attention to subtle shifts of mentality and present technical, mind-control-type methods for bringing about psychological stability. Like the 'new thought' and 'positive thinking' that has been popular in the United States since the end of the nineteenth century, or the 'human potential' movement of recent years, techniques for preserving mental stability in the midst of urban living, with its isolation and stressfulness, have been linked with ethical practice.

Logical statements

What accounts for the appeal of Seichō no Ie and Sekai Kyūseikyō? They, too, stress miracle belief and preach practical ethics for living. In this respect they have something in common with PL. Yet they also have a slightly different appeal: their systematic, logical statements. The founder of Seichō no Ie, Taniguchi Masaharu, and the founder of Sekai Kyūseikyō, Okada Mokichi, both were culturally refined men blessed with a gift for writing discourse in a coherent way. In this they were both quite different from other founders. In the cases of female founders most at home in the world of oral tradition, or male founders lacking in literary knowledge, the words they left behind are not too logical, but what they want to say is conveyed through delicate nuances. This makes translation of their teachings extremely difficult. Also, such religious groups tend to be averse to logical explanations of their teachings and to learning. Typical examples of this are the groups in the Reiyūkai family tree. These groups are not suited for expansion to other cultures when one considers the importance of transmitting teachings in a readily understandable form. In contrast, Seichō no Ie and Sekai Kyūseikyō are able to draw non-Japanese to the world of their teachings through written expression that, while easy to understand, is logical and coherent, rather than a delicately nuanced mode of expression that is bound to one determinate culture.

In addition, I believe that Seichō no Ie's stress on the importance of members reading its literature is one of the very important points of its appeal. In present-day urban society, being proficient in written expression and having a habit of reading is an important condition for social success. As was true in Japan in the 1930s, in a society where urbanization advances rapidly, religions that make positive use of easily comprehensible literature as a tool for propagation are, by that fact alone, already attractive. Also, if easy-to-read, easy-to-understand doctrinal literature is available in translation, the message can get across even without the mediation of close person-to-person contact. In propagation to people of a different language, and in an age of cultural diversity, propagation that relies on the medium of literature that is not so bound by the delicate nuances of a specific culture is especially effective.[10]

A positive approach to religious pluralism

What was said in the preceding section could almost be said about Sōka Gakkai as well.[11] But there is one important difference between Sōka Gakkai and Seichō no Ie, Sekai Kyūseikyō, and PL. This is the attitude towards other religions, especially the attitude towards the traditional religion dominant in the overseas country. Seichō no Ie, Sekai Kyūseikyō, and PL take a positive attitude to the dominant traditional religion and allow their members to continue to belong to, for example, the Catholic Church. This attitude is based on the idea that all religions are in fact rooted in the same reality and seek the same thing. They preach that their religion and Christianity are not fundamentally different, but they are merely complementing and perfecting what was lacking in the earlier Christian religion. They therefore adopt a flexible policy of leaving such things as rites of passage to the Catholic Church. This line of thinking is readily accepted by people who have taken on traditional Catholic views and rites out of custom. Also, the adoption of such a generous attitude has the additional benefit that it avoids the troubles that arise when people with many ties to a traditional religion sever those ties to join these new religious groups.

Sōka Gakkai, on the other hand, demands exclusive commitment. Its members must sever their relations with their traditional religion. This can be the cause of troubles with the traditional religious bodies, with relatives, and with neighbors. In this respect, Sōka Gakkai can be described as putting itself in a slightly unfavorable position.

Yet, seen from another perspective, these two types of groups have something in common: both assume the coexistence of diverse religions, both have prepared coherent statements for handling this situation and have prepared positive measures to cope with it.[12] People in present-day society are placed in circumstances that make them keenly aware of the coexistence of diverse religions. For a person to choose one from among the different religions and be committed to it, something is needed that will convince the person. By insisting that other religions are wrong and that it is correct, Sōka Gakkai is showing one type of a response to the pluralistic coexistence of religions. What this means is that Seichō no Ie, Sekai Kyūseikyō, and PL on the one hand, and Sōka Gakkai on the other, are adopting differing approaches to a situation they all consciously recognize, that of the coexistence of diverse religions.

I have attempted to explore the appeal of Japanese new religions to local residents by analyzing the features of those groups that have succeeded in expansion into other cultures. It is necessary, though, to consider also the basic feature shared by all the new religions of Japan, that of their being this-worldly oriented religions.[13]

To be this-worldly oriented first of all implies that a systematic conception of salvation provides the framework for these religions of magical, this-worldly salvation. In Japan's new religions, the healing of sickness, harmony in the family, and success in one's work are directly linked to the highest goal of belief in salvation. Secondly, it means putting weight on self-help and effort in one's present life. This is closely connected with the PL characteristic described earlier. An extremely large number of Japanese new religions do not preach reliance on the power of God, the power of Buddha, the power of this or that holy person, but preach that happiness cannot be attained unless one changes one's own mental attitude and manner of daily life.

This-worldly orientation in the above two meanings is linked with an immanentist view of the divine that recognizes the divinity of the human being and recognizes divinity in existence in the present world in general. These characteristics were lacking in traditional religions with their strong tendency to be affirmative with regard to the other world and negative toward this world. It is easy to understand why such this-worldly orientation and an immanentist view of the divine are attractive to people living in a competitive society where industrialization and urbanization have advanced and changes are extreme.

Cultural discord due to expansion overseas and religious unification

It has been reported many times that religious groups propagating their religion in other cultures have attempted to adapt themselves to the respective alien cultures. PL, for example, takes a variety of steps to make their translations of documents readily understandable to the local people. It has also been reported that they have introduced elements that differ significantly from the way ceremonies and assemblies are conducted in Japan (Nakamaki 1989: 440–45). Seichō no Ie is said to have omitted from its translation of *Seimei no jissō* and other documents passages that might encounter resistance from Brazilians. The NSA has also made repeated efforts to Americanize; one example is its 'pioneer spirit' catch-phrase in connection with its active involvement in the Bicentenary of American Independence (Williams 1989).

Apart from these attempts to adapt on the part of the religious groups themselves, there can be spontaneous changes made to the contents of teachings or practice by the non-Japanese members of the groups. Consciously or unconsciously, local religious culture or local ways of group management can be introduced, leading to ways that differ from the parent body in Japan. If steps are taken to ensure control by dint of force, discontent can arise among local believers, and this in turn can even lead to a splitting off of whole groups. While adaptations made by religious groups are done for the sake of more effective propagation, at the same time they can be viewed as strategies to control local believers within the framework of the larger group. This means that new religions accepted by people of alien cultures have to face new problems of cultural discord and religious unification as a result of their adaptations.

Even within Japan itself it is not unusual for groups of believers in a particular religious organization to deviate from the regulation of the central body, or even split off entirely. Reiyūkai and Sekai Kyūseikyō, for example, have seen large numbers of groups escape control of the central body – some have branched off completely – and perhaps there are but few examples of medium-sized groups that could not be classified as branches from larger groups. In the case of groups overseas, it is probably even more difficult to maintain control, given the geographical and cultural distances separating them.

Deviation of overseas believer groups from the control of headquarters in Japan already occurred in various places around the time of the Second World War as a result of loss of contact. In Brazil a group of Ōmoto followers that included a large number of non-Japanese was beginning to form from around 1930, but contact with Ōmoto headquarters ceased after government oppression of the group within Japan in 1935 (Maeyama and Smith 1983). The group of believers in Brazil developed rather independently and began to engage in activities similar to those of such popular Brazilian religions as spiritism and Umbanda. After the war, contact with headquarters was restored, and organizational affiliation was formally renewed, but the contents of its religious activities underwent no change; headquarters has done almost nothing to intervene.

In the case of Tenrikyō in Taiwan, contact with headquarters was cut after the war, and the Chiaitungmen church, which was run solely by local believers, adopted *poe* (divination stones) and the drawing of lots to divine the right times to pray, the offering of gilt paper to gods and ancestors, and other elements of Chinese folk religion (Huang 1989). But with the resumption of operations of the Tenri propagation office in Taiwan in 1967, slowly but steadily the church was restored to something similar to what exists in Japan. Still, it is said that some subordinate missionary stations even now maintain deviant elements. In Korea, where anti-Japanese feelings run high, problems of this sort are even more serious, and control by headquarters is a difficult matter, including the problem of church unity within Korea itself.

A recent example of discord occurred in Sōka Gakkai's overseas organization. NSA (Sōka Gakkai in the U.S.A.), which achieved explosive growth at the end of the 1960s, attempted to hand over leadership of the local organization to non-Japanese (Williams 1989). But the new leadership stratum made up principally of non-Japanese did not like the central-administrative, organization-mobilizing nature of the group and attempted to adopt policies that set a value on the autonomous activities of regional groups and on democratic procedures for running NSA as a whole. This happened to coincide, however, with a sudden slowdown in NSA growth and even signs of decline. From the 1980s, under the guidance of headquarters, there was a return to a central-administrative, organization-mobilizing type of religious group along with a return to a leadership setup in which Japanese formed the core. In the process, a group of people, mainly whites who for a time had been in leadership positions, separated and began independent activities. While detailed information is not available, a similar large-scale secession has also occurred in Indonesia.

Judging from the experiences of groups splitting away from parent bodies within Japan, we can anticipate that the problem of regulating overseas believer groups will occur often in the future. There will no doubt be some groups in which the overseas believers will be numerically stronger. There is already a faction, the Shinseiha, within

Sekai Kyūseikyō in Brazil, that is larger than its sponsoring body in Japan. Also, the sources of propagation activity have shifted in recent years with, for example, Brazilian members of Seichō no Ie and Sekai Kyūseikyō doing successful missionary work in Europe, and with a Korean member of Tenrikyō propagating in Argentina.[14] At present, it appears that in most of the groups the authority of Japanese propagators is preserved, but it is only a matter of time before local propagators will have more say. In the future, financial aid coming from headquarters will undoubtedly decrease when Japan's status as an economic superpower begins to decline. When that happens, the question will surely arise, how will the central body in Japan be able to maintain control over religious bodies overseas? It is impossible to predict whether or not it will be able to maintain its present unity as a single multinational organization. New religions that have expanded overseas can be compared to multinational enterprises, it has been argued, and they can be characterized as multinational religions (Inoue 1985; Nakamaki 1986, 1989), but when separations occur overseas and a religion ceases to be a single organization, we shall have to think again about the appropriateness of this designation.

Significance from a history of religions perspective

The expansion of Japan's new religions into other cultures from the 1960s on was founded on the imperialist-inspired invasions before the war as well as massive migrations from Japan, which continued even after the war. Without these two factors there probably would not have been such an extensive expansion into other cultures. It is also clear that Japan's economic prosperity is another contributing factor to recent expansion into other cultures. The success of Sekai Kyūseikyō and Sōka Gakkai in Thailand, for example, cannot be fully comprehended unless one takes into account the huge economic influence wielded by Japanese businesses in the country and the financial and spiritual help liberally poured into Thailand from Japan for the sake of propagation. In a certain sense, then, the expansion into alien cultures of Japan's new religions must be seen from one viewpoint as the fruit of the growth in economic and military influence of the Japanese.

Still, the expansion into alien cultures from the 1960s on also has to be grasped in the light of the rapid expansion in cultural exchange worldwide, with movements of personnel and information on the increase. This is also linked with a spread of cultural tolerance;

societies that previously were closed to other religions have in the past twenty years become open to missionary activity. In recent years places like the Soviet Union and Eastern Europe have been thrown open as markets where propagation can be freely conducted, and China will no doubt follow. We can expect that places for extensive activity will open anew to those religions in the world that favor propagation and evangelism, and that they will expand.

What sorts of religions will be active in these new markets and vying for results from missionary activity? There are four categories: (1) the Catholic Church, Eastern Orthodox Church, and Islam will probably extend their influence to neighboring regions by enlarging their present bases; (2) the various Protestant sects will probably show growth in Catholic areas and other regions where traditional Christian culture still has strong influence; they will also probably grow in places like Korea and ethnic Chinese societies, where the influence of Confucianism, which shares the Protestant character of a religion of moral duties and stress on scriptures, is strong; (3) loosely organized religious philosophies that are mystical and psychotherapeutic in character, such as the 'New Age' in the United States of America and the Anthroposophie movement in Germany, will probably gain wide acceptance among people in the higher education class; and (4) new religions that have been born in various parts of the globe, have the potential for huge development side by side with all of the above, especially as a force to compete with the Protestant sects.[15]

The most conspicuous cradles of these new religions have been the United States and Japan. The new religious groups originating in the United States are also often called 'cults': the Mormons, Jehovah's Witnesses, Scientology, etc. The Unification Church that was born in Korea is also powerful. The Wat Dhammakaya movement begun in the 1960s in Thailand is an example of a new religious movement with a high potential for spreading to other countries. Seen in a global perspective, Japan's new religions have much in common with these religious groups and movements.

As I suggested above, Japan's new religions have garnered great success in societies where urban populations have increased as a result of industrialization. Again, in those societies where industrialization has already been attained and the loneliness of urban living has deepened, they are considered to have the potential for a certain degree of success in missionary activity. In such societies the new religions try to indicate concrete, practical guidelines for overcoming the problems isolated individuals face in ordinary daily life. And they offer such people spiritual support for self-help and mutual-support communities. In doing this, they offer something people can hang on to as they acquire moral self-discipline and continue to live as urban middle-class citizens. Furthermore, they have more this-world intentionality than sects, and they try to respond to urban residents' this-worldly aspirations.

In a world community characterized by increasing industrialization and urbanization, the demand for religions that fulfill such functions will probably increase. The various new religions in Japan have, alongside cults originating in the United States, been in the vanguard in various regions throughout the world, nurturing and storing up the cultural resources for meeting that demand.

14 New Religions and This World

New religions and new new religions

Since the early 19th century, Japanese society has witnessed the birth of various religious movements that have advocated the salvation of individuals and gained support and followers, mainly among common people. These movements have taken root in society as organized religions. Thus, a number of new religions have emerged, resulting in the coexistence of various religions and in the popularization of religious leaders.[1] The new religions have their own doctrines, practices and organizational styles somewhat different from those of traditional religions. While many of them consider themselves to be new religious creations, some regard themselves, rather, as having returned to the origin of existing religions. Even in such cases, modern elements are incorporated in the main components of their movements and organizations. Several hundred religious movements and/or organizations are regarded as belonging to the new religions in contemporary Japan.

These new religions have reflected the changing times in the course of their development. The first period (circa 1800–1890), represented by Kurozumikyō, Tenrikyō, Konkōkyō and Honmon Butsuryūko, and the second period (circa 1890–1920), represented by Ōmotokyō, were followed by the third period (circa 1920–1970), which was the time when the new religions reached their prime. It was during this period that Sōka Gakkai (the largest new religion in modern Japan), Reiyūkai, Risshō Kōseikai, Bussho Gonenkai, Myōchikai Kyōdan and other groups derived from Reiyūkai, Perfect Liberty Kyōdan, Seichō no Ie, Sekai Kyūseikyō, En'nokyō, Zenrinkyō and others all made a great leap forward. During this period, Tenrikyō, Konkōkyō and other religious groups that were founded in the first period and had gained strength during the second, were able to consolidate their positions. Thus, the third period can be characterized as the time when all the new religions established themselves on firm ground.

However, most of the new religious bodies that had been formed by the third period fell into stagnation after 1970. Several religious bodies saw a significant reduction in the number of their followers. Many of them entered a defensive, retrogressive period after the peak of their development. On the other hand, there were some new religious movements during this period that have many characteristics in common with those new religions that experienced their prime by 1970. Therefore, they can be categorized as belonging to another phase of the new religious phenomenon, or the fourth period of new religions.

The media call the religions emerging during this fourth period the 'new new religions' in order to highlight their topicality as opposed to those who had already peaked.[2] It is not correct to assume that this term, 'new new religions,' indicates the advent of entirely new types of religion, dramatically different from the preceding 'new religions.' In many respects, the new religions of the fourth period bear characteristics similar to those of the previous periods. There are, however, some significant differences, which became more explicit in the 1990s.

In this chapter I shall discuss the characteristics, particularly beliefs about salvation, of the new new religions (the fourth-period new religions), taking as examples the God Light Association (GLA), which enjoyed rapid growth around 1970, and Kofuku no Kagaku (The Institute for Research in Human Happiness, IRH), which gathered strength around 1990. The founder of IRH was at one time impressed by the books written by the founder of GLA. Thus it is not strange that the movements share some components in their teachings. But there are also contrasting elements that differentiate the doctrines of the two religions, which may be recognized as reflecting the social tendencies and popular sentiments of 1970 and 1990. By comparing these two religions, we may gain some knowledge about new trends in religious movements, and changes in the social situation and people's thinking between the 1970s and the 1990s.

It is not my intention to claim that these two are representative new new religions, nor that they are sufficient for us to grasp the major characteristics of the new new religions. The purpose of this paper is to find some clues for the future study of the characteristics of the new new religions as a whole by focusing on one strand of them.

GLA's beliefs concerning salvation

Takahashi Shinji (1927–1976) was born to a poor farming family in Saku Heights, Nagano Prefecture in central Japan.[3] He was educated at a military preparatory school and joined the military to serve as an airman during the Second World War. After the war, he underwent training in electric applications and started an electronic parts manufacturing business at the age of 25. He was an active, hard-working manager of a small-to-medium-size factory. In 1968, when he was 40 years old, he experienced esoteric phenomena while he was worshipping the Buddha and meditating with his wife and her younger brothers. Through this series of experiences, he came to believe in the existence of the spirit as an independent entity, separate from the body, and that *jitsuzaikai* (the Real World) is the rightful home of the spirit. He realized that one should maintain harmony in one's mind and nurture the senses of love and benevolence in order to enhance one's mind to the state of *bosatsu* (Bodhisattva) or to the higher state of *nyorai* (Tathagata Buddha) – both higher entities in the Real World. In 1968, Shinri no kai (the Divine Truth Association) was formed in Tokyo to spread this belief; it was renamed Dai Uchu Shinkōkai (the Great Universal God Light Association) in the following year and, finally, the God Light Association in 1970.

From the beginning, Takahashi Shinji was eager to spread his teachings through meetings and books, and was reluctant to organize the religious body even after the rapid increase in the number of followers. After his death from sickness in 1976 at the age of 48, his eldest daughter, Takahashi Keiko, succeeded as leader of the movement, and it has continued with the name of the GLA Sōgō Honbu and a nominal membership of 12,981 as of 1990. Some disciples did not follow Takahashi Keiko after the founder's death, and formed their own sects. There is now no large religious body that believes in the original teachings of Takahashi Shinji; none the less, quite a few people, regardless of their sectarian affiliations, have been influenced by the founder through listening to his talks, or reading his writings.

In what follows, the features of GLA teachings in the 1970s will be discussed, drawing on Takahashi's books – in particular, the three volumes of *Kokoro no hakken* (Discovery of the mind): *Shinri hen* (Divine truth) (1971a), *Kagaku hen* (Science) (1971b) and *Genshō hen* (Phenomenal witness) (1973a).

The existence of the soul and of the Hierarchic Other World adjacent to the Phenomenal World

Our spirit exists independently of our bodies. After death, the spirit (also called a photon body) continues to exist apart from the vessel called the body (also called a body boat). The actual world, *genshōkai*

(Phenomenal World) with which we are familiar is not the one and only world: *jitsuzaikai* (the Real World) is just next to it. It is this Real World to which the spirit is directed after death. When one brings one's heart into harmony following the direction of Takahashi Shinji, one can experience an 'opening of the spiritual path.' When one directs one's spirit to the 'dome' leading to the Real World, and communicates with one's guardian spirit and subconscious, memories of past lives are resuscitated.

The Real World comprises six strata. The supreme stratum is *nyoraikai* (the World of Tathagata Buddha) to which belong the "great leaders' spirit of light at the upper high stage" of the three beings of Shakyamuni, Jesus Christ and Moses, and the "great leaders' spirit of light at the lower high stage" with the 423 bodies of *nyorai* (Tathagata Buddha). These spirits dominate both the Real and the Phenomenal Worlds. The second stratum is *bosatsukai* (the World of Bodhisattva) in which nearly 20,000 *bosatsu* or "leaders' spirits of the high stage" exist. The *bosatsu* guide human beings in the Phenomenal World while training themselves in pursuit of spiritual enhancement. The third stratum is *shinkai* (the World of Gods), where there exist around 150 million angels of light who have returned to the Real World after having reached the stage of enlightenment through knowledge, just as philosophers and scientists do. The fourth stratum is *reikai* (the spiritual world), where those spirits of a higher level than the common people exist and protect people in the Phenomenal World, serving as their guardian spirits. The fifth stratum is called *yukai* (the Astral World); it is a harmonious world with no war and in which people know how to be satisfied with their lives. Yet it is still close to the Phenomenal World and near to human life. From here, many people go out into the Phenomenal World for self-training. The lowest stratum is *jigokukai* (the World of Hell) where people live with pain even after death, haunted by unharmonious memories of their past lifetime.

The spirit has eternal life in the Real World with these six strata from which a person is born into the Phenomenal World to train him or herself. In other words, the cycle of life is repeated, but when a person is born, his or her memory of life in the past is lost.

The history of God, Buddha and the universe

God is the 'great consciousness,' or 'great divine spirit of the great universe,' which has the same expanse as the universe itself. Below the great divine spirit of the great universe is El Ranty, the Spiritual

Sun and the authentic Messiah. Jesus in the Akasha line, Shakyamuni (Buddha) in the Cantare line, and Moses in the Moses line are branched spirits of light. A buddha is an enlightened person, or a person who has reached the stage of being inseparably unified with God's great consciousness. When the soul of a person is enhanced, he or she climbs up the ladder of the Real World to approach the stage of Buddha's enlightenment. Human beings follow the path of evolution through the cycle of rebirth of life.

El Ranty from Star Beta arrived on earth 365 million years ago with the original human beings, but soon returned to heaven. After a long passage of time, civilized societies were formed, and the rise-and-fall cycle of civilized societies was repeated on the Mu continent, the Atlantis continent and others. Takahashi Shinji is the personification of El Ranty, and manifests the soul that was once born as Buddha Shakyamuni. In other words, he is the true Messiah.

The enhancement of the soul as the purpose of life, and its realization through mind-rectification

Human beings are born into the Phenomenal World because it is a suitable training ground to enhance one's soul. The hardships that people are faced with in this world are given as trials or training opportunities for upgrading their souls. All individuals select by themselves their own hardships in their lives, the outline of which is determined at the time of birth. Thus, one should not impose the causes of one's own hardships upon someone else; rather, one should accept them willingly for one's own training.

The soul, which has eternal life in the Real World, can be enhanced by rectifying one's heart. Having a right heart or a wrong heart also affects one's fate in the Phenomenal World. Having a wrong heart implies a state of mind that is self-centered, clings to specific things, or is possessed with worldly desires; it connotes an unharmonious heart, anger, jealousy, hatred, and irritation. People with this state of heart tend to draw misfortune and sorrow upon themselves. Because the devil spirits in the world of hell can easily possess a person with an unharmonious heart, misfortune often falls upon that person.

A right heart connotes a harmonious and impartial heart filled with benevolence and love. The norm for practices for daily life based on the right heart is manifested by the Eight Paths of Righteousness: Right View, Right Thinking, Right Words, Right Behavior, Right Living, Right Effort, Right Mind, and Right Meditative Concentration. A person's heart is purified through reflecting on his or her heart and behavior (*zenjo meisō*) based on these norms. In the teachings of GLA, this act of purifying one's heart through introspection on one's past life and the way one lives one's present life is considered to be the most important practice for the followers.

Although the heart's being right or wrong affects one's life regarding whether one will be fortunate or unfortunate, the purpose of life does not lie in individual happiness in this world. The components of life in the Phenomenal World (that is, birth, ageing, disease and death) are all causes of pain. The eventual achievement of happiness in this world lies in transience. It is the enhancement of the transmigrating soul, with its own home in the Real World, that is required for building an unshakeable foundation for eternal happiness, hence the real purpose of life. Nevertheless, each person is charged with the mission to build Utopia on earth, and is supposed to make every effort to spread harmony among the hearts of all people, thereby bringing about a harmonious society on earth.

Criticism of present society and other religions

The reality of present-day society is far from what human society should be like. People have succumbed to materialism, and are frantically searching to satisfy their desires. Rank, prestige and wealth have become the goals of life. Discrimination based on race and rank abounds. Hatred and conflicts prevail, while benevolence and love are driven away.

A brief introduction to one of Takahashi Shinji's novels, *Ai wa nikushimi wo koete* (Love transcends hatred) (1973b), may illustrate his criticism of the present society.

A woman from Taiwan married to a Japanese man was cruelly treated by their neighbors. Their son suffered discrimination as a boy. When he grew up, he kept his mixed birth a secret in order to escape further discrimination, and led a vicious life in his frantic search for wealth and power. His goal was retaliation against the people who had mistreated him. But then he fell seriously ill, losing consciousness for some time. When he was somewhere beyond this world, he reflected on his past life, repented with the desire to have his heart purified, and was awakened to the concept of being thoughtful of others around him. Takahashi's shrewd criticism of the present society is contained in this story. His critical vision also extended to contemporary religions, which rarely advocate a way of life in which people should upgrade themselves by seeking harmony in their hearts and living a right life. Rather, the dominant religions are those that promise worldly benefits, or those that claim salvation from without by relying on God and Buddha rather than on one's own efforts. Some adopt a blind or fanatic belief, and others resort to ritualism and intellectualism. All these depart from the proper function of religion: to upgrade one's heart through one's own training and practice.

The task of building Utopia may involve the reform of the social and religious features of present-day society. Takahashi, however, does not make any proposals about how to reform society. He advocates a non-activist approach in that the reform of one's heart should change religion and, eventually, society.

Kōfuku no Kagaku's beliefs concerning Salvation

Ōkawa Ryūhō, the founder of Kōfuku no Kagaku (IRH), was born in a small town in the Tokushima Prefecture of Shikoku Island in the western part of Japan. He was brought up in the family of a salaried worker with a moderate income. His father had a deep interest in philosophy, religions and politics. He was involved in religious activities such as Christianity and Seichō no Ie, and edited a local magazine of the Japanese Communist Party. Ryūhō displayed brilliance from his time in elementary school. He graduated from the prestigious Law Faculty of Tokyo University in 1981, and was employed by Tōmen, a major trading house.

Through the influence of his family, he became interested in religion from his early days. In particular, he was impressed by Takahashi Shinji's books, which he read just before starting his employment. He came to believe that he could open up a spiritual path, and report the words of the spirits of different dimensions. After publishing the words of eminent spirits of the Real World in such books as *Nichiren no Reigen* (Nichiren's spiritual words), *Kukai no Reigen* (Kukai's spiritual words) and *Kiristo no Reigen* (Christ's spiritual words), he resigned from the company in 1986 to found a new religion, 'Kōfuku no Kagaku' (IRH), in Tokyo. As dozens of his books became best sellers, his name came to attract public attention.

The growth of the organization was remarkable. Its nominal membership grew to seventy-odd thousand by July 1990, and 1,520,000 by July 1991. We may guess the active membership from the fact that the movement had the strength to mobilize tens of thousands of followers to attend its large rallies. In the autumn of 1991, they staged a loud protest against Kōdansha, a major publishing house, accusing it of having criticized and defamed the founder Ōkawa in an allegedly false article in one of its magazines. This protest was attacked in turn by the media, damaging the movement's public image. As of 1993, the organization maintains the strength to mobilize tens of thousands at any one time.

Ōkawa wrote a number of books, three of which, *Taiyo no hō* (The laws of the sun) (1987a) *Ogon no hō* (The laws of gold) (1987b) and *Eien no hō* (The laws of eternity) (1987c) are said to set forth his basic philosophy. To familiarize oneself with his ideas about society and politics, *Utopia kachi kakumei* (Utopian value revolution, 1989) and *Frankly Speaking* (1993) are essential reading. A convenient introduction to the teachings published by the organization is *Shinri yōgo no kiso chishiki* (Basic knowledge about God's truth terminology, 1990). In what follows, I shall discuss, on the basis of these books, IRH's beliefs about salvation.

The existence of the soul and of the Hierarchic Other World adjacent to the Phenomenal World

IRH shares with GLA the belief in the existence of spirits, and of a hierarchic world adjacent to the Phenomenal World. Here the Phenomenal World is called the three-dimensional world, and further dimensions from the fourth to ninth are believed to exist: the fourth dimension being *yukai* (the Posthumous Realm), the fifth *reikai* (the Spiritual Realm), the sixth *shinkai* (the Godly Realm), the seventh *bosatsukai* (the Bosatsu Realm), the eighth *nyoraikai* (the Nyorai Realm), and the ninth *uchukai* (the Cosmic Realm). Within the six strata of the Real World, the World of Hell is considered to belong to *reikai*, and *uchukai* is above *nyoraikai*. The teaching is more elaborate in that it preaches that there are more than ten dimensions in the world, and that, at the thirteenth dimension, Macrocosmic Consciousness is to be attained, after which Divine Consciousness is to be attained at an even higher dimension.

IRH's beliefs about the nature of each world, and the numbers and names of spirits in each world, are to some degree different from those of GLA. The act of opening the spiritual path is practiced by at least some members of IRH, but not with any great frequency. Rather, the existence of the world of different dimensions has been 'verified' by Ōkawa Ryūhō himself interacting with various spirits, and speaking and writing their words for his audiences and readers.

The history of God, Buddha and the universe

IRH's doctrinal theories of the history of the universe, pre-history and the history of humanity are elaborated upon at greater length than those of GLA. About 100 billion years ago, God, as a conscious Being, resolved to create the three-dimensional universe. About 80 billion years ago, the 13-dimensional universe was created. After the creation of the 12- to 10-dimensional consciousness, the Big Bang occurred within the 13-dimensional body of consciousness 40 billion years ago; hence, the emergence of three-dimensional space. This event was followed by the birth of the sun, planets, earth and living things on earth; and then the process of creating human beings began 600 million years ago, assisted by nine-dimensional divine spirits.

During this process, spirits of various other stars cooperated, the most important being El Miore (El Cantare) of Venus. El Cantare, ranking in the supreme position among the nine-dimensional divine spirits, was the main planner in the creation of humanity. He was the messiah who would later be incarnated as Hermes in Greece, as Buddha in India, and now as Ōkawa Ryuhō in present-day Japan. About 600 million years ago, El Cantare planned the creation of humanity. Then about 365 million years ago he invited from a star 60 million people who would become the ancestors of humanity on earth. The leader of these people was El Ranty and part of his soul was to become Takahashi Shinji in 20th-century Japan. Later, however, during the process of evolution of humanity, some of these people misused their free will. Thus, about 120 million years ago, the world of hell also emerged as a result of the upheaval caused by Lucifer.

Throughout the past million years, a number of civilizations have appeared, the first being the Gondarna civilization, starting about 750,000 years ago. There followed the rise and fall of the Mutram, Lemuria, Mu, and Atlantis civilizations, then, eventually, the present civilization. The Mu civilization lies at the source of Oriental civilization, while that of Atlantis is the source of today's Occidental civilization. The religion that integrates these two major civilizations, represented by Buddha and Hermes respectively, was born in Japan, IRH.

The enhancement of the soul as a purpose in life, and its realization through mind-rectification

According to IRH belief, the purpose of life is to upgrade one's soul, which is supposed to exist eternally in the Real World. For this purpose, reflection upon oneself, and the harmony of heart, benevolence and love are required: the Middle Way and practice of the Eightfold Path must be sought. However, daily moral practices and *kokoro naoshi* (mind-rectification) are manifested as 'the quest for the right mind' and its actualization: the Fourfold Path in the teachings of IRH. In the Fourfold Path, elements that differ from those to be found in GLA are also included.

The Fourfold Path consists of the paths of 'love,' 'knowledge,' 'reflection,' and 'development,' presenting a set of methodologies for true human happiness. 'Love' and 'reflection' are stressed in the teachings of GLA. 'Knowledge' and 'development,' teachings newly introduced by IRH, are scarcely touched upon in GLA teaching.

'Knowledge' means knowledge about 'God's Truth,' or acquiring the knowledge considered to be right from IRH's viewpoint. It actually means that one needs to deepen one's perception of spiritual knowledge, centering around the teachings on the mind, and of the history, religions, thoughts and philosophy, politics and economics that are discussed in Ōkawa Ryūhō's publications. Followers are encouraged to read a number of his books, and to sit the 'National Accrediting Examination for Truthology.' Having sufficient knowledge of God's Truth is considered to be a requirement for spirits in the six-dimensional world of *shinkai* (the Godly Realm).

'Development' implies the need to endeavor with a high sense of mission in pursuit of 'public happiness' beyond the level of 'personal happiness' obtained through reflection and love in one's immediate community. Purifying one's heart through reflection often makes the individual introverted. However, one should go beyond introversion to work actively upon the society in which one lives. In addition to Oriental meditative attitudes, bright and positive Greco-type attitudes are required. 'Infallible thinking' is recommended as being instrumental in producing positive, outward-looking attitudes. This positive way of thinking teaches that one can always learn something, even through failures and discouraging events, and advance while also nourishing one's soul through those events.

Visions for building Utopia

The building of Utopia that is advocated by GLA is given a concrete guiding principle by IRH, which encourages followers to work upon society with their positive attitudes. IRH encourages the 'Utopian Value Revolution' to change entirely the present social order, including politics, economics and education, and to promote an order emphasizing religious values.

In politics, for example, elements of moral excellence should be incorporated into the democratic mechanism. In the economy, divine values should be applied to price, interest rate and tax systems in place of the simple exchange of equivalents. In education, the purpose of life, the importance of love and the value of eternal life should be taught as high priorities. In the field of bioethics, IRH is opposed to the notion of recognizing brain-death. It launched a campaign against the recognition of brain-death (as a premise for organ transplants), criticizing modern medicine for attempting to transplant internal organs, as this results in shocks to the soul while it is in the process of departing from the flesh after cessation of the heartbeat.

IRH is particularly concerned with controversial discussions in the fields of thought, religion and journalism, in which the social activism of this movement is manifested. What was most radically expressed through its protest against Kōdansha Publishing, and its court battle, was its criticism of the media of today. The media is devoted to dragging down influential personalities; they cater to public jealousy, and drive the public into witch hunting. The critical and disrespectful attitudes of the media towards religions are also to be condemned. The media, as well as public consciousness, must be reformed to show respect to religions, and to respect worthy persons. IRH also asserts that even though freedom of speech is admitted, the freedom of advocating materialism should be limited to some extent. From IRH's viewpoint, the confrontation with Kōdansha is not a defensive and retaliatory action against the criticism of their founder, but an action motivated by pursuit of the goal of *yonaoshi* (world-renewal).

Characteristics of beliefs about salvation in GLA and IRH

GLA and IRH share a number of characteristics with the new religions of the first to third periods in that (1) they contain both Buddhist ideas and beliefs in deities and spirits in the other world as components of their belief systems; (2) they regard the whole body of the universe as the manifestation of God (the originator), and count on divine power, light and life contained in the universe; (3) they perceive human beings as sharing the attributes of God, and ask individuals to have self-awareness as such, and to make efforts to enhance themselves; (4) they consider that one's state of mind determines one's fate, and emphasize *kokoro naoshi* (mind-rectification) as a way to enhance it; and (5) they consider

271

that spirits of the deceased, animal spirits, and so on affect the fate of people in the present world, and pay due consideration to control of these spirits. These characteristics can be observed in many, if not all, new religions in Japan.

Some distinct points about 'new new religions' are different from former new religions. The most outstanding difference is the stress on life in the different worlds beyond this world, rather than advocating solely this-worldly salvation.

In earlier new religions, there is concern about the Spiritual World, but limited to the belief that beings in the Spiritual World affect the fate of humans in this world. If there is concern about the Spiritual World at all, the purpose of life is believed to be attaining a happy communal life in this world. This-worldly benefits such as healing sickness are valued, not downgraded as the realization of materialistic, physical and temporary benefits, but celebrated as the manifestation of ultimate salvation. Agony in this world is to be overcome within this world in order for one to attain sublime happiness. This concept of this-worldly salvation is the major feature of the view of salvation prevalent in the former new religions.

In contrast, GLA and IRH advocate that the soul has eternal life in the Real World. In accordance with the view of early Buddhism, they set forth the notion of 'transience' – that this world is but a temporary home.

A lengthy time-span, during which the soul is supposed to go through the cycle of 'transmigration' for self-improvement, is imagined by GLA and IRH so as to emphasize the mutability of life in this world. The term 'happiness' is used to express the goal of life, but it is not considered attainable during one's present lifespan. Rather, it is for the sake of enhancement of the soul with eternal life that the trials through hardships in this world should be considered meaningful.

This concept, which is focused on an elevation beyond the present world, is related to the belief held by members of some new new religions that places a strong emphasis on the independent soul with eternal life, which is thought to be as important as, and sometimes more important than, the communal life of family, relatives, local community, colleagues and others in the present world. For the transmigrating soul, interaction with people in this world is transitory. Utopia building, which is the goal of public life in this world, is achieved somewhere beyond the limited human relationships of the present life. The hope of finding ultimate salvation in lively, peaceful, warm-hearted communal life with other people, which was found in the former new religions' beliefs about salvation in this world, is somewhat relativized.

The followers of GLA and IRH are largely from generations that exhibit introversive tendencies and find mutual dependence or reliance in communal life to be troublesome. They value independence and individual responsibility, reflecting on one's past quietly, and they favor finding comfort within one's solitary soul. Although similarly preaching the need for 'mind-rectification,' earlier new religions place optimistic expectations on pleasure in human relations, while GLA and IRH cast cool eyes on human relations in this world, and are more interested in a search for inner peace, yearning for the eternal home of the soul (another world).

One reason for the spread of such a view might be that the privacy of the individual has been held in high regard since Japanese society achieved a certain level of material affluence. A supporting factor might be a marked increase in the number of persons who have acquired stoical, self-disciplinary attitudes from early childhood, reflecting the competitive, ability-oriented tendency in Japan. It may also mirror the mounting skepticism toward infinite progress and prosperity in this world among people who have come to question the quality of the progress and prosperity they achieved through the country's modernization process. Against such a background can be discerned a mental tendency to return from modern, this-world-oriented attitudes to the worship of the world-after-death, or an attitude valuing the world-outside-this-world that is to be found in an historical religion (in this case, primitive Buddhism).

Finally, a difference between GLA and IRH must be touched upon. It relates to the evaluation of the social order in the present world. GLA poses questions about the social order based on wealth, rank and power. Inequality in the distribution of wealth, and discrimination against others because of racial and ethnic differences are targets for their criticism. Dignity and equality of all people before God (the Spiritual Sun) are emphatically advocated. In IRH, however, excessive democracy and the collapse of moral order due to a stringent egalitarianism are criticized along with lack of respect for religions due to excessive freedom for the satisfaction of desires and materialism. IRH has common points with some recent anti-liberal sentiments that hope to recover morality and religiosity against anarchical freedom, and to restore dignity and divine order to advanced industrial society.

The difference in the views of society between the two religions should first be considered to reflect the difference in personal style and preference of the two leaders, Takahashi Shinji and Ōkawa Ryūhō. That the two movements, sharing some concepts concerning salvation, had a considerable number of supporters around 1970 and 1990 respectively may, however, mirror some aspects of the transition of Japanese society and its people's sentiments during that period. In other words, it is a shift from hope for a Utopia of horizontal solidarity to hope for a Utopia with a religio-moral social system. It signals the conservative inclination of a society after it has attained a certain level of affluence wherein the public have various kinds of vested interests. It is also a Japanese-style manifestation of negating some aspects of modern values, a tendency that is becoming apparent in other parts of the world in the 1980s and 1990s.

15 New Spirituality Movements and the Spiritual Intellectuals

New Age and new spirituality movements

A study of both elite and popular culture in Japan reveals that interest in religious and spiritual themes has increased significantly since the late 1970s. Some individuals seem to have only superficial interest in the occult and magic, participating in little more than divination on the streets and Ouija boards in classrooms. Others, by contrast, are seriously interested in sophisticated religious ideas, systematic worldviews, and religious practices.

Many of those with a more serious interest, however, are not likely to be involved in organized religions. Established Buddhist sects have long been declining. On the whole, the new religions established since the nineteenth century have not recorded growth since around 1970. Rather, an increasing number of people are now involved in an individualistic spiritual quest utilizing media and various networks outside of organized religions. Religious ideas and practices can be learned through the books and videotapes marketed in various shops, through seminars and workshops, and through loosely connected small groups or networks. The goal of these individualistic seekers is quite different from that of organized religions, so they would rather use the term 'spirituality' than 'religion' to designate their common interest.

Many participants and observers use the term 'Spiritual World' to refer to the individuals and small groups comprising these amorphous movements. This term was first used in 1978 by a Tokyo bookstore that set up a 'Spiritual World' section of books. Many bookstores subsequently followed this pattern and today most large bookstores in urban areas have a 'Spiritual World' corner with a selection of books that resembles the New Age section in American bookstores. One will find, for example, books by Shirley MacLaine and Colin Wilson, books by channelers, books by Osho Rajneesh and Krishnamurti, books by and on Swedenborg and Rudolf Steiner, books on meditation and healing techniques, books exploring the relationship between Eastern mysticism and contemporary psychotherapy, and books representing the 'New Science' (i.e., New Age Science).

Many of those interested in an individualistic spiritual quest would feel comfortable with the term 'Spiritual World.' Others, however, would resist this designation to represent their values and worldviews. This probably resembles the situation in the United States, where some of those interested in an individualistic quest would not be content with the term 'New Age.' I would like to propose the term 'new spirituality movements' or 'new spirituality movements and culture' or 'new spirituality movements/culture' to designate the wide range of individualistic spiritual quest developing in many parts of the world, especially in advanced industrial societies. This term would include the 'Spiritual World' in Japan and the 'New Age' in the United States. These new spirituality movements share many features in common and may be seen as representing one new global religious culture.[1]

The central element in these movements is a concern for the 'transformation of consciousness.' Participants attach a high value on realizing and approaching deeper or higher levels of consciousness by using various techniques and disciplines, such as meditation and bodywork. This dimension of consciousness is different from the ordinary and cool one. It is understood that through these disciplines one will enter a deeper level of consciousness or mind leading to one's own soul and eventually the authentic self, sometimes referred to as 'the Higher Self.' The soul may be independent of the body and connected to worlds before and after this life. Also, the soul is not necessarily restricted by the boundary of the individual mind and body but connected with nature and even the entire universe outside of the body. By promoting the transformation of consciousness and harmonious relationships with others and the natural environment, individuals not only improve their own lives but contribute to the transformation of the whole world and universe. The spread of this new level of consciousness and new style of life may enable the human race to overcome the impasses of modern civilization, eventually leading to the next stage of the evolutionary process. These are the basic ideas common to the various strands of the new spirituality movements.

Although not so individualistic in their orientation, some new religions share these ideas with the new spirituality movements. The Rajneesh movement, for example, can be included in the new spirituality movements because it advocates similar ideas and practices. On the whole, however, new religions do not fit in this category because of their systematic teachings and rituals, hierarchical and bureaucratic organizations, and veneration of a sacred founder. These common features of organized religions, both traditional and new, appear restrictive or even authoritarian to participants in the new spirituality movements. Therefore, only loosely or informally organized new religions can be included in the category of new spirituality movements.

Figure 15.1 illustrates the relationship between the four terms discussed above: Spiritual World, New Age, new spirituality movements/culture, and new religions. The Spiritual World and New Age share many common elements. The terms essentially refer to the same phenomenon but reflect the difference in language used by participants. In fact, there are only minor differences between New Age phenomenon in the West and Spiritual World phenomenon in Japan, resulting primarily from differences in cultural background. The difference between these two emic concepts is indicated by the two circles slightly off center from each other.

New spirituality movements and spiritual intellectuals in Japan

Among the various differences between American and Japanese new spirituality movements, perhaps the most important one is that Japanese new spirituality movements/culture have inherited a great deal from the dominant religious culture, whereas American movements differ significantly from the dominant Judeo-Christian traditions. The

Figure 15.1: NSMC, New Age, Spiritual World and NRMs

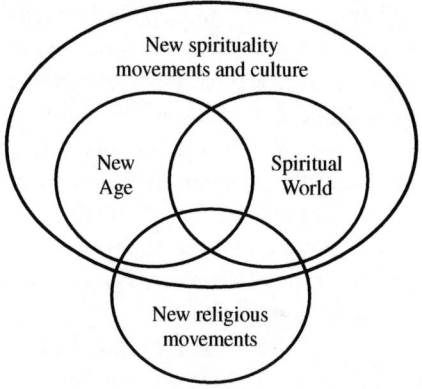

Judeo-Christian religious traditions are basically antagonistic to the premises of the new spirituality movements. Buddhist, Shinto, and folk religious traditions in Japan, by contrast, share more similarities than differences with the new spirituality movements/culture. The new spirituality movements in Japan, therefore, do not appear very 'new' nor do they appear to challenge the established religious traditions.

Continuity between the dominant religious culture and the new spirituality movements/culture can be seen in the following areas. First, as a form of popular religion, new spirituality movements share many common elements with Japan's folk religion, which has a long history of its own. The New Age practice of channeling, for example, is not very different from shamanistic practices in Japanese folk religion. These practices are still present throughout Japan, even in urban areas. Consequently, it is often difficult to determine whether a person is influenced primarily by traditional shamanism or New Age-type channeling imported from the United States in the 1980s.

Second, the new spirituality movements/culture are in basic continuity with organized religions. Shinto, as well as most of the Buddhist sects and new religions, share many ideas and practices with the new spirituality movements. Kukai (774–835), the founder of the Shingon Buddhist sect in Japan, for example, is regarded as one of the superheroes of the new spirituality movements. Some of the new religions do not hesitate to incorporate ideas and terms of the 'New Science' and many of their followers are also avid readers of the new spirituality movement books.

Third, the new spirituality movements/culture are not isolated from the dominant intellectual world of Japan. Since the late 1970s, scholars and intellectuals tend to mention religion and spirituality much more often than before when referring to the Japanese cultural tradition or to the problems of contemporary society. Many well-known writers mention values and ideas similar to those of the new spirituality movements/culture. Some even refer positively to the 'Spiritual World' with a tone of great hope for a bright future. I will refer to these scholars and writers as 'spiritual intellectuals.' In Japan, spiritual intellectuals are not regarded as outside of the mainstream intellectual culture. Through the works of these intellectuals at least some of the new spirituality movements/culture are seen as representing a contemporary manifestation of the revival of the traditional religious culture of Japan and the East.

It should be noted that these spiritual intellectuals are different from religious intellectuals (Christian intellectuals, for example, who have been influential in modern Japan). Religious intellectuals usually base their views on one particular religious tradition, while spiritual intellectuals construct their views from various indigenous and foreign sources (though drawing primarily from Eastern religious traditions). In Japanese society religious pluralism is widely accepted and adherence to one religion is viewed as rather odd. Therefore, spiritual intellectuals are more popular and influential today than religious intellectuals.

There are a number of spiritual intellectuals actively speaking on religion and spirituality in contemporary Japan. While some stand outside of the new spirituality movements/culture, others are often participants. Some of the better known spiritual intellectuals include: Iwata Keiji, Umehara Takeshi, Kamata Toji, Kawai Hayao, Kurimoto Shin'ichiro, Nakazawa Shin'ichi, Yamaori Tetsuo, and Yuasa Yasuo. Their academic backgrounds vary, but include religious studies, philosophy, ethics, anthropology, and psychology. Whatever their field, however, none are content to write for a narrow academic audience. Their writings include normative ideas and admonitions, and readers are encouraged to expect the end of modern Western civilization and the advent of a new spiritual era. The publications of these spiritual intellectuals may be understood as providing the ideological foundation for the new spirituality movements/culture. In addition to their role as spokespersons for the new spirituality movements/culture, these intellectuals are also engaged in a wide-range of other activities.

While spiritual intellectuals have a vast number of readers, the number of those who actually become involved in the new spirituality movements would be considerably smaller. Nevertheless, when we take into consideration the influence of the spiritual intellectuals, it is clear that Japan's new spirituality movements/culture have a large body of sympathizers. The movements certainly have some important meaning for the future of Japanese thought and politics. In the following sections of this chapter I will describe in some detail two influential spiritual intellectuals in order to show how they are connected to the new spirituality movements/culture and related to the wider Japanese mentality.

Umehara Takeshi and the theory of Jōmon animism

Umehara Takeshi (1925–), after studying philosophy at the University of Kyoto, taught at Ritsumeikan University and Kyoto Municipal

University of Art, and was subsequently elected as President of the latter university. From 1987 he served as the first Director of the government-funded International Center for the Study of Japanese Culture. Although Umehara's academic training was in Western Philosophy, he became more interested in Buddhist philosophy and Japanese thought in his thirties. This interest is reflected in his earlier writings, including *Butsuzō: Kokoro to katachi* (Images of Buddha: Their spirit and form, 1965) and *Jigoku no Shisō* (Thoughts on hell, 1967).[2] While Umehara was already interested in religious thought by this time, his interest was primarily in Buddhism as an existential philosophy and was not yet directed toward the new spiritual ideology.

From around 1970 Umehara began publishing many popular books and his interest began to shift in a new direction. He began studying the history of ancient Japan with a particular interest in the seventh and eight centuries. His books *Kakusareta jujika* (The hidden cross, 1972), on Horyūji Temple and Prince Shotoku, and *Minasoko no uta* (The song from the bottom of the water, 1973), on the famous poet Kakinomoto Hitomaro, proposed unique interpretations of various problems of ancient Japanese history. Although his scholarship and bold conjectures were criticized by historians and specialists in the field, these books became best sellers and were well-known and referred to with the appellation 'Umehara's ancient history.'

In *Onryō to Jomon* (Grudging spirits and Jomon, 1979), Umehara summarized his earlier work and interpretations of Japanese history around the theme of the belief in grudging spirits. According to this work, Japan's early history was shaped by many powerful individuals, or individuals who sought power. Some had achieved great things and had been highly respected, but were later killed by their enemies. Those who killed them and many others feared vengeance from their grudging spirits and therefore enshrined them as deities. In many cases, however, the truth surrounding these great figures was concealed by those who subsequently took power. Umehara attempted to show that these great figures, for whom important records seem to be missing, were in fact tragic heroes who had died unhappily and were deified because of their tragedies.

In these works Umehara provided a new perspective on Japanese political and cultural history. These works do not contain, however, a clearly articulated normative viewpoint with religious and spiritual admonitions.[3] It was not until the end of the 1970s that Umehara began to fit the image of a spiritual intellectual. This was after he began his study of the Ainu people, a minority group regarded by many as the original inhabitants of northern Japan. Through his study of Ainu people and culture his views began to resemble in many respects those of the new spirituality movements.[4]

Jomon culture as the original Japanese culture

According to Umehara, the foundation of Japanese culture and religion is to be found in Jomon culture, which developed a unique earthenware culture more than ten thousand years ago. Jomon was a hunter-gatherer culture, but different from all other hunter-gatherer cultures because it also had the highly developed technique of making complex earthenware. Much later, around 300 B.C., a new culture based on rice cultivation was brought by immigrants from the Asian continent. This new 'Yayoi' culture soon spread to most parts of the country. Most scholars, especially those specializing in folk culture and beliefs, had assumed that Japanese were originally rice cultivators and that the main stream of Japanese culture and religion flowed from this source.

Umehara, however, challenged this assumption and argued that the Jomon hunter-gatherer culture was primary and that the rice-cultivation culture was a secondary one built upon this foundation. The roots of Japanese religiosity, therefore, cannot be found in such foreign religions as Buddhism, Confucianism, or Taoism, nor in the later forms of Shinto that were influenced by these foreign religions. Rather, the animistic faith of the Jomon people is the original Japanese religion and the authentic form of Shinto.[5]

Since the Yayoi era the culture of most areas of Japan, from the Kanto area of the island of Honshu to the island of Kyushu, was influenced by the rice-cultivation culture to such an extent that it has become difficult to see the original Japanese culture. It is in the peripheral areas to the north and south that the original Japanese culture and authentic Japanese religion have been preserved. The Ainu people on the northern island of Hokkaido, although they are now few in number, are struggling to preserve the Jomon hunter-gatherer culture. The influence of this original culture is also apparent to a lesser extent in Tohoku (the north-eastern area of the island of Honshu), but the rice cultivation culture of central Japan is clearly dominant. In the southern islands, however, this original Jomon culture has been preserved by the Okinawan people. In sum, Umehara argues that the original culture of Japan has been preserved primarily in the culture and religion of the Ainu and Okinawan peoples.

The original Japanese religion

What are the basic characteristics of the original Japanese religion? What is authentic Shinto or Japanese animism? According to Umehara, there are two central features of this original religion of Japan. First, the original Japanese believed that not only human beings but all animals and plants have their own spirit. They believed, for example, in the forest spirit. Generally speaking, people from hunter-gatherer cultures (including the Ainu) regard the forest with deep awe. When most of Japan was covered by deep forests during the Jomon era, people venerated the spirits of trees and forests. One can decipher, for example, patterns symbolizing tree spirits in some of the Jomon pottery. Even today many of the Shinto shrines are still surrounded by trees. Veneration of wooden pillars can also still be seen in many parts of Japan. Cultivators, on the other hand, used the earth for their own purposes and cut down and burned these trees. In other words, cultivation culture is based on the human drive to dominate nature. This is in contrast to the awe of nature found in the culture of the forest. Belief in the forest spirit represents an attitude of respect for all living things and a desire to coexist with the whole of nature.

Second, the original Japanese viewed life and death as a movement back and forth from this world and the other world. By life they understood that a soul had entered a body and death meant that the soul had left the body and traveled to the other world. These two worlds are interrelated and very similar, and therefore should not be understood in the same way as heaven or hell, which are entirely different from this world. The view that one will either go to heaven or hell according to one's conduct in this world is a common teaching of many religions. Umehara confesses he finds this belief rather unattractive because it leads to the exclusivistic idea that only believers of a particular religion can be saved. In Umehara's view religion for the Japanese should not be such a self-centered and exclusivistic kind.

At death the soul leaves its body and travels to the other world. There it is warmly welcomed by the ancestors. Souls travel to the other world in the shape of birds and are thought to ascend to this world through a bridge symbolized by wooden pillars. Ancestors or souls in the other world watch-over and protect their descendants in this world. Each year they return to this world for the New Year festival, Bon festival, and at the spring and autumn equinoxes. The souls in the other world are also given another life in this world, descending and entering a woman's womb and starting life anew as another person. The period between death and rebirth varies from several years to several tens of years. Umehara suspects that the interval between death and rebirth is shorter for those who do more good things in this life.

This view of life and death or the view of the other world (as Umehara prefers to refer to it) can be observed in the Bear Rite, the most important ritual among the Ainu people. The purpose of the Bear Rite is to kill bears and send them back to the other world. People offer wine, fish, and grains as gifts, with the understanding that the bear will carry them to the other world. The bears, receiving these gifts in the other world, naturally believe that the world is abundant and send many bears back in return. The Ainu believed that human beings would be able to catch many bears in the years following the observance of this ritual.

Umehara summarizes the original beliefs of the Japanese in the following two points: (1) all beings in the world are spiritual and therefore equal; and (2) the spirits or souls of all beings travel between these two interdependent and similar worlds. These beliefs are still widely held by contemporary Japanese. This is partly because Buddhism in Japan incorporated so many aspects of this original Japanese religion in the course of indigenization. Japanese Buddhism differs from the original Indian Buddhism because it adapted so completely to the native animistic way of thinking. Even the thought of such important figures in Japanese Buddhism as Prince Shotoku, Saicho, and Shinran reflects the two features of original Japanese religion noted above.

Umehara and the new spirituality movements

For the most part Umehara stresses the uniqueness of the original Japanese religion over against foreign religions, but occasionally he adds that its main features were shared with many other cultures prior to the stage of cultivation. He also admits that he personally finds these beliefs attractive and suggests that it is this type of religion that will provide direction for the future of the human race. Umehara moves beyond mere description and analysis to depict the ideal religion for the next stage of evolution.

Although Umehara's version of the ideal religion does not completely correspond to the ideal of spirituality advocated by many of the new spirituality movements/culture, both share the following beliefs and concerns: (1) animistic monism: the belief that the human soul is a part of the spiritual being or reality of the whole universe; (2) an interest in

---

the cycle of life and death; a belief in the other world and life after death; a belief in reincarnation; (3) a sense of familiarity with the other world or other dimensions of reality and a belief that interchange between these various dimensions or levels of reality is possible; (4) a critical attitude toward restrictive morality and the exclusivistic ideas regarding salvation held by historic and new religions; (5) an affirmative and optimistic attitude toward life and the body; and (6) an emphasis on harmony with the natural environment and a concern for ecology.

While Umehara shares much in common with these movements (in fact, it is difficult to find areas of disagreement), the typical concern of the new spiritual seekers in ideas and practices related to healing and the transformation of the body and consciousness is lacking in Umehara's work. These ideas and practices are primarily related to religious disciplines and meditation techniques, an area largely ignored by Umehara.

In short, Umehara regards himself essentially as a philosopher, one who must think deeply and speak clearly regarding the fundamental problems of the world and human life. He has long believed that his task is to establish a comprehensive worldview from a Japanese viewpoint for the contemporary world. The pursuit of this task has resulted in many works that incidentally serve as an ideological support for the new spirituality movements.

Yuasa Yasuo and the theory of 'chi'

Yuasa Yasuo (1925–) studied ethics and economics at the University of Tokyo before beginning his teaching career at the University of Yamanashi. After periods of teaching at the University of Osaka and the University of Tsukuba, Yuasa assumed his position at Oberlin University. Although ethics was his primary field, Yuasa also pursued the study of economics. This was partly because Marxism was very popular at the time, but also because he thought economics was necessary to understand the structure of society. Ultimately, he could not develop a sustained interest in economics and returned to his former field of ethics, philosophy and intellectual history.[6] His early books are *Keizaijin no moraru* (The morality of economic man, 1967) and *Kindai Nihon no jitsuzon shisō* (Existential thought in modern Japan, 1970).[7]

During the 1970s and 1980s Yuasa taught Japanese studies at the University of Osaka and published the following books in the field of Japanese intellectual history: *Kamigami no tanjo: Nihon shinwa*

284

no shisōshiteki kenkyū (The birth of the gods: An intellectual history of Japanese mythology, 1972); *Watsuji Tetsurō* (1973); *Kodaijin no seishin sekai* (The spiritual world of ancient people, 1980); *Nihonjin no shūkyō ishiki* (Religious consciousness of the Japanese, 1981); and *Tōyō bunka no shinsō* (The depths of Eastern culture, 1982). Like his earlier work on existentialism (1970), these volumes are regarded as orthodox academic studies in intellectual history; however, his interpretations are viewed as somewhat unique because of his stress on the role of religious experience, the close attention he gives to the problems of the body and ascetic disciplines, and in his application of Jungian psychology.

Yuasa's interest in ascetic disciplines and Jungian psychology can be traced back to his youth. His parents once belonged to a new religion called Hito no Michi Kyōdan, a group that was organized in 1924 and became the object of government persecution in 1937. They were subsequently involved in smaller movements, such as Shizensha and Tamamitsu Jinja. Yuasa himself participated in some of their activities, including yoga, and was deeply impressed by religious healing. At one time he also assisted in the research of Motoyama Hiroshi, the adopted son of the foundress of Tamamitsu Jinja, who had been studying parapsychology quite seriously in his own Institute for the Psychology of Religion (Motoyama 1975). Yuasa also had a great interest in parapsychology, but he knew that it was not a subject viewed with any seriousness by the academic community at the time. Consequently, he set aside his interest in parapsychology and pursued the study of mainstream intellectual history. Studies in ascetic disciplines, Jungian psychology, and theory of the body provided him with the material needed to bridge his interests in orthodox research in intellectual history and unorthodox research in parapsychology. Sometime later a broader range of intellectuals and the general public would become interested in bridging these areas.

Yuasa's publications on ascetic disciplines, theory of the body, and Jung began to appear in the late 1970s. These works include *Shintai: Tōyōteki shinshinron no kokoromi* (The body: An essay on Eastern philosophy and the science of mind and body, 1977), *Ki, shūgyō, shintai* (Qi, ascetic discipline, and the body, 1986), *'Ki' to wa nanika: Jintai ga hassuru enerugi* (What is 'qi': The energy emanating from the human body, 1991), and three books on Jung. While the work on Jung is not unrelated to our topic, the three books on ascetic disciplines, body and 'qi' are closely connected with the new spirituality movements and deserve particular attention.

From ascetic discipline and body to 'qi'

Yuasa's theoretical interest in ascetic disciplines and the body is rooted in the Eastern religious traditions. Ascetic disciplines such as meditation, walking and fasting, play an important role in the religions of Hinduism, Buddhism, and Taoism. Ascetic disciplines are the practical methods for the cultivation of one's self and spirit. Although the cultivation of self may first appear to refer to the mind, Eastern traditions regard the mind and body as inseparable and view physical training as an essential part of the discipline. In the Eastern context, therefore, ascetic discipline can be defined as the method for cultivating one's self and spirit through physical training.

With this understanding of the way ascetic disciplines work, it is apparent that modern Western philosophy is seriously disadvantaged. Since Descartes modern Western philosophy has been based on a mind-body dualism that separates and places them in opposition to one another. Another pillar of Western philosophy is the stress on self-consciousness that results from this separation or dualism. Behind the Cartesian dualism that tends to create an isolated self also lies the Christian dualism that opposes spirit, which can ascend to the divine realm, and body, which is always the cause of sin. Dualism in the West is also related to the modern scientific method that sharply separates subject and object and assumes that precise knowledge only comes from the detached observation of an outside object by an isolated subject.

According to Yuasa, this Western worldview based on the modern scientific methodology has come to a dead end. He suggests that a new perspective based on a theory of ascetic discipline and the body will provide the direction for a way out of this predicament. In his attempt to construct a new theory of the body Yuasa utilizes ideas and insights from various Eastern religions, Japanese Buddhist leaders, modern Japanese philosophers, and Jungian depth psychology. Since Western philosophy and science provide the foundation for all of our theoretical thinking today, his work also includes a critical examination of recent philosophy and physiology. This he regards as a necessary step in order to persuasively present to contemporary intellectuals the truth he has personally experienced.

In recent Western philosophy, Bergson and Merleau-Ponty both contributed significantly to the theory of the body. Both attempted to go beyond a dichotomizing dualism, beyond the idealism and materialism, which locates either mind or body above the other. By showing the importance of the relationship between body and mind, they opened a new horizon with relational dualism. Their attempt to relate mind and body, however, was limited to only one level of their relatedness, i.e., to the level of awareness and memory. This level has been referred to as the 'surface structure of the psychosomatic relationship.' Viewed from the structure of the body this level is under volitional control and composed of the kinetic-sensory circuit nerve system, and is centered in the cerebral cortex.

Twentieth century physiologists such as Pavlov, Canon, and Selye, however, showed empirically that there was a deeper level of relationship between mind and body, i.e., the 'basic structure of the psychosomatic relationship.' This level connects the mind and the internal organs and is composed of the autonomic nerve system with its center in the subcortical areas. This level constitutes the instinct-emotion circuit. According to depth psychology, this level is the unconscious mind and is therefore not subject to volitional control.

Eastern ascetic disciplines attempt to control the psychosomatic relationship of the level that is beyond ordinary consciousness. In order to show empirically how the mind and body are related in Eastern ascetic disciplines, it is necessary to demonstrate with concrete data what is happening at the basic structure of the psychosomatic relationship and how the surface and basic structures are related to each other. 'Qi' is the central category used by Yuasa in his effort to deal with this problem.

The popularization of 'qi' and the new spirituality movements

In ordinary usage 'qi' means 'air' or 'state of mind.' In ancient Chinese philosophy 'qi' referred to the vital energy that fills each human body as well as the whole universe. According to the Chinese medical system, every human body has eight or twelve 'lines' (*keiraku*) beneath the skin that connect with numerous points (*tsubo*) on the surface of the skin. It is assumed that 'qi' is always flowing through these lines and is closely related to human health and the life force. In Chinese medicine, therefore, a system of healing was developed that aimed at controlling the flow of 'qi.' This is done by stimulating various points (*tsubo*) and lines (*keiraku*) on the skin by acupuncture or moxibustion. This form of Chinese medicine has been practiced by many people in Japan, even after the introduction of modern Western medicine. Although never incorporated into the established medical practices and institutions, the concepts of 'qi' and 'tsubo' have long been regarded as reliable ideas.

In the 1980s the concept of 'qi' began to attract widespread interest. This explosive spread of interest can be attributed to the development of Japan's new spirituality movements that found 'qi' and 'qigong' to be attractive ideas and practices for cultivating spirituality. 'Qigong' refers to both the 'work of qi' and the 'discipline of qi,' and was used for the first time by a Chinese therapist in 1956. 'Qigong' is divided into the two sub-categories of 'inner qigong' and 'outer qigong.' 'Inner qigong' refers to individual practice and the cultivation of 'qi' energy within one's own body. 'Outer qigong,' on the other hand, refers to the practice of highly trained or exceptionally gifted practitioners who are able to cure clients by the power of 'qi' emanating from their bodies. Breath control, meditation, and body work are the disciplines of 'qigong.' In essence, 'qigong' means to cultivate the ability to feel and emanate 'qi' as an 'unobservable' power or energy, and to use this to cure diseases, to promote health, and to increase various abilities of mind and body.

During the past decade 'qi' and 'qigong' have been the two key words used in Japan to reorganize Chinese and Taoist systems of medicine and physical disciplines. 'Qigong' had already become quite fashionable in China by the early 1980s, but it did not begin to spread in Japan until the mid-1980s under the guidance of Chinese practitioners and some Japanese who had studied with them and developed their own disciplines. Since that time many how-to books for cultivating 'qi' have been published and intellectual and academic interest in 'qi' has increased. According to Yuasa, attempts to measure 'qi' through scientific procedures were begun in China as early as 1977, and since then the scientific study of 'qi' has advanced considerably. By the late 1980s even the general public in Japan had become interested in the problem of 'qi.' Exceptional 'qigong' practitioners were invited to be guests on various television programs and asked to investigate and determine whether 'qi' existed or not. Today 'qi' and 'qigong' remain fashionable topics for many Japanese.

There are many aspects to the current popularity of 'qigong.' On the one hand, it can be seen as one element in the revitalization of magical and occult interests in popular culture. On the other hand, it can also be seen as part of the new spirituality movements/culture in Japan. The following are common features found both in the new spirituality movements/culture and in the more general interest in 'qi' and 'qigong': (1) an interest in levels of reality other than the one grasped by ordinary senses and consciousness; (2) pursuit of the transformation of mind and body through controlled breathing, meditation, and body work as well as a strong interest in healing; (3) an approach to the sacred based on direct experience and transformation of both mind and body, rather than through learning doctrines and pursuing ethical conduct; (4) an optimism and hopefulness regarding the possibility of integrating scientific knowledge and spiritual experience.

Yuasa'a role in the popularization of 'qigong'

For a number of years Yuasa devoted considerable attention to Chinese medicine and when 'qi' became the focus of scientific study in China in the late 1970s he recognized its significance and played a major role in introducing these research findings to Japanese intellectuals and the general public. In fact, he may be regarded as one of the key figures responsible for the recent 'qigong' craze. Without denying his role as a popularizer of 'qigong,' we must add that his main contribution has been in clarifying from a much broader perspective the meaning of 'qi' and 'qigong' in relation to contemporary science and philosophy. According to Yuasa, the theory of 'qi' is closely connected to the major task of contemporary philosophy and science; that is, overcoming the dualism of modern Western science.

The 'qi' that flows through the *keiraku* lines is understood to be interrelated not only with the state of the skin, but also with the state of the inner organs and maybe even interrelated to the 'qi' that exists outside of the body. If one can empirically show this connection between the skin and the inner organs as assumed in the theory of 'qi,' one will have demonstrated the existence of an unknown circuit between the two levels of psychosomatic relationships, i.e., the conscious surface structure and the unconscious basic structure. Furthermore, if one can measure concretely the power of 'qigong' practitioners and observe the work of 'qi' outside of the body, one will prove that unconscious information or energy is exchanged between the body and the environment. In this way, therefore, through 'qi' research it will be possible to create a new theory of psychosomatic relationships as well as a new theory of 'mystical power.' Yuasa expects that 'qi' research will lead to a new stage for parapsychology that will substantiate the existence of parapsychological interaction between an individual's mind and physical beings.

In contemporary Japan, popular interest in 'qi' and 'qigong' includes a new style of unsophisticated magical curiosity that has existed in various forms for some time. This form of interest does not really represent anything new and lacks a systematic worldview. Yuasa's version of 'qi' research and theory, on the other hand, represents a new systematic spiritual philosophy based on empirical, physical, and physiological findings. He has contributed significantly to the theoretical foundations for 'qi' movements that now constitute an important part of Japan's new spirituality movements/culture.

New spirituality movements and the rise of spiritual intellectuals

It was in the late 1970s that Japan's new spirituality movements/ culture became visible and began to attract a considerable number of participants. Before that time there had been some smaller movements, but they did not appear to represent a social force that was likely to endure. The bimonthly *Tama* magazine, for example, a 'general psychical magazine' that carried on the tradition of modern spiritualism and psychical research, began publication in 1966 but folded in 1968 for lack of readers. It resumed publication in 1979, but with content that represented the new spirituality movements/culture (Uritani 1989). The successful republication of this magazine indicates that there was already a sizable number of participants in the new spirituality movements by this time.

Similarly, as early as the 1960s there had been some intellectuals whose thought resembled that of the more recent new spirituality movements/culture. Yuasa Yasuo, for example, already had a serious interest in spiritual healing and parapsychology in the 1950s and 1960s. Also in the 1960s an influential anthropologist by the name of Iwata Keiji began praising the popular animism found in Japan and various other areas in Asia.[8] But it was not really until the late 1970s that a significant number of intellectuals became engaged in spiritual discourse and began writing books and articles that supported the ideas and practices of the new spirituality movements/culture. In 1979 the Japanese translation of Fritjof Capra's *The Tao of Physics* was published and became the first best-seller of the New Age science in Japan. That same year *Agama* magazine began publication and carried many popular and theoretical articles that helped popularize the new spirituality movements in the 1980s. It is also interesting to observe that 1979 is also the year that Umehara Takeshi, the well-known writer and scholar considered earlier, discovered the original Japanese animism in Ainu culture.

Thus, as the new spirituality movements/culture grew and became visible, a cluster of spiritual intellectuals also appeared and offered intellectual support to these popular movements and culture. These spiritual intellectuals have become quite numerous and are not far from the mainstream of Japan's academic (particularly the humanities) and journalistic communities. Some of them, like Umehara and Yuasa, are erudite and creative, and highly respected by many academies and the general public.

The fact that many spiritual intellectuals supported the new spirituality movements/culture undoubtedly contributed to the growth of these movements. However, the appearance of support from the cultural mainstream has made it somewhat difficult for these movements to consolidate a clear and distinct identity. Many Japanese, for example, may seriously discuss reincarnation and experiment with healing by 'qigong' without any awareness that they are participating in some kind of movement. This is because the new spirituality movements are largely congruous with the mainstream culture of Japan. In other words, many of the ideas and attitudes of the new spirituality movements have already been assimilated by Japan's cultural establishment.

Two examples help to illustrate this point. The first is related to 'qi' research. The Japanese Society for Mind-Body Science was established in 1991 as a counterpart to the Chinese Society for Mind-Body Science. Its aim is to study various subjects related to psychosomatic relationships, such as ascetic disciplines in Eastern religions, disciplines and techniques in martial arts and the performing arts, depth psychology, psychosomatic medicine, and parapsychology. Yuasa Yasuo played a leading role in organizing this society. If this kind of society had been organized in the 1970s, it would not have received wide support and would have been criticized as propaganda for pseudo-science. This past year, however, many newspapers carried positive articles on the establishment of this new society. This is partly because the names of many respectable scholars and celebrities appeared in the list of supporters. The Society's office was first located at Sophia University, one of the most renowned private universities in Tokyo. One of the six emeritus advisors is a former foreign minister, Okita Saburō, and one of the six current advisors is the famous Catholic novelist Endō Shusaku.

The second example is related to a dispute over bio-medical ethics. Since the 1970s there has been an ongoing debate in Japan on whether brain death should be acknowledged as human death. Medical doctors seeking to promote organ transplants have argued for the acceptance of the concept of brain death, but have met with considerable resistance. In order to reach a final decision and establish some policy on this issue, the National Diet organized the 'Special Research Committee for Brain Death and Internal Organ Transplants' in 1990. The final report of the committee was submitted in January 1992. Umehara Takeshi was one of the fifteen members of this committee. The final report acknowledges brain death as human death, but a minority opinion was included that rejected this conclusion. Umehara was the chief proponent of the minority view and made a strong argument against the concept of brain death. He maintained that the idea of death should be decided by cultural tradition, rather than by scientific procedures, and that the concept of brain death does not fit the traditional Japanese ideas regarding life, death, and the soul. This viewpoint is based on his theory of the original Japanese religion developed from the late 1970s and has many similarities with the thought of the new spirituality movements/culture.

These two examples clearly illustrate that the new spirituality movements/culture have been building a firm position in the cultural mainstream of Japan. Their power and influence, however, should not be exaggerated. We must continue to follow the changing status of the spiritual intellectuals to keep some sense of the future direction of Japan's new spirituality movements/culture.

16 'New Age Movement' or 'New Spirituality Movements and Culture'?

In my research I specialize in modern Japanese religions. In the late 1980s, I noticed that a phenomenon similar to one often called the 'New Age movement'[1] in North America and Europe was occurring also in Japan, and since that time, I have focused my efforts on explaining the phenomenon from an academic point of view. In 1996, I published a book in Japanese entitled *Whither the Spiritual World? New Spirituality Movements in the Contemporary World*, compiling all the research of the past decade.[2] In the book, my discussion of the proper name for the phenomenon took up many pages. My conclusion was that the term 'New Age movement' was unsuitable as an academic term. What term then should be used instead? I would like to propose the use of 'new spirituality movements and culture.' This article is intended to explain the reasons behind this proposed renaming.

In Japan, the term 'New Age movement' is not used frequently. The more usual term is 'Spiritual World.' If you go to a large bookstore, you will find a section for 'Spiritual World' right next to the one for 'Religions.' In this section are books on healing, self-transformation, reincarnation and Karma, near-death experiences, *qigong*, yoga, meditation, shamanism, animism, evolution of consciousness, occult experiences, transpersonal psychology, holistic medicine, 'new science' and various other similar topics. Many are translations of books published in the West. But even more are based on Japanese or Asian traditions, or deal with newly developed concepts in present-day Japan. Those who are interested in these books are people who themselves are in quest of something spiritual or healing. At the same time, they are aware of being involved in the cultural world of the present. This cultural world is defined as the 'Spiritual World.'

First, a brief note on one example, Tenkawa Benzaitensha, a well-known spiritual site of the Spiritual World in Japan, in order to delineate a concrete picture of the movement of the Spiritual World (Kamata 1991; Shimazono 1996: Ch. 12). Tenkawa Benzaitensha is an old shrine located in the mountains of Yamato, the center of ancient Japan (present-day Yoshino county in Nara prefecture). Several important historical figures are said to be closely linked to the shrine: Emperor Tenmu (672–686), who helped develop a centralized government under the Yamato court in the 7th century; the ascetic practitioner, En no Gyōja, who is considered the founder of mountain asceticism in the 7th and 8th centuries that syncretized Shinto and Buddhism; and Kukai (774–835, founder of the Shingon sect of Buddhism), one of the greatest leaders in the early days of introduction of Buddhism to Japan. Tenkawa Benzaitensha was devastated after the Meiji Restoration in 1868, when traditional Shinto-Buddhist syncretic religious activities were outlawed as part of the government's bid to modernize the nation by adopting a policy of separating Shinto and Buddhism. The first signs that this shrine was about to revive were seen only after the end of the Second World War. In the 1980s, it emerged into the limelight as a spiritual site for the Spiritual World. By 1985, Tenkawa Benzaitensha was known as 'the Roppongi of the Spiritual World,' a reference to the nightspot district in downtown Tokyo popular with the young and the fashionable.

Kamata Tōji, a Shinto and religious scholar who is commonly acknowledged as a promoter of the Spiritual World movement, sees three stages in the revival of Tenkawa: first, the 'discovery' of Tenkawa by persons with spiritual mediumistic powers; second, the 'response' to Tenkawa by artists; and third, the 'quest' by young people. From the 1950s to the 1970s, the shrine was assigned mystic significance by and attracted people with spiritual mediumistic powers and enthusiasts interested in new religions and folk religions (first stage). In the 1980s, artists with a strong inclination toward the Spiritual World, such as the musicians Miyashita Fumio and Hosono Haruomi, cartoonist Minouchi Suzue, and film director Tatsumura Hitoshi, were among the regular visitors here, seeking inspiration or a source for their creative works (second stage). Young people began to visit the shrine in the 1990s, partly influenced by the successful film 'Tenkawa Densetsu Satsujin Jiken' (The Legendary Tenkawa Murder), some in a serious quest for personal identity, and others searching for an exciting extraordinary experience (third stage).

Kamata first visited the shrine in 1983 and was charmed by the personality of Chief Priest Kakisaka Mikinosuke. He would later find a 'channel to a super-religion' at this shrine. In 1992, when the shrine faced a debt problem for the construction of a new shrine hall, a fund-raising organization called 'Tenkawa Benzaitensha

Sūkeikai' (Reverence Association for Tenkawa Benzaitensha) was set up to organize various events. Kamata was the driving force behind the movement to support Tenkawa Shrine and committed himself to planning and implementing fund-raising events. The events, combinations of round-table discussions, study meetings, film screenings, music and entertainment performances and martial arts shows, were organized at Tenkawa or sometimes in Tokyo and attracted many participants and spectators. The contributions and speeches given by the scholars, artists, writers, and movement leaders who participated in or supported the events were collected in the book *Tenkawa Mandala: Channel to a Super-Religion*, edited by Kamata and Tsumura in 1994. In his appeal to supporters to hold events, Kamata said:

> I can't believe in a religion. But the gods and the Bodhisattva (Buddhist saints) exist. Or I have to think they exist, but I don't believe in any religious authority and doctrine. Rather I believe in the impulse, force, pain, and agony of a religion trying to transcend religions, and the light of sagacity that radiates in the process. To me, Tenkawa is a channel appearing in front of me to lead the way to such a super-religion…Once upon a time, Tenkawa was the center of syncretized Shinto-Buddhism and the base of the Ancient Shinto (*Koshintō*). Mount Misen of Tenkawa was the symbol of the religion and the magnetic field for religious creations. Tenkawa accepted all the pain and diseases of people of each era. It was the magnetic field for super-religious and nature-worshipping creations and at the same time it served as an 'asile' (asylum) that accepted those who were defeated in power struggles. Knowing of the reason for the pain of Tenkawa and treating the diseases that emerged there might lead us to heal the pain and disease of our society and the world…Fortunately, there are many people connected to Tenkawa. The act of looking at the connections and re-connecting them would help initiate a process to solve Tenkawa shrine's financial problems and untangle the root of evil of our society, the first step for a religion to transcend religions. (Kamata and Tsumura 1994: 25–27)

The second editor of *Tenkawa Mandala* is Tsumura Takashi, a writer and activist with a great interest in ecology. He leads the Kansai Qigong Association to promote *qigong*. He began visiting Tenkawa with members of his association in 1991. For Tsumura, *qigong* is not just a physical exercise for health maintenance, but also something with a spiritual dimension, 'transcending religion.' During their visit to Tenkawa, Tsumura remarks, the *qigong* movement found the momentum to go beyond physical health concerns and become more concerned with spiritual social reform. The term 'spiritual social reform' suggests the prevalence of 'deep ecology.' The core of Tsumura's belief in *qigong* as a 'super-religion' is located here. 'If we want *qigong* to take deep root in the life of the Japanese, we must understand the ultimate essence of the *qi* culture of Japan.' The movement maintains that the source of Japan's *qi* culture is to be found in the 'deep ecological' Shinto of Tenkawa, just as in the religious life of the Ainu ethnic group (Kamata and Tsumura 1994: 273–87). Through the connection with Tenkawa, Tsumura appears to be attempting to develop the spiritual aspect of *qigong* and to bring it closer to the spiritual tradition of the Japanese.

This example shows only one aspect of the movement of the Spiritual World in Japan, in this case, the stream emphasizing the tradition of Japan. It is not intended as a typical picture of the new spirituality movements and culture. There are other streams from sources in the United States or India, for example, or in contemporary psychology and psychotherapy. The diversity of the movements of the Spiritual World in Japan should be kept in mind when reading this chapter.

'Movements' or 'movements and culture'?

The term 'Spiritual World' was first used around 1978 (Shimazono, 1996: Ch. 10). Without doubt, a similar phenomenon in the United States exerted substantial influence on that in Japan. However, elements introduced from India and China, and elements derived from Japanese tradition, also played significant roles. For example, Zen and Tantric Buddhism, Taoism and Shinto occupy important positions as subjects taken up in the Spiritual World. The term 'Spiritual World' implies that an ancient spiritual tradition has been revived in a new form. On the contrary, however, there is also a strong belief that the Spiritual World denotes a completely new world that has developed from a combination of traditional religious systems of the past and modern rationalism. This concept implies, to some extent, that the Spiritual World represents the civilization of a new age which will follow the current 'modern' age.

It is inappropriate to equate the phenomenon of the Japanese Spiritual World with the New Age movement in the United States. Neither is it correct to view them as independent phenomena. They are similar phenomena, and contain elements that overlap as well as unique characteristics. Are these phenomena so different in nature as to warrant different names? Should there be a term that encompasses these phenomena and their substantial commonality? Both 'New Age movement' and 'Spiritual World' are terms with broad meanings that imply various phenomena defined collectively and vaguely. If this is correct, it is natural to use a more inclusive term (Shimazono 1996: Ch. 3). Such a term would be very helpful in making a comparative study of the phenomena in North America, Europe and Japan where these trends are the most conspicuous.

There is another difficulty in using terms such as 'New Age' and 'Spiritual World' for academic purposes. There are many people who believe and practice concepts that are very close to 'New Age' or 'Spiritual World,' but who dislike being regarded as participants in these phenomena. This is particularly true with the 'New Age' label. It is better that they be grouped together under a common term, since they are similar in terms of cultural and religious phenomena. Using 'New Age' or 'Spiritual World' might encourage those who positively adopt these terms to label themselves as if they were representatives of the category.

Other characteristics of the new phenomena may be overlooked if these terms are used. So I would like to propose the use of the term 'new spirituality movements and culture (new spirituality movements/ culture).' Using 'movements' in the plural shows that the term embraces various types of 'New Age' and 'Spiritual World' groups. This broad category can also include other groups with common characteristics – whatever the terms used to describe them outside Europe, North America and Japan. The word 'spirituality' is used because many people in these movements consider that they belong to a new age of 'spirituality' that is to follow the age of 'religion' as it comes to an end. 'Spirituality' in a broad sense implies religiousness, but it does not mean organized religion or doctrine. Rather, it is used to mean the religious nature expressed by an individual's thoughts and actions. Another common element for many of these movements is a sense of a revival of something religious in a broad sense for the individual in the present times. Thus, the term 'new spirituality movements and culture' might be the right term to express their characteristics.[3]

Why use 'movements and culture,' rather than simply 'movements'? Many participants in the 'new spirituality movements and culture' believe that they are part of a new current to reform the world and further the evolution of human beings. Since they have high aspirations and act to inspire enthusiasm in their adherents, the phenomena take on the characteristics of 'movements.' However, few supporters are willing to take part in collective actions. They are satisfied with feeling that their inner self changes through participation, and dislike acting with others or assuming a position of responsibility for colleagues or others. It is often believed that the accumulation of many individuals' transformation in consciousness will automatically lead to a transformation in consciousness for all human beings. This individualistic inclination with little joint activity suggests a classification as a 'culture' rather than a 'movement.' 'Culture' here means aspects of the production or consumption of culture, rather than active individual practices. As the phenomenon has facets of both 'movement' and 'culture,' it is appropriate to call it 'new spirituality movements and culture.'

Since these movements feature an element of cultural consumption, it is logical to describe them in economic terms, for example as 'consumer religions.' The phenomenon contains many factors that cannot be understood from the viewpoints of capitalistic production and consumption of religious culture. There exist movements networking small numbers of people without regard to economic efficiency, advertising or mass-market sales. Once people assume spiritual practices, many maintain these practices without continuing the consumption of commodities. As the leisure time of contemporary society is not entirely occupied by commodity consumption, 'new spirituality movements and culture' cannot properly be understood only as the consumption of merchandise.

The 'movement' aspect of the 'new spirituality movements and culture' has something in common with the new religious movements. The term 'new religious movement' usually means a group of people with a clear system of theory and practice and a religious organization. Some groups among the 'new spirituality movements and culture' have a specific system of theory and practice. Thus, groups that are rightly classified as new religious movements are included within the term. However, many individuals who practice or sympathize with some of the new spirituality movements and culture are content with personal acts in search of their inner selves and continued practices to deepen themselves spiritually, without a systematic order as a group. These individuals lack the basic preconditions of an new religious movement, such as a shared system of theory and practice, affiliation with a religious organization, and concerted action to achieve shared goals. This feature suggests that a great portion of the new spirituality movements and culture cannot be categorized as a new religious movement. The relationships between the terms 'new spirituality movements and culture,' 'new religious movements,' 'New Age' and 'Spiritual World' are shown in the figure in the previous chapter.

The difference between new spirituality movements and culture and new religious movements can be seen in the intensity of the concept of salvation (Shimazono 1992a). The new religious movement demands earnest self-searching from its followers to realize the limits of humanity and the current world, and preaches that the organization's system of theory and practice will enable the followers to overcome such limitations. The followers of a religious group are forced to live up to the tenets of the system; in other words, they are obliged to follow certain disciplines, obey the rules of the group, perform duties, and share certain common values with the other followers. They are asked to nurture a sense of solidarity with other persons as beings who are burdened with limits.[4] In contrast, the supporters of new spirituality movements and culture find the sense of salvation irrelevant, and they tend to avoid any set of concepts leading to salvation (i.e. discipline, obedience, obligation, service and solidarity). The fact that new spirituality movements undertake few collective actions and have little sense of fellowship is associated with this apathy towards salvation. They often identify themselves as a 'spirituality movement' or a 'culture' that is different from 'religion,' an assertion due in part to their aversion to the beliefs of salvation-seeking religions. I discuss this point further in the next section.

Characteristics of the concepts and practices of the new spirituality movements and culture

The new religious movement has other distinctive characteristics, of course, but I consider its primary characteristic to be its emphasis on seeking salvation, just as Buddhism, Christianity, Islam and other historic religions do. What are the characteristics of the concepts and practices of the new spirituality movements and culture?

First, they believe that they manifest a new worldview, representing a new movement or culture that overcomes the defects of both traditional religions and rationalist modern science. They find the present world to be deadlocked, because of the dominant culture of traditional religions and modern science; they try to find ways out via alternative lifestyles. This can be seen, in one way, as a manifestation of the idea that we are in the process of transition to 'the postmodern civilization,' a consciousness prevalent in the contemporary world.

There are some who identify the source of this concept far back in the past. Even so, they are greatly preoccupied with the concept that new meaning is to be found in old beliefs and matters after the age of modern rationalism.

How will the change occur? According to believers, change is brought about by individuals who experience spiritual, conscious, psychological or physical change. The new spirituality movements and culture, in this sense, are movements and culture aimed at self-transformation. Their supporters are interested in gods and spiritual beings outside themselves, in a Higher Self or Oversoul, *qi* or cosmic energy, ETIs, cosmic consciousness, and so on. In addition, and more important, they emphasize changes experienced in one's soul, heart, consciousness and body. Altered states of consciousness, in particular, are seen as intense transforming experiences. In order to experience these changes, they practice meditation, breathing, visualization, bodywork, and the like. These activities are adopted from the shamanistic practices of Native American, tribal and ethnic religions of the world, or from traditional religions in India, China and Japan. Some of them are devised from new psychological knowledge.

An individual's experience of transforming him/herself can be either a special spiritual experience or, more commonly, a moment of encouragement within ordinary life. For example, some folk health-care methods and psychological therapies differing from those recommended by medical doctors belong to the new spirituality movements and culture. Some people undergo training in yoga and *qigong*, practicing them only for health-care purposes. Others accept Jung's psychological therapy as a tool to treat neurosis. Yet again, there are some people who find deep spiritual and/or ideological significance in these practices and concepts. And in between these extreme attitudes, there may be people at all levels of interest from the casual to the dedicated. It is said that the difference in the level of interest is affected by the degree of influence from the new spirituality movements and culture.

A similar observation is true with contemporary leisure or amusement culture. Elements of the new spirituality movements and culture are often adopted as motifs in films, videos, comics, science fiction, video games, etc. Magazines on the occult, fortune-telling, and New Age music have much in common with the new spirituality movements and culture. They do not claim to be part of the new spirituality movements and culture, but they certainly form the base of the pyramid, and serve to prepare people to enter the new spirituality movements and culture. Just as a European folk culture centering on the worship of saints formed the base of Catholic Christianity, modern popular health/therapy cultures and magico-religious popular cultures underpin the new spirituality movements and culture.

For those who find spiritual meaning in the new spirituality movements and culture, as opposed to simple health or recreational pleasure, the point is not 'salvation' but 'self-transformation' and a 'transformation of civilization.' In a salvation religion, an important element of one's religious life is undergoing individual transformation through conversion, purification, religious awakening, and enlightenment. Many salvation religions consider that this transformation should not be limited to individuals, and desire that the human community should embody their religious ideas. The idea of the millennial kingdom is a typical example. For salvation religions, however, such transformation is not limited to changes within the same horizon of this world, but involves non-continuous changes including transfer to an entirely different horizon. As a premise, there exists a domain of 'transcendence.' What elements of this 'transcendence' are present as part of salvation religions but are lacking or limited in the new spirituality movements and culture (Shimazono 1992a, and 1996)?

One such element is an acute awareness of human suffering. As the sources of suffering are largely evil deeds performed by individuals, awareness of human evil is considered to be part of the awareness of suffering. Salvation religions also hold that many, even all people share serious suffering, hence the great importance of love, benevolence and a sense of solidarity, mutual help and compassionate behavior among suffering people. Contrary to this, people in the new spirituality movements and culture do not consider that all humanity is either evil or suffering. If some individuals happen to be faced with suffering or evil, it is attributed to vicious elements in modern society or from past civilization, and is not inherent to human nature. Efforts to liberate oneself from such viciousness should be experienced as a process of self-transformation. Therefore, they can hardly be associated with an idea that one should always keep other people's suffering in mind and positively collaborate to aid them in the fight against it (Shimazono 1996: Ch. 5).

Another difference is the concept of personified agents, such as gods and the sacred Other. God, Buddha, and the founder in salvation religions have few or none of the negative properties usually present in humanity, such as evil, worldly desires, or vicious states of mind, which are sufferings per se and possible causes of greater sufferings. In this sense, there is a great disparity between human being and personified beings. Salvation is provided by personified gods and/or the sacred Other or by their mediation. In contrast, the new spirituality movements and culture have no personified God or sacred Other (such as Buddha or the founder) as the transcendent being. Some, however, exhibit strong interest in spiritual beings who have many properties not present in humankind, such as extra-terrestrial intelligences or people with special abilities. Some movements presume the existence of the non-personified presence or principal, such as the Great Soul, Gaia, Great Nature, or the Cosmic Soul, and place emphasis on intercourse with these presences. Rarely found are personified agents with holy properties sharply different from ordinary human beings, in other words, a transcendent God, gods or a sacred Other.

As explained above, salvation religions and the new spirituality movements and culture are distinguished by (1) a strong awareness of human suffering, and (2) the concept of personified agents such as God, gods or a sacred Other. Both (1) and (2) are found in salvation religions, but absent in new spirituality movements and culture. Of course, the new spirituality movements and culture are also concerned with transcendence, in that they presume the existence of beings or worlds beyond the real world, which individuals try to approach by self-transformation. This transcendence cannot be described as 'strong.' It is not always easy, however, to distinguish between 'strong' and 'feeble' transcendence. There may be some cases, for example, in which awareness of human suffering and the concept of personified agents with powers far beyond humankind can be observed in a hardly noticeable form. Some organizations among the new religions of Japan (such as Byakkō Shinkōkai, World Mate and Ijun) and several of the new religions in the West (such as Osho Rajneesh Movement and Transcendental Meditation) are cited as examples that are positioned on the borderline between salvation religions and the new spirituality movements and culture.

In Buddhism alone, elements of 'strong' and 'weak' transcendence are embraced. In the sense that the Buddha passing into Nirvana is considered to be a sacred Other far above humankind, I categorize Buddhism as a salvation religion with strong transcendental elements. But if we interpret Buddhism as a teaching that every person can undergo the Buddha's enlightenment as one's own experience if one follows the righteous paths based on the truth, then Buddhism is rather close to the new spirituality movements and culture. Significantly, some persons involved in the new spirituality movements and culture are so sympathetic to Buddhism that they consider their own quest in the new spirituality movements and culture as merely a new evolution of Buddhism for the contemporary world.[5]

New spirituality movements and culture as global phenomena

The phenomenon has evolved in step with increasing globalization, with advances in the communication media in particular. Those who are committed to the new spirituality movements and culture often obtain information from books and audiovisual materials (video, cassette tapes, broadcasting) and personal computers in their own homes, rather than through group interaction or person-to-person contact. Even if they attend meetings, seminars or workshops, the emphasis is placed on individual practices rather than group activities. Apart from a small number of paid staff who instruct and demonstrate practices, the majority of followers consider themselves part of the audience, information customers, and have no sense of belonging to a particular organization, sect or church. Thus, they understand the new spirituality movements and culture to be a loose network of like-minded individuals.

The volume of information and culture shared globally through communication media is rapidly increasing. The national or local culture is firmly maintained within this expanding information and cultural complex, but is increasingly mixed with other elements on a global scale. Globally influenced culture and information have rapidly spread across national borders. New spirituality movements and culture can be considered to comprise part of the new body of global information and culture. Although 'global,' the locales of transmitters and receivers can often be clearly distinguished. Needless to say, the United States represents a very important source of information. But Europe, Japan and India are also generating and transmitting culture and information of this sort. In the future, China could grow to be a major source. Thus, the new spirituality movements and culture is a global phenomenon, with many centers and facets.

Being multi-faceted and multi-centered implies that national and local cultural characteristics may be reflected in the new spirituality movements and culture. So far, throughout the entire new spirituality movements and culture, the influence of the New Age movement in the West is strong. But we should refrain from concluding that the characteristics of the New Age movement are equally represented by the new spirituality movements and culture in general.

The new spirituality movements and culture in Japan show remarkable continuity with traditional religious culture and conflict little with the dominant religious culture of contemporary Japan. Several intellectuals active as leaders of mainstream culture express views close to those held by supporters of the new spirituality movements and culture as we have seen in the previous chapter. On the other hand, there are many similarities found in the philosophy and practice of long-cherished folk religions, Shinto and Buddhism, on one hand and the new spirituality move-ments and culture on the other. It is often observed that the shamanist and divination culture encompassing the folk-religious tradition has taken on a modern outlook by incorporating techniques and vocabulary borrowed from the new spirituality movements and culture. It is also fairly common for the new spirituality movements and culture to incorporate a nationalist tendency (Shimazono 1995, 1996: Ch.3, and 1997). They maintain animism is most suitable for the postmodern world since it advocates harmony with nature without forcing others to obey or excluding them. They also hold that the core of Japanese religious culture is characterized as animistic, which is sharply contrasted with Christianity, Islam and Buddhism with their unecological tendency. The practice of *qigong* is gaining popularity not only in Japan but also in China and Korea. Animism, *qigong* and the like function to inspire pride in the common traditions of East Asian nations. Economic and industrial leaders are showing strong interest in this aspect of Japanese new spirituality movements and culture. No similar phenomenon occurs among the majority of residents of Western countries.

The presence of nationalist tendencies in the new spirituality movements and culture implies that the generally accepted notion of a strong individualistic tendency within the phenomenon should be modified. Of course, it is not totally wrong to consider the new spirituality movements and culture as generally inclined to individualism. The individualistic nature of this movement and culture is closely associated with its global, multifaceted, multi-centered nature. Apart from a few leaders and administrators, many of the adherents are linked with various global information and cultural resources. They have no exclusive relations with a specific community, or with a particular system of theory, doctrine or rituals. In this it differs from a traditional religion, which is administered by a clerical and intellectual elite, and supported by a community of followers. The social organization of tradition or cultural transmission[6] supports the claim made by individuals that their movement should not be identified as a religion.

The phenomenon can certainly be classified as a religion in its broadest sense. Yet there are grounds for the people involved to claim that their movement is different from a religion. Considering that many of them believe their acts to be deeply bound up with their own identity from a 'spiritual' and not 'religious' view, and taking into account emic elements of their self-understanding, it is appropriate to classify them within the new spirituality movements and culture.

Notes

Introduction
Translated by Edmund Skrzypczak.

1. For more on the meaning of the term, see Inoue et al. 1989, Shimazono 1992a, and Mullins et al. 1993, all of which aim at presenting the whole picture. Some historians maintain that the term 'popular religion' is more appropriate than the term 'new religion,' and that such religion begins as far back as the Fuji-kō in the 18th century (see Shimazono 1995d). On the 'new new religions' see Shimazono 1992b and 2001.
2. This quotation is taken from *Honda Yōichi sensei iko* (Manuscripts of our teacher, Honda Yōichi).
3. Kana, as opposed to difficult Chinese characters, are writing symbols that anyone with even a minimum of education would be able to read.

Chapter 1

1. The reader will soon realize that this paper is written with a strong awareness of the difference between the sociology of religion in Japan and in Europe. It is only two decades since Japanese sociologists of religion began interacting with their European colleagues to create more frequent opportunities for learning from each other. Differences in the style of research have also been made clear through personal contacts as well as by reading papers from both European and Japanese colleagues. I belong to the second generation of researchers blessed with mutual learning opportunities, and I feel a great debt of gratitude to the first generation of researchers who paved the way to increase the academic exchange between Japan and Europe. It is a great honor for me that this chapter was first contributed as part of a collection on the occasion of the retirement of Prof. Karel Dobbelaere, who has supported the academic exchange among the first generation of Japanese scholars. One of the first generation sociologists of religion with whom Prof. Dobbelaere cherished a warm friendship was Prof. Anzai Shin, to whom many students of the second generation pay deepest respect and affection. Prof. Anzai passed away on 1 January 1998. We mourn the loss of our respected colleague and appreciate his great achievements. This chapter was originally dedicated to

the memory of the friendship between Prof. Dobbelaere and Prof. Anzai. The original Japanese text was translated by Ms. Chine Hayashi.

2. Papers examining the history of sociology of religion in Japan include Yamanaka and Hayashi 1996; another on the history of research on new religions specifically is by Inoue et al. (1981).

3. New religions that developed rapidly after the 1970s are often called 'new new religions.' It is not by accident that many new new religious organizations are enmeshed in long-lasting conflicts with the public. See Shimazono 1992b, 1995b, 1998 and 2001.

Chapter 2

Translated by W. Michael Kelsey and Jan Swyngedouw from 'Nihon no kindaika katei to Shūkyō' (Religion and the process of Japanese modernization). Jurisuto 21 (1981), pp. 66–72.

1. These are greed, regret, partiality, hatred, animosity, anger, covetousness and arrogance.

Chapter 3

This article was translated by Hayashi Takahiko.

1. This is a term used by the philosopher Karl Jaspers, and refers to a transformative moment in the history of civilizations taking place between 800 and 200 BC. Jaspers argues that fundamental religious and philosophical questions were raised at this time, determining the direction of human civilization to today (Jaspers 1949).

2. See Jaspers 1932. For a relation of his theory to the study of religion, see Wakimoto 1983.

3. This point is analyzed in Shimazono 1979, 1982a, and 1982b.

4. Max Weber, "Religionssoziologie" from *Wirtschaft und Gesellschaft*, (1922).

5. On Durkheim, see also Miyajima 1987.

6. See the following: Lefebvre 1947, Shimoda 1986, Morris 1987, Nietzsche 1906.

7. 'Affluent society' is a term popularized by John Kenneth Galbraith (1958).

8. In regard to Europe, see Cohn 1970.

9. In regard to this section of the chapter in general, see also Wilson 1979.

10. See, for example, Toulmin 1982, Capra 1982, and Kawai 1986.

11. For example, see Watanabe 1990.

12. These terms are used in Toulmin 1982 and Albanese 1990.

13. Among the new religions in Japan in recent years we can see attempts to

unify at a deeper level the beliefs of salvation religion and the ideas of the new spirituality movements and culture, as, for example, in Worldmate (previously named Cosmomate) under the direction of Fukami Tōshū.

14. See the critique of expressive individualism in Bellah et al. 1985.

Chapter 4

1. In a public survey, about 3.3 percent of the respondents said that they were members of Sōka Gakkai. (NHK Hōsō Yoron Kenkyūjo [Public Opinion Survey Center of the National Broadcasting Company] 'Zenkoku kenmin ishiki' [Attitudes of the people in the prefectures of Japan] survey, conducted in 1978.) Because members of new religions in Japan usually do not like to admit that they are members of these groups, the actual number of believers of Sōka Gakkai is somewhat larger than this. In contrast, those who voted for the Kōmeitō – most of whose supporters are Sōka Gakkai members – in the national constituency in the 1986 election of the House of Councilors was 12.97 percent. Of course this percentage is higher than the percentage of the actual members of Sōka Gakkai. On the other hand, no surveys are available for the number of members of other new religions. But from observations of the activities of new religions in some local areas, a rough guess can be made that members of all other new religions are not fewer than those of Sōka Gakkai.

2. In counting 'syncretic Shintoist' and 'Lotus Sutra-based' as two major clusters of new religions, I am following Murakami Shigeyoshi (1980a). This is not Murakami's unique classification, however, as other writers use similar classifications.

3. For the history of Honmon Butsuryūshū, see Murakami 1976.

4. For the history of Reiyūkai, see Mizuno 1985 and Hardacre 1984.

5. For the history of Sōka Gakkai, see Murakami 1967, and Uefuji and Ono 1975.

6. For an overview of Nichirenism in modern Japan, see Tamura and Miyazaki 1972, and Tokoro 1972.

7. The following are the main sources on Reiyūkai's nationalism: for Nishida Toshizo, see Yugi 1984; for the thought of Kubo Kakutarō and his collaborator, Bekki Sadao, in the years around 1928 and 1929, see the following three pamphlets: *Hotoke no daiji daihi to unmei* (Buddha's great mercy and human fate), *Shōwa no Hokkekyō to Jofukyo Bosatsu* (Jofukyo Bosatsu and the *Hokkekyō* in the Showa Era), and *Hotoke wa messhi tamawazu* (Buddha does not perish) in Reiyūkai shi shiryo hensan iinkai 1988. Umezu 1988 offers an analysis of these pamphlets. For the years after 1934 you can see *Dainippon Reiyūkaihō,* the group's periodical, at Reiyūkai's headquarters in Tokyo.

8. The following are main sources on Sōka Gakkai's nationalism: for Makiguchi's thought, Makiguchi 1984, 1984, 1988; for Toda Jōsei, see Toda 1960 and 1963; on the problem of the national Precept Platform, see Nishiyama 1975.

9. Regarding Reiyūkai's laicism and experientialism see Shimazono 1988. The main sources used in the above article are Kotani 1958, Kubo 1972, and *Dainippon Reiyūkaihō*. For activities related to experience stories in new religions, see Chapter 9 of this volume.

10. For popularism in Sōka Gakkai, in addition to the sources listed in note 8 above, see also Sōka Gakkai Kyōgakubu 1951, Tokyo Daigaku Hokkekyō Kenkyūkai 1962, and Sōka Gakkai Kyōgakubu 1971. The contents of *Shakubuku kyōten* changed several times. I have seen the third edition (1961) and the thirty-ninth edition (1969).

11. See Ōmura and Nishiyama 1988, as well as Chapter 8 in the present volume.

Chapter 5

1. Reiyūkai was founded by Kubo Kakutarō and Kotani Kimi, who held the inaugural meeting of the present Reiyūkai in 1930, although its predecessor, bearing the same name, had been formed already in 1924. There are many religious groups that originated as schisms from Reiyūkai, and the more important of these include Risshō Kōseikai, Busshogonenkai, Myōchikai, Reihōkai, Kōdō Kyōdan, Shishinkai, Fumyōkai Kyōdan, Daiekai, and Myōdōkai.

2. As I mentioned in the previous chapter, Umezu (1988) also provides a useful analysis of this material.

3. Millennialism (or millenarism, millenarianism) was originally a term associated with Christian doctrine, but it has now become established as a general term used in the social sciences. According to Y. Talmon, for example, millenarian religious movements are those 'religious movements that expect imminent, total, ultimate, this-worldly, collective salvation' (Talmon 1968). I have dealt with the millennialism of Japan's new religions in Shimazono 1982b and in Chapter 7 of the present volume. An interesting discussion of the relationship between the millenarian thought of religious movements in modern Japan and its historical milieu may be found in Tsushima 1985.

4. A study of the significance of the idea of expedient or skilful means (*upaya*) in the Lotus Sutra in relation to the coexistence of diverse philosophies and beliefs may be found in Pye 1978. My review of this book appeared in *Shūkyō kenkyū*, No. 254 (1982).

5. See Tokoro 1965 and Takagi 1982.

6. Contained in *Shishiō zenshū* (Complete works of Shishiō [= Tanaka Chigaku]), part 1, Vol. 3 (Shishiō Bunko 1932). A summary of Tanaka's life and thought may be found in Tanaka 1977.

7. Contained in *Shishiō zenshū*, Part 1, Vol. 1 (Shishiō Bunkō 1932).

8. See Chapter 3 in Takeuchi 1978.

9. Kubo Tsugunari, the second president of the Reiyūkai, who is also a Buddhist scholar specializing in the study of the Lotus Sutra, takes the view that the essence of Mahayana Buddhism lies in laicism; see Kubo 1978: 272. However, the term 'laicism' as used by Kubo has a broad meaning, closer to 'popularism' as defined in this chapter.

Chapter 6

1. For the expansion of Japanese new religions abroad, see Inoue 1985, and Nakamaki 1968. See also the special edition of the *Japanese Journal of Religious Studies* on the subject, 18 (2/3) 1991.

2. For an explanation of the term 'this-worldly salvation,' see the introduction to Shimazono 1992a, and Chapter 3 of this volume.

3. The translation 'life-force' is meant to draw attention to the particular sense that has been given to *seimei*, one of the ordinary Japanese words for life.

4. Makiguchi's thought is treated in Seikyō Shinbunsha 1972a and Miyata 1993. In Shimazono 1992e, I have tried to lay out the characteristic ideas of Sōka Kyōiku Gakkai in its formative period. Asai (1968) argues that there are inconsistencies between Makiguchi's value theory and Nichiren Shōshū doctrine, as well as between Makiguchi's thought and the life-force theory of later Sōka Gakkai.

5. For Toda's life and thought, see Higuma 1971, Tōkyō Daigaku Hokkekyō Kenkyūkai 1975, Uefuji and Ōno 1975, and Nishino 1985.

10. Toda Jōsei Zenshū Shuppan Iinkai 1982: 12. The original existence, in Nichiren Shōshū's doctrine, is thought to predate even the *Kuon jitsujō* or 'True Attainment of the Remotest Past' of the Lotus Sutra.

11. Concerning the position of Nichiren Shōshū within the Nichiren sects, see Shigyō 1952 and Mochizuki 1958. Murakami 1967 also gives a concise treatment of this point.

12. In addition to the books by Shigyō and Mochizuki cited in the previous note, see Horigome 1976 and Ōhashi 1978.

13. In Nichiren's *Kaimokushō* this is called the true law of *ichinen sanzen* hidden in the deeper meaning of the *Juryōbon*.

14. Tōkyō Daigaku Hokkekyō Kenkyūkai's *The Doctrine and Practice of Sōka Gakkai* (1975) contains a penetrating analysis of the characteristics of Toda's life-force theory.

Chapter 7

I am greatly indebted to Michael Newton for reading the first draft of this chapter and offering suggestions for its improvement.

1. According to Yonina Talmon, millennialistic (millenarian) religious movements are those 'religious movements that expect imminent, total, ultimate, this-worldly, collective salvation' (Talmon 1968).

2. Millennialistic traditions in Japan's folklore have been studied extensively by Miyata Noburo (1975a, 1975b, and 1980).

3. This point is discussed in Yasumaru and Hirota (1966) and Miyata (1980).

4. Yasumaru and Hirota (1966) is the only existing study of the refinement of the folkloric millennialistic tradition into organized thought in new religions.

5. Few references are made in this chapter to the historical background of the movements. A handy introduction in English is Murakami (1980b).

6. English-language works on Tenrikyō's history, doctrines and religious activities include van Straelen (1957); Tenrikyō Overseas Mission Department (1966); Tenrikyō Church Headquarters (1967; 1972a); and Ellwood (1982). Tenrikyō scriptures in English translation are Tenrikyō Church Headquarters (1971 and 1972b). *Osashizu* and *Kōki* can be read only in Japanese, in Tenrikyō Kyōkai Honbu (1948–1949) and Nakayama (1957).

7. Age is reckoned in this chapter in the traditional Japanese way of counting the years of one's age, that is, counting a fraction of a year as one full year.

8. In the same source, the number of believers in 1928 is given as more than 4 million. On the other hand, the statistics for 1980 show about 2,592,000 believers (Bunkachō, 1982). It is unlikely that believers decreased dramatically between 1928 and 1980; the statistics for 1928 seem to be highly exaggerated.

9. As far as I know, there have been no studies of Honmichi in English. Honmichi Kyōgibu (1972), Murakami (1974) and Umehara (1977) give descriptions in Japanese of Honmichi's history. Three important pamphlets from Honmichi in the early Showa period (*Study Data*, *Letters*, and *An Announcement for the Patriots*) are reprinted in Tanigawa et al. (1971). I am greatly indebted to Murakami's work.

10. For the *Mikagura-uta* and the *Ofudesaki* I used the English translations published by the Tenrikyō Church Headquarters (1972b and 1971).

11. The number is that of each *tanka* in each Part.

12. In the original translation by the Tenrikyō Church Headquarters, 'foreigners' and 'Japanese' are 'the people of the region where My teachings spread

later' and 'the people of the region where My teachings spread early.' Corresponding Japanese words are simply *kara* and *nihon*.

13. As to the relationship between *Ofudesaki* and *Kōki*, see Shimazono 1981 and 1982b.

14. In the summary of *An Announcement for the Patriots* there are eight items, the first of which – general remarks on God – is omitted here, for it has little to do with millennialism.

15. Mass pilgrimages to the Ise shrine occurred about every 60 years in the Tokugawa period, giving rise to a folk belief that God gives humanity abundant benefits at this interval. 1928 was the sixty-first year after 1867 when a big mass pilgrimage called *Eejanaika* had occurred.

Chapter 8

1. This chapter is an expanded version of a paper presented in June 1986 at the 34th Congress of the Kanto Association of the Sociology in Hitotsubashi University. It was translated from the Japanese by James W. Heisig.

2. Martin Buber's work is still worth reading in this context (Buber 1923).

3. See, for example, Hunter 1983 and Michaelson and Roof 1986.

Chapter 9

1. The present chapter is based on two previously written essays. See Shimazono and Inoue 1985, and Shimazono 1988b. Also Shimazono1984 and 1986 deal with related problems. Since I do not treat the concrete types and contents of testimonies in the new religions in the present chapter, the reader is referred to these essays.

2. There may have been an opportunity for talking about conversion in the cult groups (*kō*) of the Pure Land Shin sects, but probably this was not a regular custom. According to Morioka Kiyomi, who made a comparative study of the *o-za* in the Pure Land Shin sect in Noto Peninsula and the *hōza* in Risshō Kōseikai, personal sufferings and troubles are not thematized in the dialogues of faith of the *o-za*, and even if the 'self-awareness of being wicked' is stressed, this remains limited to the conceptual level. Morioka explains: 'If what and who is evil would be concretely pointed out in front of neighbors and conclusions made about someone's ugliness and dreadfulness of heart, one could no longer feel at ease in that place. One might come to hate such people who expose evil and criticize their hypocrisy. The social organization of the village believers who sustain the *o-za* would face dissolution. Therefore, the stimulation of the awareness

of being wicked does not exceed the level of conceptual general theory' (Morioka 1975: 190).
3. See Shimada 1983, esp. pp. 47–50, for such a process as occurring in meetings of the Yamagishikai.

Chapter 10

1. For alternative medicine in the United States, see Andrew Wile 1983 and Robert C. Fuller 1989. For alternative medicine movements in Japan from the 1920s to the 1930s, see Tanabe Shintarō 1989.
2. The following books are recommended for their treatment of a phenomenon similar to AKMs: Roy Wallis 1979 and Kano Masanao 1983. 'Rejected knowledge' in the former and 'popular scholarship' in the latter have much in common with the 'alternative knowledge' mentioned in this chapter, despite some subtle differences.
3. The close relationship of NRMs in modern Japan with folk religions and syncretic religions are described in some detail in Shimazono 1992a.
4. New spirituality movements in contemporary society, closely related to AKMs, are recognized as being close to the orthodox knowledge system in Japan, and they sometimes work in collaboration with nationalism. See Shimazono 1995c and Chapters 15 and 16 in this volume.
5. Shimazono 1992a has presented a perspective for seeing the massive growth of new religious movements in Japan in terms of the multiplicity and popularity of religious groups and deep-rooted folk religions.
6. Reference books for alternative agriculture movements in the West and Japan include Kokumin Seikatsu Center 1981, Tamanoi Yoshiro et al. 1984, Kume Hayami 1984 and 1986, Yasuda Shigeru 1986, and Bruege 1984.
7. More information on Shimamoto Kakuya's life and his agricultural method can be found in the following books: for his life, Shimamoto Kakuya 1984; for his thought, Shimamoto Kakuya 1975; for his agricultural method in the early days, Shimamoto Kakuya 1949 and 1952. For the movement's present agricultural method, see Shimamoto Kunihiko 1987. The description in this chapter is based on these books and information obtained by interviewing Shimamoto Kunihiko.
8. This is a summary of Shimamoto 1975. Incidentally, the concept outlined here has something in common with the 'vitalistic conception of salvation' found in other new religious movements. See also Tsushima et al. 1979.
9. The main characteristics of new spirituality movements are outlined in Shimazono 1992a. For the revival of nature religion (nature theology), see Stephen Toulmin 1982. With regard to the connection between nature

religion and the New Age, an interesting description can be found in Albanese 1990.

Chapter 11
Translated from the Japanese by Jan Swyngedouw.

1. The other types are the conversionist, revolutionist, introversionist, reformist, and utopian sects.
2. My description of the concept of manipulationist sects is based on Wilson 1970 and 1973. An earlier work (Wilson 1967) lists only four types, among which the one then called 'gnostic' corresponds to the manipulationist type.
3. I have dealt with this point in two (Japanese-language) essays: Shimazono 1988a and 1989.
4. Before adopting the term 'therapeutic,' Rieff spoke of 'psychological man.' See Rieff 1959 and Homans 1979.
5. My main sources on Yoshimoto Ishin include Miki 1976, Yoshimoto 1977 and 1983, and Takemoto 1984. The contents of Yoshimoto 1977 are almost the same as those of Yoshimoto 1965.
6. Yoshimoto 1980 contains articles and descriptions taken from newspapers, magazines, dictionaries, and other general publications which speak positively about Yoshimoto Naikan.
7. Yoshimoto 1983 refers to Naikan as 'a way which corresponds to all religions.' Moreover, the idea that Seichō-no-Ie and Hito no Michi Kyōdan are not 'religions' or that they are 'ways corresponding to all religions' has been proposed from time to time.

Chapter 12
Translated from the Japanese by Mark Mullins and Paul Swanson.

1. On Japanese new religions abroad, see the following chapter.

Chapter 13
This article first appeared in the special issue on 'Japanese New Religions Abroad' edited by Mark R. Mulling and Richard F. Young, Japanese Journal of Religious Studies 18/2–3 (June–September 1991), pp. 105–32. It was translated from the Japanese by Edmund R. Skrzypczak.

1. The history of the overseas expansion of Japan's New Religions can be found in summary form in Inoue et al. 1990: 608–57.
2. One exception was Ōmoto. More will be said about this group in the sections below.

3. Most of what follows is based on information I received and materials presented to me when I visited, in summer and autumn 1990, the headquarters of Sōka Gakkai, Seichō no Ie, Sekai Kyūseikyō (Shinseiha), PL, Tenrikyō, and Sūkyō Mahikari.

4. Sōka Gakkai's overseas organizations are known by a variety of names. In this study I shall refer to them all simply as 'Sōka Gakkai,' except for the organization in the United States, which is widely known as NSA.

5. The following description is dependent on Williams 1989.

6. One can obtain some idea of conditions during this period from Yamamoto 1982 and Huang 1989.

7. For a consideration of these features of Brazilian culture and their relationship to features of the religious situation, with a comparison with the United States and Japan, see Nakamaki 1986: 204–28.

8. For a work that presents this point of view, see Shōji 1986.

9. See Seichō no Ie Honbu 1980, Maeyama 1983, and Matsuda 1988 and 1989. Stark and Roberts (1982) point out that sometimes a new religious movement that began in a large-scale society is forced to remain a minor movement there, and so early hopes wither and die, but when it shifts to a small-scale society it reaps unexpected success – that is, supported by many influential members at first, it develops into a powerful, prestigious religion in that small society. The assumption that another religion might have reaped the greatest success in Brazil if it had become the most influential in the Japanese community is not completely groundless.

10. The leader of Seichō no Ie's Brazilian propagation program, Matsuda Miyoshi, has written that 'another unique and absolutely decisive factor in Seichō no Ie's enlightening not only of Brazil but also of the whole world, is the new campaign method of propagation through the written word. There can be no denying that Seichō no Ie's spread to the most distant land from Japan, Brazil, in the very same year Seichō no Ie began in Japan (1930), its spread to the remotest corners of Brazil, and the fact that the Brazilian translation of *Seimei no jissō* was widely diffused and became a pillar of strength, are all due to the power of propagation through the written word' (Matsuda 1989: 331–32).

11. This also has a bearing on what I said earlier: Seichō no Ie, Sekai Kyūseikyō, and Sōka Gakkai have in common the fact that they were founded by men of intellectual ability familiar with history, religious doctrine, modern thought, and scientific statement. This sort of religious group forms a large type within the new religions, standing alongside the 'indigenous-emergent type' that a fairly unlettered founder began from a folk-religion background, and the 'moral-cultivation type' in which popular ideas of character building and virtue come to be linked to a salvation belief – a type that can be called

the 'intellectual-thought type.' Further, the groups in the Reiyūkai tradition and most of the groups derived from Shinnyoen fall midway between the 'indigenous-emergent type' and the 'intellectual-thought type,' so they belong to a fourth type we might refer to as an intermediate type. According to my tentative classification of the new religions, most of the religious groups that have succeeded in expanding into alien cultures belong to the 'intellectual-thought type.' In contrast, the lack of success overseas of the quite numerically large 'intermediate-type' groups is particularly striking (Shimazono 1990: 216–23).

12. For the philosophy of Ōmoto, which was the source of Seichō no Ie's and Sekai Kyūseikyō's idea that all religions are the same, see Young 1988.

13. The brief discussion that follows can be fleshed out by consulting Tsushima et al., 1979.

14. Nakamaki (1989: 445–47) draws attention to this aspect of PL.

15. Stark and Bainbridge (1985) divide religious groups in contemporary North America and Europe into three categories and attempt to depict the ways in which they have taken turns being influential. The categories are: 'church,' 'sect,' and 'cult.' 'Cult' is subdivided into 'cult movement,' 'client cult,' and 'audience cult.' I have made four categories, but they are not that far apart from Stark and Bainbridge's. I have singled out their 'cult movement' and taken it to be 'new religions.' Again, what I have placed in my third category to a great extent overlaps with their 'audience cult' and 'client cult,' though not completely.

Chapter 14
Translated by Ms. Hayashi Chine.

1. For general characteristics of Japanese new religions, see Shimazono 1992a, and for the new religions' beliefs about salvation, see Tsushima et al. 1979.

2. One book which contributed greatly in propagating the term 'new new religions' is Muroo 1984. For perceptions of the new new religions, see Shimazono 1992a, 1992b, 1992e, and 2001.

3. For a detailed description of GLA and Takahashi, see Numata 1988.

Chapter 15

1. I have discussed the terms New Age, the Spiritual World, and the new spirituality movements in the following books and article: Shimazono 1992a, 1992b, 1992c, 1996 and 2001.

2. Books by Umehara discussed in this paper are as follows: Umehara 1965, 1967, 1972, 1973, 1979, 1983, 1988–1989, 1989, 1991, and 1992.

3. In the foreword to his *Nihon bunkaron* (1976), Umehara explained that in the future he would return to the philosophical problems that he was working on before he began his historical studies.

4. This may be seen in a number of Umehara's works (1983, 1988–1989, 1989, 1991, and 1992).

5. For a critical discussion of this point see Hosokawa 1991.

6. See the 'Postscript' in Yuasa's *Keizaijin no moraru* (1967).

7. Books by Yuasa discussed in this paper are as follows: Yuasa 1970, 1972, 1973, 1977, 1978, 1980, 1981a, 1981b, 1982, 1986, and 1991.

8. See, for example, Iwata 1970, 1973, 1976, and 1979.

Chapter 16

1. The following research works published in the West inspired me in considering phenomena in Japan: Chandler 1988, Bednarowski 1989, Melton 1990, Albanese 1990, Lewis and Melton 1992, York 1995, and Heelas 1996. Reference materials in Japanese are omitted.

2. See Shimazono 1996. Prior to this publication, the outline of the contents of the book was published in Shimazono 1992a and 1992b, and a paper originally published in the journal *Syzygy* that is presented as Chapter 15 of this volume. Originally *'shin reisei undō'* was rendered into English as 'new spiritual movements' but the preferred term is now 'new spirituality movements and culture.'

3. The preference for 'new spirituality movements and culture' over 'new spiritual movements' was presented in my previous book in Japanese (1996), but it is developed more emphatically in this chapter.

4. Max Weber (1920–1921) called this 'the religious brotherhood ethic.'

5. For example, Okano Moriya, president of Sangraha Institute of Psychological Research, which attempts to spread self-transforming experiences through workshops, etc., considers his own attempt to be an integration of transpersonal psychology and the ideas of *vijinana-vadin* from Buddhism. Ken Wilber of the United States also takes a stance close to Okano (Okano 1995, Wilber 1996).

6. This term is based on Redfield's discussion of 'great tradition' and 'little tradition' (1956).

References

Ahlstrom, Sydney E. (1972), *A Religious History of the American People,* 2 volumes, New Haven: Yale University Press.

Albanese, C. L. (1990), *Nature Religion in America*, Chicago: The University of Chicago Press.

Anderson, Benedict (1983), *Imagined Communities: Reflections on the Origin and Spread of Nationalism,* London: Verso and New Left Books.

Aoki Shigeru (1955), *Kasaoka Konkō daijin* (Konkō daijin of Kasaoko), Kasaoka: Konkōkyō Kasaoka Kyōkai.

Asai Endō (1968), 'Sōka Gakkai no shutsugen to mondaiten' (The emergence of Sōka Gakkai and its problems). In Mochizuki Kanko, ed., *Kindai Nibon no hokke bukkyō* (Lotus Sutra Buddhism in modern Japan), Kyoto: Heirakuji Shoten.

Bakhtin, Mikhail (1984), *Rabelais and His World,* (tr. Helene Iswolsky), Bloomington: Indiana University Press; originally published in Russian in 1965.

Bednarowski, Mary F. (1989), *New Religions and the Theological Imagination in America*, Bloomington: Indiana University Press.

Bellah, Robert N. (1957), *Tokugawa Religion: The Values of Pre-industrial Japan.* Chicago: The Free Press.

Bellah, Robert N. (1970), 'The religious evolution,' in *Beyond Belief: Essays on Religion in a Post-Traditional World,* New York: Harper & Row.

Bellah, Robert N. et al. (1985), *Habits of the Heart: Individualism and Commitment in American Life,* New York: Harper & Row.

Blacker, Carmen (1975), *The Catalpa Bow: A Study of Shamanistic Practices in Japan*, London: George Allen & Unwin.

Bromley, David G. and Anson D. Shupe, Jr. (1981), *Strange Gods*, Boston: Beacon Press.

Bruege, P. (1984), *Die Anthroposophen,* Reinbek bei Hamburg: Rowohlt.

Buber, Martin(1923), *Ich und Du,; Zwiesprache,* Frankfurt am Main: Insel.

Bunkachō (1982), *Shūkyō Nenkan* (Religions Yearbook), Tokyo: Gyōsei.

Bunkachō (1987), *Shūkyō Nenkan* (Religions Yearbook), Tokyo: Gyōsei.

Capra, Fritjof (1982), *Turning Point*, New York: Simon and Schuster.

Chandler, R. (1988), *Understanding the New Age,* Dalas: Word Publishing.

Cohn, Norman (1970), *The Pursuit of the Millenium*, Oxford: Oxford University Press.

Durkheim, Emile (1915), *The Elementary Forms of the Religious Life*, trans. Joseph Ward Swain, New York: George Allen & Unwin Ltd.

Egawa Shōko (1991), *Kyūseishu no yabō* (Ambition of the savior), Tokyo: Kyōiku Shiryō Shuppankai.

Ellwood, Robert S., Jr (1982), *Tenrikyō: A Pilgrimage Faith*, Tenri: Oyasato Research Institute, Tenri University.

Freud, Sigmund (1912–13), *Totem und Taboo*, Wien: Internationaler Psychoanalytischer Verlag.

Fujiwara Satoko (1995), *'Kagami to yōgo: Aum Shinrikyō jiken niyotte shūkyōgaku wa ikani kawatta ka'* (Mirror and advocacy: How religious studies has changed by the Aum Shinrikyo Incident), *Tōkyō Daigaku Shūkyōgaku Nenpō* (The Tokyo University Religious Studies Yearbook) 13: 17–31.

Fukushi Masahiro, Shikata Yasuyuki, and Kitabayashi Toshinobu (1992) *Yōroppa no yūki nōgyō* (Organic Agriculture in Europe), Tokyo: Ie-no-Hikari Kyōkai.

Fukushima Masato (1989), *'Mō hitotsu no "meisō": Toshi to iu keiken no kaidoku kōshi'* (Yet another way of meditation: A framework for understanding the urban experience), in Tanabe Shigeharu, ed., *Jissen shūkyō no jinruigaku* (The anthropology of practical religion), Kyoto: Kyōto Daigaku Gakujutsu Shuppan.

Fuller, Robert C. (1989), *Alternative Medicine and American Religious Life*, Oxford: Oxford University Press.

Fukuoka Masanobu (1983), *Shizen nōhō: Wara ippon no kakumei* (Natural Agriculture: A revolution by a single rice-straw), Tokyo: Shunjūsha.

Galbraith, John Kenneth (1958), *The Affluent Society*, Boston: Houghton Mifflin.

Girard, Rene (1972), *La violence et le sacré*, Paris: B. Grasset.

Hardacre, Helen (1984), *Lay Buddhism in Contemporary Japan: Reiyūkai Kyōdan*, Princeton: Princeton University Press.

Heelas, Paul (1996), *The New Age Movement*, Oxford: Blackwell.

Higuma Takenori (1971), *Sōka Gakkai, Toda Jōsei*, Tokyo: Shinjinbutsu Ōraisha.

Homans, Peter (1979), *Jung in Context: Modernity and the Making of Psychology*, Chicago: University of Chicago Press.

Honmichi Kyōgibu (1972), *Honmichi gaikan* (An outline of Honmichi), Takaishi: Honmichi Kyōgibu.

Hori Ichirō (1971), *Nihon no shamanizumu* (Shamanism in Japan), Tokyo: Kodansha.

Horigome Nichijun (1976), *Nichiren daishōnin no kyōgi: Nichiren shōnin to Hokkekyō* (The teachings of Nichiren: Nichiren and the Lotus Sutra), Tokyo: Nichiren Shōshū Bussho Kankōkai.

Hosokawa Ryoichi (1991), '*Umehara Takeshi shi no Nihonjin no "anoyo" kan ni yosete'* (A comment on Takeshi Umehara's theory of the Japanese view of 'the other world'), *Rekishi Hyōron* 490.

Howard, Albert (1940), *An Agricultural Testament*, London: Oxford University Press.

Huang Chih-huei (1989), 'Tenrikyō no Taiwan ni okeru dendō to juyō' (Evangelism and acceptance of Tenrikyō in Taiwan), *Minzokugaku kenkyū* 54/3: 292–306.

Hunter, James D. (1983), *American Evangelicalism*, New Brunswick: Rutgers University Press.

Inoue Nobutaka (1985), *Umi wo watatta Nihon shūkyō* (Japanese religions abroad), Tokyo: Kōbundō.

Inoue Nobutaka (1992), *Shinshūkyō no kaidoku* (Explication of new religions), Tokyo: Chikuma Shobō.

Inoue Nobutaka, et al., eds. (1981), *Shinshūkyō kenkyū chōsa handobukku* (A handbook for survey research on new religions), Tokyo: Yuzankaku Shuppan.

Inoue Nobutaka, et al., eds. (1990), *Shinshūkyō jiten* (New religion encyclopedia), Tokyo: Kōbundō.

Ishibashi Tomonobu (1927a), 'Kakuretaru Nihon no meshia-kyō – Isson-kyō no kyōdan seikatsu to sono shinkō naiyō' (A hidden Messiah religion in Japan: The way of life of the Isson-kyō and what it believes), Part I, *Shūkyō kenkyū new series* 4/4.

Ishibashi Tomonobu (1927b), 'Kakuretaru Nihon no meshia-kyō – Isson-kyō no kyōdan seikatsu to sono shinkō naiyō' (A hidden Messiah religion in Japan: The way of life of the Isson-kyō and what it believes), Part II, *Shūkyō kenkyū new series* 4/5.

Iwata Keiji (1970), *Kami no tanjō* (The birth of the gods), Tokyo: Tankosha.

Iwata Keiji (1973), *Sōmoku chūgyo no jinruigaku* (An anthropology of grass, trees, insects and fish), Kyoto:Tankosha.

Iwata Keiji (1976), *Kosumosu no shisō* (Thought on the cosmos), Tokyo: Nihon Hoso Shuppan Kyōkai.

Iwata Keiji (1979), *Kami no jinruigaku* (An anthropology of the gods), Tokyo: Kodansha.

Jaspers, Karl (1932), *Philosophie: II. Existenzerhellung*, Berlin: J. Springer.

Jaspers, Karl (1949), *Vom Ursprung und Ziel der Geschichte*, Zürich: Fisher.

Kamata Tōji (1991), 'Shin Shin-Butsu Shūgō no Jikkenjo: Tenkawa Benzaitensha' (Testing ground of new Shinto-Buddhism syncretization), in Sasaki Kōkan, ed., *Bukkyō to Nihonjin 12: Gendai to Bukkyō* (Buddhism and the Japanese 12: Contemporary Buddhism), Tokyo: Shunjūsha.

Kamata Tōji and Tsumura Takashi, eds. (1994), *Tenkawa Mandala: Cho-Shukyo e no suiro* (Tenkawa Mandala: Channel to a super religion), Tokyo: Shunjūsha.

Kanda Hideo (1990), *Nyorai-kyo no shisō to shinkō* (The ideology and beliefs of Nyoraikyo), Tenri: Tenri University Oyasato Research Institute.

Kano, Masanao (1983), *Kindai Nippon no minkangaku* (Popular scholarship in modern Japan), Tokyo: Iwanami Shoten.

Kawai Hayao (1986), *Shūkyō to kagaku no setten* (The Intersection of religion and science), Tokyo: Iwanami Shoten.

Kokumin Seikatsu Center, ed. (1981), *Nippon no yūki nōgyō undō* (Organic Agricultural Movements in Japan), Tokyo: Nihon Keizai Hyōronsha.

Kōmoto Mitsugi (1978), 'Minshū no naka no senzokan no ichisokumen' (One aspect of the view of ancestors among the masses), in Sakurai Tokutarō, ed., *Nihon shūkyō no fukugōteki kōzō* (The complex structure of Japanese religion), Tokyo: Kōbundō.

Konkōkyō Honbu Kyōchō (1953), *Konkō daijin*. Okayama: Konkōkyō Honbu Kyōchō.

Kotani Kimi (1958), *Watashi no shugyō seikatsu sanju-go nen* (The Thirty five Years of My Life of Ascetic Discipline), Tokyo: Reiyūkai Kyōdan.

Kubo Tsugunari, ed. (1972), *Kotani Kimi shō : Ten no ongaku* (From the words of Kotani Kimi: The music of heaven), Tokyo: Hotoke no Sekai Sha.

Kubo Tsugunari (1978), *Zaikeshugi Bukkyō no susume* (An invitation to laicist Buddhism), Tokyo: Inner Trip Sha.

Kumamoto Nichinichi Shinbun, ed. (1992), *Aum Shinrikyō to mura no ronri* (Aum Shinrikyō and the logic of the village), Fukuoka: Ashi Shobō.

Kume Hayami (1983), *Nippon no shizen nōhō* (Natural agriculture in Japan), Tokyo: Kosei Shorin.

Kume Hayami (1984), *Sekai no shizen nōhō* (Natural agriculture in the world), Tokyo: Kosei Shorin.

Kume Hayami, ed. (1986), *Gendai no shizen nōhō: Zōshu to shūdanka* (Natural agriculture in contemporary society: Profit increase and transforming to collective farming), Tokyo: Kosei Shorin.

Lefebvre, Henri (1947), *La pense de Karl Marx,* Paris: Bordas.

Lewis, James R. and J. Gordon Melton, eds. (1992), *Perspectives on the New Age*, Albany, NY: SUNY Press.

Luckmann, Thomas (1967), *The Invisible Religion*, New York: Macmillan.

Maeyama Tadashi (1983), 'Japanese religions in southern Brazil: Change and syncretism,' *Latin American Studies* (University of Tsukuba) 6: 181–238.

Maeyama Takashi and Robert J. Smith (1983), 'Ōmoto: A Japanese "new religion" in Brazil,' *Latin American Studies* (University of Tsukuba) 5: 83–102.

Makiguchi Tsunesaburō (1984, 1984, 1988), *Makiguchi Tsunesaburō zenshū dai 8, 9, 10 kan* (Collected works of Makiguchi Tsunesaburō, vols. 8, 9, 10), Tokyo: Daisan Bunmeisha.

Maruyama Masao (1974), *Studies in the intellectual history of Tokugawa Japan*. Tokyo: Tokyo University Press.

Matsuda Miyoji (1988), *Burajiru dendō no hanseiki* (An incomplete record of evangelism in Brazil), Tokyo: Nihon Kyōbunsha.

Matsuda Miyoshi (1989), *Hikari wa kokkyō wo koete* (The light crosses national boundaries), Tokyo: Nihon Kyōbunsha.

Matsuno Junko, ed. (1984), *Shinshūkyō jiten* (Dictionary of new religions), Tokyo: Tōkyōdō Shuppan.

Melton, J. Gordon (1990), *New Age Encyclopedia*, Detroit: Gale Research Inc.

Michaelson, R. S. and W.C. Roof, eds. (1986), *Liberal Protestantism*, New York: Pilgrim Press.

Miki Yoshihiko (1976), *Naikan ryōhō nyūmon: Nihonteki jiko-tankyū no sekai* (Introduction to Yoshimoto Naikan: The world of the Japanese search for the self), Osaka: Sōgensha.

Miyajima Takashi (1987), *Dyurukemu riron to gendai* (Durkheim's theory and the present), Tokyo: Tōkyō Daigaku Shuppankai.

Miyata Noboru (1975a), *Miroku shinkō no kenkyū* (A study on Miroku [Maitreya] belief) (revised edition), Tokyo: Miraisha.

Miyata Noboru (1975b), *Kinsei no hayarigami* (Fashionable gods in the Tokugawa Period), Tokyo: Hyōronsha.

Miyata Noboru (1980), *Atarashi Sekai eno inori: Miroku* (Prayer to the future world: Miroku [Maitreya]), Tokyo: Kosei Shuppansha.

Miyata Kōichi (1993), *Makiguchi Tsunesaburō no shukyō undō* (The religious movement of Makiguchi Tsunesaburō), Tokyo: Daisan Bunmeisha.

Mizuno Yasuharu (1985), *Reiyūkai: Kubo Kakutarō no shōgai* (Reiyūkai: Kubo Kakutarō's Life), Tokyo: Kodansha.

Mochizuki Kankō (1958), *Nichiren kyōgaku no kenkyū* (A study of Nichiren doctrine), Kyoto: Heirakuji Shoten.

Morioka Kiyomi (1962), *Shinshū kyōdan to ie seido* (Shin sect religious organization and the household system), Tokyo: Sobusha.

Morioka Kiyomi (1970), *Nihon no kindaika to Kirisutokyō* (Japan's modernization and Christianity), Tokyo: Hyōronsha.

Morioka Kiyomi (1975), *Gendai shakai no minshū to shūkyō* (People and religion in contemporary society), Tokyo: Hyōronsha.

Morioka Kiyomi (1984), *Ie no henbō to senzo no matsuri* (The changing forms of the 'ie' and ancestor observances), Tokyo: Nihon Kirisukyōdan Shuppankyoku.

Moroi Masaichi (1953), *Kaitei Seibun iin* (Posthumous publication of the writigs of Seibun or Moroi Msaichi), revised ed., Tenri: Tenrikyō Dōyūsha.

Morris, Brian (1987), *Anthropological Studies of Religion*, Cambridge: Cambridge University Press.

Motoyama Kinue (1975), *Tamamitsu Jinja kyoso jiden* (The autobiography of the foundress of Tamamitsu Jinja), Tokyo: Shūkyō Shinri Shuppan.

Mullins, Mark (1993), 'Christianity as a New Religion,' in *Religion and Society in Modern Japan*, Mullins et al. eds., Berkeley: Asian Humanities Press.

Mullins, Mark R. (1998), *Christianity Made in Japan: A Study of Indigenous Movements*, Honolulu: University of Hawai'i Press.

Mullins, Mark, Shimazono Susumu, and Swanson, Paul, eds. (1993), *Religion and Society in Modern Japan*, Berkeley: Asian Humanities Press.

Murakami Shigeyoshi (1967), *Sōka Gakkai=Kōmeitō* (Sōka Gakkai and Kōmeitō), Tokyo: Aoki Shoten.

Murakami Shigeyoshi (1971a), *'Konkō daijin oboe'* (Konkō Daijin's memoirs), in *Minshū shūkyō no shisō, Nihon shisō taikei 67* (The ideology of folk religions, Japanese thought, volume 67), Murakami Shigeyoshi and Yasumaru Yoshio, eds., Tokyo: Iwanami Shoten.

Murakami Shigeyoshi (1971b), 'Isson Nyorai Kino to Nyoraikyō/Isson Kyōdan' (Isson Nyorai Kino and Nyoraikyō/Isson Kyōdan), in *Minshū shūkyō no shisō, Nihon shiso taikei 67.* (The ideology of folk religions, Japanese thought, volume 67), Murakami Shigeyoshi and Yasumaru Yoshio, eds., Tokyo: Iwanami Shoten.

Murakami Shigeyoshi (1974), *Honmichi fukei jiken* (Honmichi's *lèse majesté* incident), Tokyo: Kōdansha.

Murakami Shigeyoshi (1976), *Butsuryū kaido Nagamatsu Nissen* (The Founder of Butsuryū, Nagamatsu Nissen), Tokyo: Kodansha.

Murakami Shigeyoshi (1979), *Gendai Nihon no shūkyō mondai* (Religious issues in contemporary Japan), Tokyo: Asahi Shinbunsha.

Murakami Shigeyoshi (1980a), *Shinshūkyō: Sono kōdō to shisō* (New religions: Their behavior and thought), Tokyo: Hyōronsha.

Murakami, Shigeyoshi (1980b), *Japanese Religion in the Modern Century*, trans. H. Byron Earhart, Tokyo: University of Tokyo Press.

Muroo Tadashi (1984), *Shinjinrui to shūkyō: Wakamono wa naze shin shin shūkyō ni hashiru no ka* (The new humanity and religion: Why young people run to the new new religions), Tokyo: Toki no Keizaisha.

Naito Kanji (1941), 'Shūkyō to keizai rinri: Jōdo Shinshū to Omi shonin' (Religions and Economic Ethics: Jōdo Shinshū and the merchants of Omi), *Nenpō shakaigaku* (Sociology yearbook) 8.

Nakamaki Hirochika (1986), *Shinsekai no Nihon shūkyō* (Japanese religions in the new world), Tokyo: Heibonsha.

Nakamaki Hirochika (1989), *Nihon shūkyō to nikkei shūkyō no kenkyū* (Studies of Japanese religions and Japanese-derived religions), Tokyo: Tōsui Shobō.

Nakamura Hajime (1989) et al, eds, *Iwanami bukkyō jiten* (Iwanami Buddhist dictionary), Tokyo: Iwanami Shoten.

Nakamura Kōzō (1992), *Amerika no yūki nōgyō* (Organic agriculture in America), Tokyo: Ie no Hikari Kyōkai.

Nakayama Shōzen (1957), *Kōki no kenkyū* (A study on Kōki), Tenri: Tenrikyō Dōyūsha.

Nakayama Tarō (1930), *Nihon hujoshi* (The history of Japanese female shamans), Tokyo: Parutosusha.

Naruse Muneo (1989), *Tōitsu Kyōkai no hanzai: Reikan shōhō to shōkyō rengō* (The crimes of the Unification Church: Extrasensory sales and the anti-Communist alliance), Tokyo: Hachigatsu Shokan.

Nietzsche, Friedrich (1891), *Zur Genealogie der Moral*, z. Aufl., Leipzing: C.G. Naumann.

Nishino Tatsukichi (1985), *Denki Toda Jōsei* (The biography of Toda Jōsei), Tokyo: Daisan Bunmeisha.

Nishiyama Shigeru (1975), 'Nichiren Shōshū Sōka Gakkai ni okeru "honmon kaidan" ron no hensen' (Changes in the 'honmon kaidan' theory of Nichiren Shōshū Sōka Gakkai), in Nakao Akira ed. *Nichirenshū no shomondai* (Problems of the Nichiren sect), Tokyo: Yuzankaku Shuppan.

Nishiyama Shigeru (1985), '*Sengo shinshūkyō no henyō to shinshinshūkyō no taitō*' (The transformation of postwar new religions and the emergence of the new new religions), *Shūmu jihō* 73.

Numata Kenya (1988), *Gendai Nihon no shin shūkyō* (The new religions in contemporary Japan), Osaka: Sōgensha.

Ōhashi Jijō (1978), *Bukkyō shisō to Fujikyōgaku* (Buddhist thought and the Fuji sect doctrine), Tokyo: Nichiren Shōsha Busshō Kankōkai.

Okano Moriya (1995), *Wakaru yuishiki* (An understandable exposition of *Vijinana-vadin*), Tokyo: Mizu Shobō.

Ōkawa Ryūhō. (1987a), *Taiyō no hō* (The laws of the sun), Tokyo: Tsuchiya Shoten.

Ōkawa Ryūhō (1987b), *Ōgon no hō* (The laws of gold), Tokyo: Tsuchiya Shoten.

Ōkawa Ryūhō (1987c), *Eien no hō* (The laws of eternity), Tokyo: Tsuchiya Shoten.

Ōkawa Ryūhō (1989), *Utopia kachi kakumei* (Utopian value revolution), Tokyo: Tsuchiya Shoten.

Ōkawa Ryūhō (1993), *Frankly Speaking*, Tokyo: Kōfuku no Kagaku Press.

Ōkawa Ryūhō, ed. (1990), *Shinri yōgo no kiso chishiki* (Basic knowledge about God's truth terminology). Tokyo: Kōfuku no Kagaku Press.

Ōmoto Honbu, ed. (1975), *Ōmoto annai* (Guide to Ōmoto), Kameoka: Ōmoto Honbu.

Ōmura Eisho and Nishiyama Shigeru, eds. (1988), *Gendaijin no shūkyō* (Contemporary religion), Tokyo: Yuhikaku.

Ōtsuka Hisao (1948), *Kindaika no ningenteki kiso* (The human foundation of modernization), Tokyo: Hakujitsu Shoin.

Pye, Michael (1978), *Skilful Means,* London: Duckworth.

Reader, Ian (1996), *A Poisonous Cocktail?: Aum Shinrikyō's Path to Violence*, Copenhagen: Nordic Institute of Asian Studies.

Redfield, Robert. (1956), *Peasant Society and Culture,* Chicago: The University of Chicago Press.

Reisman, David (1956), *The Lonely Crowd,* New Haven: Yale University Press.

Reiyūkai, ed. (1976), *Bessatsu hyūman: Shakaden kara no shuppatsu* (Supplement to human series: Starting from the Shaka Hall), Tokyo: Hotoke no Sekaisha.

Reiyūkai shi shiryo hensan iinkai ed. (1988), *Reiyūkai shi shiryō, ichi no yon* (Sources on Reiyūkai's history, vol. 1–4), Tokyo: Reiyūkai.

Rieff, Philip (1959), *Freud: The Mind of the Moralist*, New York: Viking Press.

Rieff, Philip (1966), *The Triumph of the Therapeutic*, New York: Harper & Row.

Rodale, J.I. (1945), *Pay Dirt*, Emmanus, PA: Rodale Press.

Saki Akio (1960), *Shinkō shūkyō: Sore o meguru gendai no jōken* (New religions: Their surrounding contemporary conditions), Tokyo: Aoki Shoten.

Sakurai Tokutarō (1974, 1977), *Nihon no shamanizumu* (Shamanism in Japan), 2 vols., Tokyo: Aoki Shoten.

Sasaki Kokan (1980), Shamanizumu (Shamanism), Tokyo: Chuōkonronsha.

Sasaki Yūji (1981), *'Wagakuni ni okeru fusha no kenkyū'* (The study of mediums in Japan), in Sasaki Yūji, ed.*Gendai no esupuri 165: Shamanizumu* (L'Esprit d'aujourd'hui: Shamanism), Tokyo: Shibundō.

Seichō no Ie Honbu (1980), *Seichō no Ie gojūnenshi* (Fifty years of Seichō no Ie history), Tokyo: Nihon Kyōbunsha.

Seikyō Shinbunsha, eds. (1972a), *Makiguchi Tsunesaburō,* Tokyo: Seikyō Shinbunsha.

Seikyō Shinbunsha, eds. (1972b), *Shosetsu ningen kakamei* (Human revolution), Tokyo: Seikyō Bunko.

Seikyō Shinbunsha, eds. (1980), *Jinseishō: Ikeda Daisaku Shingenshū* (Snatches of life: Proverbs of Ikeda Daisaku), Tokyo: Seikyō Shinbunsha.

Sekai Kyūseikyo, Inc, The Founder's Biography Editing Committee (1981), *Tōhō no Hikari* (Light from the East), 2 volumes, Atami: Messianica General.

Seto Mikio (1974), 'Kinsei kōki Ōtani mura no shakai keizai jōkyō ni tsuite: Akazawa Bunji ni okeru rinriteki jissen no haikei' (On the social and economic conditions of Otani Village in the late modern period: The background of Akazawa Bunji's ethical practice), *Konkōkyōgaku* 14

Shigyō Kaishū (1952), *Nichirenshū kyōgakushi* (A history of Nichirenshū doctrine), Kyoto: Heirakūji Shoten.

Shimada Hiromi (1980), *'Karada no kyūsai to kokoro no kyūsai: Iryō shūkyōgaku e'* (The salvation of the body and the salvation of the mind: Toward a medical science of religion), in Shūkyō shakaigaku kenkyūkai, ed. *Shūkyō no imi sekai* (The religious world of meaning), Tokyo: Yūzankaku Shuppan.

Shimada Hiromi (1983), 'Inishieshon to taiken' (Initiation and experience), *Shūkyō kenkyū* 257: 31–54.

Shimada Hiromi (1992), *Kamigami no tsugō* (The gods' convenience), Kyoto: Hozokan.

Shimada Hiromi (1997), *Shūkyō no jidai to wa nan datta no ka* (What was the Age of Religions?), Tokyo: Kodansha.

Shimamoto Kakuya (1949), *Kōso no ōyō to nōgyō* (Application of enzymes and agriculture), Kameoka: Aizen Mizuhokai.

Shimamoto Kakuya (1952), *Biseibutsu nōhō* (Microbiological agriculture), Kameoka: Aizen Mizuhokai.

Shimamoto Kakuya (1975), *Tamatebako* (Treasure box), Minakuchi: Shimamoto Kunihiko.

Shimamoto Kakuya (1984), *Daichi no sakebi: Shimamoto Kakuya no shōgai* (A call from the Earth: The life of Shimamoto Kakuya), Minakuchi: Kōso no Sekaisha.

Shimamoto Kunihiko (1987), *Shimamoto biseibutsu nōhō* (Shimamoto's microbiological agriculture), Tokyo: Nōson Gyoson Bunka Kyōkai.

Shimazono Susumu (1977), 'Kamigakari kara tasuke made: Tenrikyō no hassei josetsu' (From divine possession to salvation: An introduction to the origin of Tenrikyō), *Komozawa daigaku bukkyōgakubu ronshū* 8.

Shimazono Susumu (1979), 'The Living *Kami* Idea in the New Religions of Japan,' *Japanese Journal of Religious Studies*, 6: 389–412.

Shimazono Susumu (1980), 'Shūkyō no kindaika: Akazawa Bunji to higara-hōi shinkō' (The modernization of religion: Akazawa Bunji and beliefs in lucky and unlucky days and directions), in Gorai Shigeru et al., eds. *Kōza Nihon no minzoku shūkyō 5: Minzoku shūkyō to shakai* (Essays in Japanese folk religion 5: Folk religion and society), Tokyo: Kōbundō.

Shimazono, Susumu (1981), 'Shinshūkyō no shūkyōishiki to seiten' (Religious consciousness in new religions and the scriptures), pp. 298–312 in Ikeda Hidetoshi et al. eds, *Nihonjin no shūkyō no ayumi* (Steps in Japanese religious history), Tokyo: Daigaku Kyōikusha.

Shimazono Susumu (1982a), 'Karisuma no henyō to shikōsha shinwa' (Transformation of charisma and myths of the supreme person), in Nakamaki Hirochika ed., *Kamigami no sōkoku* (Conflict of the gods), Tokyo: Shinsensha.

Shimazono Susumu (1982b), 'Tenrikyō ni okeru kyūsaishi shinwa' (Myths of salvation history in Tenrikyō), in *Tetsugaku shisō ronsō* (Journal of philosophy and thought), published by University of Tsukuba, Department of Philosophy, 1: 17–28.

Shimazono Susumu (1984), 'Shinshūkyō-kyōdan ni okeru taikendan no ichi: Myōchikai, Risshō Kōseikai, Tenrikyō' (The place of testimonies in the new religions: Myōchikai, Risshō Kaseikai, and Tenrikyō), *Tōkyō daigaku shūkyōgaku nenpō* 2: 1–20.

Shimazono Susumu (1986) 'Shūkyō-gengo to shite no taikendan: Reiyūkai kyōdan o rei toshite' (Testimonies as religious language: The case of Reiyūkai and its offshoots), in Tōkyō Gaikokugo Daigaku Kaigai-jijō Kenkyūsho, ed. *Shōwa rokujū-nendo tokutei kenkyū-hōkoku* (Report on special research projects during Showa 60), Tokyo: Tōkyō Gaikokugo Daigaku.

Shimazono Susumu (1987), 'Kyōso to shūkyō teki shidōsha sūhai no kenkyū kadai' (Issues in the research of worship of founders and religious leaders), in Shūkyō shakaigaku kenkyūkai ed., *Kyōso to sono shūhen* (Founders and their surroundings), Tokyo: Yūzankaku shuppan.

Shimazono Susumu (1988a), 'Seichō no Ie to shinri ryōhōteki sukui no shisō: Taniguchi Masaharu no shisō keisei katei o megutte' (Seichō no Ie and the idea of psychotherapeutic salvation: The formation of Taniguchi Masaharu's thought), in T. Sakurai, ed. *Nihon shūkyō no seitō to itan* (Orthodoxy and heresy in Japanese religion), Tokyo: Kōbundō.

Shimazono Susumu (1988b), 'Shin shūkyō no taiken shugi: Shoki Reiyūkai no baai' (Experience orientation of the new religions: The case of early Reiyūkai), in Murakami Shigeyosi ed., *Taikei Bukkyō to Nihonjin 10 minshū to shakai* (Buddhism and the Japanese people, vol. 10, masses and society), Tokyo: Shunjūsha.

Shimazono Susumu (1989), 'Toshigata shinshūkyō no kokoronaoshi: Hito-no-Michi Kyōdan no shinriryōhōteki kyūsai-shinkō' (Healing of the mind in new urban religions: Psychotherapeutic salvation beliefs in Hito no Michi Kyōdan), in Y. Yuasa, ed. *Taikei Bukkyō to Nipponjin 3: Mitsugi to shugyō* (Buddhism and the Japanese people, vol3: Secret Rituals and Ascetic Practices), Tokyo: Shunjūsha.

Shimazono Susumu (1990), 'Oshie no ruikei' (Types of teaching), in Inoue Nobutaka et al., ed. *Shinshūkyō jiten*, Tokyo: Kōbundō.

Shimazono Susumu (1992a), *Gendai kyūsai shūkyō ron* (On contemporary salvation religions), Tokyo: Seikyūsha.

Shimazono Susumu (1992b), *Shin shin shūkyō to shūkyō būmu* (New new religions and the religious boom), Tokyo: Iwanami Shoten.

Shimazono Susumu (1992c), 'Shinshūkyō igo no shūkyō undō' (Religious movements 'after' new religions), *Imago* (Seidosha), Vol. 3, No. 2.

Shimazono Susumu ed. (1992d), *Sukui to toku: Shūyōdan Hoseikai no shinkō kōzō* (Salvation and virtue: Creedal structure of Shūyōdan Hoseikai), Tokyo: Kōbundō.

Shimazono Susumu (1992e), 'Shin shūkyō no taishu jiritsu shisō to ken'ishugi' (Thoughts on self-reliance for the public and authoritarianism in the new religions), *Rekishi Hyōron* (Review of History) no. 509.

Shimazono Susumu (1992e), 'Seikatsuchi to kindai shūkyō undō: Makiguchi Tsunesaburō no kyōiku shisō to shinkō' (Practical knowledge in daily life and religious movements: The educational philosophy and faith of Makiguchi Tsunesaburō), in Kawai Hayao, ed., *Iwanami kōza Shūkyō to kagaku*, vol. 5, *Shūkyō to shakai kagaku* (Religion and science, vol. 5: Religion and the social sciences), Tokyo: Iwanami Shoten.

Shimazono Susumu (1995a), 'In the wake of AUM: The formation and transformation of a universe of belief', *Japanese Journal of Religious Studies* 22: 381–415.

Shimazono Susumu (1995b), 'Shūkyō kyōdan no naiheika to kindai jiyūshugi' (The closedness of religious organizations and modern liberalism), *Shūkyō hō* (Religious Law) 14.

Shimazono Susumu (1995c), 'Nihonjinron to shūkyō' (Japan theory and religion) *Tōkyōdaigaku Shūkyōgaku Nenpō* 13: 1–16.

Shimazono Susumu (1995d) 'Minshū shūkyō ka, shinshūkyō ka' (Popular religion or new religion?), in Edo no shisō henshū iinkai (Edo Thought Editorial Committee), ed. *Edo no shisō* (Edo thought), no. 2, Tokyo: Perikansha.

Shimazono, Susumu (1996) *Seishin sekai no yukue: Gendai sekai to shin reisei undō* (Whither the Spiritual World?: New spirituality movements in the contemporary world), Tokyo: Tōkyōdō Shuppan.

Shimazono Susumu (1997), 'Gendai Nihon no han-sezokushugi to nashonarizumu' (Anti-secularism and nationalism in contemporary Japan), in Nakano Takeshi et al., eds., *Shūkyō to nashonarizumu* (Religions and nationalism), Kyoto: Sekai Shisōsha.

Shimazono Susumu (1998), 'The commercialization of the sacred: The structural evolution of religious communities in Japan', *Social Science Japan Journal* 1.

Shimazono Susumu (2001), *Posutomodan no Shinshūkyō : Gendai nihon no seishinbunka no Teiryū* (New religions in the postmodern age: Undercurrents of the Spiritual Culture of Contemporary Japan), Tokyo: Tōkyōdō Shuppan.

Shimazono Susumu and Inoue Nobutaka (1985), 'Kaishinron saikō' (A new look at theories of conversion), in Ueda Shizuteru, and Yanagawa Keiichi, eds. *Shūkyōgaku no susume* (An exhortation to religious studies), Tokyo: Chikuma Shobō.

Shimoda Mikio (1986), *Marukusu shugi to shūkyō* (Marxism and religion), Tokyo: Seishin Shobō.

Shōji Kōkichi, ed. (1986), *Sekai shakai no kōzō to dōtai*, Tokyo: Hōsei Daigaku Shuppankai.

Shūkyō Shakaigaku Kenkyūkai (Association for the sociology of religion), ed. (1992), *Ima shūkyō wo dou toraeru ka* (How can religions be studied today?), Tokyo: Kaimeisha.

Sōka Gakkai Kyōgakubu ed. (1951), *Shakubuku kyōten* (A guidebook for doctrinal persuasion), Tokyo: Sōka Gakkai.

Sōka Gakkai Kyōgakubu (1971), *Sōka Gakkai nyūmon*, (An introduction to Sōka Gakkai), Tokyo: Seikyō Shinbunsha.

Stark, Rodney and W.S. Bainbridge (1985), *The Future of Religion,* Berkeley and Los Angeles: University of California Press.

Stark, Rodney and Lynne Roberts (1982), 'The arithmetic of social movements: Theoretical implications,' *Sociological Analysis* 43: 53–67.

Suzuki Hiroshi (1963–1964), 'Toshi kasō no shūkyō shūdan: Fukuoka-shi ni okeru Sōka Gakkai'(A religious group of the urban lower class: Sōka Gakkai in Fukuoka City), *Shakaigaku kenkyū* (Sociological studies) 22, 24, 25

Suzuki Hiroshi (1968), 'Toshi kaso no shūkyō shūdan: Fukuoka-shi ni okeru Sōka Gakkai' (A religious group of the urban lower class: Sōka Gakkai in Fukuoka City), in Nakano Takashi, et al., ed. *Kyōzai shakaigaku* (Teaching materials, sociology), Tokyo: Yuhikaku.

Takagi Hiroo (1958), *Shinkō shūkyō: Taishū o miryō suru mono* (New religions: What captivates the masses), Tokyo: Kōdansha.

Takagi Hiroo (1959), *Nihon no shinkō shūkyō: Taishū shisō undō no rekishi to ronri* (Japan's new religions: The history and logic of movements based on the thought of the masses), Tokyo: Iwanami Shoten.

Takagi Yutaka (1982), *Kamakura Bukkyō shi kenkyū* (Studies in the history of Kamakura Buddhism), Tokyo: Iwanami Shoten.

Takahashi Shinji (1971a), *Kokoro no hakken shinri hen* (Discovery of the mind: Divine truth), Tokyo: Sampō Shuppan.

Takahashi Shinji (1971b), *Kokoro no hakken kagaku hen* (Discovery of the mind: Science), Tokyo: Sampō Shuppan.

Takahashi Shinji (1973a), *Kokoro no hakken genshō hen* (Discovery of the mind: Phenomenal witness), Tokyo: Sampō Shuppan.

Takahashi Shinji (1973b), *Ai wa nikushimi wo koete* (Love transcends hatred), Tokyo: Sampō Shuppan.

Takemoto Takahiro, ed. (1984), *Meisō no seishin ryōhō: Naikan ryōhō no riron to jissen* (Mental therapy of meditation: The theory and practice of Naikan therapy), Tokyo: Shibundō.

Takeuchi Hiroshi (1978), *Nihonjin no shusse kan* (Japanese views of success in life), Tokyo: Gakubunsha.

Talmon, Yonina (1968), 'Millenarism,' in *International Encyclopedia of Social Sciences,* Vol. 9, New York: Macmillan and Free Press.

Tamanoi Yoshirō, Sakamoto, K. and Nakamura, H., eds. (1984), *Inochi to nōhō ronri: Toshika to sangyōka o koete* (The logic of life and agriculture: Beyond urbanization and industrialization), Tokyo: Gakuyo Shobō.

Tamura Yoshirō (1987), 'Japanese Culture and the Tendai Concept of Original Enlightenment,' *Japanese Journal of Religious Studies* 14: 203–10.

Tamura Yoshirō and Miyazaki Eishu, eds. (1972), *Kōza Nichiren ron: Nihon kindai to Nichiren shugi* (Lectures on Nichiren, vol. 4, Japan's modernization and Nichirenism), Tokyo: Shunjusha.

Tanabe, Shintarō (1989), *Yamai to shakai: Healing no tankyū* (Diseases and society: A quest for healing), Tokyo: Kōbundō.

Tanaka Kōho (1977), *Tanaka Chigaku,* Tokyo: Shin Sekai Sha,

Tanigawa Ken'ichi et al. eds. (1971), *Nihon shomin seikatsu shiryō shūsei. 18: Minkan shūkyō* (Materials for the common people's life in Japan. Vol. 18: Popular religions), Tokyo: San'ichi Shobō.

Tenrikyō Kyōkai Honbu (1949), *Tenrikyō Kyōten* (The Doctrine of Tenrikyō), Tenri: Tenrikyō Doyūsha.

Tenrikyō Church Headquarters (1967), *Life of Oyasama, the Foundress ofTenrikyō,* Tenri: Tenrikyō Church Headquarters.

Tenrikyō Church Headquarters (1971), *Ofudesaki: The Tip of the Divine Writing Brush,* Tenri: Tenrikyō Church Headquarters.

Tenrikyō Church Headquarters (1972a), *The Doctrine of Tenrikyō,* Tenri: Tenrikyō Church Headquarters.

Tenrikyō Church Headquarters (1972b), *Mikagura-uta: The Songs for the Tsutome,* Tenri: Tenrikyō Church Headquarters.

Tenrikyō Dōyūsha, ed. (1929), *Tenrikyō kōyō, Shōwa yonenban* (The elements of Tenrikyō), Tenri: Tenrikyō Dōyūsha.

Tenrikyō Kyōkai Honbu, ed. (1948–1949), *Osashizu* (8 vols), Tenri: Tenrikyō Dōyūsha (Tenrikyō Church Headquarters).

Tenrikyō Overseas Mission Department, ed. (1966), *Tenrikyō: Its History and Teachings.* Tenri: Tenri Jihōsha.

Toda Jōsei (1960), *Toda Jōsei sensei kantogen shū* (Toda Josei Sensei's forwords), Tokyo: Sōka Gakkai.

Toda Jōsei (1960), *Toda Jōsei ronbunshū* (Essays by Toda Jōsei), Tokyo: Shūkyōhōjin Sōka Gakkai.

Toda Jōsei Zenshū Shuppan Iinkai, ed. (1982), *Toda Jōsei zenshū* (The collected works of Toda Jōsei), vol. 2, *Shitsumonkai hen* (Answering questions from the believers), Tokyo: Seikyō Shinbunsha.

Toda Jōsei Zenshū Shuppan Iinkai, ed. (1987), *Toda Jōsei zenshū* (The collected works of Toda Jōsei), vol. 7, *Kōgi hen III* (Lectures, part III), Tokyo: Seikyō Shinbunsha.

Tokoro Shigemoto (1965), *Nichiren no shisō to Kamakura Bukkyō* (Nichiren's thought and Kamakura Buddhism), Tokyo: Fuzanbō.

Tokoro Shigemoto (1972), *Kindai shakai to Nichirenshugi* (Modern society and Nichirenism), Tokyo: Hyoronsha.

Tōkyō Daigaku Hokkekyō Kenkyūkai (1962), *Nichiren Shōshū Sōka Gakkai*, Tokyo: Sankibo Busshorin.

Tōkyō Daigaku Hokkekyō Kenkyūkai, ed. (1975), *Sōka Gakkai no rinen to jissen* (The doctrine and practice of Sōka Gakkai), Tokyo: Daisan Bunmeisha.

Toulmin, Stephen (1982), *The Return of Cosmology*, Berkeley and Los Angeles: University of California Press.

Tsushima Michihito (1985), '*Shūmatsu yogen shūkyō no keifu*' (The genealogy of apocalyptic religions), *Shinri to sōzō* 24.

Tsushima Michihito (1989), 'Shinshūkyō ni okeru "bankyō dokon" shisō to shūkyō kyōryoku undō no tenkai' (The 'thousands of religions, one root' idea in the new religions and the evolution of the religious cooperation movement), in Central Academic Research Institute, ed. *Shūkyōkan no kyōchō to kattō* (Harmony and discord among religions), Tokyo: Kōsei Shuppansha.

Tsushima Michihito et al. (1979), 'The vitalistic conception of salvation in Japanese new religions: An aspect of modern religious consciousness,' *Japanese Journal of Religious Studies* 6: 139–61.

Turner, Bryan S. (1975) 'Confession and social structure,' in *A Sociological Yearbook of Religion in Britain 8*. London: SCM Press.

Uefuji Kazuyuki and Ono Yasuyuki, eds. (1975), *Kakumei no taiga: Sōka Gakkai yonjūgonen shi* (The story of a revolution: The forty-five-year history of Sōka Gakkai), Tokyo: Seikyō Shinbunsha.

Umehara Masaki (1977), *Tenkeisha no shūkyō: Honmichi* (The religion of the revealed: Honmichi), Tokyo: Kōdansha.

Umehara Takeshi (1965), *Butsuzō: Kokoro to katachi* (Images of Buddha: Their spirit and form), with Mochizuki and Sawa, Tokyo: Nihon Hōsō Shuppan Kyōkai.

Umehara Takeshi (1967), *Jigoku no shisō* (Thoughts on hell), Tokyo: Chuō Kōronsha.

Umehara Takeshi (1972), *Kakusareta jūjika* (The hidden cross), Tokyo: Shinchōsha.

Umehara Takeshi (1973), *Minasoko no uta* (The song from the bottom of the water), Tokyo: Shinchōsa.

Umehara Takeshi (1976), *Nihon bunkaron* (A discourse on Japanese culture), Tokyo: Kōdansha.

Umehara Takeshi (1979), *Onryō to Jomon* (Grudging spirits and the Jōmon), Tokyo: Asahi Shuppansha.

Umehara Takeshi (1983), *Nihon no shinso* (The depths of Japan), Tokyo Kōsei Shuppansha.

Umehara Takeshi (1988–1989), *Nihon no boken* (The adventures of Japan), 3 Volumes, Tokyo: Kadokawa Shoten.

Umeahra Takeshi (1989), *Nihonjin no 'anoyo' kan* (The Japanese view of the other world), Tokyo: Chuō Kōronsha.

Umehara Takeshi (1991), *'Mori no shisō' ga jinrui o sukuu* ('Forest thought' will save the human race), Tokyo: Shōgakukan.

Umehara Takeshi (1992), *Nihonjin no tamashii* (The soul of the Japanese), Tokyo: Kōbunsha.

Umezu Reiji (1988), 'Reiyūkaikei shinshūkyō undō no hassei: Sono shisōteki sokumen o chūshin ni' (The emergence of new religious movements related to Reiyukai: Mainly on their thought), in Kōmoto Mitsugi, ed. *Ronshū Nihon Bukkyō shi dai kyukan: Taisho Shōwa jidai* (Papers on Japanese Buddhism, vol. 9, Taisho and Showa Eras), Tokyo: Yūzankaku Shuppan.

Uritani Yuko (1989), *Shinsō jiko no hakken* (The discovery of the deeper self), revised edition, Tokyo: Tama Shuppan.

Ushio Kitarō (1934), 'Otasuke' ni tsuite' (About *otasuke*), *Yamato Bunkwa* 2: 93–120.

van Straelen, Henry (1957), *The Religion of Divine Wisdom: Japan's Most Powerful Religious Movement,* Kyoto: Veritas Shoin.

Waga Shinya (1978), *Tōitsu Kyōkai: Sono kōdō to ronri* (The Unification Church: Its behavior and logic), Tokyo: Shinkyō Shuppansha.

Wakimoto Tsuneya (1983), *Shūkyō o kataru* (Narrating religion), Tokyo: Nisshin Shuppan.

Wallis, Roy, ed. (1979), *On the Margins of Science: The Social Construction of Rejected Knowledge,* London and New York: Routledge.

Watanabe Yoshio (1990), *Minzoku chishiki ron no kadai* (Issues in theories of folk knowledge), Tokyo: Gaifūsha.

Weber, Max (1920–1921), 'Zwischenbetrachtung: Theorie der Stufen und Rich-tungen religiöser Weltablehnung,' *Gesammelte Aufsätze für Religionssoziologie Vierte Auflage*. Tübingen: Mohr.

Weber, Max (1922), 'Religionssoziologie', from *Wirtschaft und Gesellschaft,* Berlin; J.C.B. Mohr (Paul Siebeck).

Weber, Max (1958), *The Protestant Ethic and the Spirit of Capitalism,* New York: Charles Scribner's Sons.

White, James W. (1970), *The Sōkagakkai and Mass Society,* Standford: Stanford University Press.

Wilber, Ken (1996), *A Brief History of Everything*, Boston: Shambhala

Wile, Andrew (1983), *Health and Healing,* Boston: Houghton Mifflin.

Williams, George M. (1989), *Amerika ni okeru shūkyō no yakuwari* (The role of religion in America), Tokyo: Ushio Shuppansha.

Wilson, Brian, ed. (1967), *Patterns of Sectarianism*, London: Heinemann.

Wilson, (1970), *Religious Sects*, London: Widenfeld and Nicolson.

Wilson, Brian (1973), *Magic and the Millennium*, London: Heinemann.

Wilson, Brian (1979), 'The new religions,' *Japanese Journal of Religious Studies* 6: 193–216.

Yamada Yutaka (1983), 'Healing, conversion, and ancestral spirits: Religious experiences among the Japanese-American members of the Church of World Messianity in Los Angeles, California,' in Yanagawa Keiichi, ed. *Japanese Religions in California*, Tokyo; Department of Religious Studies, University of Tokyo.

Yamaguchi Hiroshi (1993), *Kenshō: Tōitsu Kyōkai* (Verification: The Unification Church), Tokyo: Ryokufu Shuppan.

Yamamoto Soseki (1982), *Kaisei no bōkensha: Sai Sai-kan* (Choi Jae-Whan: An adventurer in renewal), Tenri Tenrikyo Dōyūsha.

Yamamuro Gunpei (1899 [1992]), *Heimin no fukuin (The Gospel of the common people),* 526th edition, Tokyo: Kyūseigun Kyōkyūbu.

Yamanaka Hiroshi and Hayashi Makoto (1996), *'Nihon ni okeru shūkyō shakaigaku no tenkai'* (The evolution of the sociology of religion in Japan), *Aichi Gakuin University Literature Faculty Bulletin* 25.

Yanagawa Keiichi and Morioka Kiyomi, eds. (1979), *Hawai nikkei shūkyō no genkyō to tenkai* (The current situation and future prospects for religion among Hawaiian Japanese-Americans), Tokyo: Tōkyō Daigaku Shūkyōgaku Kenkyūshitsu.

Yanagawa Keiichi and Morioka Kiyomi, eds. (1981), *Hawai nikkeijin shakai to nikkei shūkyō* (Japanese-American society and Japanese-American religion in Hawaii), Tokyo: Tōkyō Daigaku Shūkyōgaku Kenkyūshitsu.

Yanagita Kunio (1913–1914), 'Hujo kō' (Consideration of female shamans), *Kyōdo kenkyū* (Provincial studies) 1.

Yasuda Shigeru (1986), *Nippon no yūki nogyo: Undō no tenkai to keizaiteki kōsatsu* (Organic agriculture in Japan: The evolution of the movement and its economic consideration), Tokyo: Diamondsha.

Yasumaru Yoshio (1974), *Nihon no kindaika to minshū shisō* (Japan's modernization and popular thought), Tokyo: Aoki Shoten.

Yasumaru, Yoshio and Hirota Masaki (1966), 'Yonaoshi no ronri no keifu: Maruyamakyō o chūshin ni' (A genealogy of the logic of 'yonaoshi' : Focusing on Maruyamakyō), *Nihonshi Kenkyū*, Vols. 85–86

Yoneyama Yoshio (1988), *Shūkyō jidai* (Religious Age), Tokyo: Shobunsha.

York, Michael (1995), *The Emerging Network: A Sociology of the New Age and Neo-Pagan Movements*, London: Rowman & Littlefield.

Yoshida Teigo (1973), 'Jujutsu' (Magic), in Oguchi Iichi and Hori Ichirō, eds. *Shūkyōgahu jiten* (A dictionary of religious studies), Tokyo: Tōkyō Daigaku Shuppankai.

Yoshimoto Ishin (1965), *Naikan yonjūnen* (Forty years of Naikan), Tokyo: Shunjūsha.

Yoshimoto Ishin (1977), *Naikan no michi* (The way of Naikan), Yamato Kōriyama: Naikan Kenkyūjo.

Yoshimoto Ishin (1980), *Naikan nijūgonen no ayumi* (Twenty-five years of Naikan), Yamato Kōriyama: Naikan Kenkyūjo.

Yoshimoto Ishin (1983), *Naikan e no shōtai* (Invitation to Naikan), Osaka: Tokishobō.

Young, Richard F. (1988), 'From *gokyō-dōgen* to *bankyō-dōkon*: A study in the self-universalization of Ōmoto,' *Japanese Journal of Religious Studies* 15: 263–86.

Yuasa Yasuo (1967), *Keizaijin no moraru* (The morality of the economic man), Tokyo: Hanawa Shobō.

Yuasa Yasuo (1970), *Kindai Nihon no jitsuzon shisō'* (Existential thought in modern Japan), Tokyo: Sōbunsha.

Yuasa Yasuo (1972), *Kamigami no tanjō: Nihon shinwa no shisōshiteki kenkyū* (The birth of the gods: An intellectual history of Japanese mythology), Tokyo: Ibunsha.

Yuasa Yasuo (1977), *Shintai Tōyōteki shinshinron no kokoromi* (The body: An essay on Eastern Philosophy and the science of mind and body), Tokyo: Sōobunsha.

Yuasa Yasuo (1978), *Jung to Kirisutokyō* (Jung and Christianity), Tokyo: Jinbun Shoin.

Yuasa Yasuo (1980), *Kodaijin no seishin sekai* (The spiritual world of ancient people), Tokyo: Minerva Shoten. Originally in 1973 by San'ichi Shobō

Yuasa Yasuo (1981a), *Watsuji Tetsurō: Kindai Nihon tetsugaku no unmei* (Watsuji Tesurō: The fate of modern Japanese philosophy), Tokyo: Minerva Shoten.

Yuasa Yasuo (1981b), *Nihonjin no shūkyō ishiki* (Religious consciousness of the Japanese), Tokyo: Meicho Kankōkai.

Yuasa Yasuo (1982), *Tōyō bunka no shinsō* (The depths of Eastern culture), Tokyo: Meicho Kankōkai.

Yuasa Yasuo (1986), *Ki, shūgyō, shintai* (Qi, ascetic discipline and the body), Tokyo: Hirakawa Shuppan.

Yuasa Yasuo (1991), *'Ki' to wa nanika: Jintai ga hassuru enerugi* (What is 'qi': The energy emanating from the human body), Tokyo: Nihon Hōsō Shuppan Kyōkai. Tokyo:

Yugi Gibun (1984), *Nishida Mugaku kenkyū nōto* (A Research Note on Nishida Mugaku), Tokyo: Sankibō Busshorin.

Zaidan hojin Yano Tsuneya Kinenkai, ed. (1981), *Sūji de miru Nihon no hyakunen* (Japan's century in statistics), Tokyo: Kokuseisha.

Index

Agonshū, 170
Ahlstrom, Sydney, 214
Ainu, 27, 280–3, 290, 296
Alternative agriculture
    movements
    See also Shimamoto Kakuya
    development of, in the
        world, **201–2**
    in Japan, **202–3**
Alternative knowledge
    movements (AKMs), 195
    See also Alternative
        agriculture movement
    and agriculture, 200
    and modern knowledge,
        197–8
    and new spirituality
        movements, **209–10**
    and religious movement,
        196–7
    and their interrelations,
        208–9
    future for, **210–1**
    in modern Japan, **198–200**
Alternative medicine, in the
    United States, **195–6**
Akazawa Bunji (Konkō Daijin),
    45–6, 179–80, 186
Animism
    and nationalist tendency
        of new spirituality
        movements, 304
    as belief in spirits, 167
    Iwata Keiji and, 290
    Umehara's study of, 282, 290
Anthroposophie movement, 259
Anzai Shin, 306–7c1n1
Ascetical ethos, 174

decline of, 175
Association of People Thinking
    about Life and Death, 24
Aum Shinrikyō, 4, 7, 24–5,
    36–9, 233
Axial age, 53, 307c3n1

Baha'i Faith, 3
Bakhtin, Mikhail, 102
Bekki Sadao, 93, 104
Belief in spirits
    and modern urban society,
        171–5
    and return to religion, 167
    popular culture and revival of,
        176–7
    rebirth of, in new religions,
        168–71
Bellah, Robert, N., 42, 57–8,
    216
Berger, Peter, 176
Bergson, 286
Blacker, Carmen, 31
Buber, Martin, 312c8n2
Buddhism (Buddhist sects)
    See also Lotus Sutra, Lotus
        Sutra-based new religions,
        Mahayana Buddhism
    and funeral and ancestor rite,
        7–8, 13, **77**
    and new spirituality
        movements, 64, 278, **302–3**,
        317c16n5
    as representative historic
        religion, 57–8
    characterization of suffering
        in, 53
    destroying authority of, 247